A cross the line

Tales of the First Black Basketball Players
in the ACC and SEC

Revised and Updated

Barry Jacobs

LYONS
PRESS

Essex, Connecticut

An imprint of Globe Pequot, the trade division of
The Rowman & Littlefield Publishing Group, Inc.
4501 Forbes Blvd., Ste. 200
Lanham, MD 20706
www.rowman.com

Distributed by NATIONAL BOOK NETWORK

British Library Cataloguing in Publication Information available

Library of Congress Cataloging-in-Publication Data

Names: Jacobs, Barry, 1950- author.
Title: Across the line : tales of the first black basketball players in the ACC and SEC /
    Barry Jacobs.
Description: Revised and updated. | Essex, Connecticut : Lyons Press, [2022] |
    Includes bibliographical references and index.
Identifiers: LCCN 2022019783 (print) | LCCN 2022019784 (ebook) | ISBN
    9781493069217 (trade paperback) | ISBN 9781493071296 (epub)
Subjects: LCSH: African American basketball players—Biography. | African American
    college athletes—Biography. | African American college students—Biography. |
    Discrimination in sports—United States. | Racism in sports—United States. |
    College sports—United States. | Atlantic Coast Conference—History. |
    Southeastern Conference—History.
Classification: LCC GV884.A1 J34 2022 (print) | LCC GV884.A1 (ebook) | DDC
    796.357092/396073—dc23/eng/20220625
LC record available at https://lccn.loc.gov/2022019783
LC ebook record available at https://lccn.loc.gov/2022019784

♾™ The paper used in this publication meets the minimum requirements of
American National Standard for Information Sciences—Permanence of Paper for
Printed Library Materials, ANSI/NISO Z39.48-1992.

To those who dared be first.

The heart which is greater than the intellect is not that which beats in the chest.

Kim Stanley Robinson, *The Years of Rice and Salt*

CONTENTS

Acknowledgments   ix

Introduction: The Way of Things   xi

PART ONE: VANGUARD

1. An Uneasy Fit   1
   Billy Jones and Pete Johnson, University of Maryland

2. Forms of Hell   23
   Perry Wallace, Vanderbilt University

3. Between Worlds   51
   C. B. Claiborne, Duke University

4. Fall from Grace   75
   Henry Harris Jr., Auburn University

5. The Loneliest Number   97
   Charles Scott, University of North Carolina

6. Door Jamb   123
   Wendell Hudson, University of Alabama

PART TWO: CHANGING OF THE GUARD

7. Pipe Dream   147
   Norwood Todmann, Wake Forest University

8. Prisoner of Choice   169
   Tom Payne Jr., University of Kentucky

9. Friendly Bounce   195
   Al Heartley, North Carolina State University

10. Penn Pall   217
    Ronnie Hogue, University of Georgia

11. Forbidden Territory   241
    Craig Mobley, Clemson University, and Casey Manning,
    University of South Carolina

12. All in the Family   269
    Collis Temple Jr., Louisiana State University

13. Shooting the Hoop   291
    Coolidge Ball, University of Mississippi

PART THREE: REAR GUARD

14. Expected Difficulty   311
     Al Drummond, University of Virginia

15. Moving On   331
     Wilbert Cherry and Larry Robinson, University of Tennessee

16. Later Gators   349
     Steve Williams and Malcolm Meeks, University of Florida

17. Sneakers   367
     Larry Fry and Jerry Jenkins, Mississippi State University

Appendix   383

Bibliography   387

Index   403

About the Author   421

ACKNOWLEDGMENTS

The price of gasoline and the amount of gray in my hair increased considerably over the 13 years I worked on this book. What remained steadfast throughout was the support and cooperation I received from friends and strangers.

Particularly helpful were the sports information staffs and library archivists at the University of Alabama, Auburn University, Clemson University, Duke University, the University of Florida, the University of Georgia, the University of Kentucky, Louisiana State University, the University of Maryland, the University of Mississippi, Mississippi State University, the University of North Carolina at Chapel Hill, North Carolina State University, the University of South Carolina, the University of Tennessee, Vanderbilt University, the University of Virginia, and Wake Forest University. The staff at the main branch of the Hyconeechee Library in Hillsborough, North Carolina, under the direction of Brenda Stephens, was invariably helpful as well.

Charles Bloom and DeWayne Peevy at the SEC office and Brian Morrison, Barb Dery, and Fred Barakat at the ACC office repeatedly provided assistance. The sports information offices at Florida State University and the Georgia Institute of Technology also pitched in when asked.

I interviewed more than 150 people for this book. (But who's counting?) They are listed in the bibliography. I was most appreciative of their time, honesty, and willingness to direct me to others who might be helpful. I was inspired by many of them.

Pete Gaudet, Jeff Jones, Kim Morris, and Buzz Peterson were gracious hosts and guides. Tom Konchalski assisted my early efforts to identify pioneering players, sharing his encyclopedic basketball knowledge with characteristic generosity. Bill King, Jerry Ratcliffe, John Rose, and Ken Tysiac readily made an extra effort to provide information I might otherwise have missed. Ron Beck at the Green River Correctional Complex cleared a path when I needed to get behind bars.

Donna Baker and Dianne Reid were good enough to read significant portions of the manuscript. Moses Carey and Steve Halkiotis served as occasional sounding boards. Ron Morris lent not only a friend's enthusiasm but a professional's insights. Everyday assistance was lent by Bernice Jacobs, Jim and Sharon Kirkman, Ian Rankin, Edward Draper-Savage, Teresa Snipes, Emily Love, Ford, Grant, Jackson, and Truman. The staff of Orange County government, led by manager John Link, was quite accommodating of the demands placed upon my time.

John Thorn's vision helped this project get off the ground, and Jack Semonche made sure it took flight. Tom McCarthy, Sarah Mazer Zink, Josh Rosenberg, Eugene Brissie, and Chris Fischer, my successive editors, were supportive, enthusiastic, and displayed a light touch I appreciated. The belief and persistence of my agent, Andrew Blauner, helped book and author bridge some gloomy chasms to end up in print.

Bob and Julia Lackey generously shared their support and their Pawleys Island home, where I spent several weeks sitting on a soundside porch, reading and perspiring in peace. Charlie Riley shared his love for, and knowledge of, the game of basketball, particularly the New York variety. Robin Jacobs shares most everything there is to share, for which I am eternally grateful.

INTRODUCTION: THE WAY OF THINGS

We started working the rows of tobacco at dawn, stripping the broad leaves from their stalks and piling them neatly on a wagon. All too soon even the birds and insects fell silent, overwhelmed by breathless heat and humidity that soaked clothes with sweat, making them cling like heavy, fabric skin. The only oasis was the pause at midday to enjoy a homecooked meal of, say, stewed tomatoes, beans and fatback, sweet potato casserole, steamed cabbage, Brunswick stew, salad greens, cornbread, rolls, homemade lemonade, cake, and ice cream.

The small log house where we loaded our plates with food offered scant relief from the stifling North Carolina summer, especially with the wood cookstove dominating the kitchen. Yet, it gradually dawned on me, it was neither heat nor diet that kept a white coworker from entering the house or dining at a shaded table outside with the four of us, two Black and two white. Instead, the invisible barrier, woven like a thread through the currency of daily life, was race.

Chip Connor told a similar, if reversed, story about the habits of separation where he grew up in southern Virginia several decades earlier. "When you talked about older Black folks in the forties and fifties, when I was really a kid, I can remember, if you worked in the fields and it came time to eat lunch or to cut a watermelon or something, the older ones would take theirs and go sit somewhere else to eat," said Connor, a former

University of Virginia player and assistant coach. "The older ones, that's apparently what they felt like they were supposed to do."

The dictates of race, so deeply ingrained they became self-enforcing, have shaped American society from colonial times to the present. "In all the relations of life and death, we are met by the color line," Frederick Douglass wrote in the 19th century. "The problem of the 20th century is the problem of the color line," William Edward Burghardt (W. E. B.) Du Bois famously wrote in his book *The Souls of Black Folk*.

For whites, beneficiaries of the established order, the line was comfortably invisible. "Never thought about it being anything," said Jimmy Davy, a sportswriter from Nashville. "You were born, and you grew up, and that's the way it was, and you didn't have to figure out that's the way it was." For Blacks, subordinated by rote, the color line was as omnipresent as the air they breathed.

"You always knew what your place was, because those policies and that conduct that was expected was always very clear," said Cleveland Sellers Jr., a South Carolina native, prominent college protester, director of African American studies at the University of South Carolina, and then president of Voorhees College in Denmark, South Carolina, his hometown. Second-class status for African Americans was a matter of law, custom, and enduring prejudice, as mockingly outlined by John Hope Franklin, the eminent Black historian. "Physiologically they were inferior, emotionally they were juvenile, and intellectually they were hopelessly retarded. Fortunately for them, the argument went, they were the chattel of an aristocracy characterized by talent, virtue, generosity, and courage."

That self-impressed aristocracy launched a War for Southern Independence in 1861 in a vain attempt to preserve slavery and the society it supported. Defeated white supremacists rose from the ashes to reimpose their worldview, gradually extending segregation and the sham of separate but equal throughout the old Confederacy and beyond.

"By 1910, in the estimation of a visitor, race relations in the South had become a 'state of war,'" Leon F. Litwack wrote in *Trouble in Mind*, a masterful book on the segregated South. "This 'war' black men and women were clearly losing; indeed, it had become a virtual rout. The other side owned the land, the law, the police, the courts, the government, the armed forces, and the press. The political system denied blacks a voice; the educational system denied them equal access and adequate resources; popular culture mocked their lives and aspirations; the economic system left them little room for ambition or hope; and the law and the courts functioned effectively at every level to protect, reinforce, and deepen their political powerlessness, economic dependence, and social degradation."

At various places and times, African Americans were forced to use separate schools, libraries, beaches, parks, swimming pools, water fountains, entrances, Bibles, churches, cemeteries, mortuaries, hospitals, ambulances, doctors, transportation, hotels, movie theaters, and restaurants. They were excluded from neighborhoods, juries, jobs, unions, fraternities and sororities, civic groups, and of course, sports teams. They could not walk through certain parts of town, expect to be addressed as Mister or Missus, or try on clothes in a department store. Twenty-nine states from Oregon to Alabama, the Dakotas to Virginia, enacted laws prohibiting marriage between Blacks and whites.

Segregation in public education was nearly as widespread. John McLendon, a Black man and future Hall of Fame basketball coach, reported that fellow University of Kansas students fled a campus swimming pool when he entered the water in the 1930s. When I attended high school in the late 1960s in Levittown, New York, no Blacks were among nearly 2,000 students because restrictive covenants prevented their families from purchasing homes in the area.

Well into the 21st century, African Americans traversed Southern cities and towns in the shadows of statues honoring Confederate heroes, erected long after the Civil War. Only recently have many of these nostalgic manifestations celebrating a heritage of white supremacy been removed by local edict or crowd action, frequently over the objections of state legislators. As this is written, the federal government contemplates a new nomenclature for Southern military installations named for Rebel generals.

The scale of virulence by which separation was enforced was not necessarily a function of geography. But the South, including border states such as Kentucky and Maryland, could be counted on to be especially unbending, unforgiving, and unapologetic in preserving the racial status quo. Blacks responded by building their own institutions, economy, and support system. Serendipitous benefits accrued from opportunity's chronically narrowed focus. Distinctive styles of artistic expression evolved, including a form of basketball familiar to modern fans that stressed full-court play, athleticism, and aggressiveness. Self-sufficient enterprise emerged.

Communities formed protective cocoons in which African Americans could function safely. Lack of job options actually enabled school systems to nurture educational excellence in some instances despite minimal funding. "I went to Jim Crow schools from the time I entered school up till high school," said Chester Grundy, a Louisville native and senior diversity adviser to the dean at the University of Kentucky's College of Medicine. "If you looked at these schools, you would say, 'Oh, those poor Black kids, getting that inferior education.' But when I was in school, particularly from the time I entered kindergarten through junior high, all my teachers had advanced degrees. I had a math teacher in the eighth grade who was a dissertation short of a PhD from Columbia. My uncle had a degree in pharmacy from Purdue, and he taught eighth grade science."

Horizons for Black ambition expanded fitfully following World War II. The U.S. Supreme Court ruled against racial segregation on matters from interstate commerce to graduate school enrollment, and in 1948 an executive order from President Harry Truman integrated the military. Sports played a role, with Jackie Robinson very publicly breaking the color barrier in 1947 with Major League Baseball's Brooklyn Dodgers.

The mortal blow to white hegemony was struck when the Supreme Court unanimously decided in *Brown v. Board of Education of Topeka* that separate education is inherently unequal. At the time of the May 1954 ruling, no university or college in the Atlantic Coast Conference or the Southeastern Conference—which between them covered nine of the eleven states of the old Confederacy—had integrated either its undergraduate student body or its athletic program. Many officials, especially in the South, reacted to Brown by dragging their feet with the determination of football receivers trying to stay inbounds, making a sham of the court's admonition to end segregation "with all deliberate speed." Leaders at institutions of higher learning joined the resistance but increasingly recognized that failure to comply with the court threatened federal funding, academic stature, and athletic competitiveness.

Grudgingly, with occasional violent accompaniment, schools in the SEC and ACC desegregated their undergrad ranks. Where once the best African American athletes either left the region or attended historically Black schools, now they began crossing the color line at major Southern schools previously reserved for whites.

The blade of integration cut both ways. The same sharp edge that cleared a path into the white world forever altered the landscape, helping to hasten the demise of profitable Black business districts, self-supporting Black communities, and talent-laden Black athletic programs. "All of the great athletes, they went white," said Harvey Heartley, who coached at the high-school level in North Carolina and later in the historically Black Central Intercollegiate Athletic Association (CIAA). "So, you lost your teachers, you lost your students, and you lost your athletes. We didn't get replacements, so it was like cutting your wrists. You knew eventually that your program had to die."

By 1965, every school in the ACC and SEC had African American undergraduates. By the fall of 1972, every varsity basketball program was desegregated. Maryland's Billy Jones broke the ACC color barrier in 1965–66. Seventeen seasons later, more than half of the ACC's players were Black, including all five starters on a North Carolina State squad that won the NCAA title. The SEC's first Black player was Perry Wallace, a high-school valedictorian and All-American who joined the Vanderbilt varsity in 1967–68. Seven seasons later Alabama won the conference title with five Black starters, undermining an informal quota system limiting African Americans' opportunity on the court.

Today the preponderance of players in both leagues are Black. "Take away every Black player that played in the ACC last year," said Billy Packer, a Wake Forest alumnus and former college basketball TV analyst, "and put them in the CIAA, and tell me where the talent would be."

Yet only 8 of 29 head coaches in the two leagues (27.6 percent) were African American entering the 2022–23 season. Prior to both conferences' recent expansions in the mid-2000s, the proportion was 10 Black head coaches at 22 schools (45.5 percent). That decline is in keeping with national trends in Division I athletics and in pro football and baseball. According to a 2021 report from the Institute for Diversity and Ethics in Sport (TIDES), the SEC and ACC currently have three African American athletics directors between them. As with all but one power conference, neither the ACC nor SEC has ever had a Black or female commissioner.

Most SEC and ACC schools at one time belonged to the Southern Conference, an all-white association so large and unwieldy it instituted a postseason basketball tournament in 1921 to determine its champion. The SEC broke away from the Southern first, starting in 1932 with a dozen members, two more than when desegregation hit. Disorder accompanied integration at the University of Alabama, the University of Georgia, and the University of Mississippi; the transition occurred without overt violence at Auburn University, the University of Florida, the University of Kentucky, Louisiana State University, Mississippi State University, the University of Tennessee, and Vanderbilt University, the only private school in the conference.

The SEC's most notable athletic trait has been its prowess in football, in which a majority of its core members laid claim to national championships, and the manner in which Kentucky dominated conference basketball fortunes. Running afoul of NCAA regulations has been a league constant as well, with half the membership recently on probation.

Kentucky's Wildcats have achieved more victories than any other program in basketball history. UK has reached seventeen Final Fours, emerging with eight NCAA titles, most recently in 2008. "Big Blue" became a national power under Hall of Fame coach Adolph Rupp, who retired in 1972. The other nine schools active in the SEC during the mid-sixties and early seventies have combined for 12 Final Four visits and a pair of national titles in men's basketball by Florida in 2006 and 2007. (Arkansas, a post-integration SEC addition along with Missouri, South Carolina, and Texas A&M, won in 1994 and had two other Final Four visits as an SEC member.) Between 1953 and 1978, a period when there was no SEC basketball tournament, Kentucky went to 18 NCAAs compared to 8 trips for the league's remaining schools. Four of those Wildcat appearances came because other SEC members declined to enter integrated postseason competition.

Seven breakaway Southern Conference members formed the ACC in 1953, retaining a postseason tournament to determine a basketball champion. Early on, the single-elimination ACC tournament was much maligned but soon became a lucrative and often dramatic signature event. Now every Division I conference holds a similar tournament. The eight ACC members at the time of desegregation, some of them still colleges, were Clemson University, Duke University, the University of Maryland, the University of North Carolina at Chapel Hill, NC State University, the University of South Carolina, the University of Virginia, and Wake Forest University. (South Carolina withdrew from the conference in 1971 and joined the SEC twenty years later. Maryland went to the Big Ten in 2014.) Duke and Wake are private schools.

At its founding the ACC boasted national football powers in Clemson, Duke, and Maryland. The league periodically achieves excellence in that sport, and over time has added nine members, primarily to bolster football. But despite ongoing efforts to highlight football, TV's darling, the ACC remains best known for basketball, in which it is perennially a national leader. Duke and North Carolina, the dominant basketball programs, have captured 11 of 15 NCAA men's titles earned by schools then in the ACC. The pair won six NCAA championships since 2001—Duke most recently in

2015, UNC in 2017. Virginia, an ACC member since December 1953, was the ultimate victor in 2019.

Of 47 Final Four visits achieved by programs that were ACC members at the time of desegregation, 38 (84 percent) represented the Blue Devils and Tar Heels. The North Carolina program—built by Hall of Famers Frank McGuire and Dean Smith and run for eighteen years by Hall of Famer Roy Williams (who retired in April 2021)—is second to Kentucky in all-time basketball victories. The Blue Devils rank fourth in total wins, elevated by their recently retired coach Mike Krzyzewski, a Hall of Famer whose teams won five national titles and more games than anyone in NCAA history—1,202 in 46 years at Army and Duke through the 2021–22 season.

Commitment to basketball varied widely within both leagues during the desegregation era, prior to rich television contracts, saturation media coverage, and multimillion-dollar paydays derived from NCAA participation. SEC schools frequently regarded basketball as a filler between football activities. The difference in prestige between the sports was so pronounced, Mississippi formally proclaimed during the early sixties that its head basketball coach had been promoted—to direct the freshman football squad. The founding ACC schools outside North Carolina were little better in terms of committing resources to basketball.

What was constant across the SEC and ACC was a lack of eagerness to bring in Black athletes. Typically, years passed between a school's undergraduate desegregation and the addition of an African American varsity basketball player. A canary-in-the-mine factor came into play at schools such as Ole Miss, where athletic officials privately acknowledged evaluating the racial transition in basketball before risking disharmony in football.

Schools were more or less evenly divided across the two leagues in choosing whether to venture first across the color line in basketball or football. Basketball, with its smaller squads, did offer a greater likelihood of an immediate competitive return with the addition of a single player. That impact was enhanced if one subscribed to the widespread belief that it was safer and wiser to choose a racial pioneer who was "a superstar, high school All-American, that type of reputation," said C. M. Newton, the former Kentucky player and Hall of Fame basketball coach at Alabama and Vanderbilt.

Certainly, it appeared the SEC heartily embraced that standard of overt superiority, where trailblazing basketball players at 9 of 10 schools made all-conference, compared to only North Carolina's Charles Scott in the ACC.

Talented African Americans flooded the ACC in the second wave of recruits. Gilbert McGregor, an early African American basketball player at Wake Forest, said whites simply were more comfortable accepting a person of color if he possessed extraordinary abilities. "That's the Black person you can relate to. Nobody wants to get in there and relate to the Black person that's just human."

Universities that were the northernmost outposts in their respective leagues each broke the ice with a pair of Black freshmen, Maryland in 1964 and Vanderbilt in 1966. Most often, however, basketball pioneers arrived alone on campuses where African Americans constituted a miniscule portion of the student body. Early arrivals usually came from totally segregated backgrounds, requiring a major social and academic adjustment to their surroundings. Even those who had been among the first Black students to attend white schools in their hometowns, frequently an unpleasant experience, found themselves on uncertain ground.

"It was constantly getting used to, constantly trying to adjust to that particular environment," said Ernie Jackson, an early Duke football player from South Carolina. "I talk to my kids these days, and it's very difficult for them to even imagine the way it existed at that particular time, and how difficult it was just trying to leave the Black world that you'd existed in for a long period of time and get acclimated to the white world that you found yourself thrust into."

The adjustment was complicated for basketball players because, as desegregation unfolded, they were more likely to bear the brunt of doubt and hostility. "There's no hiding a basketball player," said Wendell Hudson, the Alabama pioneer. "You know who they are. You know where they're from. You know what color they are." Basketball is easily the most intimate of major team sports. Games occur in enclosed spaces. Fans sit close to the action. Players wear no obscuring helmets or pads; uniforms are little more than glamorized underwear.

"One can see muscles flexing and faces contorting in concentration or frustration," said the 1973 University of Mississippi yearbook. "The players aren't little blobs of color that are glimpsed occasionally from the vantage point of Section A, row 43, seat 15, student section, PLEASE DO NOT SPIT ON THE BAND, but are actual, honest-to-god real-life people who are recognizable as such."

Many teams played in bandbox arenas in the 1960s and 1970s where individual spectators could readily make their voices heard, touch performers on the sidelines or pelt them with debris, as Black pioneers discovered to their dismay. Furthering a sense of isolation in those situations, associates tended to unconsciously tune out abuse directed not at them but at the sole dark-skinned person in their midst. "It had to be a huge deal for Al Drummond and for Billy Jones," said ex-Virginia player Dan Bonner, recalling the first Black players at UVa and Maryland, respectively. "It had to be a huge thing for them, and yet the people that were there, that were with them, that should have been the closest people to them in the world, their teammates, it just wasn't a big deal to them."

Pride, lack of trust, and basic male reticence led players to keep inner conflicts and the sting of racism hidden from white associates. "I internalized it, and I would never cause a problem, because I was taught that," said Pete Johnson, who entered Maryland with Jones. "In looking back, I was always proud of the fact that we were never the reason for a situation, and when we saw a situation, we would always back out of it and move around it." Their coach, Herman "Bud" Millikan, "definitely didn't see it because we didn't bring it up." Nearly until his death in 2010, Millikan claimed to be unaware Johnson and Jones encountered race-tinged problems at College Park.

Coaches worked to downplay differences, clinging to the assurance that they treated everyone alike. Superficially equitable, that attitude led to unanticipated troubles on the road and to routine failures to establish support systems to help Black pioneers cope with problems on campus, from antagonistic professors to hesitant roommates to an absence of dating options. Compounding the difficulties for trailblazing players, they were frequently regarded by Blacks and whites as representatives of their entire race, a heavy burden for anyone, let alone a teenager away from home for the first time. Remarkably, most became uncomplaining role models. "Those thoughts don't go through your mind at that time, that you are inspiring other people to do things or that you are satisfying other people or you are giving other people inspiration," said Charles Scott, the North Carolina icebreaker. "You don't understand the politics of what you are adding at that time."

Political correctness has become a dismissive term for form's precedence over substance in how we speak and act, commonly in response to the concerns of minorities. Back in the turbulent sixties, the only political correctness on many historically white Southern campuses was an orthodoxy of exclusion. There were no accepted methods for discussing, understanding, and bridging racial divides, let alone agreement that such efforts were desirable. The weight of habit and custom worked against African Americans, as did an older generation of athletic officials in positions to ease their transition.

Kentucky football integrated during the mid-sixties, yet years passed before Adolph Rupp, the South's preeminent basketball coach, did likewise with his program. The oft-advanced explanation was that Rupp and others such as Clemson athletics director/football coach Frank Howard were merely products of their times, with no obligation to lead a thorny transformation. That neatly ignored the powerful dictum that Martin Luther King Jr. articulated: "Non-compliance with evil is just as much a moral duty as is compliance with good."

The arrival of Black athletes on campus confronted coaches, administrators, and teammates with unexplored differences in language, custom, history, symbol. From use of the word "boy" to playing "Dixie" to waving Confederate flags to rules governing facial hair and Afros, new sensitivities were required. The disconnect between white comfort and Black experience had to be addressed. "You do not take a person who, for years, has been hobbled by chains and liberate him, bring him up to the starting line of the race and then say, you are free to compete with the others, and still justly believe that you have been completely fair," said President Lyndon Johnson as he pushed through landmark legislation protecting civil rights and voting rights.

College athletics, basketball in particular, advanced that adjustment. Strong affiliation with a favorite college is a pervasive trait in a region where professional sports had a minimal presence at the dawn of integration. Seeing an African American on "your" team made him tougher to objectify, and in turn made it more difficult to dismiss or demean Blacks at opposing schools. "That's a huge wall that's been broken down, because in the old days the rednecks would have rooted against that guy," said Farra Alford, Hudson's teammate at Alabama.

"It has had a tremendous impact," Duke's Krzyzewski said of his sport. "Coach K" played at the U.S. Military Academy in the late sixties. "When you watch a basketball game, what you've seen is African Americans and whites hugging one another, on a team together, laughing with one another, crying with one another, being people with one another. That's out there. You're advertising that . . . It's like having an infomercial about how people should be."

Perhaps because history is by its nature a story fashioned in retrospect, its outcomes known, the temptation is to underestimate the tensions and uncertainties that basketball's trailblazers faced as they crossed racial lines.

Distance in time also diminishes a sense of danger. We know Perry Wallace's worries he would be shot on a basketball court were unfounded, that the tears Mildred Hudson shed over her son's prospective fate at Alabama proved unwarranted, that Black students were not run down by cars at Clemson or subjected to more than epithets at NC State the night Martin Luther King Jr. was assassinated. But icebreaking players operated with no assurance that their defiance of racial norms would go unpunished. Today's relatively free intermingling within the precincts of daily life seemed a distant dream in 1970, as unreal as pervasive, enforced racial exclusion seems now.

"My daughters, for example, as we talk about the forties and the fifties, often tell us what they wouldn't [tolerate]," said Harold White, a retired associate athletics director at the University of South Carolina who grew up in strictly segregated circumstances in Columbia. "And, thank goodness, people gave their lives so that they could make statements like that, so they won't have to experience those things. My grandchildren will even have experiences that my children didn't have. So, we're not there yet, but Lord knows we've made great progress."

Alterations in basketball's racial fabric occurred with a mixture of agonizing slowness and stunning rapidity. Perry Wallace's career at Vanderbilt was illustrative. Auburn's Henry Harris was the SEC's only other Black player during a varsity career in which Wallace admittedly walked on eggshells to avoid confrontation, denying himself the latitude to play with the same abandon as opponents. That competitor's privilege was wielded with impunity by Georgia's Ronnie Hogue, LSU's Collis Temple Jr. and others who played within a year or two of Wallace's 1970 graduation. By 1978, the majority of starters were Black at all but two SEC schools. (Vanderbilt, Wallace's alma mater, was among the exceptions.)

Few subsequent players knew Wallace's story or that of ACC groundbreaker Billy Jones. By modern standards, their contributions and those of basketball's other Southern trailblazers occurred in a media vacuum. In fact, the first Black players in the ACC and SEC remain an invisible fraternity, largely unknown to each other or to anyone beyond the squads on which they played. They did not realize that they faced many of the same personal challenges. They did not know that many of their number shared a residual weight of bitterness and alienation spawned in those difficult days. They were unaware that several of the earliest pioneers self-destructed; that universities in supposedly tolerant communities were among the least welcoming; and that, despite playing at Deep South schools where campus integration met vigorous opposition, Alabama's Hudson and Mississippi's Coolidge Ball spoke most favorably of their college days.

Nor do many contemporary players realize that the ACC and SEC traditionally barred Black participation, or that daring young men of their age went to considerable lengths to quietly storm a barrier now all but forgotten.

"Not everybody understands the people that came before them, the price they paid," said Collis Temple III, who played at LSU a generation after his father broke the ice. "I think they should care because these men, they changed the college game, they changed the game in the SEC, they changed the game at their respective schools. They paved the way for every African American player that is at those schools today. I think players should understand their heritage, understand where it's come from, and respect it and know it."

Gaps in awareness about basketball's pioneers reflect a broader, glaring absence. Histories of the civil rights era examine many factors in the success and failure of "The Movement," but beyond mention of baseball's Jackie Robinson such accountings rarely consider the role of sports in advancing race relations. Robinson, who attended UCLA and later served as an officer in the U.S. Army, appropriately became a symbol of determination, pride, and achievement. But one pioneering SEC player noted that, in his view, Robinson was insulated to an extent by an attentive press corps and by the Dodgers' professional organization. Nor was the adult Robinson required to compete simultaneously in an academic setting. Other than spring training in Florida, he rarely traveled in the South, where he would be exposed to what writer Marshall Frady described as its "lingering romance of violence, a congenital love for quick and final physical showdowns."

Crossing racial borders at the region's major white universities was a difficult proposition long after Robinson broke into the major leagues. Recognizing that reality, Georgia native John Guthrie likened basketball's SEC and ACC pioneers to Rosa Parks, whose refusal to move to the back of a Montgomery, Alabama, bus sparked a watershed boycott in December 1955. "They just opened up the doors," said Guthrie, a successful head coach at the University of Georgia. "What they did for college basketball in the South is obviously just like what the woman did that jumped on the bus in Montgomery, and, to a degree, like what Dr. King's movement was. It was nonviolent, obviously, and it was providing opportunity for people—as it should have been. They were doing something lofty; that was good."

Thanks to risks taken more than 50 years ago, competitive virtue is now celebrated, regardless of race, and amply rewarded. Athletics has become a national meeting ground, the venue in which the myth of the melting pot comes closest to realization. "Bill Russell once said that the reason he liked it was because it was about numbers, while much else in life was politics," Bill Bradley wrote of basketball in *Values of the Game*. "The implication was that given the politics of life in America, a Black man would not be able to rise with his ability, because somewhere along the line racist thinking and racists [*sic*] acts would subvert his achievement, whereas in basketball you got the rebound or you didn't. The ball went in or it missed. There were no artificial barriers between ability and reward."

Of course, where race is concerned barriers may be subtle, so interwoven in our activities that they are nearly invisible to those not directly affected. Black players from Solly Walker of St. John's in the early fifties to Georgia's Ronnie Hogue in the early seventies insisted, for instance, that game officials tended to unfairly penalize them in the South. The truth in such instances is impossible to ascertain, although we've learned that the relentlessness of prejudice justifies suspicion. Was Norwood Todmann benched at Wake Forest to avoid having three Black starters, as teammates believed? Was Perry Wallace struck in the brow by a purposeful blow in his first visit to Ole Miss? Did Charles Scott lose in voting for 1969 ACC player of the year because media members had a racist agenda? Why, decades after equality supposedly was achieved, have neither the ACC nor SEC extended more than a taste of authority to African Americans at athletics' highest decision-making levels, with little discussion about their absence?

Only now, more than a half-century after a dispersed group of singular young men crossed the racial divide in the South to play basketball and pursue a college education, after the Black Lives Matter movement called out racism that kills the innocent and maims the spirit, does the depth of the pioneers' unsung achievements come into clearer focus. They and their sport have come a long way, and we have so far yet to go.

Hillsborough, North Carolina
July 2022

CHAPTER 1
AN UNEASY FIT

Billy Jones, University of Maryland, 1964–68
Pete Johnson, University of Maryland, 1964–69

The one thing that doesn't abide by majority rule is a person's conscience.

Harper Lee, *To Kill a Mockingbird*

The distinction was apparent but unspoken as members of the University of Maryland basketball squad trooped into a New Orleans hotel dining room.

Billy Jones, on the Maryland varsity after a year with the freshman squad, stood only 6-foot-1, boasted no national reputation, had no roots in Louisiana. He played sparingly in 1965–66. Yet his presence among the sweat suit–clad Terrapins was a powerful statement in a state that banned athletic competition between blacks and whites, and in a city grudgingly acceding at that moment to court-ordered voter registration for disenfranchised African Americans.

The Terps were in New Orleans as 1965 ended to play Houston and Dayton in the Sugar Bowl Tournament, prelude to the more prominent New Year's Day football contest of the same name. Jones, a Maryland native, was barely seated for the team meal when, as he recalled decades later, "Out of the kitchen comes the chef. He comes out and shakes my hand and goes back. Doesn't say anything. Just shakes my hand and goes back. Politely. Here comes another guy a couple of minutes later. Several people [all of them African Americans] came out of the kitchen at intervals and shook my hand.

"I knew what they were doing. Other folks didn't. 'Do you know those people?' they asked. 'Nah, I don't know them.' They were acknowledging the fact that here's this black guy in uniform in a scenario that's not typically seen down here."

The following year Jones would be joined in the Atlantic Coast Conference's varsity ranks by teammate Julius "Pete" Johnson, who red-shirted his sophomore year after a season on the freshman squad, and by Duke's Claudius Claiborne. Two years later Perry Wallace broke the color barrier in the Southeastern Conference. But in that 1965–66 season, much to his surprise, Jones stood alone—the first African American to play basketball for a high-profile, historically white university south of the Mason-Dixon Line.

"I was really naive. I knew that," Jones says of his status as the ACC's first black basketball signee. "But I didn't make a big deal about it because I honestly thought that other schools were going to do the same thing. To me it was like the ACC had this agreement that we could do this now so everybody can start doing it. That's what I honestly thought. I was a 17-year-old. I am the first to sign. OK. Fine."

The flood Jones expected proved only a trickle; his college career concluded with barely half of all ACC squads integrated. Six seasons after Jones's debut, the University of Virginia became the final ACC program to include an African-American player on its varsity team.

Nor did Jones's groundbreaking role in the ACC command particular attention at the time, or in the decades since. Without overt drama or conflict, the media looked elsewhere. "I'm positive in my mind that, had I gone into detail about how mistreated the University of Maryland and/or Billy Jones were, and had I spewed on and on and on about numerous instances of encountering prejudice, why, there'd have been much, much written," says former Maryland coach Herman "Bud" Millikan. "Where, because of Billy being like he is, it was dropped. Had there been turmoil, it would have been news. Because there was not, why, it wasn't news, and I give credit to Billy Jones."

Contrary to Millikan's assertion and most historical accounts, Jones and cohort Pete Johnson did endure considerable grief playing at College Park. But they purposely hid their troubles from the Terrapins coach and those beyond a small circle of African-American friends. "I was always proud of the fact that we were never the reason for a [racially charged] situation, and when we saw a situation, we would always back out of it and move around it," Johnson says. "We didn't go to [Millikan] complaining about all this stuff, so he thought everything was fine, and in that sense it was."

Given Jones's relatively low profile and Johnson's virtual anonymity, popular credit for breaking the ACC color barrier routinely goes to Charles

Scott, who enrolled at the University of North Carolina two years after Jones arrived at Maryland. This misperception in part reflects the stronger impression made by Scott, a riveting All-American who enjoyed a productive career in professional basketball. North Carolina also did a far better job of marketing Scott over the years, an effort augmented by misinformed commentary on television and from other media outlets.

There also was a sense that breaking barriers in Maryland, a state that never left the Union during the Civil War, surely was less difficult than in North Carolina, an original member of the Confederacy. "I've had people call me because they've gotten into arguments—I'm serious, arguments—about Charlie Scott being the first black player," Jones says with some amusement. Even his daughter got drawn into a discussion of the subject at a wedding. "She kind of addressed them in a very nice way, then gave me a phone call," Jones says.

"I always thought that they needed to get credit; those two guys [Jones and Johnson] didn't get the credit, nor did Bud get the credit, that they deserved," says Hall of Famer Gary Williams, Maryland class of 1967 and the school's men's basketball head coach from the 1989 through 2011 seasons. "Back then it wasn't as liberal, probably, so nobody said, 'What a great thing you've done'—not just for allowing integration to happen, but because obviously then the other schools could break the barriers. Nobody wanted to be first. Bud was first. So he deserved a lot of credit for that." One person who did grow up admiring Johnson and Jones was Orlando "Tubby" Smith, a native of southern Maryland with his own basketball aspirations. He played at High Point College in North Carolina and later became the first African-American head basketball coach at the University of Georgia and then the University of Kentucky, where he presided from the 1998 through 2007 seasons before moving to the University of Minnesota and then High Point University.

The University of Maryland's leadership role in accepting and advancing minorities continued for some 30 years. The school became the first in the ACC or SEC to have an African-American assistant basketball coach when George Raveling was hired in 1969. It also remains the only school in either conference to have an African-American chancellor, with John B. Slaughter directing the university from 1982 to 1988. In 1986 Maryland hired the ACC's first Black head basketball coach, Bob Wade, and in 1994 Debbie Yow became the first female director of athletics in the ACC or SEC.

O

Historically, however, the state of Maryland was no bastion of progressive racial attitudes. Border states such as Maryland, Kentucky, and Missouri seethed with pro-slavery sentiment during the mid-19th century. Thus president-elect Abraham Lincoln sneaked through Baltimore in the dead of night in February 1861. Two months later rioters attacked a trainload of Union troops from Massachusetts passing through the city. The incident inspired a young Baltimore native living in Louisiana to pen "Maryland, My Maryland," which remains the state song and is played at University of Maryland athletic events. Set to the tune of "O Tannenbaum," the song became a Confederate favorite. Among its lyrics: "She is not dead, nor deaf, nor dumb / Huzza! she spurns the Northern scum!"

Slave conditions were often as bad in parts of Maryland as anywhere in the Deep South, as reported by fugitives such as Frederick Douglass. Some claimed that only South Carolina's slave code was more draconian. Not until October 29, 1864—when the Civil War was nearly over and almost two years after Lincoln issued the Emancipation Proclamation—did Maryland become the first border state to abolish slavery. Later it voted against ratifying the 15th Amendment, which extended voting rights to African-American men.

Lynching remained a part of Maryland's racial landscape well into the 20th century. The most notable modern instance occurred in late 1933, within the lifetime of Jones's and Johnson's parents. A mob of 4,000 to 5,000 men, women, and children in Princess Anne—home today to the historically black University of Maryland–Eastern Shore—lynched George Armwood, a suspected African-American criminal. Then they tore apart and burned his dead body, evincing the kind of savagery celebrated in postcards, photographs, and gruesomely detailed newspaper accounts decades earlier in the Deep South. When local authorities balked at making arrests related to the lynching, Governor Albert Ritchie sent the National Guard to enforce the law. A crowd gathered to protect the nine individuals taken into custody, and firemen called onto the scene turned their hoses not on unruly civilians, as was the plan, but on the Guardsmen.

To its credit, the University of Maryland at College Park admitted an African-American man, Donald Murray, to its law school not long after Armwood was lynched. And within months of the May 1954 U.S. Supreme Court ruling in *Brown v. Board of Education*, the former Maryland Agricultural College enrolled a pair of African Americans, becoming the first Southern state university to integrate its undergraduate student body.

Yet the *Brown* decision was hardly embraced within the state at large. For a time following the ruling, a thousand white students per month fled the public school system in Baltimore, Maryland's largest city. Alabama Governor George Wallace, making his first run for national office, found enough kindred spirits in Maryland to garner 43 percent of the vote in the state's 1964 Democratic presidential primary, compared to 30 percent in racially uneasy Indiana and 34 percent in Wisconsin. Denouncing "pointy-headed liberals" who favored civil rights, Wallace found particularly strong support on the Eastern Shore in places like Cambridge, an area from which thousands had marched to serve the Confederacy during the 1860s.

"Wallace astounded political observers not so much by the percentage of votes he could draw for simple bigotry," Theodore White argues in *The Making of the President 1964*, "as by the groups from whom he drew his votes. For he demonstrated pragmatically and for the first time the fear that white working-class Americans have of Negroes."

University of Maryland athletics moved ahead with integration anyway. The autumn preceding Wallace's near-triumph, Darryl Hill transferred to Maryland from the Naval Academy, becoming the first African American to play football at a white school in the South. (Hill, who himself suffered instances of overt racial prejudice as he traveled around the ACC during his playing career, was honored by making the coin toss at the expanded conference's first intra-league football championship game in December 2005.) Then, during the spring in which Wallace polled strongly in Maryland, Jones and Johnson became the school's first African-American basketball signees. Chris Richmond, a black junior-college graduate with local roots, also went out for the basketball squad in the fall of 1964. He was cut prior to the start of the season and never officially played in a Terrapin uniform.

Johnson signed to play at Maryland shortly after Jones, with whom he matriculated and eventually played in the backcourt. But while Jones knew that he was breaking the color barrier, Johnson did not. He felt cheated when he found out.

"As a matter of fact, it didn't even occur to me until I saw the article in the paper that said it," recalls Johnson, a soft-spoken man with an easy laugh. Bald, with gold-rimmed glasses, he often looks down as he speaks, as if avoiding confrontation. "You never thought about being a pioneer. You never thought about being someone like a Jackie Robinson. One of the things that kind of got to me was the fact that, to be a first meant that a lot of things that would happen to the second and the third and the fourth won't happen to the first."

Johnson spent half his childhood in Seat Pleasant, Maryland, at the eastern edge of the District of Columbia; there he attended segregated schools. Yet he failed to appreciate his home state's Southern orientation until subjected to an unexpected geography lesson on a school field trip to a Revolutionary War battle site. "As we crossed into Pennsylvania, we saw a sign that said YOU ARE NOW CROSSING THE MASON-DIXON LINE," Johnson said. "I said, 'My God, I didn't know that we were south of the Mason-Dixon Line.' It was funny."

Black students in Prince George's County did not begin attending high school with whites until Johnson's senior year (1963–64), nearly a decade after the *Brown* decision. As in the districts from Kansas to South Carolina that spawned the landmark desegregation suit, African-American students in Prince George's County were bused long distances to Fairmont Heights High, often passing white schools as they went. "The school was so far away that some of the ballplayers never played because they couldn't get home," Johnson said.

Johnson's parents, Julius and Susie Johnson, had come to the D.C. area to escape such inequities. They hailed from Statesboro, Georgia, northwest of Savannah, where his father had advanced to the eleventh grade and his mother finished the ninth. That was above-average schooling for African Americans in the rural South, where the accent was more on training than education. After their move Julius Sr. became an automobile mechanic and opened his own business. The Johnsons spoke little of life in Georgia, other than telling their son and daughter about going to town on Saturdays and being forced to go to the back of a restaurant to order their fish sandwiches.

"They never said anything about race relations," said Johnson Jr., who moved so fast as a high school ballplayer that he was nicknamed Peter Rabbit (and thus called Pete).

The family first lived in the Capitol Hill section of D.C. in integrated circumstances, the realities of racism kept mercifully at bay. "I just thought everybody was as happy as we were," Johnson said. "I had white friends, and we would play and run. I never saw a difference; they never saw a difference." That sheltered existence was shattered when the family moved to Seat Pleasant and Johnson's mother sent her nine-year-old son to the store. His path took him past an apartment complex where a half-dozen white teenagers loitered on the sidewalk. Thinking nothing of it, Johnson walked between them and immediately was accosted. But just when the jostling began, one of the boys intervened, calling off his friends. "I can't even remember his face," Johnson said. "I just remember what he did and what he said. And then he put his hands on my shoulders and told me to go home. At that point, on my way home, I realized that there was a problem. That's when it hit me."

Ronnie Hogue, a resident of the District of Columbia and the first African-American player at the University of Georgia, came to a similarly sobering realization about his home turf. "At first I was brainwashed and thought all the bad people were in the South," he said. "Maryland was just as bad as Georgia."

Billy Jones ("William is so aristocratic and formal," he protests) was a sixth grader when he enrolled in an integrated school, moving race to the forefront of his experience. Jones grew up in East Towson, an African-American enclave on the outskirts of Baltimore where his family had lived since 1903. Racial separation was the order of things. The Towson Theater, six blocks from his house, wasn't integrated until Jones was a senior in college. Fittingly, the first film shown to an integrated audience was *To Kill a Mockingbird*, Harper Lee's story of racial prejudice in the Deep South.

"Baltimore and Washington were as segregated as Mississippi," according to Clarence "Big House" Gaines, an athletic hero at Morgan State in Baltimore who subsequently became a Hall of Fame basketball coach at Winston-Salem State University in North Carolina. "I left in 1945 to come down here. A Black woman couldn't try on a hat in Baltimore in the store; couldn't stay in a hotel, either."

Jones was born in 1946 and raised by his mother, Ruth. The boy was barely out of infancy when his father, ditchdigger Ernest Jones, was killed in the collapse of a trench on which he was working. His widow, "a very proud lady," according to Jones, supported her son and four daughters by laboring as a maid in West Towson. "We had necessities, but I didn't realize I was poor until I got to high school," Jones said. "Kids had cars. Kids go on vacations. Kids do this at Christmas; kids do that at Christmas. They go away for the summers. That was all foreign to me. I learned to make do with what we had."

The disparity only whetted Jones's appetite to leave West Towson, where talent was frequently squandered and, he says, "People who went off to college were legendary." Jones readily reeled off the names of those who made good their escape. His basketball heroes, in fact, were All-America Oscar Robertson of Cincinnati and David Bishop, a local product who prospered at Virginia State University.

Jones believed that responses to the racism inherent in daily life separated youngsters who escaped from those who "never got a job other than wearing a uniform with their name on it and working for somebody in a parking complex." He said, "I think a part of it was that in some ways, the system of bigotry beat them down. They just did not have any more resistance."

By contrast forceful and direct, Jones found his resolve strengthened by a policeman who off-handedly called him a "monkey"; a store employee who shadowed him simply because of his skin color (a slight he says he still endures); teachers who automatically doubted his intelligence; and strangers who spat in his face. "It taught me an awful lot in terms of just plain perseverance—just hang tough, do what you have to do to stay focused," said Jones, later manager of cast services at Disney World in Orlando, Florida. "If I had responded to that stuff, I'd still be fighting. I wouldn't have had time to do anything else."

Sports in particular were an avenue to equality and self-confidence at Towson High. Jones played football, basketball, and lacrosse but would have stood out anyway, given that his large senior class contained only a handful of African Americans. He was the only Black quarterback in his league and believes that he was the first African American to play lacrosse in Baltimore County. Lacrosse was not without racial undercurrents; Jones was twice hit in the groin with a stick while playing against one particular school, actions that he suspected the opposing coach countenanced.

Jones's college choice came down to Michigan or Maryland, where he was already familiar with the campus. "My whole point was, I'll swap my basketball for a degree," he said. "That was my mind-set. I don't have aspirations to go to the NBA. All I know is, I'll go down there and play my heart out for Coach Millikan, and in return I'll get a degree. That's my focus: I want to get a degree."

For Millikan, Jones's race was not a factor in extending an offer. "To me he was just a very deserving young man who could play basketball and deserved an opportunity to get an education," the coach said. "By God, I was right!"

Johnson, who did have pro aspirations, toyed with the idea of following his hero, Dave Bing, to Syracuse. The streak-shooting second guard decided instead to stay close to home, where friends and family could see him play and media coverage was likely to be substantial.

Neither players' parents shared concerns with Millikan about the dangers facing their sons as they crossed the color line, according to the coach. "I don't know that anything came up," he said. "I can't recall that anything was ever said to me, inquiring from me, 'Well, what will happen?' Had they asked, I would have said, 'I probably don't know what will happen, other than the fact that he will be treated exactly the same as everybody else that's on our squad. If we are going to go into a place to stay, we will go into a place to stay. If we go into a place to eat, we will go into a place to eat. That's the only thing I know. There will be no difference whatsoever.'"

Jones appreciated the quiet protection, the tacit support. But both he and Johnson said their coach's insistence on treating them no differently than their teammates was myopic, no matter how well-intended. Like it or not, they stood inescapably apart as visible exceptions to white society. "We were not normal, and we shouldn't have been treated as normal because it was an abnormal situation, especially for the first time," Johnson said.

Jones said: "I give Millikan credit. He didn't have to do what he did. He offered an opportunity. He didn't know how to do it. How do you practice riding a bike until you get up on one? It's like raising kids; there is no rehearsal for raising kids. So he didn't know exactly what to do. I sympathize in a way, empathize with him in a way. Back then the philosophy was to treat all people the same.

"We know in human psychology that's not the way you treat people—you treat people the way they want to be treated. The paradigm has switched, but in his mind he was doing the right thing. Your moral fibers tell you what to do; his moral fiber was operating correctly. He didn't understand the scenario. I *am* different. When somebody tells me, 'I never see you as a black person,' my message to them is 'Then you don't see me, because I *am* Black. You're really not seeing me. I understand what you're trying to say. I can appreciate that. But the reality is I am Black. I want you to understand that and see that, deal with it.'"

The civil rights movement forced whites to confront the issue of race. Otherwise, it remained abstract to those who never knew or competed athletically against African Americans while growing up. "I don't think back then you gave much thought to the racial situation in this country," Gary Williams says of his own post–World War II childhood, "because everything was so separate that you never had to deal with it." Williams, who played at

Maryland from 1964 to 1967, grew up in Collingswood, New Jersey. He encountered Black players only in pickup basketball action in Trenton and Camden. "I don't think there were any Black kids in our high school," he said. "How'd that work? But that's the way it was."

At first, Williams did not notice that the university he attended had only a smattering of African Americans or that the league in which he competed had none at all. "In the ACC, you played like 16 league games, but you didn't play against any Blacks," he said. "I didn't think about it then. I don't think many major Southern universities had a lot of Black students back then. It wasn't any different than Carolina or other places like that, I'm sure."

Millikan, from all-white environs in Missouri, says he tried for years to recruit African-American players on Maryland's home turf, from Elgin Baylor to John Thompson to Bing. But the university had too few Black undergraduates to foster a welcoming environment, and its basketball program was seriously handicapped in other aspects as well.

Early in Millikan's tenure, which began in 1950, boxing matches at Ritchie Coliseum—an on-campus arena seating 4,200—drew larger crowds than the basketball games that followed. "By the time the teams warmed up," said Millikan of his first and only head coaching assignment, "most of the crowd was gone." Maryland didn't offer a full scholarship until 1953–54, when senior All-America Gene Shue received one. Millikan did not have a full-time assistant coach until 1962. "Shoot, we hardly had lockers individually," said the coach who exclaimed "Hell's fire!" when irked. Meanwhile, league rivals in North Carolina had embraced the sport. North Carolina, Wake Forest, and Duke all had appeared in at least one Final Four by 1964.

In December 1955 the Terrapins moved to the 14,500-seat Student Activities Building (officially named for Judge William P. Cole Jr. and thereafter better known as Cole Field House, the building was repurposed as a football practice facility in 2021 and renamed the Jones-Hill House in honor of its pioneering Black players in basketball and football). Among East Coast facilities, only New York's Madison Square Garden was larger. State high school championships were played at Cole, introducing players like Jones and Johnson to the College Park campus, where both won prep titles in their respective divisions. But Millikan found the benefits minimal and focused his recruiting on Pennsylvania and New Jersey. "There wasn't a basketball player in Maryland, hardly," he said. "The only thing they played was lacrosse at that time."

Even with its handicaps, Maryland basketball got off to a good start under Millikan, considered a potential successor to Hall of Famer Henry "Hank" Iba, for whom he played and worked as an assistant at Oklahoma A&M (now Oklahoma State). Millikan's only previous head coaching experience was at the high school level, but during his first season at Maryland the disciplined Terrapins led the nation in field goal accuracy, making 39.8 percent of their shots. Moreover, the Terps were the only non–North Carolina team to capture an ACC title in the league's first 17 years, winning the 1958 conference tournament. They finished in the upper division of the eight-member ACC in six of the league's first seven seasons before falling off the pace.

The program hit a low point in 1963, its second consecutive eight-win season. Millikan was hanged in effigy on campus, a common expression of student dissatisfaction in those days. "Those hangings in effigy were strictly the work of a small group of campus beatniks," Jim Kehoe, chairman of Maryland's athletic council, said dismissively. Yet Kehoe, the school's long-time track coach before becoming its athletics director in 1969, agreed with those who found fault with Millikan's coaching: "I thought he was one of the outstanding coaches in America, but, frankly, he couldn't recruit. He never got the big man. Basketball was moving into a time when everybody was high scoring, and Bud stuck with the Iba concept."

By the time Millikan was forced out following the 1967 season, fan support had dissipated to such an extent that the atmosphere at Cole was "disheartening," noted Kent Baker in *Red, White and Amen: Maryland Basketball*. "ACC rivals played before packed, howling, reassuringly partisan audiences. Comparatively, Maryland played in a morgue."

Millikan's program briefly regained its footing in 1964–65, when Jones and Johnson were freshmen. The Terrapins finished 18–8 and tied for second place, ending a three-season run of losing records. That season Frank Fellows, a part-time assistant coach and professor in the college of physical education, directed the freshman team. Fellows allowed players more freedom than they would enjoy in Millikan's regimented system. Jones and Johnson appeared in every contest as the squad compiled a 9–7 record. (Fellows eventually succeeded Millikan, surviving two losing seasons as head coach.)

Johnson led the 1965 freshmen in scoring with 20.6 points per game, higher than he would ever average on the varsity. Twice he scored 29 points in a game. Johnson was sufficiently aggressive in attacking the basket to pace the team in free throw attempts, an unusual achievement for a 6-foot guard. Once he had 23 rebounds in a game. Jones was second on the freshman team in scoring with 17.3 points, second in free throw tries, and second in rebounds, with 154 in 16 games.

"Pete Johnson could have played in the NBA. I really believe that," said Williams. The intense head coach, who led his alma mater to the 2002 national championship and a school-record run of 11 straight NCAA appearances (1994–2004), had eight first-round NBA draft picks since returning to Maryland. "Billy was a good athlete playing basketball. Pete was more of a pure basketball player."

Millikan remembered Jones as "tremendously agile. Decent shooter. Smart kid, smart player. Knew how to do what he needed to do. Very competitive. He was very, very good in some of our pressing-type defenses. He helped us a lot." That help extended off the court, where Johnson came to rely personally on Jones, who had previous experience in an integrated environment. "I guess if I was there just by myself, I don't know how I would have made it," says Johnson, who served as a nondenominational minister in Maryland for more than two decades. "He would be like a big brother. He understood a lot more than I understood, and I fought against a lot of things that he didn't fight against. I didn't openly fight; I wasn't openly rebellious. I was just frustrated, and nobody knew it. . . . But I got along. I didn't create problems on the team or anything like that."

Johnson's high school coach stressed sportsmanship, perhaps recognizing that an all-Black team would undergo special scrutiny. His players were instructed to speak politely to one another as well as to others, to always hand rather than toss the ball to an official, and to never disrupt, dispute, or disrespect.

So when a racially tinged episode went unremarked prior to Johnson's freshman season at Maryland, the experience undermined his confidence in Millikan. It never fully returned. The team held a workout involving freshmen and upperclassmen that summer of 1964, the sort called voluntary but deemed mandatory. Johnson found himself matched against a white senior. "I'd just run all over him, playing defense, making it very hard for him," he said. "And then he couldn't stay with me. So he just started calling me names." Johnson played on, expecting the coaches to quash the racist banter, but nothing was said, then or later.

Jones didn't hear the comments, yet he found Johnson's recollection quite plausible. As a senior the burly guard/forward got into a locker room scuffle with a white teammate who called him a racially altered version of "Neanderthal." Millikan knew nothing of that incident, which brought anger bubbling to Jones's otherwise placid surface. "I wanted to beat him to death," he said of his teammate.

"In the heat of battle, some things would come out," Jones said of bigoted remarks. "Pete and I, I think personality-wise, are a little different. I honestly think that they [other players] may have thought if they said something to me, I would respond. I don't mind being physical. I played that way, and I really don't mind it."

Internalizing wounds and disappointments, as Johnson did, fit the strategy embraced by Maryland's first African-American players in football and basketball. They kept their own counsel, tended to their own affairs. When hassled on the College Park campus or outside their motel in Charlottesville prior to a game at the University of Virginia, they dealt with the situation without assistance or guidance from their coaches.

Blending in was hard work. There were few guideposts, few relevant examples to emulate. The outside world paid little attention to Jones, Johnson, and cohorts as they set out on uncharted racial seas. They, more than their coaches and professors, were left to measure for themselves what constituted progress or danger or wisdom.

"We'd shut the door, and we'd talk," Jones said. "It was not an easy time. It required constant adjustment and trying to see the good in stuff and not interpret something in the negative. Something happens, let's not make it a racial thing, necessarily. . . . Let's not make it an issue here, because then you get sidetracked. Am I causing myself more problems than it's worth? Am I bringing up stuff that I should be able to handle? I handled it before I met Bud, so I thought, 'I'm going to handle it now, and I'm not going to tell anybody.'"

Later, Millikan and many colleagues proudly reported that integrating their squads went well. A key indicator, in the coaches' estimation, was that their office doors were always open, yet groundbreaking African-American players voiced few complaints. Chip Connor, an assistant coach at Virginia in the early 1970s, when Al Drummond was the sole Black player on the squad, offers a typical recollection: "Drummond almost never came to the office and complained about anything. He never said, 'My social life is this or that. I'm not having a good time.' He never said anything." Jones counters rhetorically: "What are you going to say? 'Coach, I don't have a date?' What are you going to say? Seriously."

Johnson said the tension of a pioneer's role "was just well-hidden." And the tension surely was more pronounced for the cadre of young men who attended segregated schools and stepped with little preparation into a predominantly white milieu. Among the arguments mounted by the National Association for the Advancement of Colored People in the *Brown* case was that a segregated system had a deleterious effect on the self-image of African-Americans relegated to inferior schools and inferior social status, as was clearly the case under "separate but equal" policies. The insular world from which they emerged might be nurturing and protective, but it also was fraught with handicaps both physical and psychological.

"If we did it all over again, would we do it any better?" Jones wondered. "I don't know if I did all I was supposed to do, so I can't call anybody else now on what they didn't do."

Jones and Johnson both struggled academically at Maryland, at least at first. The low point of his college years, Jones said, was a disappointing freshman grade-point average that he soon righted. He would go on to earn both an undergraduate and a master's degree. Johnson, on the other hand, stayed in academic trouble and never graduated. When he and Jones were sophomores, Millikan asked Johnson to redshirt so that he could get up to speed academically. That meant the guard would sit out the 1965–66 season without losing any playing eligibility under NCAA regulations then in effect. Reluctantly, Johnson acquiesced.

Consequently, for an entire season Jones stood alone, feeling "somewhat abandoned" by Johnson. He became the first African-American to play in an ACC varsity basketball game when the Terrapins lost, 65–61, at Penn State on December 1, 1965.

That year, and in ensuing seasons when Johnson joined Jones on the varsity, white teammates and coaches did their best to remove hurdles and to address prejudices before they harmed the two Black players. Or, at least, they tried within a limited spectrum of understanding. "Billy and Pete could take care of themselves," Williams said. "We made sure they weren't ganged up on—like rough, elbow stuff in a game—because they were black. The only overt situation I ever saw was when we played Duke one Saturday night. We were taking the train back to D.C. overnight, and we had walked into the train station [in Durham]. They had a little lunch place. They had a white place to eat and a little Black stand where you could get stuff to go. This was back in 1967, I guess, and they wouldn't serve Billy there where we were. So we all just left. That was the only thing like that. Nobody ever kept us out of a hotel room because of having Black guys."

Jones appreciated that Williams and others took him "under their wing" by tending to his welfare. He later heard of situations in which Millikan changed team plans out of similar sensitivity. But for all the concern, Jones says, those around him inhabited a separate universe, one in which they took for granted freedoms he dared not assume. "You had to always be conscious of where you were," Jones said. "That's something other players didn't have. They never thought about it."

Jones assiduously avoided situations on the road that might prove confrontational. When teammates tried to include him in outings, he often excused himself and stayed in his room, pleading the press of schoolwork. "I was more concerned with that person off the street starting something with me than I was with somebody during the game itself," Jones said. "Fifteen thousand people and the officials, what are they going to do to me? Other than call me a name, what are they going to do to me?"

Certainly there was plenty of name-calling. Johnson remembers students at a North Carolina school—he thinks it was Duke—chanting "Leroy! Leroy!," a derogative term for African Americans. "They thought that was so very funny," he said. Williams has ugly memories of Clemson and the University of South Carolina, which Johnson says were "the worst" places to play. "I'm not sure there had ever been a Black player in their gym, let alone playing on a team," Williams said of the ACC's original southernmost outposts. "It was tough. You could hear stuff from the stands. You know, the usual name-calling. Yelling stuff at us, too, the white guys, for playing with those guys."

Jones might dismiss the dangers posed by hostile fans, yet both he and Johnson admit to having altered their play on the road. Jones says that he first circumscribed his conduct in high school, quickly calculating the costs and benefits of chasing a ball into the stands. "Sometimes you'd kind of let it go and get back, as opposed to getting in that stand and getting punched," he says. "I guarantee that doesn't exist for Gary. He never thought of that. Never, ever crossed his mind."

Life on the road accented the separateness of Maryland's Black players. They were surrounded by white people day after day, traveling places where few African Americans ventured. Sometimes the sense of isolation grew so heavy that Johnson and Jones sought out predominantly Black schools in the cities they visited just "to see some Black people," Jones says.

Returning to College Park was not altogether comfortable, either. During his senior year Jones was quoted publicly as saying that bias against African Americans "absolutely" existed at the University of Maryland, particularly when it came to the social scene. Campus life revolved around fraternities, yet Jones was never invited to a frat party, let alone rushed by one of the many fraternities. That remained true his senior season, when he was a team co-captain and yet, unlike his white counterparts, was not avidly sought for social functions. "You felt like you were a partial citizen," Jones said. "You were a noble but partial citizen. That's not the greatest of feelings."

Games provided a respite, one denied to Johnson during 1965–66 while he sat out. Jones ran into a backstop support early that same season, suffered a hairline fracture in his foot, and missed nine games in December and January. Maryland finished the season with a 14–11 record. Jones was injured and unable to play in New Orleans when his presence in the hotel dining room so pleased African Americans on the kitchen staff.

Jones was back in the lineup, injury undiagnosed, well in advance of the 1966 ACC tournament, held for the last time at Raleigh's Reynolds Coliseum on the North Carolina State University campus. There, during the Dixie Classic holiday tournament in December 1958, fans had hectored Oscar Robertson, a Black player for the University of Cincinnati. The crowd reaction was far different when Jones took the Reynolds floor as a substitute in the Terps' ACC tournament opener, a 77–70 loss to North Carolina. On that early March evening, he was accorded a polite ovation that went unremarked by the sports media. Jones cherished the moment, if only as validation from a corps of knowledgeable and ultimately accepting fans. "I really felt that the fans appreciated basketball, and that was my read on why I got the hand when I went into the game," Jones said. "I think it was acknowledging the fact that this young Black kid had survived the season."

The season ended in a more emphatic manner two weeks later at Cole Field House. Texas Western (later the University of Texas–El Paso), employing an African-American starting five, upset lily-white Kentucky, coached by Adolph Rupp, to win the NCAA championship. The game proved pivotal to changing perceptions. Texas Western entered the NCAA Tournament with a 23–1 record. Coach Don Haskins's Miners played tough defense, allowing but 62 points per game, 8 fewer than Kentucky. Yet they were given little chance of winning the title, largely due to a stereotypical view of black players' capabilities. "The Miners," wrote James H. Jackson of the *Baltimore Sun*, "don't worry much about defense" but instead "try to pour the ball through the hoop as fast as possible . . . The running, gunning Texas quintet can do more things with a basketball than a monkey on a 50-foot jungle wire."

There were, in fact, two styles of play prevalent in college basketball at the time. Most white teams played a deliberate, patterned style predicated on screens and passes, with two distinct guards, two distinct forwards, and a center. Iba, Rupp, and Long Island University's Clair Bee were the leading practitioners of this style. All are in the Basketball Hall of Fame. "Everything was a pattern," Big House Gaines, the former Winston-Salem State coach, said. "If you didn't run a pattern, you were playing what they called niggerball." African Americans tended to play a more up-tempo, aggressive game. "We have always played 94–40, smoke and smother," said Harvey Heartley, former head coach at St. Augustine's College in Raleigh, North Carolina, alluding to the dimensions in feet of a basketball court. "What that meant was we were going to come after you from baseline to baseline for 40 minutes."

Millikan, recommended for the Maryland job by Iba, most decidedly believed in pass and screen, to the chagrin of many players. "I disagree wholeheartedly that it's slowpoke, I'll put it that way," Millikan said of his attack. "We wanted to make sure we had the ball with us." Maryland proved to be Millikan's only college head coaching assignment. By the time he completed his 17-year tenure at College Park, his approach—which included Iba's practice of having players lie on their stomachs on the court during timeouts to combat crowd noise—was a bit anachronistic.

Jones and Williams went on to become coaches. Both credit Millikan for teaching them the importance of defense, which the Terps prosecuted in a tough, disciplined, up-tempo manner. That was in distinct contrast, however, to their deliberate offense. "The offense style didn't complement the defensive style," Jones said. "One was very, very aggressive, in-your-face, go-at-you, and the other was walk it down and run through nine options."

"You played a certain way," Williams said. "That was the way Hank Iba played, and that was the way we were going to play. In other words, we played what we called a 'white style' back then. There's no doubt about it.

We made a lot of passes. We weren't allowed to go between our legs or behind our backs. [Millikan] was much more comfortable if you set up every time rather than run a fast break. We played with our back foot on the top of the circle. That's where our man-to-man defense started. That's where Oklahoma A&M started their defense. That's all we did, but we did it well."

Certain players, usually forwards, were the designated shooters in Millikan's system. Everyone else was expected to fill a subordinate offensive role. Jones and Johnson were not among the anointed and thus were castigated during games for taking shots they had mastered in high school. Millikan yelled, waved his arms, threw towels, or otherwise took pains to express his displeasure. Jones still vividly recalls such an instance at Wake Forest, where the team benches were located along the baseline. "So, if I face the basket, I'm looking right at Coach Millikan. I can remember getting the ball, faking one way and wheeling, going the other way on the dribble, and shooting about an 8-foot, left-handed hook. Coach jumps up and tells me, 'No!' He screams 'No!' at me." Incidents of that sort severely eroded confidence, to the point that Johnson and Jones discussed transferring to another school.

Jones used the experience to shape his coaching philosophy. He believed that Williams likewise embraced a fast-paced offense based on the disappointments of playing Millikan's way. "Part of my philosophy was to build players' confidence, to make sure they had enough shooting drills to give enough confidence to take the shots, enough confidence to make decisions," said Jones, who was an assistant coach at American University, San Diego State, and Stanford before directing the University Maryland–Baltimore County basketball program for a dozen years.

Johnson likewise was limited by Millikan's system. "Pete was a pretty jump shooter and really slick with the ball," Jones said. "That was Pete's game. I think he was ahead of his time when it came to offensive skill. He really was. There weren't that many players playing that way. But taking your man and breaking him down one-on-one, that was not part of Bud's offense."

The result was confusion, frustration, and resentment on Johnson's part. Dissatisfaction affected his schoolwork and soured his view of Millikan's coaching. He felt insulted, not instructed, when he tried to rise to an occasion during a game—he'd done repeatedly in high school—only to be reprimanded for his shot selection. He speculated that his redshirt season, his failure to start games, and his playing time were attributable to his skin color. He wondered why Maryland recruited him, only to impose a style adverse to his game and professional aspirations. Once admittedly "so cocky" about his abilities that "nothing could ever destroy that," Johnson fell into a prolonged funk. "There was a conflict going on between the things I knew I could do and wanted to do, and [the things I] couldn't do and they didn't want me to," Johnson said. "Boy, I was so frustrated. There wasn't much room in the system to use your abilities, and I wanted to. So you get to the point where you leave this off, and you leave that off just to get on the court and to fit in. After a while of not practicing those things, they become kind of dormant."

For all that, Johnson enjoyed a successful career. He appeared in all 75 games Maryland played from the 1966–67 through 1968–69 seasons. He scored in double figures each year, including his junior season, when he recorded a team-high average of 15.0 points per game. Jones, who sometimes played at forward, managed only a 2.8-point average in 1965–66, his first year on the varsity. He became a starter as an upperclassman, recording consecutive double-figure scoring averages in 1966–67 and 1967–68. Both players believe that they also had a major impact forcing turnovers, blocking shots, and making assists, statistics that went widely unrecorded in college basketball until the 1980s.

Johnson made peace with his Maryland athletic career when, after working for the recreation department in Washington, D.C, he was called "to carry the gospel of Jesus Christ to a lost world." As a minister he found grist for numerous sermons in his Maryland experiences. A favorite topic is comportment "even in the face of defeat," he said, "and how to honor those that have authority over you. Even if things aren't going your way, you still honor those that are above you."

Jones also found "lessons to be learned" from a career that others call modest but he deems impressive, considering that "there wasn't one damn play designed to go my way."

Politics was a major part of Jones's college experience; he supported the black student movement on campus, savored an eloquently inspirational speech at Ritchie Coliseum by Muhammad Ali, and closely followed riots in D.C. that reflected the anger and disenfranchisement of a near-powerless African-American majority. He struggled, as did most pioneering Black athletes, to balance a burgeoning sense of racial identity with the athlete's inherent respect for authority—not to mention fear of losing his scholarship.

Viewed through a militant's lens, Jones found himself and Johnson wanting in their acceptance of Millikan's edicts about playing the game. "We didn't challenge," Jones said. "We didn't test authority. 'You just tell me how hard, and I'll run. You just tell me how hard, and I'll do it, Coach.' That's who we were. We were gullible. I wish I had been more challenging, if you would, to authority. Probably would have gotten thrown off the team, but I wish I had been."

Some four decades later, Jones believed a different challenge to authority is in order. The levers of power almost completely eluded the grasp of African Americans in the Atlantic Coast Conference for a long time after its founding in 1953. All but Duke of the original eight ACC members have had a Black head basketball coach. Football coaches saw a similar but less sweeping rise in diversity on the sidelines. Craig Littlepage, hired at Virginia in 2001, was the first Black director of athletics in conference history. Currently Virginia and Duke have two of the handful of female Black ADs in the country.

The league office has had a few Black assistant commissioners, and no publicly articulated policy on tapping African Americans to fill decision-making roles. Black head coaches in any sport remain anomalies, as do African Americans in a position of authority within their athletics departments. Jones was attuned to this failure on many levels: as a pioneer in athletic race relations, as someone with an affinity for the conference, and as a self-described mentor and coach at Disney for "people who are not from privilege" but are eager to advance within the corporate world. Yet he was not an advocate of affirmative action, resenting those who erroneously assume that his admittance to Maryland was a product of preferential treatment rather than merit.

Nor would Jones, honored as an ACC basketball "legend" in 2007, compel the conference to embrace diversity. "It's not part of your vision if you're forced to do it. Trust me, if you're forced to do it, you're not putting the same passion and commitment into it." Instead, Jones challenged the ACC's "good old boys" to recognize the wisdom embodied in Disney's stated commitment to "ensure that inclusiveness is woven into your fabric." Just as the South, once an economic and social backwater, advanced after it accepted the need to employ every available human resource, so the ACC would improve itself by embracing the full gamut of those it educates.

"The playing field is easy," Jones said, knowing just how difficult it was in his day. "You need athletes. They produce dollars. College Park will reap tremendous benefit from what their football and basketball programs have done. If you're smart, you leverage every talent that comes along. If you don't trust in the people that you educate, I don't think you have much credibility as far as your education.

"There's talent out there, and I'd say, ACC, make me proud. Make yourself proud. We've done the player side. We've done one more story about Billy Jones's role. We're tired of hearing that story. Let's get some stories about people in administration now."

CHAPTER 2
FORMS OF HELL

Perry Wallace, Vanderbilt University, 1966–70

If someone says, "I love God," and hates his brother, he is a liar; for he who does not love his brother whom he has seen, how can he love God whom he has not seen?

1 John 4:20

Perry Wallace stood alone as halftime wound down that February night in 1968, beset by a boisterous crowd of 8,500 in an arena he found "a hellish, hellish place." Vanderbilt University teammates, coaches, and support staff, apparently oblivious to his fate, had returned to the playing floor at Tad Smith Coliseum on the Oxford campus of the University of Mississippi. That left Wallace, brow bloodied from an opponent's blow delivered in the first half, to travel alone from locker room to court, past a gauntlet of overhanging fans who screamed loudly for his return.

"I looked out the door and I saw our team warming up, and I could hear the catcalls," he told an interviewer several years later. "You could hear the catcalls over the radio, people told me. They were hollering, 'Where's the nigger? Where's the nigger? Is he scared? Did he quit?' I stood there and looked out, and I said, 'Who is on *my* side?'"

This was no rhetorical question.

Barely five years had passed since deadly rioting rocked the Ole Miss campus upon James Meredith's court-ordered enrollment as an undergraduate student. Federal troops had been withdrawn from campus two and a half years before Perry Wallace came to town. As late as the mid-1960s, according to an Ole Miss history professor, "A white man could literally kill a Black person in Mississippi without much fear of reprisal."

Wallace, a native of Nashville, Tennessee, and a former musician, knew well the haunted melody he called "the song of the South." From the

23

moment he had signed to attend Vanderbilt, breaking the color barrier in the Southeastern Conference, Wallace had dreaded this visit to Ole Miss, a task that deterred others from blazing the trail he cut from 1966 through 1970.

Sure enough, the sophomore heard Rebel fans threaten to lynch him, beat him, castrate him. They cheered his mistakes, pelted him with objects, followed cheerleaders in organized chants of abuse and ridicule. "I got spat on at halftime by four generations of one family," Wallace recalled. Ole Miss was not unique in extending so vile a welcome, just a bit more relentless, organized, and menacing. "Certain places [made you feel as if] you had just gone to hell," Wallace said. "These were cracker boxes in all kinds of ways, I guess you might call it, because they were right there on you and you heard everything that they said. You ran down the floor near the sidelines on a fast break, and you were 3 feet from somebody with a Rebel flag calling you a bunch of names."

For all its intensity, Wallace's sense of isolation was not peculiar to the moment.

"People not supporting me and all that—a lot of that didn't surprise me because it was wide open. All kinds of things were possible," Wallace said. "I could get shot. I would [worry about it]. Whether it was founded, you didn't know. But you have a right to wonder, and in the absence of knowing, when this is the first time that this had been done, you've got people screaming and threatening to do all kinds of stuff. . . . You know that there are a bunch of people that would love to see you die. There's a whole bunch of them in a society where killing some Black folks and having some Black folks die, or the value of black life, that wasn't considered anything very important."

Wallace went on to enjoy one of the better halves of his career that night at Oxford, and to make a lasting mark on the basketball court. Playing at a distinct disadvantage as a 6-foot-5 center, he nonetheless started and led the Commodores in rebounds every year he was on the varsity. At the conclusion of the 2021–22 season, Wallace, an all-conference player as a senior, still ranked second at Vanderbilt in career rebounds (894) and rebounds per game (11.5) behind Clyde Lee, a two-time SEC Player of the Year.

Wallace's SEC trials ultimately left few overt wounds, the blow to the head at Ole Miss being the most memorable exception. Long afterward, before a Washington, D.C., classroom as a tenured professor of environmental, business, and international law at Washington College of Law at American University, Wallace showed no sign of being haunted by his experiences. Lecturing on such topics as buy-and-sell agreements, his rich voice accompanied by the cricketlike chirps of students' laptops, he was a commanding but unthreatening presence, a large, round-cheeked man with a ready smile and a genial manner.

Yet speak with Wallace, and it becomes clear that he paid a price for his pioneering role in SEC sports. Snubs were far more common than acts of acceptance. Only a handful of people reached out or offered support. Most of those at and around Vanderbilt, a private university catering to the Southern elite, knew African Americans as laborers and servants, if they knew them at all. Accustomed to a segregated universe in which Blacks and whites moved in separate orbits, they had no experience of meeting African Americans on equal terms.

Wallace discovered this bitter truth firsthand while enrolled in a summer program for incoming Vanderbilt freshmen. Years earlier, when recruited to play for Nashville's prestigious all-Black Pearl High School basketball team, Wallace had readily acceded to his father's requirements that "you keep your studies up and keep going to church and acting like you've got good sense." Once at Vanderbilt he dutifully began attending a nearby church of the same fundamentalist, conservative denomination to which his family belonged. "Religion was a big part of my life," Wallace said. "It was very, very important, and I thought, well, I could just dress up each Sunday and go right out of the dorm and go right across the street to the Church of Christ. I would go in and sit in the back."

It wasn't long before a deputation of parishioners politely met him at the door as he arrived. "They had a difficulty, and they explained it to me: It was that older people in the church were very disturbed by my being there, and they said that they were not going to leave bequests in their wills to the church. I found that very interesting, and I said, not with any sarcasm, 'It seems to be that it's about the money.' So I agreed—I agreed not to go to church that day. I went on out. They were nice. It was cordial, but it was frank; it was blunt. The result was blunt."

Wallace's rejection at the church door reflected an enduring national phenomenon. Of nearly 100,000 white churches in the South surveyed in 1959, fewer than two dozen had Black members. Baptist minister Robert Seymour, who worked with University of North Carolina coach Dean Smith on integration in Chapel Hill, tells of several African Americans who showed up to worship at a white Southern church, only to be chastised: "If you were Christians, you wouldn't be here." (Segregated worship remained so ingrained, particularly in the South, that in August 2003 a Black Louisiana minister offered a cash bounty to whites who would attend his church.)

Religion was one of many realms in which Wallace, like other pioneering Black players, endured awkward, often stinging isolation. On-court abuse only added to their difficulties. Incidents like the Ole Miss game "really symbolized something to me, and it was the importance of having my own internal, independent system for handling [those kinds of situations]," Wallace said. "Without question, it would be easy [for the white players] to walk back into that gym and not get all that close to me, because I'm the one that's getting screamed at."

Bob Warren roomed with Wallace when the team was on the road and played alongside him in the frontcourt. Warren grew up in tiny Hardin, a town in western Kentucky, and had met only two African Americans before attending Vanderbilt. "I had been taught as a child that there was no difference, so for Perry to be my roommate was a privilege," he says.

Warren played in the 90–72 Vanderbilt victory at Oxford in 1968. He recalls that the crowd "either cheered or booed every time" his Black teammate took a shot, but he cannot remember whether success or failure elicited a positive response.

Neither Warren nor anyone else associated with Vanderbilt thought to aid Wallace by following the example of Harold "Pee Wee" Reese, another white product of western Kentucky. During a baseball game in Boston two decades earlier, Reese had placed a friendly arm around the shoulder of pioneering Brooklyn Dodger teammate Jackie Robinson to stifle heckling from the crowd. "I didn't have a clue as to what was going on," said Warren, who was two years ahead of Wallace and a fellow engineering major. "I'm sorry to this day that I didn't understand to the degree that I do now. I'm very sorry that I couldn't be more of an encouragement to him, because it was tough."

One reason Warren failed to bridge the chasm of experience and sensitivity was that Wallace kept his own counsel, choosing his words and company carefully. "When he was around me, he didn't give any indication, through what he expressed verbally, that there was a whole lot going on there," Warren said. "He never, not once, as a roommate said anything negative to me about anybody. And he was very quiet, just a gentleman."

That temperament, camouflaging powerful pride and determination, made Wallace the ideal person to break the racial barrier in the SEC, according to both Blacks and whites. "He was very even-keeled and always thought things through," said Roy Skinner, the Vanderbilt head coach from 1961 to 1976. "The way he conducted himself commanded respect." Yet, unlike the Brooklyn brain trust that guided Jackie Robinson's odyssey, Skinner gave little thought to Wallace's personality while recruiting him to play in the SEC, the southernmost major college league. "No, I wasn't that smart," the coach said. "It just happened. I just recruited a good basketball player and a good person."

Skinner had little experience with African Americans growing up in Paducah, in western Kentucky. "It was very segregated," he recalled of his hometown in a border state presumably less racially rigid than Tennessee, a member of the old Confederacy. "Black people had their own schools. Blacks and whites didn't play each other at all. Didn't even think about it." Paducah produced another college coach at mid-century: "Big House" Gaines, coached at historically black Winston-Salem State University for 47 years. (Gaines, who died in April 2005, earned a spot in basketball's Hall of Fame after becoming the second coach to reach 800 career wins; Kentucky's Adolph Rupp was first.) "We never really experienced the hardcore segregation—the Ku Klux Klan, people running you to the back of the bus, and all that sort of thing," Gaines said of Paducah. "There were just certain unwritten laws or customs that you followed. If you went to the movie, you went to the balcony."

Raised in a world comfortably compartmentalized for whites—and having coached only in Kentucky, South Carolina, and Tennessee—Skinner gave no thought to the special pressures that Wallace would face. "The catcalls and the things at the games, I just hadn't anticipated anything like that," Skinner admitted. "To me [having an African-American player on the team] wasn't a big deal, and I was surprised that it was at some of the other places. I shouldn't have been."

Cornelius Ridley, Wallace's coach at all-Black Pearl High School, offers a different take on Vanderbilt's recruitment of the hometown hero. "Perry was a fine gentleman, a fine gentleman and a scholar," Ridley said of the valedictorian in a class of 441. "It was a perfect fit. He wasn't one of these guys who was going to run after girls. He wasn't going to do anything. He'd play basketball, get in his work."

Perhaps even more importantly, Wallace was apt to avoid behaviors that would provoke racist whites. As Ridley perceived Vandy's interest: "We're going to integrate with a Black guy, but we want the Black guy to be the perfect guy. We don't want him bringing any excess baggage with him. He's got to be willing to be called names, you know, and not retaliate. A level-headed person. Good family background. I think they did all that; they checked him out."

Jimmy Davy, who covered sports for Nashville's *Tennessean*, met informally with Wallace to talk through the pros and cons of attending Vanderbilt. He was pleased when Wallace decided to stay in Nashville. "He was perfect in terms of personality, hometown celebrity, academic achievement," said Davy, a Nashville native. "If you had to come up with a model to be the first anything to break a social barrier, he was perfect. And I think handled himself really well.

"The SEC owes Perry Wallace. He could have been the wrong guy and delayed for a number of years the active, aggressive recruitment of African-American kids. There was absolutely nothing to dislike about Perry Wallace. Even if you were a bigot, you had to like Perry Wallace."

Wallace certainly had the respect of other players. His 1969–70 team-mates elected him their squad captain, and he was voted the SEC Sportsman of the Year in 1970. He also made the dean's list, won an award as Vanderbilt's most outstanding engineering student, and was elected to the engineering honor society while completing a double major in engineering mathematics and electrical engineering with a B average. Vanderbilt students named Wallace the 1970 Bachelor of Ugliness, a signal honor reserved for a senior and marked by the awarding of an inscribed Bowie knife.

During his varsity career Wallace faced only one African American from another SEC school, Auburn's Henry Harris. Yet he helped break a logjam, countering a decades-old trend that saw gifted African-American athletes in the South routinely go to historically Black schools or flee north or west to play on integrated squads. Within four years of Wallace's 1970 graduation, more than half of SEC basketball recruits were African American. In 1977 Alabama won the conference title with an all-Black starting five. And by 1978 eight of ten SEC schools had at least three Black starters, and 83 percent of the league's recruits were African American.

Wallace had arrived at Vanderbilt two autumns after it accepted its first Black undergraduates. He took his pioneering role to heart, carrying it as banner and burden at a time when universally integrated basketball squads seemed a distant dream. "You've always got to act a certain way," he said. "The good thing about that is that it does keep your standards high; it does give you a certain sense of the importance of reflecting certain standards. Obviously the bad part of it is the pressure, the constant pressure, including how it feels if you make a mistake or something doesn't pan out."

One measure of Wallace's suitability for the conflicted and repressed atmosphere in which he operated was the contrasting fate of the other African-American player with whom he entered Vanderbilt. Northerner Godfrey Dillard, a 6-foot-1 guard, lasted two years before transferring to Eastern Michigan. Dillard, product of a Catholic high school, had known whites only as equals and thought nothing of speaking his mind and standing his ground. "If somebody said something to me, I'd cuss them out," he said. "If a student came up to me and bumped me in the elevator or was drunk and breathing his alcohol in my face, I would tell him to get out of my face."

Dillard went to Vanderbilt believing that it gave him "the opportunity to do something special on behalf of people of color," he said. Those were heady times on campus, as the growing militancy of young civil rights leaders intersected with mounting student anger directed at the Vietnam War and with a surging awareness of the repression of women. Dillard became president of the school's nascent Afro-American Association and in the spring of 1967 invited incendiary Black leader Stokely Carmichael to speak on campus. That sparked a furious local backlash and a confrontation over free speech in which Vanderbilt chancellor Alexander Heard sided with the students.

Dillard edited *Rap from the 11th Floor*, a free newspaper chronicling the concerns of the school's several dozen Black students, and spoke to the faculty on the need for change in campus attitudes. "All of Vanderbilt's Black students in those days were basically middle-of-the-road," said Bev Asbury, former university chaplain. "There was not a radical among them. But there were people of conscience and deep conviction, and he was one of them."

Comparing himself to Wallace, Dillard said, "I was from Detroit. I was big-city. I had played ball with white boys all my life. I talked trash, and I backed it up. I was much more aggressive, much more outgoing. In that sense, Perry was much more of the typical Southern Black person who had adjusted or who had found a balance in terms of dealing with the racist environment that he grew up in."

Predictably, Dillard earned a reputation as a troublemaker. "Although I grew up in a racist environment as well up here in the North, I certainly did not have the history of lynchings and the all-Black schools and the feelings of inferiority that may have grown from that," he says. "I didn't have all of that. I was a very proud young Black athlete. On a mission."

Dillard was simply too brash for a world defined by centuries of second-class Black citizenship, unanswerable violence, and institutionalized segregation. "A man who knows the South can sense the feelings of it, can sense danger when the ways of the South are challenged, can sense how far one can go safely," wrote John Ehle in a civil rights history from the era. Wallace was attuned to those nuances, even if Dillard was not.

Wallace remembers Dillard as exhibiting "the same sense of spunkiness and spirit as almost any white boy at Vanderbilt." But those attributes proved confusing, then confounding, for an African American on a historically white Southern campus. "In hindsight, I probably should have said, 'Am I here to be a politician, or am I here to be an athlete?'" says Dillard, who went on to become an attorney and was named Michigan's 1999 Lawyer of the Year. In 2003 he played a role in fashioning a case for the University of Michigan's race-based admissions policy that was upheld by the U.S. Supreme Court. "But I was politically active even before I got there, and I was committed. I was seriously committed, and I didn't let people turn me around."

Dillard insists that he was driven away after failing to heed Skinner's warnings to quit his political activities, and that he transferred on the eve of the 1968–69 season to preserve his sanity and academic career. The coach says that Dillard wasn't an SEC-caliber player, particularly after he sustained a knee injury (just before his sophomore season) that forced the guard to sit out a year.

"If you weren't controlled and you had just normal, natural reactions, that was going to lead to the type of conflict that would make it all fall apart," Wallace said of the tensions of the time. "The fact is that you needed someone that was not going to fly off the handle, who was going to understand the way the South had operated and try to provide some sort of transition. If we're talking about evolution as opposed to revolution, that means something. That means some attempt for a smoother transaction, and it also means a certain amount of taking of the weight."

Wallace's endurance derived from a lifetime of navigating the racial waters of Nashville, a city that, despite its reputation for moderation, was thoroughly and sometimes brutally segregated. "It was still a terribly segregated time," Asbury said. Hired by Heard to facilitate campus integration, the Georgian arrived at Nashville in January 1967, midway through Wallace's and Dillard's freshman year. He stayed for three decades. Nashville "was just as incorrigibly corrupt and set in its ways as any city in the South," he said.

Still, Nashville prided itself on the achievements reflected in its nick-names. The capital city—a center of trade, publishing, and education—dubbed itself the "Athens of the South" after a replica of the Greek Parthenon was constructed on its outskirts to celebrate the Tennessee centennial in 1897. Downtown came to be called the "Wall Street of the South" due to its concentration of banking and insurance companies. The city's plentitude of places of worship suggested the "Protestant Vatican" and the "buckle of the Bible Belt." And the rise of country and western music and the fame of the Grand Ole Opry led to the moniker "Music City." (Nashville's 100,000-watt radio station WLAC also had broad impact. Beaming rhythm and blues from Mexico to Canada, it promoted a style of music virtually frozen out of mainstream radio in segregated America.)

The city boasted 16 colleges and universities, including Meherrin Medical College and Fisk University, the latter the alma mater of inspirational black leader W. E. B. Du Bois. Both schools were among the finest historically Black educational institutions in the nation.

African Americans in Nashville were not prevented from voting, as in most Southern communities. They consequently had political clout, with their support spelling the difference in a 1951 mayoral race won by Ben West. Nine years later, confronted by sit-in demonstrators, the Vanderbilt grad's grudging support helped break the back of segregation in downtown retail establishments. African Americans served on the Nashville board of education and were members of the police force and fire department, anomalies in the segregated South. Two Black residents were elected to the city council in 1951, products of a local act establishing district representation that West had championed when serving as a state senator.

Despite those cracks in the edifice of segregation, leading one critic to denounce Nashville as "the very citadel of carpetbag liberalism," Wallace grew up in a setting where discrimination and racial separation remained interwoven in the fabric of civic, social, religious, and educational life. "By the 1950s, the races in Nashville had never been more segregated," argued Don Doyle in *Nashville Since the 1920s*. Jobs were strictly stereotyped, with African Americans relegated to menial tasks. Segregated buses, movie theaters, bathrooms, parks, and buses, along with all the other accoutrements of Jim Crow, were firmly in place.

"It's just how it was," said Davy, the white sports reporter. "Never thought about it. You were born and you grew up, and that's the way it was, and you didn't have to figure out that's the way it was. You didn't really know the other side, how they felt or anything."

Nashville did offer youngsters informal exceptions to the South's general ban on interracial competition, according to Davy. "In the summer we used to go to the old Nashville baseball park, Sulphur Dell it was called, on Fifth Avenue North. It was in an industrial neighborhood. Kids would go down there and play ball in the summertime—Black and white. Junior Gilliam, who later played for the Dodgers, played down there. There was a trainer down there [actually, a masseuse] named Willy White who sort of opened the ballpark and was there all day; he didn't go with the team on the road trips. [Blacks and whites] played ball with each other. You know, friends.

"When September 1st came, Labor Day, we went back to school. [The Black kids] all went to a Black school, and we always went to North High, which was all-white. It was just the sort of thing you'd do: 'See you next spring.'"

Tolerance of such impromptu competitions typified the fact that "Nashville was not a hard town," said Cornelius Ridley, the former Pearl High School coach. Ridley grew up on 12th and Jefferson in the heart of the inner city's Black community. "By having the colleges here—by having Vanderbilt, Fisk, Tennessee State—there was a lot of interaction between the professors and the university community," he said. "Even before integration they had a race relations institute where people from all over the United States came to Fisk. The way people thought of each other wasn't like it was in the Deep South. . . . They integrated here far quicker than they did a lot of places, though we did have our share of bombings and that sort of thing when the schools were integrated."

Ridley also recalled, "If you were Black and an outstanding citizen, you could interact with white people on the same basis." Still, the realm of whites was fraught with limitations and danger, and Nashville's Black enclave compensated by providing what freedoms and bounties it could. Wallace remembered that enclave as "rich in offerings. Because of the racial harshness at the time, staying in the Black community gave you a lot of protection. And since you did have movies and social events and universities and games and athletics and the whole deal, you could live a pretty good life."

Wallace's parents, Perry Eugene Sr. and Mattie Wallace, came to Nashville from rural Rutherford County, Tennessee, near Murfreesboro, about a half-hour drive southeast of the capital. Both were raised on farms. Neither got past the eighth grade in an era when separate and unequal education was routinely imposed on African Americans trained primarily for work in field and factory.

During the 1940s the average school term for Southern African Americans was at least 20 days shorter than that for whites; in many rural districts the school year for Black students lasted no more than four months. In 1950 nearly a third of Tennessee counties offered no education for African Americans beyond elementary school, tracking a regionwide trend in which the median schooling for Blacks was 5.9 years compared to 9.3 for whites. Only 14.4 percent of African-American children in the South had graduated from high school at mid-century, and the majority of Black men living on Tennessee farms had less than a fifth-grade education as late as 1960. "In these days," the U.S. Supreme Court wrote in its 1954 *Brown v. Board of Education* decision, "it is doubtful that any child may reasonably be expected to succeed in life if he is denied the opportunity of an education."

Yet Perry and Mattie Wallace did succeed. They raised four girls and two boys (Perry Jr. was the youngest). Mrs. Wallace kept house and did occasional domestic work. Wallace Sr. started his own brick-cleaning business, helping new suburban homeowners to burnish their dreams.

The value of cultivating one's mind was among the key lessons the Wallaces imparted. Mattie Wallace enjoyed reading and made a point of perusing each book her boys and girls brought home from public school. Her husband read the newspaper daily and liked to discuss the ways of the world. All of their children went on to graduate from college. "My folks were humble people who worked hard and really believed in education," Perry Wallace said. "The notion of continuing to learn and continuing to grow was something that I got from them." He cited as an example teaching himself French while in his 30s, mastering the language sufficiently well to travel to France to read, review, and discuss a friend's doctoral dissertation. Wallace also studied voice and learned to sing opera in Italian and German.

Perhaps surprisingly, it was Wallace's "old-fashioned, hard-core conservative" father who introduced his son to music as a serious pursuit by bringing home a trumpet when the boy was in elementary school. Soon young Perry was practicing three hours a day (when no one else was home, by popular request). Wallace learned selections from a variety of works, including the Giuseppe Verdi opera *La Traviata*. He took private lessons from an assistant band director and accomplished jazz musician at nearby Tennessee State.

Wallace also began enjoying basketball during his elementary school years, overcoming shyness, asthma, and his father's general disapproval of sports. Perry Jr. stood about 6-foot-2, admired pro center Wilt Chamberlain, and could dunk by the eighth grade. "Some guys just have spring in their legs," said Ridley, who scouted the youngster in junior high. "You never would have thought it because he had pretty large feet, but he had good spring."

Wallace entered Nashville's public schools in the fall of 1954, several months after the U.S. Supreme Court mandated equal educational opportunity in *Brown*. Yet he never attended an integrated school until he enrolled at Vanderbilt. The grudging response in Nashville was typical of the state: In 1959, when Wallace entered sixth grade, only 169 of Tennessee's 146,700 African-American children went to schools that were even marginally integrated.

By the time Wallace was ready for high school, his family had moved to Clay Street in a mixed-race neighborhood 100 yards from North High. No matter. Wallace was sent to Pearl, several miles distant. (When the dictates of segregation in Topeka, Kansas, similarly forced elementary school student Linda Brown to bypass a more convenient school, it spawned the case that gave the *Brown* decision its name.)

Assignment to Pearl High was far more privilege than punishment for a teenager in Nashville's African-American community. Pearl was considered the city's elite Black high school academically and athletically. Designed by McKissack and McKissack, the nation's first architectural firm owned by an African American, Pearl was relatively modern and well equipped. The building, now Martin Luther King Magnet at Pearl High School, was added to the National Register of Historic Places in 2002.

The Pearl faculty was heavy with spouses of professors at Nashville's nearby Black colleges and universities, and the school produced a wealth of accomplished students as well as famous musicians and athletes, among them pro quarterback Joe Gilliam. But during Wallace's youth Pearl was best known for its basketball program, supported by a sophisticated feeder system from the junior-high level. "I inherited a great program," said Ridley, who attended Pearl and returned as coach in 1961. "You had to be loony to screw up a program like they had there. All the Black kids in North Nashville came to high school there." When Loyola of Chicago won the

NCAA basketball championship in 1963, it employed four African-American starters. Two, Vic Rouse and Leslie Hunter, were Pearl grads.

Black basketball had a rich tradition in Nashville beyond Pearl High. Tennessee A&I hosted an annual tournament for African-American high schools to determine a national champion. The school, later renamed Tennessee State, broke new competitive ground itself in 1953, sending the first Black team to an integrated national college basketball tournament. Spurned by the prestigious NCAA, historically Black schools turned to the National Association of Intercollegiate Athletics for national competition. The NAIA was not entirely welcoming, either, lumping all Black teams into a single district, Division 29. Undaunted, Tennessee A&I squads coached by future Hall of Famer John McLendon marched to three consecutive NAIA championships from 1957 through 1959. The Tigers thereby quietly produced the first Black college teams in any sport to win a national title against white competition. The star of those squads, guard Dick "Skull" Barnett, became a key component of the New York Knickerbockers' 1969 NBA championship squad.

Pearl High held its own in North Nashville's basketball pantheon. Media coverage of local Black athletics was spare, yet playing for Pearl spoke loudly in the community. Sporting Pearl's gaudy red-, white-, and blue-striped uniform, reminiscent of that worn by the Harlem Globetrotters, was an advertisement of excellence. "That was the ultimate goal," said Davy, among the few white reporters to venture into the town's Black basketball venues. "When you did that, and you wore that uniform and played for Pearl High School, in your neighborhood you had made it. They didn't need to read it in the paper. They didn't need to hear about it on the radio. They didn't need to watch it on television."

Wallace had never contemplated wearing a Pearl uniform, other than as a trumpet-playing member of the band, until a strange and wonderful thing happened. "Mr. Ridley, the coach of the Pearl High basketball team, came to see me," Wallace recalled, a sense of awe coloring his voice some 40 years after the fact. "I wasn't ready for that. I was surprised. I was shocked. It never occurred to me that he had actually watched me play and remembered it." Wallace won his father's blessing by promising to comport himself properly. Then Wallace worked to embrace the stern coach's assessment that he could develop into a "real basketball player."

As Wallace puts it, "The sky opened up." His junior year, the Pearl basketball squad finished 26–3 and won the 1965 Tennessee Secondary School

Athletic Association (TSSAA) tournament for Black teams. His senior season, the Tigers were even more dominating. "They were strong, they were physical, and they were good players," Ridley recalled. Vanderbilt's Skinner, watching from a vantage point across town, considered Pearl a "super" team. Every 1966 Pearl starter and several reserves earned college scholarships, among them Ted "Hound Dog" McClain, who attended Tennessee State and played eight years of pro ball. Wallace won high school All-America honors. "He was a great rebounder and a great defender," Ridley said.

Like many of the best Black teams, Pearl ran the fast break and pressed relentlessly. "You had to have a pressing team because most teams we played would come out, and they'd stall and hold the ball and do everything to try to keep it close, to get you where it was a free-throw-shooting contest," Ridley said. "So you had to have an up-tempo team in order to beat them."

The style was widely denigrated by whites, but it worked. Pearl was undefeated as it entered the 1966 TSSAA state tournament, the first in which Black schools competed against white schools for the title. Pearl benefited in this mixed setting from Ridley's sensitive handling of his squad's pioneering role, and from a signature pregame ritual craftily cultivated to intimidate opponents. In an era when few white players dunked at the high school or college level, the Tigers lined up in size order, largest to smallest, and after performing the usual warm-up drills, each player dunked. The aerial assault was punctuated by a 5-foot-7 guard who shocked onlookers by soaring above the rim to complete the procession. "We used to scare them all to death," Ridley said with satisfaction.

Some teams would not watch Pearl during warm-ups, a sports equivalent of Lot's averted gaze to avoid corruption. Ridley was ready to rub salt in the wounds of those who did look. "There was one game where [Ridley] told us, 'When you go out there, I want everybody to do three sets of regular layups,'" Wallace remembered. "'After that I want everybody to slam. No layups. I want you to slam, and if you can do some backwards dunks, if you can do some hook dunks, if you can do some cup-the-hands and just some real serious slams, just do that.'

"And we did that. And then a voice said, 'Hey, look! Look at the other team.' We looked down, and they were just mortified. They had stopped shooting layups to watch us dunk."

Pearl dominated the competition en route to a 31-0 record, the state championship, and an enduring place in Tennessee basketball lore. The final victory was secured the same day that Texas Western, with an all-Black starting five, shocked lily-white Kentucky to win the NCAA championship. Wallace savors the message implicit in the dual titles. "I think people had to see a bunch of strong, young Black men who walked above the rim, who were not scared or shuffling," he said. "This was new stuff, even if it was quote-unquote 'only' in sports. Just the sight of it was very new and probably a little bit unsettling."

Bob Warren, Wallace's eventual teammate at Vanderbilt, watched Pearl in the TSSAA tournament. "Of the leapers that I had been exposed to at the college level, of course Perry was just head and shoulders above anything I'd ever seen," he said, no pun intended. With his natural talents, basketball pedigree, good grades, and gentlemanly demeanor, the thickly built, 217-pound Wallace drew interest from some 100 schools. He was so perfect a recruit that Davy called him "Mr. America."

Interest from Michigan, Iowa, and Purdue—Big Ten universities with strong engineering programs—brought Wallace's long-held dream of escaping the South within reach. But his outlook shifted after a few campus visits on which he encountered Black student-athletes tucked into dubious classes, nearly illiterate but eligible, or purposefully disconnected from the rest of campus life. "Basically, for a lot of the Black athletes, it was the new plantation," Wallace said. "They were there very much like slaves. They lived in their own world."

Wallace turned his attention to Vanderbilt, one of his most ardent pursuers in a saga well-chronicled by Nashville newspapers and the *Hustler*, Vanderbilt's student paper. "That was a big deal; everybody looked at it as if it was going to open up Vanderbilt," said Davy, who covered the story. "Vanderbilt and everybody else had played second fiddle in basketball to Kentucky for so many years. [The recruitment of Wallace] looked like opening the door."

The Commodores were usually competitive in SEC basketball under Bob Polk and then Skinner, a four-time SEC coach of the year (1965, 1967, 1974, and 1976). During Skinner's 16 seasons Vanderbilt finished in the top half of the league 13 times, including first place in 1965 and 1974. His overall record at Vanderbilt was 278–135, a 67.3 percent success rate. Skinner suffered his sole losing season in 1970, Wallace's senior year, but still managed to hand Kentucky its only defeat until postseason.

Vanderbilt's chancellor encouraged the taciturn Skinner to recruit Black players; for several years he sought Northern recruits to no avail. "I couldn't recruit them because Vanderbilt was in the South, and I guess they had too many questions about going to Alabama and Mississippi and some of the other schools in the Southeastern Conference," Skinner said. "I didn't realize it at the time, but after Perry came to Vanderbilt, yes, they were justified."

A contemporary Associated Press story quoted Wallace thinking long and hard "about being the first Negro boy in the SEC." (Two Black football players enrolled at Kentucky the same fall semester that Wallace and Dillard arrived at Vanderbilt; neither lasted past the first game of the 1967 season.) Wallace later said he overlooked "the risks associated with the integration thing" because he wanted to get a quality education and remain near his elderly parents, both of whom died before he completed his undergraduate studies.

Presaging the rocky path ahead, some Vanderbilt alumni encouraged Wallace to enroll while others protested his recruitment. "It took a great deal of courage for Perry Wallace to sign," Davy insisted. "Because of who he was. He was a shy kind of kid. He didn't look like a guy that would do it to be any kind of great social crusader; that wasn't part of his consideration. If it did open the door, which it did, then good. I think that he would tell you that he wasn't thinking in terms of any historical thing. He was just a kid looking for an opportunity that was unusual, that had come open to him to get this great education and have it paid for. I think everything else was a by-product of his looking at an opportunity."

Up in Detroit, Godfrey Dillard's decision to sign with Vanderbilt precipitated death threats at games and turmoil at home. "I've often said that if my father had been alive, he would have never let me go," Dillard said. "My mother was scared to death." Natives of Arkansas and Louisiana, respectively, Dillard's parents had experienced firsthand the difficulties of being Black in the South.

○

Vanderbilt, the only private university in the SEC, was founded in 1875 by railroad robber baron Cornelius "Commodore" Vanderbilt to educate the South's well-to-do whites. The intimate campus, where humans share paths with half-tame squirrels and brick buildings vie for light with magnolias and dogwoods, was surrounded at construction by a stone fence to keep cows off the grounds. By the mid-20th century Nashville had grown to surround the campus, and Vanderbilt sought greater national stature. B. Harvie Branscomb, former dean of the Divinity School at Duke, was hired as chancellor in 1945 and inherited a student body dominated by Tennesseans. By 1963, when Branscomb was succeeded by Heard, a product of the University of North Carolina, 58 percent of undergraduates were from out of state. Vanderbilt's broadened aspirations were substantially underwritten by national funding sources, moving one dean to quip that Branscomb arranged for Commodore Vanderbilt's statue to face north, "toward the Ford Foundation."

Conscious of pleasing such patrons, and given legal cover by a string of U.S. Supreme Court decisions preceding *Brown*, Vanderbilt's School of Religion quietly admitted a Black graduate student, Tennessee minister Joseph A. Johnson, in 1953. The decision did not sit well with segregationists. Justification for the move was denounced as "spurious and indeed absurd" by Donald Davidson, a professor of English literature at Vanderbilt. In 1955 he became head of the Tennessee Federation for Constitutional Government, which opposed federal intervention in Southern race relations. Late in the 1950s, when several Ole Miss graduates challenged the fitness of a professor at their alma mater, they noted dismissively that he held several degrees from Vanderbilt, "well known for its integrationist sentiments."

"The issue was the violation of tradition: blacks being treated as if they were white," explained Melissa Fitzsimons Kean in a doctoral dissertation on the desegregation of private Southern universities. Segregationists, echoing the slippery-slope argument favored by present-day gun control opponents, believed that "even the smallest crack in the edifice of institutional segregation represented a real threat, an exception to the rules that would ultimately bring the rules crashing down," Kean said. "To them, quite reasonably, Vanderbilt's action would seem a calculated betrayal of southern tradition, done for the approval of northerners in exchange for money."

Vanderbilt's School of Religion was again engulfed in controversy with the advent of the sit-in movement in 1960. Civil rights advocates had used sit-ins since 1943 to desegregate restaurants and lunch counters. The tactic did not capture national attention, however, until a quartet of African-American college students employed it on February 1, 1960, at a Woolworth's in Greensboro, North Carolina, just down the street from the office of the Atlantic Coast Conference.

Within weeks sit-ins spearheaded by well-dressed, well-behaved Black college students had spread throughout Southern cities, Nashville included, precipitating arrests, media coverage, and counter-demonstrations by sometimes-violent whites. In 1930 an estimated 75,000 people attended lynchings in the United States; some 30 years later, approximately 70,000 participated in sit-ins. Some critics, including former President Harry Truman, insisted that the sit-ins were engineered by communists, a spin applied in some quarters to tarnish any civil rights effort.

Workshops in nonviolent tactics were hosted in Nashville starting in 1958, and the city experienced test sit-ins at lunch counters late in 1959. From these experiences Nashville's colleges produced a cadre of prominent civil rights leaders, notably John Lewis, Diane Nash, Marion Barry, and James Lawson. Lawson, a conscientious objector who refused to fight in Korea, was a graduate student in religion at Vanderbilt. He had been to India to study the movement of Mohandas Gandhi and counseled others in nonviolence. Soon after demonstrations began in Nashville, Lawson, who had not participated, was quoted advising students "to violate the law" when it seemed a "gimmick" to oppress their race.

His comments precipitated a barrage of front-page editorial criticism from the *Nashville Banner*, a pro-segregation newspaper whose publisher sat on the Vanderbilt Board of Trust. Another board member was the owner of a local store targeted by demonstrators. The publisher wrote that Lawson had "forfeited his privilege to further education at Vanderbilt." The university and Branscomb underlined those words by expelling Lawson after he refused to voluntarily withdraw less than a semester from graduation. The bulk of the faculty at the well-regarded Divinity School resigned in protest, earning Vanderbilt much adverse reaction beyond Nashville.

Two years later, as civil rights demonstrations continued in the city, Vanderbilt students voted against admitting Black undergraduates. But campus sentiment for racial exclusion was weakening. The *Hustler*, which had called for Lawson's ouster, changed its tune under the editorship of Lamar Alexander—a future governor of Tennessee, U.S. Secretary of Education, and erstwhile presidential candidate—and supported an open admissions policy. So did the Vanderbilt faculty.

Finally, with federal funding in jeopardy, six Black undergraduates were admitted to Vanderbilt in the class of 1964–65. Wallace and Dillard, athletic pioneers in the SEC, arrived in the autumn of 1966 among a dozen Black freshmen, part of a miniscule representation in a student body of nearly 6,000. "It was a tough place" for Black students and for those who rocked the boat, said Bev Asbury. "It was rougher than I expected it to be."

Asbury received a bracing lesson in campus realities when the chancellor's office asked him to visit a trustee being treated at Vanderbilt University

Hospital. The chaplain was the rare white at the school actively reaching out to African-American students. He also was an outspoken opponent of the Vietnam War on a campus where students demonstrated in favor of America's role in the conflict.

Asbury arrived at the hospital room to find the trustee drunk and threatening. "He wanted me to resign because I was an embarrassment to the university because of my stance on race and the Vietnam War," Asbury said. "I allowed as how I was not going to do that and I wanted to defend the integrity of what I was doing. Then he said that he was a powerful person in a powerful position in Washington, D.C., and that he knew how to arrange to have people killed—and that he would have me assassinated.

"I said something to the effect that I thought we ought to pray. As I recall, I had a prayer for peace, love, and integration with him. Then I called the chancellor's office and let him know what had happened, and he apologized for the trustee's behavior."

The chaplain found such attitudes typical of veteran members of the board of trustees at the time. No wonder Wallace kept a low profile in the manner of an infantryman scuttling through a trench under fire. "You don't just kind of up and become OK with race," Wallace said. "I guess I have a long-lost book I'm trying to write, and there's one chapter that's going to be entitled 'What the Toms Knew.' It's easy to look from the outside and talk about how brave you ought to be and how you ought to get up in people's faces and that kind of stuff. But, you know, the [Uncle] Toms were Toms for a real reason. There was real danger, real horror"—he elongates the word *horror* for emphasis—"that awaited. If you were not going to just go up North, if you were going to try to stay there in the South, there was no such thing as, 'Yeah, I'll fight them off.'"

Wallace felt the need to explain his approach at Vanderbilt, moved by African Americans who have questioned his lack of militancy. He placed himself in the low-key mold of prominent black leaders such as politicians Colin Powell and Condoleezza Rice, businessmen Bob Johnson of Black Entertainment Television and Ken Chenault of American Express, and studiously apolitical basketball star Michael Jordan. "It's harder to agitate inside and get out alive," Wallace said. "It's easier if you're Jesse Jackson and those folks, but you can't use those same kinds of tactics if you're on the inside."

Certainly attending Vanderbilt meant working from the inside. Allies were few. Threats to the psyche, if not the body, were a fact of daily life. And matters frequently worsened during basketball season, when the Commodores took to the road. "These were painful, stressful, traumatic experiences, where every day you walked out into some form of hell," Wallace said. Students at Vanderbilt, as at many Southern universities, hung Confederate flags from their dorm windows, the same symbol proudly affixed to the helmets of police who beat civil rights demonstrators. Derogatory remarks were not uncommon, even in an academic setting. One Black freshman reported to Asbury that upon walking into an English class, his professor looked up and said, "Well, I'll be goddamned! They let the niggers in after all."

Wallace, alternately acclaimed and ignored, told an interviewer late in his senior year that he was "lonesome" at Vanderbilt. Hallmates in his dorm intentionally treated him to stony silence for an entire year, intensifying the sense of isolation. A teammate joked about picking cotton and "the old slave breeding grounds" while a coach listened and laughed along. Campus social life revolved around sororities and fraternities closed to African Americans. Dillard joined a fraternity at Fisk.

"Over the years many people knew my name but they were not interested in knowing me," Wallace told reporter Frank Sutherland, later the editor of the *Tennessean*. "On the dormitory halls I got to know some people but there were others who condescended, people who were used to Blacks who cut the grass and who swept floors. They respected my basketball ability but they still consider me a person who sweeps floors."

Well-meaning whites sometimes added to the sense of alienation, as Wallace recalled in a subsequent interview. "There was a friend of mine who wanted to show me and some of his other Black friends off to his parents," he told Sam Heys of the *Atlanta Constitution*. "He brought them over and then he said to me, 'Say something. Just say something.' Because he wanted to show his parents that I could speak grammatically correct English."

○

Discomfort with diversity long outlived Wallace's time on campus. Nearly two decades passed before the first Vanderbilt sorority was integrated; there were only 149 African-American students at the school when Pi Beta Phi admitted a Black member in January 1987. The next month swastikas appeared on a Jewish fraternity house. Asbury fought for three decades to create a center on campus for Jewish students, a goal realized after he left in 1996.

More than half of all Black Vanderbilt undergraduates surveyed in 1989 said that they were racially harassed on campus. Black football alumni considered forming their own organization in 1990 because they did not feel welcome returning to the school. That same year a sorority required pledges to dress as aborigines in blackface. Controversy arose in 1991 over university officials' continued membership in exclusionary clubs. The Princeton Review polled 40,000 students at 286 colleges in 1993 and ranked Vanderbilt fifth-worst for "most-strained race and class relations."

The same lack of progress held true in athletics. Wallace had far more impact paving the way for Black players elsewhere in the SEC than he did at Vanderbilt. "Funny thing about the first school to integrate and all," Cornelius Ridley said in a 2001 interview. "Today, it's still considered the worst place for a Black to go because of that social situation."

Davy remembers traveling to Los Angeles in 1974 with a Commodore squad so thoroughly white that a fan yelled, "My God, it's the Russians!" The school's athletics director acknowledged as late as 1991 the need to combat the "perception that this is a white, elitist campus." That year, only 10 of 209 nonfootball athletes at Vanderbilt were Black.

African Americans constituted 5 percent of undergraduates at Vanderbilt during the 2002–03 academic year, the same proportion as in 1985 and about half the representation at Emory and Duke, two comparably sized and respected private Southern universities. It has since closed the gap.

Wallace has given Vanderbilt's racial climate deep consideration, and he speaks of his experiences with uncommon insight and an almost thespian flair. "The fundamental fact is that all of that stuff is insane," Wallace said of life within the maelstrom. "You've got somebody that curses at you, spits at you, and you just keep moving. Somebody threatens your life, but you don't say anything. People are screaming and hollering at you, and you don't have any response to that. That's insane, but you have to be insane in a productive manner. That's one way to describe it."

○

Wallace's productivity on the basketball court was readily apparent. He was powerful, lithe, quick, persistent. Playing in an era when NCAA rules rendered freshmen ineligible for varsity competition, he led the Vanderbilt freshman squad to an 8–7 record, averaging 20.3 rebounds (the team high) and 17.3 points per game (tied for best). "Perry brought the fans to their feet time after time with his dazzling play featuring his personalized 'dunk shot,'" gushed the 1967 school yearbook.

Wallace debuted on the road at Western Kentucky, and, according to Skinner, the undersized center dominated 7-foot Jim McDaniels, later an All-American and a pro. Wallace's 31 rebounds against Kentucky Wesleyan broke Clyde Lee's Vanderbilt freshman mark. But Wallace's most impressive achievement was simply appearing on courts where an African-American player's presence was previously forbidden. Ole Miss cancelled a visit from Vanderbilt's freshmen without explanation, perhaps to avoid hosting Wallace and Dillard. That left it to Mississippi State to provide the Commodore freshmen with a full blast of racist bile, delivered on February 27, 1967.

Legal and political resistance to interracial progress was fierce in Mississippi. The 1963 Mississippi State basketball squad had to sneak out of the state to play an integrated opponent in the NCAA Tournament. "The revolution that so profoundly changed American race relations between 1954 and 1964 stopped at the borders of Mississippi," Anthony Lewis wrote in 1968. "Northerners who were concerned with the problem felt, when they visited Mississippi, that they had strayed into another time, another country."

Dillard and Wallace came to 5,000-seat Maroon Gym in Starkville less than four years after MSU's team had fled town to make its NCAA appearance. They found the arena filled to capacity for the preliminary game between freshman squads. "You could feel the fans breathing; they were that close to you," said Dillard. "I would take the ball out of bounds, and they would throw drinks at me, throw things at me. Toward the end of the game [the referees] weren't even letting me take the ball out of bounds."

Both players were shaken, Wallace told *Versus Magazine* interviewer Dave Sheinin in 1989. "The fans were calling us niggers, coons, shoe polish, threatening our lives, saying why don't you go to Jackson State?" Wallace said, referring to an all-black college in Mississippi. "The gym was this old, decrepit, cold, concrete, airplane-hangar-type gym. The whole experience sticks out in my mind. My mother had just been put in the hospital."

Wallace and Dillard were so nonplussed by their treatment that they sat together in the locker room at halftime, holding each other's cold hands while freshman coach Homer Garr instructed the team. No one else mentioned the crowd's behavior. "When you see a purple man and nobody else sees him, you begin to wonder," Wallace said.

The following season, and in years to come, Dillard was not by Wallace's side to provide emotional support or to dilute a crowd's unwanted attention.

That was the case at Oxford in 1968 when an Ole Miss big man hit Wallace during the first half. "I'd gotten the rebound, and the player just came up and it seemed like he just poked me right in the eye. I had gotten the rebound. People were going back up the floor, and I got poked in the eye. And what was amazing to me was that the play seemed to come right back down the floor, and the referee didn't call a timeout for an injury. I stood there holding my eye for I don't know how long."

Davy noted that the also-ran Rebels "were pretty much football players who played basketball, and they roughed up everybody." But, like Wallace, he was schooled in the nuances of Southern racial politics. "Because of the situation, it said racism," Davy confirmed. "You would have to think [that Wallace] certainly felt it was racial."

Vanderbilt's team trainer treated the wounded sophomore at halftime, then waited with everyone else as Wallace made his solitary return to the court. Wallace not only endured the intimidating stroll without flinching, but also broke out of a slump and dominated the game as the Commodores won handily. "He just turned it on and got every rebound that came off the boards," Skinner remembered. "He just took over. He was so strong and such a tremendous leaper."

Robert "Cob" Jarvis, an Ole Miss assistant coach at the time, recalled that he was "awed" by Wallace that day: "He scared me to death the way he'd get off the floor and get those rebounds." But Jarvis denied that the Vanderbilt player was mistreated by fans. "If they did, it wasn't where I could hear them. I think later on he did make some comments about that, but I never did see anything really get out of hand towards him."

Wallace finished the game with 14 points, 11 rebounds, and a reinforced sense of pride. "That was just a super-outrageous situation, and it really was a question of do-or-die. I had to reach and get something, and I did," he said. "My eye was still messed up, and in the second half I came back in and probably played a game like I hadn't really played before.

"I actually at one point got the ball on a fast break and threw a behind-the-back pass with my left hand. That's the first one that I had ever thrown in my life, and it was the last one. A left-handed, behind-the-back pass. I don't know where that came from. And, probably more significant in a certain way was that, as things moved along, the people in the crowd got a chance to see me do a couple of things that they hadn't been used to seeing. A lot of it had to do with my jumping—hang time and that sort of thing. And it was interesting to see that the place got quieter. It got a little quieter."

Wallace achieved that impact without resorting to the dunk, that most emphatic of offensive moves. Throwing the ball down had been an essential part of his repertoire during high school and his freshman year at Vanderbilt, but the NCAA banned the shot from 1967–68 until the 1976–77 season. Observers claimed that the ban was aimed directly at UCLA's towering Lew Alcindor (later Kareem Abdul-Jabbar), a junior in 1967–68. More generally, African Americans believed that the prohibition was an attempt by traditionalists to suppress their stylistic contribution to the game. "The dunk is one of basketball's great crowd pleasers," Alcindor said, "and there is no good reason to give it up except that this and other niggers were running away with the sport."

Skinner was among many who attributed abolition of the dunk to the influence of Kentucky's Rupp, a power in NCAA rulemaking circles. Rupp yelled at Wallace when he legally dunked during a freshman game at Lexington. And the conservative UK coach surely was not pleased when Texas Western scored its first basket of the 1966 national championship game on a monstrous dunk by confrontational Dave "Big Daddy" Lattin. "This guy was scary," Wallace said of the older player, against whom he scrimmaged one summer at Tennessee State. "He was the Mandingo."

By all accounts the removal of the dunk cost Wallace, who played around the rim but had relatively unpolished offensive moves, several points per game throughout his career. He nevertheless became the sixth player in Vanderbilt history to reach 1,000 points, scoring 1,010 in three seasons. Wallace was forced to work on other aspects of his game; each year he improved his field goal and free throw accuracy, as well as his scoring and rebounding averages.

Wallace dunked once in varsity competition—the last points he scored in his 1970 career finale against Mississippi State. That day Wallace had 29 points and 27 rebounds, personal bests and team highs for the season. His final points before an enthusiastic home crowd came on a dunk with 21 seconds to go that officials somehow failed to notice. "That was about as legal as marijuana," teammate Tom Arnholt said admiringly after the game. "Yeah, but wasn't it a beauty?"

Fans at Vanderbilt's Memorial Gym had accorded Wallace an extended ovation prior to the game, their support a bright spot he readily acknowledged. "That was what impressed me about Vanderbilt, the fans really stick with you," Wallace said in a valedictory interview with the *Tennessean*. There were ovations at other venues that year, including at

Oxford, Mississippi. Such displays suggested that spectators recognized the grace with which Wallace had endured insult, danger, and fear. Black awareness increasingly took a confrontational tone as the 1960s expired, but Wallace did not meet anger with anger. Instead, he essentially turned the other cheek.

"I didn't hate them then, I don't hate them now, I never did in between," Wallace said of his tormentors. "People have asked me, 'What do you think about those people who screamed and yelled, all that?' And sometimes they're surprised to hear that honestly, honestly, [the answer is] nothing. It's not like I'd want to go down and shine them off, or that I hope bad things happen to them or anything. Part of the process of actually either cleansing yourself or really getting through it involves not developing or harboring a bunch of anger. Part of the process is looking into the whole experience and into yourself.

"The only way you can save yourself is not to hate people, not to hate back. That's the ironic formula—that if you're going to cycle out of this, you don't get a chance to hate. The fact is that you don't need to. Sadly, the die is cast; it's an indictment of slavery and the system and the people who couldn't step up to the plate and be decent—the administrators and others who weren't willing to say to their fans and their people that this is not good behavior. And then there were people who took a dive. Ironically, they don't realize that they were playing a game called 'Who's the nigger? Who's the nigger?' And it never was me. It never was me. . . .

"If you're really, truly superior, you don't have to worry about putting anybody down, because you're on top of everything. You can be gracious. And then here they are, everybody teaming up on one guy, hoping that he fails and expressing outright hatred. Out of control. 'Who's the nigger? We gave that nigger hell!' . . . What they didn't know at the end of that Saturday night as they were going home was how much they had wounded and tainted themselves. That was a real wound, it was a quiet, silent one."

Wallace had his own wounds to contend with, as detailed in a front-page interview with the *Tennessean* two days after his college playing career ended. Headlined "Lonely Four Years for VU Star," Wallace's candid comments about his experiences rocked many associated with Vanderbilt. Until then, Wallace's athletic and academic success had been taken as evidence that "everything was peachy," Skinner said. To his credit, the coach learned from the article that Wallace "had had it a lot rougher than I had thought." A more common reaction was "a real bad taste in the mouths of Vanderbilt people that we've given him this opportunity, and here he brought up all these bad things," Davy said.

"I don't think people realized how bitter we were," Dillard said. "Mostly, I think the racist viewpoint is, 'You ought to be glad you're here. What are you complaining about? You're going to the premier university in our state. You're being given an opportunity that no black has ever been given before.'"

In his remarks to the *Tennessean*, Wallace avoided a confrontational tone or any mention of what he calls the truly "ugly" cards, letters, and photographs he had received. Instead, he utilized the interview to warn others that his groundbreaking experience had not "fixed" the racial problems at Vanderbilt or in the SEC.

"What I wanted to do was to finish my job as a pioneer," he said. "The way I describe it is that if Daniel Boone and Davy Crockett and Lewis and Clark—all those guys—had come back from their journeys and said, 'Well, everything is cool. There are no big problems out there. They've got a few rabbits along the way. All the people are friendly. Just dress casual and have a ball,' then that's a lie. You're going to get some folks hurt. I knew that if I didn't say something, there were going to be some athletes who were going to get hurt. . . . But that those who did [follow] would go in with their eyes open."

After graduation Wallace was taken by Philadelphia in the fifth round of the NBA draft. He soon quit playing ball and earned a law degree from Columbia University. He worked for the Urban League; for Walter Washington, the first elected mayor of Washington, D.C.; and as a trial attorney for the U.S. Department of Justice before becoming a full-time law professor in 1985. Yet for many in Nashville, neither Wallace's postgraduate achievements nor his historic role in desegregating sports overcame the sting of his candor. He was warned he was unwelcome in the capital city. According to Wallace, some people made it clear that he was considered "an ungrateful nigger."

Nearly 20 years passed before Wallace was invited back to his alma mater. Soon afterward, in October 1990, the Vanderbilt Student Government Association unanimously recommended naming a new student recreation center after him. A vice chancellor explained that a large philanthropic gift was required to secure naming rights, and the matter was dropped. Vanderbilt's student government resurrected the proposal in February 2003, shortly before Wallace was inducted into the Tennessee

Sports Hall of Fame. The undergraduate leadership voted unanimously to rename the school's rec center "in honor of Perry Wallace and his contributions to Vanderbilt University, southern collegiate athletics, and American society." Again, nothing came of the idea.

Instead, the school retired his jersey in February 2004, making it the third to hang in Memorial Gym after those of Clyde Lee, a two-time SEC Player of the Year, and women's great Wendy Scholtens Wood. In 2020 a street outside Vanderbilt's basketball arena was named for Wallace. "Perry Wallace is a Vanderbilt hero," said then-university chancellor Gordon Gee. "Perry's accomplishments—in the classroom, on the basketball court, and throughout his life—are an inspiration to us all." In 2021, four years after his death, the U.S. Basketball Writers Association named its annual award for courage in college basketball for Perry Wallace.

CHAPTER 3

BETWEEN WORLDS

C. B. Claiborne, Duke University, 1965–69

But under all our talk floated a latent sense of violence; the whites had drawn a line over which we dared not step and we accepted that line because our bread was at stake. But within our boundaries we, too, drew a line that included our right to bread regardless of the indignities or degradations involved in getting it.

Richard Wright, *Black Boy*

Three brick chimneys, vestiges of a bygone era in which textiles and tobacco dominated the economic landscape, tower above the oaks just beyond bucolic Ballou Park. Danville, Virginia, home of Duke basketball pioneer C. B. Claiborne, is very much enamored of its past, embodied in numerous older commercial structures retained in its faded, somnolent downtown, the array of handsome 19th-century homes along "Millionaire's Row," and an enduring pride in its standing in the annals of the Lost Cause.

Danville was a rail and warehouse center of about 6,000 residents at the time of the Civil War. Never sullied by a Union invader's hand, the river city played a central role in a final grand flourish of the dying Confederacy. The white, Italian Villa–style Sutherlin mansion, owned by Danville's most prominent businessman, served for a week in April 1865 as headquarters to Confederate president Jefferson Davis, in flight west from Richmond, the fallen capital.

Here on the bank of the Dan River, Davis issued his final proclamation as president of a putative sovereign nation. Even as Davis spoke, Robert E. Lee's Army of Northern Virginia, surrounded and virtually without provisions, limped toward surrender at nearby Appomattox. Davis exhorted the faithful "as patriots engaged in a most sacred cause" to "show by our bearing under reverses, how wretched has been the self-deception of those who have believed us less able to endure misfortune with fortitude than to encounter danger with courage." He went on to praise the South's struggle, "the memory of which is to endure for all ages and to shed ever-increasing luster on our country." Folks in Danville may have been patriotic, but they were also pragmatic, blocking the efforts of Confederate cavalry to blow up the railroad bridge across the Dan River after Davis and entourage hastened south.

The well-connected city prospered, much of the time with a Black majority, until the midpoint of the 20th century, when growth ground to a halt. Boasting 101,162 residents in 1950, Danville grew by barely 9,000 people over the next 50 years while populations boomed elsewhere in Virginia and throughout the Sun Belt.

Caught in the quiet eddies of time, Danville's past presses close, epitomized by the jaunty Sutherlin mansion, now dubbed the Danville Museum of Fine Arts and History and the William T. Sutherlin Mansion and Confederate Memorial, which is listed in the National Register of Historic Places. The house long mutely symbolized the city's racial hierarchy, serving from 1928 as the library for whites while the facility for African Americans, located just blocks away, was housed on the ground floor of a modest duplex. "When in the 1960s they integrated the library, they called it 'vertical integration,'" Lawrence Campbell, a prominent Danville civil rights leader and bishop of Bibleway Church, recalled with a laugh. "No one could sit down." No African American, that is. Lunch counters throughout the South employed the same tactic to forestall meaningful integration.

The association between the Confederacy and white supremacy was long a fact of life in Danville. African Americans familiar with the city inevitably mention, without fondness, its cherished role as "the last capital of the Confederacy," a fact touted on Web sites and tourist materials. "The Supreme Court decision in the *Brown* case was in 1954," said Hank Allen, who coached and taught in the city's Black-only schools for nearly two decades. "It didn't mean much to Danville. Danville was the last capital of the Confederacy, so Danville was a strict, conservative, segregated society. They weren't about to move; they weren't about to allow Black people equal access or equal opportunity. So they didn't do anything."

Allen quietly resisted what indignities he could, a tactic silently replicated throughout the South. "I never rode a bus or any form of public transportation when I was in Danville because I would not pay for segregating myself," said the native of New Jersey, where his teacher training wasn't enough to get a Black man a job. "I wouldn't go to the movie to sit upstairs in the balcony, either. Those things that I could control, I did." Most African

Americans in Danville, as elsewhere north and south, found it simpler to acquiesce, to live within limitations that were harsh, ingrained, and largely unspoken.

"There were places that you clearly did not go in Danville, would not walk, would not go alone. I think that was more understood" than articulated, said Claiborne, who escaped as a teenager into a world once reserved for whites. "The first time I got on the bus, it was with my grandfather, and we walked to the back of the bus and took a seat, even though this particular bus only went through the Black community. There wasn't going to be anybody else riding it. We still sat in the back. Later on that changed, but I don't ever remember questioning or being told, 'Go to the back of the bus.'"

At times this sense of second-class citizenship was enforced with casual brutality, as Claiborne experienced daily en route to his segregated junior high school. "When we got to the railroad tracks, if you were by yourself, you would wait for somebody else Black coming along," he said. "You didn't do that walk from the railroad tracks to Main Street by yourself if you were a Black kid because there were going to be gangs of white boys. We were going to get in a fight. We'd wait there, put rocks in our pockets, whatever. This was the late 1950s, early 1960s. This was a very conflictual time. I can remember, even with four or five of us, walking by that white high school right before we got to the library and having kids on the other side calling us names, maybe throwing stuff at us for no apparent reason other than we were walking down the street."

Similar harassment was routine elsewhere, as South Carolinian Kirby Higbe once attested in a radio interview. Higbe, a Brooklyn teammate of Jackie Robinson, attributed his strong pitching arm to throwing rocks at African Americans when he was growing up. But Black residents of Danville considered the racial landscape there to be less hospitable than most. "It just was a totally segregated city," said Campbell, who served as executive secretary of the Danville Christian Progress Association, a civil rights group allied with Martin Luther King Jr.'s Southern Christian Leadership Conference. "The cemetery was segregated. The water fountains, white and Black. The penal system, segregated Black and white. You name it."

King visited Danville twice in 1963, in March and July. At the time of President John Kennedy's assassination in late November, the SCLC was weighing whether to focus its efforts next in Danville or in Alabama at Birmingham or Montgomery. "When I was in Danville, Danville was as bad as Birmingham," Wyatt T. Walker, a former SCLC executive director, said in a 1991 interview with the *Danville Register*. "The police here were brutal. And your city fathers . . . city council, they were [as] intransigent as any place I've ever been. I really think Danville is one of the worst cities I've ever been in, you know, of that era, with the single exception, I think, of Shreveport, Louisiana. I know of no city where they arrested the leadership for—what was the charge?—treason. Charged with treason."

John Lewis, leader of the Student Nonviolent Coordinating Committee (and from 1987 until his death in 2020 at age 80 a U.S. congressman from Georgia's Fifth District), singled out Danville during an address on civil rights legislation at the massive March on Washington in August 1963, best remembered for King's "I Have a Dream" speech. "This bill will not protect young children and old women from police dogs and fire hoses, for engaging in peaceful demonstrations," Lewis said. "This bill will not protect the citizens of Danville, Virginia, who must live in constant fear in a police state."

Violence shook Danville during late spring in 1963, violence perpetuated by police. With little movement to integrate schools, to open public facilities to all races, or to extend equal opportunity in city employment, frustrated African Americans had taken to the streets in peaceful protest. Arrests quickly escalated into the hundreds. King said of Danville that "the arrogant refusal of the city officials to grant any of the demands of the Negro community is an affront to the whole civil rights movement."

On June 10, 1963, a protest rally at city hall in support of those who had been arrested was met with force. Mayor Julian Stinson, who had proudly vowed earlier to "not give in one inch to the law breakers," instructed the police chief to "Give them all you've got!" Beset with blasts from fire hoses, protestors huddled between parked cars along a fence by the jail. There, "uniformed and special police drove them from between the cars by scrambling over the cars and beating them with their newly made night sticks," reported the *Register*. A newspaper photographer recording the melee was arrested on the grounds that he was inciting a riot and that his flashbulb constituted an assault on the police chief. State police were brought in in an armored car, claiming a threat from snipers, and police dogs were employed.

The following week the Danville paper editorially criticized not the response of authorities but, in a refrain echoed across the South, "travelers under false banners of non-violence" who had undermined "the groundswell of good will that long prevailed in the community." Equally revealing of Danville attitudes was this June 16, 1963, newspaper photo caption: "Another in City Hall concert series as Negroes work themselves into frenzy with rocking, rolling version of their theme song, 'Everybody wants free-ee-dom.'"

Campbell, later a member of the Danville school board, says that a view of African Americans fraught with stereotypes and paternalism left whites divorced from reality. "They just did not want to believe that these Black underresourced people were rising up against the status quo," he said of the 1960s. "That's why the people across the country, especially in the South, saw Martin Luther King as being subversive, as being part of the Communist Party or something like that because, sure, these people in this community would not do this. So it took this agitator to stir us up. That was the furthest thing from the truth. I think that what the white community failed to realize is that there was a seething dislike and disdain for what Black people were going through in terms of how dehumanizing life was for them on a daily basis. [Whites] just did not want to accept that.

"Oddly enough, today it's no different."

Danville's murky horizons were far too limiting for Claiborne, who came from an old, respected, and well-educated family. "I talk about growing up in Danville like trying to get out of a paper bag," he said. "I always felt confined as far back as I can remember."

Claiborne ultimately would sacrifice the surety of a place within the black community, as well as a long-held dream of playing ball at North Carolina A&T State University, for a chance to go where no African American had gone before. A star student and athlete at Danville's John Langston High School, he chose to become the first African American to play varsity basketball at Duke University, an hour's drive down the road in Durham, North Carolina.

"In hindsight, that was probably the biggest mistake of my life," Claiborne said of his choice of Duke over A&T, a historically Black school with a coach, Cal Irvin, whom he had known and admired for years. "But it wasn't a hard decision at all because this is what I was expected to do. It was an opportunity. No one had ever had this opportunity before, so of course you take the opportunity. You don't say no to it."

The dutiful Claiborne was the only son of a disabled veteran and a mother who served as a maid to some of Danville's most prosperous white families. His younger sister was mentally handicapped and spent her life in institutions. The young man with the long face and lean frame prospered within a comfortable cocoon that included aunts, uncles, and grandparents who lived close by. The extended family closed ranks after "Pop" Claiborne, who worked as a waiter, sold novelties, and otherwise scrambled for work, died about the time his son finished grade school.

Claiborne emerged as a top student, earning a national college scholarship and a trip with his mother to meet President Lyndon Johnson at the White House. Besides serving as president of both his senior class and of the National Honor Society at Langston, Claiborne also starred on and captained championship-caliber baseball and basketball teams.

Claiborne's senior year at Langston, 1964–65, was the first in which Danville's high schools were integrated, at least in principle. (John Mercer Langston, the man for whom the school was named, became the first African-American local elected official in the United States when chosen a township clerk in Ohio in 1855. He later served as ambassador to Haiti, U.S. congressman from Virginia, first dean of Howard University School of Law, and president of Virginia Normal and Collegiate Institute, now Virginia State University. Langston also was among the first African Americans admitted to argue before the U.S. Supreme Court.) But "freedom of choice," a stratagem widely adopted throughout the South to thwart genuine racial mixing, was really a coy means of preserving the status quo. No whites chose to attend Black schools, and few African Americans elected to buck custom and risk approbation in order to attend the better-equipped, better-funded white schools. "Integration was going to the white school," said Claiborne, who stuck with teammates steered since boyhood through a feeder system that bolstered Langston athletics.

Langston basketball was quite popular; the team had its own pep band, its games were broadcast on local radio, and the Danville paper occasionally provided coverage. Another attraction was Allen, a tough, demanding, superior coach whose teams rarely lost during Claiborne's four years on the varsity. Langston was undefeated in its district and won 23 games in a row when Claiborne was a senior. "It was the best team I ever coached," Allen said. "They were just super, and they loved the game. I couldn't get them out of the gym."

Sports occasionally provided a bridge across Danville's racial chasm, though only informally. Claiborne took up basketball in the sixth grade; soon he and his friends sneaked pickup games with white boys on a shaded dirt court behind a white junior high school. The boys played baseball, too. "It was nice because it was hidden from view," Claiborne said. "The white folks couldn't see the back of the school." Not that the illicit activity escaped notice. "A few of the Black folks that lived on Holbrook Street that had big yards or high, two-story houses could see over, and they knew what we were doing," he recalled. "They would say, 'You all shouldn't be doing that. You know you're doing to get in trouble playing with those white boys out there.' We'd say, 'Yes, ma'am,' but we did that for a while. I'm not quite sure when it ended. It *did* end. It wasn't as official as the police coming, but somebody at some point noticed it."

By high school, the good-natured interracial athletic rivalry had intensified. George Washington, Danville's white high school, had a powerful basketball squad led by a pair who later played at Virginia Tech. In 1965 both schools reached the state finals in their respective, racially distinct divisions.

The teams never met officially on a basketball court, so they found an informal outlet at Ballou Park, a little more than a mile west of the Sutherlin mansion. There they put on an engaging, groundbreaking show. "Every Saturday and all day Sunday you could see some of the best basketball you'd want to see in your life," said James Slade, a coach and educator in Danville's African-American community. "Integrated teams playing each other, Black teams playing white teams."

There is no more eloquent expression of the racial climate in Danville during the tumultuous 1960s, when the barriers were shaken, or of the city's enduring tensions and prejudices, than what occurred at lovely Ballou Park. Built beside a reservoir and named after a former city engineer, the park is a rolling, wooded urban oasis with a nature center nearest West Main Street and a road meandering back to picnic areas and active recreation facilities. "At some point in the early 1960s, the park was integrated," Claiborne said. "Well, it was sort of integrated. What that meant is that if you were [Black and] in the park, you wouldn't get arrested. But, by and large, the only thing that Black people did was kind of drive through the park. Maybe you would sit there in your car and talk to your neighbor or whatever. Not many people got out of their cars. Certainly, in the back of the park where they had the tennis courts and those kinds of facilities, you didn't go."

The basketball goals were hard by the road in front, on a strip of court-size asphalt. "Anybody driving up and down West Main Street could see the basketball goals," Claiborne said. Soon it became "the thing" for Blacks and whites to go to the park on weekends to play basketball. "So we would have these pick-up games that were Langston versus GW. It started to draw more and more attention because everybody was saying these two schools have great players. We'd be playing for who's the best. It would always be highly contested."

That's when the police showed up.

Claiborne, currently a marketing professor at Texas Southern University in Houston, remembers vividly the day the balls stopped bouncing in Danville. He has a precise, meticulous manner of speech, as if he is walking carefully amid frangible words and concepts. "The first time it happened, the police just came out there and said something like, 'You all are making too much ruckus; you'd better stop playing.' So we took our balls and went home. The next time we went by, they had taken down the goals. And if you go there now, there are no goals. I don't think they ever put them back up."

Decades later, most workers at the parks and recreation office at Ballou Park did not realize that the isolated, abandoned strip of asphalt just down the hill, cracked and pocked with weeds, once served as a basketball court. Yet a visitor need only look closely to find, imprinted in the faded, graying surface, a midcourt line and center circle that once governed play. "Took the goals down: I was up there to see it, because I could not believe it," Slade said, his voice suffused with a mix of amazement, outrage, and perverse glee at the blatant foolishness of racist resistance. All that remains of that time of tentative discovery are pavement, memories, and windblown leaves. Informal separation reportedly still holds sway at Ballou, with whites frequenting the park one day per weekend, African Americans the other.

Fortunately for Claiborne, even as snags developed in Danville, broader horizons beckoned. "C. B. could have gone to any school in the country," Allen said of his star player. "Everybody wanted him—all the schools, even those that didn't play anything. Whether he played anything or not, they still wanted him academically because he was a brilliant kid. He's still brilliant."

Claiborne briefly considered Maine's Bowdoin College, where in 1826 John B. Russwurm became one of the first Black Americans to earn a college degree. But, enamored of both an education in engineering and a chance to play big-time sports, Claiborne ultimately narrowed his options to North Carolina A&T, Purdue, Wake Forest, and Duke. The two Atlantic Coast Conference schools had yet to recruit an African-American basketball player.

A local clothing store owner and Duke supporter began appearing at Langston games at a time when white spectators were uncommon. But even before that man sold the Duke coaching staff on Claiborne, Wake's Horace "Bones" McKinney came calling. McKinney had played at both NC State and North Carolina during the 1940s and had enjoyed a successful professional career with the Boston Celtics. Then he went to Wake Forest and, while serving as an assistant to head coach Murray Greason, completed studies to become a Baptist minister. Friends say he was eager to recruit African Americans almost from the time he became head coach of Wake basketball in 1957.

Under McKinney, Wake Forest reached the 1962 Final Four and appeared in five straight ACC Tournament finals between 1960 and 1964, prosperity unseen at the university before or since. But the program was tailing off by the mid-1960s, and the immensely personable McKinney would resign after the 1965 season. Duke, meanwhile, went to consecutive Final Fours in 1963 and 1964 under coach Vic Bubas.

"I remember he was just the nicest person," Claiborne says of McKinney. "This was somebody I wanted to play for. But in those days Wake Forest didn't have much of a basketball team. And they played so slow. I saw [Jeff] Mullins and [Art] Heyman playing at Duke, and I thought, 'Oh, that's the kind of game I want to play.' Duke had the image, and they had just been in the national championship, that kind of stuff. So I didn't even consider Wake Forest, although if I had picked people, I would have picked Bones in a heartbeat."

Of course neither McKinney nor Bubas would sign Claiborne or any other Black player until the private schools for which they worked integrated their student bodies. The schools, particularly Duke, were in no hurry. Like Vanderbilt, Duke was a somewhat-elite academic institution that sold naming rights to a wealthy industrialist, abandoning the name Trinity College in 1924 when James B. Duke allocated a handsome plug of tobacco money. Like Vanderbilt, Duke had an alumni-dominated board of trustees drawn from the region's upper crust. And like Vanderbilt, Duke emerged from World War II intent on assuming greater prominence among the nation's universities, which meant broadening its horizons. Leading the way was attorney Willis Smith, who became chair of the Duke Board of Trustees in 1946.

Unfortunately, Smith took the traditional view of race relations, neatly summarized in a philosophy doctoral dissertation by Melissa Fitzsimons Kean: "Black progress was possible, but only the educated white men of the South could decide how and when." Come 1950, Smith also embraced traditional demagoguery in a successful race for the U.S. Senate that ranks as perhaps the dirtiest campaign in North Carolina history.

Smith's opponent was Frank Porter Graham, the much-respected president of the University of North Carolina system who had been appointed to serve out an unexpired Senate term. "Dr. Graham is one of the most Christ-like men I have ever met," said one Senate colleague. Smith proceeded to crucify the progressive Graham in the Democratic primary, aided by unknown Jesse Helms, a zealous young supporter.

In 1948 California had become the first state to overturn a ban on interracial marriage. Two years later, the mildest mixing across racial lines was still discouraged in most of the country through law and/or custom. Social intercourse between races was derided in North Carolina, where Smith supporters circulated photos of black soldiers dancing and drinking with white women, accompanied by the admonition, "Look before you vote, and remember these persons could be your sisters or daughters under such an educational program as Graham advocates. THINK."

Smith, the underdog, forced a runoff. His supporters' smears of Graham intensified, with ads exhorting voters to sustain the work "of all those patriotic men who freed our state from Negro domination" and warning that "Frank Graham favors mingling of the races." The specter was raised of blacks working beside whites in mills and factories, sleeping in the same hotels, using the same toilets. In those precomputer days, one unattributed broadside pictured an African-American soldier dancing with a white woman who had the crudely superimposed face of Graham's wife, Marian.

Perhaps the lowest moment of the campaign came on the final day, when Graham, appearing in the furniture and mill city of High Point, was greeted by small children who chanted from the sidewalk, "No school with niggers! No school with niggers!" Less than a month later, the front page of the *New York Times* published this myth-debunking revelation: "No Scientific Basis for Race Bias Found by World Panel of Experts."

The end of Smith's tenure as a Duke trustee in 1953 did not change the tenor of race relations at the university. Land sold to faculty and staff contained restrictive covenants that excluded African Americans. Hospital wards and waiting rooms were segregated. Faculty members with black guests were required to eat in a special room on campus. The football stadium had a "colored" entrance and seating. When John McLendon, the black Hall of Fame basketball coach at Durham's North Carolina College, expressed a desire to see a game at Duke Indoor Stadium, he was told he could attend if dressed as a waiter. (The 1940-vintage building was renamed Cameron Indoor Stadium in 1972 after Eddie Cameron, a former Duke football and basketball coach and the school's longtime athletics director.)

Internal petitions to integrate the Duke Divinity School, submitted first in 1948 and repeated in 1956, 1959, and 1961, fell upon deaf ears, even when religion students at the Methodist-affiliated university declared segregation to be a "sinful" violation of Christian beliefs that caused them an "anguish of spirit."

State law required segregation, a convenient excuse for inaction at private universities even as court edicts struck down unequal access to graduate schools at public institutions. Duke president A. Hollis Edens argued in a 1953 letter to alumna Helen Morrison that integration by state schools was "an action in compliance with the law of the land," which "is much simpler than a voluntary action initiated by the institution." He also told Morrison: "In such matters I am a 'gradualist', which is a hated word in some quarters. It is my firm conviction that Duke University can and should admit negroes only when the community and constituency are prepared for it."

So gradual was Duke's preparation that another nine years passed before the board of trustees agreed to admit African Americans to the university's graduate schools. Not until the 1963–64 academic year, when Claiborne was a junior in high school and the *Brown* decision was nearly a decade old, did Duke admit its first five Black undergraduates. No floodgates opened; when Claiborne earned his degree in 1969, only eight Black students had preceded him in graduating.

Bubas recalls neither a university push for athletic integration nor a focus on desegregating his team. "I don't remember it ever coming up," he said. "The whole evolution is something that's weird. I can't trace it." Former Bubas assistant Harold "Bucky" Waters, however, insisted care was taken in choosing the first Black player. "You can't say it was like a Jackie Robinson, but clearly the first kid at Duke would be under a microscope just because he was different and the first," Waters said. "C. B. was there. He was a good player, a good student, good kid. Nice player. It was a 'Why not?' kind of thing."

Waters was dispatched to make contact with Claiborne, who saw in the crew-cut assistant many of the qualities he admired in Hank Allen, his high school coach. That affinity affected the player's decision. But Waters was gone by the time Claiborne matriculated, hired as head coach at West Virginia University. The ex-assistant said he only vaguely remembered Claiborne. Claiborne also was influenced by the enthusiasm of local hero

Bennie Dix, who played alongside Sam Jones at what is now North Carolina Central University. "He's the first one I can remember coming to me and saying, 'Oh, it's so good you got into Duke. This is great for basketball,'" Claiborne said. "He aspired to that world, but he was the generation before me, so that was literally an impossibility for him."

Claiborne was invited to attend Duke on the presidential scholarship he had earned for his exemplary schoolwork. Bubas told United Press International that Claiborne was "welcome to come out for the team and compete for a position." That freed a grant-in-aid for another athlete and placed Claiborne in an anomalous category between walk-on and recruit. There was only one definition that mattered, anyway. "It was always important that we graduate kids that we brought in, especially a minority kid, the first one," Waters said. "He more than fulfilled expectations as far as I'm concerned."

Claudia Claiborne, carried as an infant in her parents' arms to political meetings on and around the Duke campus, had a different take on her father's attractiveness to the premier ACC program of the mid-1960s. "We keep hearing about affirmative action and Black people getting whatever—getting stuff because they're Black, not because they deserve it," said Claudia, a physician who attended Yale University and the Virginia Commonwealth University School of Medicine. "Whereas he's the opposite. He should have gotten in by his grades, but if it wasn't for basketball, he wouldn't have."

Bubas never saw Claiborne in action before the player attended Duke. That lack of scrutiny was not extraordinary. Bubas often relied for player evaluations upon a group of assistants that included Waters, Chuck Daly, Hubie Brown, Fred Shabel, and Tom Carmody. (All went on to become successful head coaches at the college or pro level. Daly and Brown are in the Naismith Basketball Hall of Fame.) Yet Bubas's recruiting methods yielded extraordinary talent during his 10-season tenure from 1960 through 1969. Between 1961 and 1967 four Blue Devils—Heyman, Mullins, Jack Marin, and Bob Verga—were named consensus All-Americans and the program had the best cumulative winning percentage in the country. Heyman was the ACC Player of the Year in 1963, Mullins in 1964, and Steve Vacendak in 1966. Duke routinely and famously cast a wide net for recruits: When Claiborne joined the varsity in 1967, the stars of the team were Verga, a guard from New Jersey, and Mike Lewis, a big man from Montana.

Among Duke's attractions was an up-tempo approach on offense and defense akin to that once employed by Everett Case, an Indianan who revolutionized interest in college basketball in the Southeast after World War II. Bubas had played and later served as an assistant at NC State under Case, who died in 1965. "He loved the fast-break style of play," Bubas said. "I thought he was probably the best teacher of the fast break that I ever saw."

"We had great players, and he let them play," Waters said of Bubas. "We were averaging in the 90s back then without the three-point shot." Duke scored 92.4 points per game in 1965, the third-highest average in ACC history and long before the 3-point shot came into effect. "That year we ran more than anyone else," Bubas said. "Literally tore the ball out of the net and ran it upcourt. Took the first good shot."

Bubas "was really innovative," added Maryland's Gary Williams, who played against Duke at the height of Bubas's prowess. "He ran the multiple guards at you. Bud [Millikan] was still playing five, six, maybe seven if you got into foul trouble. Bubas, he platooned his guards. He had great guards. Vacendak was as good as anybody I ever played against. Verga was as good a shooter as there was in the country. Jack Marin was there. [Bubas] took advantage of his talent."

The Duke coach also emulated Case in cultivating a big-time atmosphere surrounding his program. "He would be the first to tell you this, but so much of the Case vision, thinking big, he got from coach," said Waters, another former Case player. Bubas ordered that names be affixed to the backs of player jerseys, an unusual practice at the time, and then improved the arena's lighting so fans and television cameras could better read the words. He copied the "straw hat band" from the University of California at Berkeley and the sideline dancing girls from UCLA. He started a coach's TV show, courted female fans, and reached out to students known for warming pennies with matches and tossing them at opposing players. Bubas soon created a heated environment at Duke Indoor Stadium that remains as frenzied as any in college basketball.

Claiborne joined the Duke program in 1965–66, when the Blue Devils finished 26–4 and reached their third Final Four in four years, losing to Kentucky in the semifinals. Freshmen were ineligible for varsity in those days, so Claiborne spent the season as a member of the Blue Imps, the Duke freshman squad that finished with a 13–3 record under Carmody. "He was just a solid all-around player," said classmate Fred Lind, Claiborne's roommate on the road and a friend to this day. "Good team player. Knew the fundamentals. He could pass, had a good pullup jump shot, and could go to the hole. Just a solid all-around game."

The pair found much in common off the court. "Both he and I were pretty serious about the studies," said Lind, a longtime public defender in Greensboro, North Carolina. "We usually brought our books on the road and did a little bit of studying, because we were missing class a lot of times."

The 6-foot-2 Claiborne appeared in every game as a freshman, his role comparable to those of the four scholarship players. Listed as a forward despite his guard's size, he ranked fourth on the squad in rebounds per game (5.4) and sixth in scoring (7.8 points). Carmody described Claiborne as "a swift, smooth ball player with a fine outside shot." He also praised him as "one of the most unselfish players I've ever coached," adding, "He is able to accept criticism graciously and is a most coachable boy."

Yet Claiborne did not readily fit in.

Freshmen played prior to varsity contests, and Claiborne could hear older Duke fans critiquing his game as he performed. "They would criticize me for dribbling through my legs or passing behind my back," he said of moves common to Black basketball players then and ubiquitous throughout the game today. "They would call them hotdog moves in those days."

Durham press reports also repeatedly invoked the player's race, as if skin color was as much a defining characteristic as being left-handed or muscular. Claiborne was the "Negro cage ace" in one story, "the 6-2 Negro guard" in another, the "Danville Negro" in a third. Even after four years in Durham, he remained "a senior Negro player." At least the media capitalized the word "Negro," unlike former university president Edens. But, as Eldridge Cleaver notes in *Soul on Ice*, use of the word carried an implicit, unflattering message: "To the white man, prefixing anything with 'Negro' automatically consigned it to an inferior category."

That separation was underlined when Duke held its 1966 postseason basketball banquet at the segregated Hope Valley Country Club, a site also favored by the football program. Claiborne was unable to attend. The use of Hope Valley by Duke organizations and the memberships of key university officers, including the president, soon became a divisive campus issue. The subject sparked a daylong campus "study-in" by the school's Afro-American Society in November 1967.

Change came slowly. Just as Duke did not rush to desegregate, so it was slow to accommodate a more inclusive vision once African Americans joined the university community. When Waters succeeded Bubas as head coach in

1969, the job brought free membership at unrepentant Hope Valley. "We had an Indian woman here at Duke, and she went to play tennis at Hope Valley" with several other women, Waters recalled. "They came back, and they got a note at the faculty club saying certainly our women's team was invited back, but this lady wasn't. I told them to take that membership and . . ."

Claiborne failed to protest his exclusion at the time of the team banquet. In retrospect, like early pioneers Billy Jones of Maryland and Vanderbilt's Perry Wallace, he laments his passivity. "I was probably much too compliant and didn't push the system enough to make more happen," Claiborne said. "Normally, I think my perspective is to try to be more, not necessarily pacifist, but more harmonious—to understand the broader sweep of things." Still, by his senior year Claiborne was deeply involved in militant campus activities and even missed a Duke game at West Virginia in order to participate in a Black student takeover of the administration building on the main campus.

Claiborne's varsity playing career was one of modest achievement. "He didn't play as much as I thought he would," North Carolina coach Dean Smith said. A torn ligament in his left knee limited Claiborne's opportunities as a sophomore, and a quiet dispute with Bubas over his Afro hairstyle sent him to the bench after a promising start to his senior season. In between, Claiborne was largely a substitute and defensive specialist, much to Allen's disgust. "Bubas never gave C. B. a chance, put it that way," he said. "He never gave that boy a chance to play basketball."

Claiborne got his first career start at forward in a home win over Penn State in January 1967, after nine players had been suspended for violating training rules on New Year's Eve. The 1966–67 team was Bubas's first in seven years that failed to win at least 20 games. The Blue Devils lost in the first round of the National Invitation Tournament to a Southern Illinois squad led by Walt Frazier, a Black Atlantan who had fled the South to play ball.

The 1967–68 team, which Bubas at the time deemed his favorite as a coach, won 22 games, finished second in the ACC and tenth in the polls, and again made the NIT. Prior to the season, Bubas praised Claiborne as "vastly improved," noting the junior's jump shot in particular. "He must learn to 'dig' in every minute of action," the coach said. That year, in a loss at Vanderbilt and a win against Davidson, Claiborne guarded centers Perry Wallace and Mike Maloy—like him, the first African-American players at their respective schools. The Blue Devils concluded the regular season by defeating powerful North Carolina in a legendary triple-overtime contest in which Lind and Claiborne played significant roles. Lind was the hero; he was carried off the court after contributing 16 points in the late going, more than he had scored during the entire season combined. "They threw me in the shower, and I didn't even feel it," Bubas told a reporter. "I've never been thrown in before. Maybe that tells you something about this group of kids."

The 1968–69 team replaced three starters and its top two reserves and finished 15–13, the worst record of Bubas's career. It would prove to be his final team. He retired after a season noted for its ups and downs and a sense of unrealized potential, marked off the court by a call from Duke's faculty to withdraw from the Atlantic Coast Conference and form a new league with more academically oriented schools. The faculty presciently argued that intercollegiate athletics had become "the tail that wags the university dog."

Claiborne was the fifth starter early in the 1968–69 season; then he went to the bench and stayed there. "He probably could have played more," Lind said. "For some reason, after Christmas our senior year, Coach just didn't put him in that much."

Claiborne did not often participate in close games during his career. Nor was he favored with playing time in postseason competition. He failed to play at all in Duke's NIT contests, including a 100–71 shellacking by St. Peter's in 1968, the worst defeat endured to that point by an ACC team in postseason action. Claiborne appeared in one of eight ACC tournament games played by Duke during his varsity career, and then only briefly in the final contest of his senior season. The Blue Devils' sole African-American player detected another persistent theme related to his playing time. "I played more minutes on the road than at home," he said. "Always. I assumed that I wasn't supposed to play in Durham, that there were people that didn't want to see me on the court in Durham. So it didn't have any-thing to do with how well I played. That was just given."

Regardless of whether the facts strictly support Claiborne's impression, his uneasy place at the table was of a piece with the experiences of Duke's other early African-American students. Demeaning suppositions were made in class. The charitable explanation was that faculty members recognized the inferiority of Black education within a separate and unequal system. "The professors were generally OK," said Josie Knowlin, who married Claiborne when both were undergraduates, "except you'd get [comments] like, 'You write really well. You speak English well.' You'd go, 'Well, yeah, it's my native tongue.'"

The disadvantages inherent in attending poorly equipped schools posed challenges as well. The teacher in Claiborne's first math class at Duke held aloft a textbook on derivative and integral calculus and asked, "How many of you used this in high school?" Everyone except Claiborne raised a hand; classwork for the semester focused on only part of the book, with the professor assuming everyone had mastered the rest.

There were times when racial animosity could be reasonably inferred from a professor's comment. During Claiborne's freshman year, all four African-American males at Duke were aspiring engineers. After one engineering class, three of them inquired together about their coursework. "Something came up where we said, 'We're trying to get a clarification because we want to get an A on the assignment,'" Claiborne reports. "And I'll never forget it: This guy who was an old professor that had been there for some time, he said, 'Don't worry about it, you won't get an A.' He didn't know anything about us. We'd asked a question about what the homework assignment was. That was my introduction to racism at Duke. Just *a priori*, 'You won't do well in this class.' Why is that? We all looked at each other, because we all came from [strong academic] backgrounds; we were expecting to do well."

Racial divisions among the predominantly Southern students were comparably pronounced, although Knowlin insisted most undergraduates "tried to be fair." She found their occasional insensitivities more a function of social class than race. "We really didn't have a whole lot of incidents," she said.

That unruffled assessment is at odds with the experience of Ernie Jackson, one of Duke's first African-American football players. Jackson entered the university in the fall of 1967 and went on to a senior season as remarkable as any in the history of modern, two-platoon football. Employed on a depleted Blue Devil squad as both a defensive back and a running back, the 5-foot-10 Jackson was an All-American, voted the 1971 ACC Player of the Year, the first African American so honored in the history of the conference. Yet his memories of Duke, where the school band still played "Dixie" at athletic contests in his early years, constitute "sort of a love-hate relationship," he said.

"I had a lot of honors there from an athletic standpoint, but the thing I recall more than anything else was when I'd walk through the dorms on the way to practice every day," Jackson said. "Most of the football players were [fraternity] members, I believe. And when you saw the Confederate flag hoisted out of their dorms all the time, it was extremely difficult to have to go to war with those guys and play with them from a teammate perspective. . . . Whenever I think about Duke, I don't think about the All-America honors, I think about the other stuff. That's the most glaring picture that comes to mind."

Such displays contributed to a sense of alienation among the handful of Black students at Duke, most of whom came from segregated settings. "It was foreign to us at first to see so many white people," Knowlin said. Further, there was a significant difference between being plunked onto campus and being assimilated into student life. There was no barber at the student union who knew how to cut a Black man's hair, no course of study with an African-American theme, no Black professors.

Understandably, Duke's African-American students tended to stick together. "We got along well as a group because we got thrown into a situation where we mostly ended up being sort of like family," Knowlin said. By the end of their college years, the small group had spawned six or seven married couples, including the Claibornes, who had three children during a 10-year marriage. "With desegregation, all you do is put bodies under the same roof," said Hank Allen, the Langdon High coach who went on a distinguished career as a professor of education at the University of Virginia. "Integration is a mentality. People misinterpret those two terms, misdefine them. They've done it all along. They're two different concepts altogether."

Furthering the sense of isolation at Duke, the university lay at arm's length from working-class Durham, a city that grew in the immediate aftermath of the Civil War from an unassuming rail stop with fewer than 100 inhabitants into a tobacco boom town. Demand for the area's new, lighter tobacco exploded after looting troops, in town for Confederate general Joseph Johnston's surrender to Union general William T. Sherman, got a taste of "bright leaf." Among those prospering most were peddler Washington Duke and his family, who rode the boom to tremendous wealth, $40 million of which was bestowed in 1924 upon what was until then Trinity College. A Gothic-style main campus, designed by Philadelphian Julian Francis Abele—an African American whose ancestry was largely acknowledged at Duke until the 1980s—was erected at a remove from downtown factories and warehouses ripe with the sickly sweet smell of flue-cured tobacco.

Despite the social and physical gulf separating the new university from the rest of Durham (a lingering rift highlighted by the racially tinged 2006

Duke lacrosse case), the school's early Black students had a ready and receptive outlet just across town. North Carolina College for Negroes, later N.C. Central, was a cornerstone of Durham's thriving African-American community and an oasis to which many Black students at Duke and nearby UNC–Chapel Hill fled. "We used to take the bus over there all the time," Jackson said. "That was our only haven."

Charles Scott, who matriculated at North Carolina a year behind Claiborne, similarly found his social life at Central. For years he and Claiborne journeyed to east Durham to play in pickup games either in the gym at Central or on the outdoor courts at nearby Hillside High School. "I went to Central almost every day," Claiborne said. "I went to Central so much that I had a meal card so I could go eat in the dining hall at Central. And I knew a lot of people over there. Sometimes I'd take my books, have lunch, and stay over there the rest of the afternoon, particularly when it wasn't basketball season."

Time spent at Central also brought Claiborne and others into contact with Durham's strong, stable, active African-American community, which had drawn praise from black visitors as diverse as militant W. E. B. Du Bois and accommodationist Booker T. Washington. In 1912 Du Bois had written an essay called "The Upbuilding of Black Durham," which was subtitled "The Success of Negroes and Their Value to a Tolerant and Helpful Southern City."

Mechanics and Farmers Bank, along with the North Carolina Mutual Insurance Company, the nation's largest and oldest Black-owned business, anchored a Durham financial district called "the Black Wall Street." The vibrant Hayti section—through which a devastating four-lane, limited-access freeway was under construction even as Duke admitted its first Black students—was known as "the Black Baltimore." And the Durham Committee on the Affairs of Black People was North Carolina's oldest African-American political organization.

Certain racial lines were not to be crossed, however. In her family history *Proud Shoes*, Pauli Murray—an African-American author, attorney, and minister who grew up in Durham in the early 20th century—recounted seeing a playmate shot dead for traversing a white man's watermelon patch. The threat of violence lingered a half-century later: At a November 1966 rally in Durham, a Ku Klux Klan leader told 2,500 people, "This is Klansville, U.S.A." Nonetheless, challenges to white hegemony came earlier in Durham, with a population that was 40 percent Black, than in many

Southern communities. Three years before Greensboro sit-ins brought civil rights struggles to the forefront of American consciousness, Durham African Americans sat-in to protest cramped, segregated accommodations at the Royal Ice Cream Company. Then came battles over the slow pace of public school integration and, later, the bitter, programmatic decimation of 500 acres of Hayti in the name of progress.

"Hayti redevelopment, presented to the people as an urban renewal project, pictured a beautiful new development with prosperous businesses and attractive new homes for about six hundred families that would be displaced," noted Dorothy Phelps Jones in *The End of an Era*. "The plum turned to a lemon when the area was leveled and two hideous buildings, Tin City, were erected for a few of the businesses. Homes became apartment housing projects." The devastation caused by urban renewal, dubbed "Negro removal" by many African Americans, was epidemic throughout the South.

External events in 1968—from the unprovoked shooting of Black college students in Orangeburg, South Carolina, to the assassination of Martin Luther King Jr.—intensified anger within Durham's Black community even as Hayti fell. The summer and fall saw a boycott of city merchants by the Black Solidarity Committee, which advocated better education and housing, equal justice, and better jobs for African Americans as well as more Black representatives on governing boards.

Activism in Durham was mirrored and supported on campus. An integrated "Silent Vigil" was held at Duke in the spring of 1968, with demonstrators calling for an end to discriminatory pay and working conditions for Black maids, janitors, and dining hall workers. Soon, professing frustration with Duke's slow response to their concerns, African-American students presented president Douglas Knight with a list of demands that included increased Black enrollment levels and course offerings, the withdrawal of campus memberships at segregated facilities, and an end to the harassment of African Americans by campus police.

Matters came to a head in February 1969 during the school's "Black Week," when speakers included Mississippi voting rights advocate Fannie Lou Hamer, future Atlanta mayor Maynard Jackson, author LeRoi Jones, local activists Howard Fuller and Ben Ruffin, and comedian/activist Dick Gregory. Speaking at the basketball arena, Gregory praised what he called "probably the most morally dedicated and committed group of youth in history" at a time, he said, when "the number one problem confronting us today is moral pollution." Then, in a remark perhaps less prophetic than informed, he asked, "Which is the mark of degeneracy—stealing drawers [in panty raids] or taking over the administration building?"

On a bitterly cold morning three days later, some 60 members of Duke's Afro-American Society occupied Allen Building, the university's administrative headquarters. Squarely in the middle of the action were senior C. B. Claiborne and his wife, Josie. The couple had met when he was a sophomore, she a freshman. "He was very tall and slender, a good-looking guy," Knowlin said. "He appeared very studious because he was an engineering major, so he was doing a lot of studying when it looked like a lot of the other guys were goofing off."

Claiborne, who cultivated a resemblance to Stokely Carmichael, was one of the few pioneering Black athletes who visibly engaged in campus protest. Most shied in the face of threats, overt or implied, from their coaches. "We were told—this is when a lot of administration buildings were being taken over all across the country—we were told by the athletic department that it was an NCAA rule that if you participated in such an occasion, you were subject to lose your [athletic] scholarship," Ernie Jackson said. Claiborne had the luxury of attending school on an academic scholarship. Further, he had grown up with protests in Danville, watching bloodied demonstrators stream through the streets toward the church that had been their staging place. He also was firmly plugged into Durham's heated politics.

And, as far as basketball was concerned, he felt he had little to lose.

"I'd had a number of run-ins with Vic about growing an Afro," Claiborne recalled. "He said, 'I support your right to do that, but if you're going to grow your hair, you won't play on my team.' And I said, 'All right, I'll sit on the bench.' I was on the bench anyway. It wasn't like I was losing a whole lot. He wasn't going to take my last piece of dignity by telling me what I had to look like. Particularly when everybody else in the country who was Black was growing Afros and still playing. And we kind of had this understanding about that, and so I continued to let my hair grow and he continued to let me sit on the bench. In practice everything was fine. I just didn't play."

Bubas has no such recollection. Regardless, Claiborne's perceived lack of a stake in his basketball fate made it easier to follow his instincts. "Those were very fervent times," he said. "I can remember saying, 'This is more important than basketball. This is something I have to be a part of.'"

Claiborne joined the Allen Building occupants, slipping in a back entrance before the occupiers chained the doors shut.

Eight hours passed. More than 100 Durham County sheriff's deputies, Durham city policemen, and state highway patrolmen gathered in the nearby Duke Gardens, waiting to storm the building. Some ominously removed their badges, hiding their identities preparatory to moving in. The atmosphere inside the building, Knowlin said, was "very tense—very, very tense—because we didn't know what to expect. This was Durham, North Carolina, and we were expecting the 'Southern' response to demonstrations. And then all during the day, we kept hearing that they were calling in the troops. So it was really tense. The initial takeover actually went a lot easier than we initially thought, because a lot of people hadn't gotten to work yet that morning. That was a little of a breather. Then everything started kicking in."

A sympathizer among Durham's Black leadership climbed in a window and warned that the police "were coming with tear gas and all that," Claiborne says. The students vacated the building through a window, women first. The police arrived within minutes and took control of the premises. More than 1,000 students, black and white, gathered on the quadrangle in front of Allen Building. The police exited the building and advanced on the crowd with clubs and tear gas, spraying the gas into the religion building and even Duke Chapel. "I can still smell the gas, see the smoke . . . [We were] wondering how our lives were going to change, because we didn't know what was going to happen next," Knowlin said. "The world's coming to an end. What are you going to do? It was a fatalistic kind of thing, a feeling that the revolution was here."

The Claibornes remained deeply involved as Duke students boycotted classes for three days and rallied on campus and off. Meanwhile, C. B. missed a basketball practice and a trip to West Virginia that resulted in a Duke loss. Four days passed before he phoned Bubas to say that he remained in school and wished to stay on the team. "I want to make it clear that C. B. has been a fine young man who has contributed much to this team," the coach said in a statement. Claiborne was on the bench in uniform the next day, and two games later he saw action in a decisive loss at NC State. A local sports columnist suggested Claiborne was "a lucky man" to escape punishment for being absent without permission.

Claiborne graduated several months later with an engineering degree, a child, and a wife. Offered essentially the same salary by the Harlem

Globetrotters and by Westinghouse, Claiborne chose the business world. Later he earned a master's degree in engineering from Dartmouth and a doctorate in business from Virginia Tech. He has since remained a college professor and "a class fellow," according to Lind, his former roommate.

Duke added a handful of Black recruits after Claiborne's graduation but went eight years before signing Philadelphian Gene Banks, its first prominent African-American basketball player. Banks was the 1978 ACC Rookie of the Year as Duke leapt from a tie for last place in the league to a berth in the NCAA title game against Kentucky. A lingering image of that season was Banks and equally fiery classmate Kenny Dennard, a white North Carolinian, hugging on the court.

The contemporary Blue Devils, arguably the nation's preeminent program under coach Mike Krzyzewski, who retired in 2022, routinely deploy five Black players at a time. Claiborne's groundbreaking role remained largely unsung. His alma mater did celebrate his groundbreaking efforts, but only alongside Clarence Newsome, a pioneering Black football player at the school long after the fact. Only in 2021 did Duke prominently honor the spirit of inclusion by selecting Nina King, an African American woman, as its athletics director. The school has yet to have a Black head coach in football or men's basketball.

As for Claiborne, he stays in shape, playing basketball and engaging in martial arts. But he stopped participating in alumni basketball games after a few appearances. "They spelled my name wrong on the jersey," he said. "That's a statement in and of itself."

That is as critical as Claiborne will get. "I don't think I've ever heard anything negative about anything ever from him," said Claudia Claiborne, his oldest daughter. "He just doesn't mention it if he doesn't like it." Unlike her father, Claudia is quick to voice her irritation with Duke. "Especially with them being so good now and so popular—and clearly Black players are an integral part of their team and their success—there should be, not a recognition of him personally, but sort of an outward appreciation or a verbal appreciation of Black basketball players in general," she contends. "That doesn't exist."

Claiborne, the man caught between worlds, seems to accept that he made little splash but was himself a bridge, narrowing a gap that could no longer be endured. "My experiences at Duke were just what you would have expected them to be given that place, given the time. So in that sense, it's certainly not exceptional," he said of his years on the Durham campus. "If there's a remarkable piece of this, it's probably that I got through it. For whatever value or benefit it has, it was sort of the cornerstone for what came later. Because there was a necessity for people to change their attitudes, or be able to adjust to the way the world was turning. And, even though they weren't ready for it then, that first step was necessary when I was there."

CHAPTER 4

FALL FROM GRACE

Henry Harris Jr., Auburn University, 1968–72

Ships at a distance have every man's wish on board. For some they come in with the tide. For others they sail forever on the horizon, never out of sight, never landing until the Watcher turns his eyes away in resignation, his dreams mocked to death by Time.

Zora Neale Hurston, *Their Eyes Were Watching God*

Henry Harris's final leap of faith embraced only gravity.

Harris had come far from rural Alabama, yet on that spring night in 1974, he apparently felt he had gotten nowhere at all. So, dressed resplendently for the occasion in a striped suit, Harris quietly opened a window and exited his disheveled dorm room at the University of Wisconsin–Milwaukee. He landed with an irredeemable thud 13 stories below, facedown on the roof of Green Commons, a four-story lounge named for the first African American to graduate from the University of Wisconsin Law School at Madison.

When Harris died he was less than two years removed from his own pioneering career as the first black scholarship athlete at a predominantly white university in Alabama.

It fell to Robert Raymond to identify his younger brother's body. "When I got to the door at the morgue, I couldn't walk in," said Raymond. "When I saw Henry laying on the table, saw his face, I froze. I couldn't walk in and identify him. It took me a year to come out of it, get back right. I quit my job in Pennsylvania and moved back to Alabama then. I don't know how to explain it. Something just happened." Raymond's voice quavered as he spoke, anguish slithering just below the surface decades after his brother's death at age 24. "My uncle went in and identified him."

The death made a brief splash in Milwaukee, where a *Milwaukee Journal* story under the headline "A Tangled Life Ended Abruptly" described Harris as a "many sided" and "complex young man." The same edition of the newspaper reported that U.S. Judge John Sirica had issued a subpoena directing President Richard Nixon to give the Watergate special prosecutor tapes and documents related to 64 conversations; that a video of a San Francisco bank robbery showed heiress Patty Hearst among the participants; and that Thomas Pynchon, winner of the National Book Award for *Gravity's Rainbow*, sent Professor Irwin Corey, a comedian, "to baffle the audience with sour jokes and convoluted grammar" at the awards ceremony.

Harris essentially was marooned in Milwaukee, where he had moved the previous summer to join head basketball coach Rudy Davalos, the lead recruiter when Harris signed with Auburn University in the spring of 1968. But Davalos left for a job with the NBA's San Antonio Spurs, citing broken promises by the UWM athletics director and a chance to return to his hometown. He never coached a game in Milwaukee. As the end of the spring semester approached, Harris, who had not graduated from Auburn, was about to lose both his free tuition at UWM and his $1,000-a-year job as a junior varsity basketball coach and intramural supervisor.

Journal reporter Bill Dwyre described Harris as a loner who struggled with his schoolwork but was well liked by colleagues and by the players he coached. Apparently unaware that Vanderbilt's Perry Wallace had broken the color line in the SEC, Dwyre wrote that Harris "reportedly was not militant about being Black, and at the same time he reportedly was in the process of writing a book about his experiences as the first Black basketball player in the Southeastern Conference." No manuscript ever surfaced.

A follow-up story in the *Milwaukee Sentinel*—accompanied by a photograph of Harris wearing a serious expression and a stylishly large Afro, a mustache, and long, wide sideburns—said he died even as Davalos had secured a playing spot for him in European pro basketball. "I feel like I have lost a son or a brother," Davalos told a reporter at the time.

"The first thing I thought was, 'What would have happened if I had stayed?'" Davalos, who retired as the University of New Mexico athletics director in 2006, said recently. "If I had stayed there, would that have happened? So I went through kind of a temporary guilt trip, which I think all of us do when something like that happens. But then I also looked at all the things I tried to do to help him. He had some problems that he wasn't dealing with properly."

Harris's brother and his uncle, an auxiliary policeman from Chicago, made inquiries into the death, which was ruled a suicide. Four empty beer cans, three plastic bags of marijuana, two burnt-down joints, two empty wine bottles, and a pipe with marijuana residue were found in Harris's room. An autopsy revealed no trace of alcohol or barbiturates in his blood.

University police reported that several hours preceding his death, Harris told a fellow student, "I feel empty, empty like a shell, and I want to die." The UWM police listed "suicide" as the "offense" investigated upon finding "the body of a N/M [Negro/Male] dead on arrival." Harris's clothing clearly indicated forethought. Still, there was no report of a suicide note.

Suicide simply did not square with the Henry Harris familiar to relatives or friends. So Raymond looked for telltale signs of murder in Milwaukee. Back in Alabama he tracked rumors, spurred by anguished voices raised at the funeral, mourners proclaiming that someone had killed his brother. "It took me a while, a year, to close out in my mind that he did kill himself," said Raymond, who returned to Auburn when Harris was posthumously honored prior to a January 2002 game. "I had played with him and grew up with him, and I didn't want to believe it. I still don't believe he killed himself. Not the person that I knew." Samuel Isaac, a teammate at Greene County Training School, had a similar reaction: "Knowing Henry, I don't think he'd do that."

Auburn associates were comparably perplexed. "For many who knew Henry Harris while he was at Auburn, it is difficult to comprehend that he would take his own life and it is equally difficult to understand why," wrote local newspaper columnist Guy Rhodes. In an interview with Rhodes, head coach Bill Lynn said Harris was a "fierce competitor and team man all the way." Perspectives on Harris remained equally positive over time. Larry Chapman, an Auburn assistant coach for part of Harris's career, recalls the player as "a brilliant guy" and "very confident." Teammate John Mengelt said Harris was a "happy-go-lucky" introvert who played hard, blended seamlessly into the Tigers basketball program, and was a "very, very tough competitor." Davalos remembered "a bubbly, smiling guy in high school" who was still "fine" at Auburn.

Auburn teammate Jimmy Walker, a white Georgian who roomed for a time with Harris, recalled "an outgoing guy. I always remember this about him: He thought he was a philosopher, and he read about Malcolm X all the time. His favorite saying was 'Everything is everything.' You'd say, 'How's it going, Henry?' 'Everything is everything.' That was his favorite statement. What that meant, I have no idea. He got into the Malcolm X stuff. We'd kid him about it; we could cut up with him. We'd say we were going to get the Ku Klux Klan on him if he didn't straighten up. Just that stuff, back and forth. He wasn't a hard-nosed guy; he could take a lot of kidding and carry on just like everybody else."

Yet Harris could not escape a ravaged knee that quickly circumscribed his lofty gifts and aspirations. The injury, incurred during a game his freshman season, limited Harris's mobility in an era before arthroscopic surgery refashioned torn ligaments and tendons to be virtually as good as new. Wearing a bulky black knee brace, Harris never quite made the splash in college augured by his high school achievements. Those included more than 3,000 varsity points scored, All-America honors, and inclusion among 20 talented prep players from around the nation in Pittsburgh's prestigious Dapper Dan Classic. Harris scored 20 points and was named Most Valuable Player in the 1968 Alabama All-Star Game, capping a senior season in which he averaged 32.4 points and 12 rebounds per contest.

"You remember guys who are good and were never able to fulfill their promise because of something like [the knee injury] happening," said Mark Murphy, who grew up around Auburn sports and graduated from the university in 1975. "People liked him a lot. He was really a favorite of the students when he was up with the varsity."

There's no doubt Harris also suffered a wound while crossing the South's racial divide. Most of college basketball's early racial pioneers endured multiple marriages and divorces. Many had such bittersweet experiences that they kept their distance from their alma maters once their playing days ended. Several failed to graduate. Several self-destructed. Tom Payne, Kentucky's first African-American basketball player, spent much of his adult life in prison for rape and parole violation. Wake Forest's Norwood Todmann reportedly spent his promise on crack cocaine. And Harris committed suicide.

"I think he'd still be alive if he had gone someplace like Iowa or Villanova," said Al Young Jr., Harris's high school coach and a longtime family friend. "And he would have played in the NBA. But he wanted to be a pioneer."

Harris developed his athletic and scholastic prowess in tiny Boligee, an agricultural community along the banks of the Tombigbee River in Greene County, on the Alabama border with Mississippi. "We picked cotton together," said Raymond, now a rewinder operator for a toilet-tissue manufacturer near Demopolis. "We'd get whipped for picking the bolls off and shooting them like we were shooting a basketball. All he did was play ball."

The town and surrounding countryside were quiet. Fishing the "Big Tom," walking, and playing sports were the primary diversions. "That was about it, because there really was nothing to do," said Raymond. "There was absolutely nothing to do. Most of the guys around got involved in sports."

Greene County was a sleepy realm of farms and laden logging trucks, camp stew and barbecue, pecans and hot boiled green peanuts. Huge catfish ponds lined the roads, their harvest sent to processing plants in Union and Greensboro. The area's heyday came long ago, in the decades preceding the Civil War. Buoyed by its waterways, warm weather, and rich, loamy soil, back then Greene County bristled with cotton, plantations, and slaves. "Every mile or two was a resplendent farm house where the planter lived in his country retirement with his family," wrote George Clark in his 1914 book *A Glance Backward,* "and around, or adjacent, were the quarters of the slaves, all of them comfortable with rare exceptions, and inhabited with a tenantry whose devotion to their masters and families was surpassed only by their industry in bringing in bountiful crops." Consistent with this idealized image of the Old South, Clark insisted that "treatment of the slaves was of the kindest and most patriarchal character."

Greene County character of a different sort emerged in separate incidents during Reconstruction. Four Black citizens were murdered in murky circumstances, as was Alexander Boyd, the white county solicitor and a Republican outsider who sympathized with African Americans. One night in 1870, Ku Klux Klan members dragged Boyd from his hotel room in Eutaw (the county seat, located 10 miles from Boligee) and murdered him. They left his body on the walkway where he died, completing the statement of intimidation.

Equal rights for African Americans came slowly. A century passed before Greene County schools were integrated, precipitating a massive exodus of white students from public education. In Harris's time, most whites attended private schools such as Warrior Academy, while African Americans in larger numbers swelled the public school rolls. Relations between the races were cordial and sometimes openly collaborative, but a marked distance endured.

"It's sort of like this: 'I don't want to go to your school any more than you want to go to my school,'" explained Bernice Young, a longtime library science teacher in the public schools and the wife of Harris's high school coach. "I go to my church; they go to their church. I'm not interested in their church, and they're not interested in mine, unless we have a meeting where we have to come together as a group." Her husband, Al, cannot recall ever having a white player on the teams he coached.

Like Harris, Al Young grew up in Boligee, where his father, Alfonso (Al Sr.), was principal of the Greene County Training School, established in 1924. After integration the former high school for African Americans became a middle school, then a K–8 charter school that closed in 2021. Harris's mother, Willie Pearl Harris, worked as housekeeper and cook for Al Sr. The Harris family lived across the street from the school, hard by the road in what Davalos said "looked to me like it was a former gas station. . . . It was just a very small block building; you walked in and kind of walked right through the house."

Harris had been an excellent student but quit school at age 15 to have her first child. She subsequently married Henry Harris Sr., a "paper wood" worker who hauled timber. He died of illness several years into their marriage. Later in life Mrs. Harris received her GED; she was contemplating a return to college when Henry, the third of her five sons, died.

Ms. Harris was a caring but strict parent, preaching "pray, work, and pay your bills" to her six children. "Henry and I went to a corner store," Raymond said by way of illustration. "One of the teachers was at the store. There was a ginger cake [gingerbread] there. Henry picked it up and put it in his pocket. Stole it. Came on back home. When we got back home, the man let the store close and came to the house. Told my mother.

"My mother went in the house, got a belt or switch or something, and walked out there and started beating Henry. She beat Henry until that man started crying and said he hated that he told her. That's the way my mother was. She said, 'We'll work and get it, or we don't get it.' Later in life she recanted. She said that she shouldn't have beat us. She said that was a slavery thing, but she didn't know any better. I think she did the right thing, because Henry and I were terrible." The mischievous brothers were kept in line by an extended family of teachers, coaches, and other adults for whom Henry became a special favorite.

Harris was a confident leader "who didn't meet a stranger," his brother said. He starred in basketball, baseball, and football; in the latter he was the quarterback and punter for four years. But basketball was his first love, even in a state where football was a form of worship. "I declare, he was good," said Isaac, Harris's Greene County teammate. "Back then, when we played the gym was always full. Everywhere we played, the gym was full. They wanted to see Henry shoot the ball. . . . He could handle the ball like a monkey handles peanuts. You couldn't get it away from him." Isaac remembered a game in which Harris scored 52 points for the Bobcats. "He was good. He was awesome. He was a Michael Jordan."

Recognizing her son's aptitude and interest, Harris's mother bought a goal and had it erected in the yard. It became the focal point of his existence. "If he had a certain move he wanted to perfect, he would go out and practice four hours a day for a whole week just to get that one move," recalled Raymond, who covered for his brother by doing both of their chores. "And once he got it, he would show it off on me or anybody else. It was like it came naturally, because he had practiced.

"He wasn't satisfied unless he shot 47 out of 50 free throws at the house. At night, everybody would get in and go to bed, and he'd still be out there. My mother would make him come indoors, beat him or whatever it would take to make him come indoors and go to sleep. He didn't care. That was all he did—practice basketball eight days a week."

Harris made the varsity as a ninth grader, the earliest possible opportunity, and soon became a star. In his senior season, the last before integration, Harris was the main man on what Al Young deemed "probably the best team I had. I think we were 30–2 or something like that. That was great. That spoiled me from then on. Never got back to that."

Young touted the teenager, the pride of his community, in letters to Auburn and Alabama, both of which had yet to sign a Black basketball player. "We didn't call them point guards then; I called it something else. Henry played that position and also played in the middle on defense," Young said. "He was a top-notch rebounder. He'd come down three-on-one, three-on-none—just that fast."

Soon the top recruits in Alabama were Harris and Isaac "Bud" Stallworth, another African American. Stallworth decided to go to Kansas after attending band camp there. Meanwhile, Auburn's assistant coaches overcame the reservations of head coach Lynn and aggressively sought to sign a Black player. "He let us have basically free rein," Davalos said. "He could have stopped it. Yeah, it was our idea, but we certainly had his blessing." Starting out of state, they brought Joby Wright and his parents from their home in Georgia to attend Auburn's football homecoming game, the passage of the Black trio through the stadium attracting "a lot of strange looks," Davalos recalled. The coaches were disappointed when Wright, a forward with questionable scores on standardized tests, ultimately chose Indiana.

That left Stallworth and Harris. Assistant coach Chapman had seen Harris play in his home gym in Boligee. "When the boys come out to warm up, there ain't no doubt who Henry was," said Chapman, head coach at Auburn University at Montgomery from 1977 through 2014. "Boy, he was so smooth. He was about 6-foot-3 and unbelievable. Good-looking athlete. I told my wife, Sarah, 'Hey, he's the real deal.' We watch the game, and there's no doubt about [his talent]. We start recruiting him. As we go forward, Rudy's really good with him. Rudy's Mexican-American. . . . I'm telling you, Henry liked Rudy. Rudy was a minority. There was trust there. When you make a decision like that, the most important thing is trust."

Part of the decision, of course, was accepting the role of trailblazer, of life in a fishbowl with many eagerly awaiting your mistakes and welcoming every flaw. "He had some concerns, but Henry was a brilliant guy. He was very confident," Chapman said. "He was a unique kid. Things didn't scare him." Perhaps the challenges ahead should have scared him. But Boligee was a dead end for an ambitious young Black man, and a basketball scholarship offered Harris a way out.

"He could do it all," Chapman said. "He could guard you. Really. He had unbelievable energy. He could run and jump. Basketball being a game of runners, it really kind of distanced him from people. He had great quickness, great skills—could shoot the ball, handle it, pass it. He did it all. How could you watch Henry and not remember everything about him? He could do it, buddy. Had the greatest hands and the greatest feet. In those days it was a half-court, kind of boring game. He added so much to probably the beginning of full-court basketball—and more exciting basketball."

High-stakes recruiting quickly engulfed Greene County and the Harris family. In an era of looser rules and widespread cheating, when Southeastern Conference basketball strained to escape the long shadows of both football and Adolph Rupp's colossal Kentucky program, Henry Harris's services were a coveted prize.

Tapping homegrown talent was a departure for Alabama basketball programs. Most SEC schools trolled basketball hotbeds Illinois, Indiana, and Kentucky for players not taken by their states' premier programs. These limited horizons occasionally yielded a John Mengelt, an Indiana shooting whiz, but more often perpetuated basketball's second-class status in the SEC.

Football preeminence was not peculiar to Auburn. "At Alabama the head basketball coach was the football trainer," said C. M. Newton, a Hall of Fame inductee as a contributor. He played for Rupp at Kentucky and later was a head coach at two SEC schools. "At Tennessee the head basketball coach was an assistant football coach—what they call the football recruiting coordinator today."

SEC basketball fitfully edged toward national and internal competitiveness in the mid-1960s. Integration provided a welcome new vein of talent to complement full-time staffs, increased funding, and new arenas. Suddenly, African-American athletes such as Harris, previously ignored by traditionally white schools in the region, were fair game.

With attention came inducements. Young Harris accompanied one coaching staff to nearby Meridian, Mississippi, and returned home "with all sorts of stuff," said Young. Money and a car were offered to Mrs. Harris, who didn't even have a telephone. "I recruited Harris," recalled George Raveling, then an assistant at Villanova. "I thought I had him. I went in there one day, and he was watching an SEC game on a black-and-white television. I came back two weeks later, and I watched it in color." Davalos dismissed the story. "That sounds like one of George's folktales," he said. "I don't remember them having a color TV."

Old racial habits also affected Harris's recruitment. White Alabamans had, in the not-so-distant past, used economic sanctions to pressure African Americans to adhere to the dictates of segregation. But when Harris became a prime recruit, a banker threatened his mother's credit if her son *didn't* attend a particular school. A competing school responded by marshaling a feed-store owner to threaten withdrawing his business from the bank.

"We probably spent more time recruiting Henry than any player while I was at Auburn," Lynn, who resigned a year after Harris finished his Auburn career, told columnist Rhodes. "He was very much respected and looked up to by his family and probably because of that stayed near home for his college career."

There was some question about whether Harris's score on a standardized test was sufficient for admission, but schools made dispensations for the high school valedictorian. Maneuvering continued until Harris was on scholarship—and off the market. "When signing day rolled around, Wimp Sanderson was down at the house," Young said of the Alabama assistant coach. "They couldn't find the boy. I think Auburn had scooted him off somewhere. Wimp was going crazy."

So Harris entered Auburn wooed, touted, and talented. "He was an all-American kid," said Ralph Foster, an African-American acquaintance from Harris's Auburn days. "He was treading in high cotton."

○

Somewhere along the way, Auburn lost its luster for Harris. Somewhere along the way, the happy-go-lucky Harris became more introverted, began fretting about ghosts and sleeping with the lights on in his dorm room to keep them at bay. A year after completing his Auburn career, Harris avoided discussing his experience there. "He didn't want to talk about the school too much. He seemed distraught about it," said older brother Raymond. "My mother said she talked to him about two hours one time to get him not to start a ruckus, not to be a troublemaker. She never told me exactly what [the issue was]; she just felt that he had been mistreated."

Brenda Temple Tull might have struck Harris's mother as a troublemaker. An older sister of Collis Temple, Louisiana State University's first Black basketball player, she was among the first African-American undergraduates at LSU. She recalled the strain on barrier-breakers as constant. Several of her Black classmates reportedly suffered nervous breakdowns. "All that pressure, all of that tension, and I was just a regular student," Tull said. "To be someone who was going to be a trailblazer—that was incredibly difficult."

Similar dynamics applied to Harris in the Alabama countryside and to African-American athletes elsewhere during the civil rights era. Among the most prominent was Louisiana transplant Bill Russell. A gangly All-American at the University of San Francisco (where he played from 1952 to 1956) and perhaps the best player in NBA history (with the Boston Celtics from 1957 through 1969), Russell decries the effect of systematic discrimination in *Go Up for Glory*, his 1966 autobiography. "AM I A FOREIGNER IN MY HOMELAND?" he asked. "Thus does the anger descend upon a man. Thus does it well up and declare the battleground. A field without banners, a fight without bugles. A deadly, personal conflict, where only a man who is a man can survive."

Perry Wallace, the only other African-American player in the SEC when Harris first joined the Tiger varsity, grappled throughout his life with the terms of survival he accepted. Wallace marveled to see Harris at Auburn, where the Vanderbilt player found the 2,500-strong crowd at the intimate Sports Arena (more familiarly called "the Barn") as mean as any he encountered.

Certainly the old military-style Quonset hut, a vestige of days when male students at the land-grant college had to take six semesters of ROTC, lent itself to the intimidation of visitors. "You'd go in for a layup, and you'd run into the crowd," recalls Herb "Hub" Waldrop, a former Tiger football player and venerable institution himself within Auburn athletics. "That's the kind of atmosphere that we had during that time. It was mostly the male students who attended the games. Very few females attended the games during those years." (Women at the state's oldest coeducational university were celebrated, however, in the *Plainsman*, the student newspaper, in a weekly feature called "Loveliest of the Plains.")

"I saw us play Kentucky one night, and there were people up in the rafters, and sparks started flying up there," Waldrop said. "I thought the place was going to burn down. It was a tremendous atmosphere." (The Sports Arena did burn down in 1996, long after it had been supplanted as the school's basketball facility.)

Wallace insisted the treatment he received at Auburn was hardly akin to the generic abuse heaped on any visitor. Nor did he believe that Harris's psyche escaped unscathed from his experience at the school. "I don't think they ever really acknowledged the connection between him committing suicide and having been there at Auburn," Wallace said. "It puzzled me to see Henry Harris at Auburn. It puzzled and discouraged me because that was an awful place. It was just as bad as it could be. And the thought that somebody was down there actually living on the campus and trying to function in that system was really scary."

Some people protested such a characterization of Auburn, both the town and its like-named university, founded in 1856 as East Alabama Male College. "There never was really a problem at Auburn," said Mark Murphy, whose seventh-grade class was the first in town to be integrated. "It was pretty calm about the whole thing. There was not a lot of tension compared to some places."

Waldrop described similarly smooth sailing. The former head trainer at Auburn University joined the athletics staff in 1960 and remembered Harris as player and person. "I've been in this program for 40-something years, and I can truthfully say that I've never known of a racial incident," said Waldrop, who kept a Bible on his desk and Christianity on his lips. "Athletes bond together. See, when an athlete walks through that door, that's not a Black athlete or a white athlete; that's an Auburn University athlete. That's the way they've always been treated, and they bonded together."

Ralph Foster, a lifelong resident of the town and a friend of the basketball program and "very liberal" Bill Lynn, ratified the notion that Auburn is a place of racial moderation, at least by Alabama standards. "Auburn has always been unique in itself because it is a very highly educated center. We don't have the overt rednecks. It wasn't a mill town, a farming town."

These claims ring a bit hollow when one considers that in 2001, members of two Auburn fraternities posed in blackface at Halloween parties; one member was dressed in Klan garb, holding a weapon and a noose around the neck of a "Black" victim. Stunningly oblivious to the implications, one fraternity posted photos of the activities on its Web site, leading to apologies, suspensions, and the establishment of the Center for Diversity and Race Relations on campus. "One reason African-American student enrollment is low is because Auburn's culture is overwhelmingly unwelcoming to anyone outside the status quo," a *Plainsman* editorial stated.

Racial peace in the city of Auburn, as elsewhere, was long secured through separation, not understanding. Railroad tracks usually provided the physical manifestation of that arm's-length arrangement. "Any time you went in the South and were heading for the black community, if you asked for directions, one thing was always going to happen," Raveling said. "Somewhere in the directions, they were going to say, 'And when you cross the railroad tracks . . .'" The arrangement, replicated throughout much of the country, carried a universal message, as Leon Litwack explained in *Trouble in Mind: Black Southerners in the Age of Jim Crow.* "The location of the black section of town, the condition of the streets, the state of sanitation, the quality of the housing, and the sharply limited access to what lay outside their neighborhood all attested dramatically to their 'place' in the larger society."

In nearby Sylacauga, roughly halfway between Auburn and Birmingham, Charles Reynolds experienced segregation from the whiter, brighter side of the coin. "It's hard to understand the power of unquestionable social customs unless you've lived with them," said Reynolds, professor of religious studies at the University of Tennessee from 1980 through 2001. "I knew when I was growing up that it was OK for me to play outside with Robert, who was the son of the family maid, who would frequently come with him to the house. She'd prepare meals, wash the clothes, all kinds of stuff. It was fine for Robert and me to be outside playing basketball or shooting marbles.

"And we could eat at the same time, but the only place we could eat together was out on the porch. There was no way, he knew and I knew, that we could sit down at the table inside and eat together. But there was no problem for one of us to be in a swing or a chair out on the porch and take our food out and eat.

"Isn't it amazing that kids at 10 or 12 years old, one white and one Black, know those boundaries and know how not to violate them? When I try to articulate that to the students today, they believe me at one level, and at another level it doesn't make sense to them. 'Well, if you can eat out on the porch, why can't you sit down at the table?' But those were two different social settings. People that worked with my dad, Blacks and whites, would sit around outside and eat their lunch together at the sawmill. There was nothing thought about it. And yet, there'd have been a killing if somebody had insisted on eating in the house together."

Togetherness wasn't all that great anyway, in Foster's estimation. Just as African Americans in Athens, Georgia, watched UGA football from a distant section called "Niggers' Roost," so Foster recalls being forced to sit in "the Hole" to watch games at what is now Jordan-Hare Stadium on the Auburn campus. (Bill Overton, a Wake Forest lineman in the mid-1960s and one of the first African-American players to compete at Auburn, remembered this section as "an old, rickety part of the stands.") Foster's memories of exclusion have an unexpectedly nostalgic flavor. "As I look back, it was more enjoyable watching the game from there than it was sitting in the stands," he said. When he was able to purchase a ticket to sit among white fans, they spurned him by shifting to leave an empty seat as a buffer, or heedlessly offended him because "nine out of ten times they were yelling foul names at the other players: 'Stop the nigger!'"

Foster spent his professional career as a teacher, coach, and administrator in public schools in Loachapoka, a heavily African-American community 6 miles west of Auburn. He helped Lynn recruit Black players but met Harris only when the athlete came to Loachapoka to date African-American women. Harris began frequenting Loachapoka during his sophomore year. "He would be gone at night doing that," Mengelt recalled. "Which, when you look back on it, I guess you can't blame him."

There were few African-American students in those days at Auburn, where black enrollment was low. Harris was the first Black athlete in any sport to earn a War Eagle scholarship. "He was the only one here," Foster said. "There was no support. And I don't know if it's here today." By 1981, nine years after Harris ended his career, every Auburn basketball starter was an African American. Yet in 1980 only 482 of 18,603 students (2.6 percent) at the university were Black.

Integration at Auburn University (the school officially adopted that name in 1960) had gone relatively smoothly, particularly compared to the University of Alabama, which greeted potential Black students with a riot in 1956 and the 1963 melodrama of Governor George Wallace making his famous stand in the schoolhouse door. "In contrast to the tension in Tuscaloosa, Auburn was almost an oasis of quietude," Tom Vaughn, an Auburn professor during the 1960s, told the *Plainsman*. (Alabama–Auburn comparisons in every realm are constant; the rivalry is "365 days a year," according to Alabama grad Paul Ellis.)

Yet Auburn shared the history of larger Alabama. At the dawn of World War II, for every $100 spent on higher education for whites in the state, $6.24 was spent on African Americans. And race-tinged tactics proved to be hoary staples of the social and political order. Sometimes the racism was colorfully cloaked, as when Governor James "Kissin' Jim" Folsom declared in 1954, "All I can say is what I told the good colored people of this state during my campaign, that they wouldn't have to go to school with us white folks."

White Southerners' enduring fixation with the so-called "race problem" left little room for tolerance, as George Wallace learned to his political detriment in 1958. After being portrayed as soft in his embrace of bigotry, Wallace privately vowed, "No other son-of-a-bitch will ever out-nigger me again." Militancy on this matter was an Alabama trademark, as was resistance to federal authority. The state motto, "We Dare Defend Our Rights," celebrates states' rights, not civil rights. Alabama so adamantly resisted federal efforts to force integration that in 1956, voters approved constitutional amendments that, among other things, relieved the state of the requirement to provide public education. To prevent racial mixing, the state was authorized to lease, sell, or give away public facilities such as parks. As late as 1961, when integration had gained at least token footholds in most states, Alabama, Mississippi, and South Carolina retained completely segregated educational systems.

"No less than the integrity and preservation of the white race was at stake," Litwack offered. "That explains why the maintenance of white domination dwarfed any other political issue. This was the litmus test for any aspiring politician, and it could make or break a person's standing in the community."

Upon learning in August 1963 that federal judge Frank Johnson had ordered the integration of public schools in Macon County, a first for Alabama, Governor Wallace had an instructive reaction. Local school officials acquiesced to the inevitable, drawing the instantaneous, calculated ire of the governor, the self-proclaimed defender of what journalist Tom Wicker called, in a 1967 article in *Harper's*, a "traditional Southern attitude toward Negroes—a mixture of contempt, distaste, amusement, affection, and appreciation for a valuable servant."

Wallace dispatched state troopers to deliver an executive order to the Macon school superintendent that closed Tuskegee High School to "preserve the peace, maintain domestic tranquility and to protect the lives and property of all citizens of the State of Alabama." The schools were closed for a week. (Summoned to the White House a year later by President Johnson, Wallace insisted, "I haven't got the political power" to dictate actions to local school boards. "Don't you shit me, George Wallace!" exclaimed the president.)

Eighteen miles up the road from Tuskegee, Auburn University had a history of quiet hostility to racial nonconformity, as demonstrated in the case of Bud R. Hutchinson. An untenured assistant professor of economics, Hutchinson was dropped from the faculty at the end of the 1957–58 academic year at the direction of Auburn president Ralph Brown Draughon. Hutchinson's offense had been a letter to the *Plainsman* in which he defended efforts by the New York City Commission on Integration to promote busing specifically and integration generally. The newspaper itself was censured by university trustees in 1961 after it predicted that Auburn would soon be integrated and declared that Freedom Riders, who were being beaten and harassed as they passed through Alabama, had "law and morality on their side." *Plainsman* editor Jim Dinsmore was suspended from his job for several months in 1962, then forbidden to return as editor. His crime was calling integration a "Christian, moral act" and Alabamans "ignorant and narrow-minded."

Less than two years later, in January 1964, Harold Franklin won a protracted legal battle and became the first African American to enroll in an Auburn graduate school. He met with no violence—unlike James Meredith, who entered Ole Miss in the fall of 1962—but there was no welcome, either. Franklin faced catcalls as he approached the library to register, and he was made to room and eat alone. He left Auburn within a year, after his academic advisor refused to let him write a thesis on the civil rights movement and the use of civil disobedience. (The first African American to graduate from Auburn was Samuel Pettijohn, who earned his bachelor's degree in 1967.)

The university hired its first African-American professor in 1968, and come that fall, Henry Harris arrived on campus. "He had to be a young man with a lot of courage to make that step," Hub Waldrop said. "There had to be something—a foundation within him. That was a tough step to make, man. He had to be somebody special."

O

Whatever difficulties Harris encountered, he largely kept to himself. "How could you talk to people about being Black, about what you were going through?" asked Charles Scott, the first Black player at the University of North Carolina. "How could you expect to answer them when they'd never dealt with that part of it? What response could you expect from them [white teammates]? What response could they give you to answer your problems?

"First of all, they were the problem. I mean, that was a significant problem—the fact that you're different and there's a different treatment going on there, there's a different scenario. There are things I can't do that you assume I can do with you. No matter what you say, off the court our lives went separate ways, and that could not be changed."

Given Jimmy Walker's account that Harris was a devotee of Malcolm X, it seems unlikely that Harris was entirely accepting of his surroundings at Auburn. Yet, typically, the whites with whom he associated had little idea of the challenges he confronted. "Being the first Black at Auburn didn't seem to be a big point with Henry," Lynn said. "The subject was seldom mentioned during our conversations. He just wanted to play basketball."

"He was the sweetest kid you've ever met," said Chapman, the freshman team coach. "All that white stuff didn't bother Henry—being the first. If it did, it didn't show. You know, it was different. Heck, you take a white person going to an all-Black school. Even now, you go into an all-Black church, you're going to feel a little [awkward]. You know what I'm saying. You don't feel intimidated, but there's a difference."

Mengelt, a year ahead of Harris, insists the school's sole Black athlete was just another player within team and dorm. "We'd play jokes on everybody, and he participated and played jokes on us." Walker recalled that, given a choice by older players of enduring a paddling or being driven blindfolded into the nighttime Alabama countryside, then left at nearby Chewacla State Park to make his way back, Harris confidently chose the walk and returned within an hour. "I'm sure that didn't sit well with him, [being left to wander] in Alabama where he wasn't familiar with the area," Walker said.

But when it came to racial sensitivity, Mengelt conceded he was in his own "cocoon" at a school that in 1970 had 100 African Americans among 15,139 undergraduates. "I guess I didn't even realize the challenges that someone like that would have to go through," Mengelt said of Harris. "Other than guys calling him names at a game once in a while and a fight breaking out, I don't remember anything that happened that I thought was because Henry was Black. But I'm sure a lot of things did. I don't even know how he was treated when he went to try to eat something, because I don't know that I was ever with him other than when we were with the team. And nobody ever said anything to us as a team. If they would have, a fight probably would have broken out in the restaurant."

Walker, who grew up in Eastpoint, Georgia, does recall such incidents. Harris, for his part, dismissed his trailblazing status. He insisted Mengelt, a Yankee with long hair and a cocky attitude, drew more jeers. "It just wasn't that big a deal," Harris said in a story written for a January 1972 Auburn game program. "To me and the other players and the coaches, I was just another basketball player."

Perhaps. But early returns indicated Harris was something special, on the court if not off it. In those days of freshman ineligibility for the varsity, Harris led the freshman squad in 10 of 11 major statistical categories, finishing second only in free throw percentage. He averaged 20.8 points and 9.7 rebounds and scored in double figures in all 19 games. "I think Henry really felt loved, and I really loved coaching him," Chapman said. "He went to Kentucky and got 40 points. *Forty.*" Actually, he scored 43. "Henry had a great freshman year, was a joy to coach. It's obvious that I didn't impede his game any."

But a mishap in the UK game did impede Harris. Lynn said the guard "fell over someone's back after making a layup." Harris landed on both knees, displacing the kneecaps. "He played in pain after his freshmen year," Lynn said. "Sometimes he could hardly walk after a game." Pain notwithstanding, the heralded newcomer impressed Auburn's varsity players, who practiced with the freshmen. "Henry played very, very hard," Mengelt said. "I think that's one thing that, more than anything, I respected about him. If guys beat on him, which we probably did (we all beat the freshmen), he would come back harder and battle you. He wouldn't go into a shell. He was a very, very tough competitor."

Chapman, the first player in Auburn history to start every game of his career, said Harris's toughness was an acquired skill. The way he told it, Harris at first played into the stereotyping that haunted African Americans for years. "When he first got here, he'd drive in the lane and they'd knock him down," Chapman recalled. "He'd lay down. Finally, I got him in my office one day and I said, 'Look, Henry. Let me tell you something now. You've got to quit that shit. You keep falling every time they touch you, and they're all going to start referring to you as the N-word. If you're hurt bad and you're down, you stay down, and I'll be the first one there—but otherwise, get your ass up and play.' From that day forward, he never laid down, and they would hit him, buddy. He would pop up. That was good advice to him."

Harris was shifted to forward as a sophomore in 1969–70, joining a varsity squad that returned starting guards Mengelt and Carl Shetler. "They didn't let Henry play his position," said Isaac, his Greene County teammate. "They held him back."

Mengelt, a junior, was the star of the team and a local hero who found Auburn "a great and special place." The top three-year scorer in Auburn history, he was the first Tiger to have his jersey number retired. He racked up a school-record 60 points in a home win over Alabama, on 23 of 44 shots. He averaged 26.8 points in those days prior to the three-pointer, easily good enough to lead the 1970 Tigers. (Amazingly, Mengelt was thoroughly eclipsed as a scorer by LSU's Pete Maravich, a phenomenon who burned the league for 44.5 points per game, still best in NCAA history.)

The 1969–70 season was a good one for Auburn. The Tigers were 15–11 overall and third in the SEC with an 11–7 record, which included a sweep of Alabama and wins at Louisiana State and Tennessee. Beard-Eaves-Memorial Coliseum, a $6 million facility that had opened in January 1969, virtually sold out when Maravich came to town on February 16, 1970; 12,468 fans packed the arena, the largest crowd in the first six years of its existence. (Maravich scored 46 points in a Tigers victory.) Mengelt made first team All-SEC. Harris, a fan favorite at Auburn, was named to the 1970 All-SEC sophomore team; he ranked second among the Tigers in rebounds (7.5) and third in scoring (12.5).

But 1969–70 also was Lynn's last winning season and the start of a slide in attendance arrested only by a coaching change. Lynn was a protégé of controlled Joel Eaves, his predecessor and, until Cliff Ellis in 1999, the only Auburn coach to win an SEC title (in 1960 with a group dubbed "Snow White and the Seven Dwarfs," after Eaves and a squad lacking anyone taller than 6-foot-4). Lynn's teams employed a controlled style that reflected his training, which included two seasons playing for Eaves and years as his assistant. "Coach Eaves would turn over in his grave if he saw how the game is today," Hub Waldrop said. "He was very basic. No fancy passes or shooting." Lynn employed Eaves's shuffle offense, designed to minimize mistakes. The team walked the ball up the court and depended on big guys who could handle the ball.

Lynn's style ill-suited Harris, who was accustomed to the more open, up-tempo style typical of African-American basketball. "Schools weren't integrated, and they just didn't see that type of ball," said Al Young, Harris's Greene County coach. "He was a run-and-gun player." That did not mean Harris was undisciplined or unskilled. Waldrop attested that he had not seen Harris's "level of skill as far as ball-handling ability, passing the ball, and those type of things." Auburn aficionado Mark Murphy concurred: "He just sort of had a flair and charisma out there. He was a solid outside shooter—sort of solid everything—but just a real smart all-around player."

Back in Greene County, Harris's legion of fans puzzled over his move to forward, the position at which he started and appeared in every game as an Auburn sophomore. Puzzlement soon turned to alarm. "There was one game on TV that we were sitting here watching," Young recalled. "They would not pass him the ball! They wouldn't pass it. Everybody called and said, 'What in the world is going on up there?'" Mengelt, later an NBA player, said nothing unusual was going on. "If we weren't passing him the ball, it wasn't because he was Black. It was maybe because nobody was passing the ball to anybody. . . . I would say that we didn't have anybody good enough to freeze a guy out."

Raymond visited Harris that year. They took in a concert by the Commodores, and Harris "seemed pretty happy," his brother said. They soon lost touch, to Raymond's regret. "He had no support system," offered Raymond. "He was under a lot of pressure. We didn't know it, though. We were just kids."

The following season Auburn slid to 11–15 overall, 8–10 in the SEC. Mengelt got a new backcourt mate, leaving Harris to perform as an undersized forward once again. Harris significantly improved his accuracy from the floor (.498) and foul line (.813), and he was third on the team in rebounding (6.4) and scoring (11.6). Meanwhile Mengelt set the school scoring record with a 28.4-point average. According to Auburn's media guide, Harris emerged as "probably the best defensive player in the SEC" that season. He usually guarded the opposition's toughest player, regardless of any size differential.

The basketball program accorded Harris several honors prior to his senior season. He was elected captain of the 1971–72 squad, and he and Lynn were featured on the cover of the media guide. With the coliseum in the background, the two sit almost touching, with Harris in Auburn warm-up garb and Lynn in a blue suit and tie, blue socks, a pink patterned shirt, and black-and-white saddle shoes. Harris has a small smile and a large Afro, and he is leaning away from his coach, whose legs are crossed and hands clasped. They do not look particularly comfortable.

Lynn had generous words for the senior—remarkable considering the physical limitations that plagued Harris for years. "He's like a cat," the coach said. "He can stay with anybody. Henry's valuable to our team offensively, defensively and as a leader. He is a good rebounder too." A profile in a 1972 game program lauded Harris for his speed, quickness, and "maneuverability," and the media guide described him as an "excellent one-on-one player who has pro type moves."

With Mengelt gone, Harris returned to guard. Anticipating the change, the media guide suddenly praised Harris as an "outstanding play-maker who sets up the offense and makes it go" and as the squad's "best ball handler." But the return to his natural position came too late. Harris underwent knee surgery during the summer between his junior and senior years and never fully recovered. "He always complained about it," Walker, the 1971 team captain, said of the knee. "He probably expected to be a little better than what he was. He was probably an above-average SEC player."

Teams did not officially keep track of steals, assists, and turnovers in those days, so there is no way to gauge objectively Harris's defensive and ball-handling contributions. His scoring and rebounding averages both dipped slightly in his senior season, as did his shooting accuracy. The team he led finished 10–16, with losses in 11 of its final 14 games.

Harris, a business major, did not graduate. He was the 110th player chosen in the 1972 NBA draft, by the Houston Rockets in the eighth round, hardly a vote of confidence. He failed to make the team.

Harris never pursued a career in vocational rehabilitation, as he once envisioned. He moved to his brother's house in Harrisonburg, Pennsylvania, in 1973 and tried his hand at Eastern League basketball while working as a hall monitor and an aide in the school system where Raymond taught industrial arts. Harris stayed in town some four months, then moved to Milwaukee to resuscitate his academic and athletic careers at Davalos's side. "I called him, and I said, 'Henry, you didn't get your degree,'" Davalos said. "'I'd like for you to be one of my assistant coaches. I'll put you on scholarship and give you some kind of stipend, and I want you to finish your degree.' He jumped at it, and he came to Milwaukee."

By April 1974 Harris was dead.

"I remember when it happened, but I don't remember the details," Hub Waldrop said. "I'm thinking that, based on where he'd come from and what he probably had to deal with, he'd reached a point where he just couldn't handle it. I'm thinking that, somewhere along the line, we might have failed him. I don't know what might have happened in his life after he left Auburn. But anytime a young man [commits suicide], you say, 'Somewhere, someone failed him,' and you replay your role in that. Somewhere there was a need, and we missed it."

CHAPTER 5

THE LONELIEST NUMBER

Charles Scott, University of North Carolina, 1966–70

One ever feels his two-ness,—an American, a Negro; two souls, two thoughts, two unreconciled strivings; two warring ideals in one dark body, whose dogged strength alone keeps it from being torn asunder. The history of the American Negro is the history of this strife,—this longing to attain self-conscious manhood, to merge his double self into a better and truer self.

W. E. B. Du Bois, *The Souls of Black Folk*

He was "Great Scott" with an exclamation point or simply "Charlie" to University of North Carolina fans. An arresting presence with a style previously unknown at a major Southern school, Charles Scott was twice voted an All-American and three times chosen all-conference. He made the U.S. Olympic squad as a sophomore in 1968 and was the ACC's scoring leader and Athlete of the Year in 1969–70, a season in which he also was an Academic All-American. "Contrary to a popular notion on the UNC campus, Scott isn't God," Charles Elkins wrote in 1970 in the Winston-Salem Journal. "But he may well be the best all-around, the most exciting player who has ever been in the ACC."

Thus Scott proved the rule—if there was such a rule—that a pioneering Black player would gain acceptance only if he was so good that no critic could reasonably dispute he deserved a scholarship. "I didn't understand the significance of the deal," Scott said, "but now that I'm older, I do. When you deal with booster clubs and alumni and you're giving that first scholarship to someone Black, and alumni think there's a white player who could have gotten that scholarship, then there's a lot of pressure."

Scott was the only one of the ACC's groundbreaking African-American players who made the all-conference team or developed a reputation that extended beyond the region. Black youngsters across the South, from David Thompson in the western North Carolina piedmont to Collis Temple in the

Louisiana bayous, watched the Tar Heels on television and saw someone to emulate. "Damn, Charlie Scott could play!" said Temple, an all-SEC big man at LSU. "He was the first 6-5, 6-6 guard. I loved Charlie Scott. I wanted to be like Charlie Scott."

The impression Scott made during his collegiate career, bolstered by a decade in professional basketball, was so strong he often is erroneously identified as the first to cross the color line in the ACC. The misconception is due in part to sloppy reporting in subsequent years, and in part to the striking lack of recognition some other conference schools have accorded their first Black varsity players.

Yet it is also true that Scott prospered on the national stage, a circumstance unique among Southern basketball's racial pioneers. Among that group of 22 players in the ACC and SEC, Scott alone appeared in more than one NCAA Tournament game. More than any other Black college ballplayer in the late 1960s, he frequented the region's television screens, appearing in 10 of 27 ACC regular-season games televised during his three-year varsity career. Thus one can argue that Scott, highly visible and highly skilled, bore the brunt of blazing a trail, even if other African Americans played at their respective schools prior to Scott's arrival at Chapel Hill.

"Charlie was the first, like the kid over there at Vanderbilt—Perry Wallace," insisted Billy Packer. The longtime college basketball television commentator was an assistant coach at Wake Forest University during the 1960s and recruited the school's first Black players. "Charlie was really the first guy that was impactful, an All-American. He was the best player on the team. There were a lot of other guys that came in early, even at Maryland, that were not athletically top guys.

"I think it's unfair to list these other guys as the first players because they weren't recruited as that. The two kids at Maryland were good, but Scott was a breakthrough player. Wallace was a breakthrough player at Vanderbilt. Charlie Scott was a breakthrough player in the ACC because he was without question a bona fide, big-time basketball player." Tellingly, in 1995 the National Association of Basketball Coaches included Scott and Wallace on its silver anniversary squad, along with Louisiana State's Pete Maravich, Niagara's Calvin Murphy, and Columbia's Jim McMillian.

Clearly, Scott's impact was substantial and enduring, regardless of how he is categorized. And while he may marvel at, and relish, the effect he had on others, Scott insisted it was largely unintentional.

"I was very naive to not notice the significance [of being the first Black player at UNC], and probably lucky that I did not really think about what it meant to so many people," said Scott, a man with a soft voice, a long face, and a small scar above the corner of his left eye. "I thought of it as going to the University of North Carolina. I didn't think of it as far as most blacks in Mississippi or Alabama or Georgia—that other states had so much invested in it, because it was a Black person being shown playing basketball where they had never seen a Black playing before. Up to this day, it is still kind of overwhelming to have people come up to me—especially Black people, but also whites—and talk about the significance that me playing had on their lives."

Scott's prominence was enhanced by another factor over which he had modest control: He arrived as the North Carolina program hit what proved to be a historic stride under Dean Smith, a young head coach who had been elevated from assistant when Frank McGuire left in 1961. (McGuire was back in the league by 1964–65 as head coach at the University of South Carolina.)

Dick Grubar was recruited a year ahead of Scott. Rival coaches sent clippings to his Schenectady, New York home, recounting the two times Smith was hanged in effigy on UNC's campus in January 1965. Grubar went to Chapel Hill anyway, in part because Smith, a "very honest, down-to-earth-type guy," offered no illegal inducements, in contrast to several other prominent suitors. "My dad might have said, 'How can you help my son?'" Grubar remembered. "And Dean said, 'Room, board, tuition, and $15 a month [in NCAA laundry money].' There it was."

While Scott played on a freshman squad officially nicknamed the "Tar Babies," Smith directed the 1966–67 varsity to a first-place ACC finish, an ACC tournament title, and a berth in the Final Four. The squad was led by upperclassmen Bob Lewis and Larry Miller, both first team all-conference players. Lewis graduated, Scott joined the varsity, Miller became a consensus All-American, and the winning continued. The Tar Heels finished first during the ACC regular season, won the ACC tournament, and advanced to the Final Four in 1968 and 1969. Duke from 1999 to 2001 is the only ACC team that ever duplicated so thorough a run of excellence. "We started the Carolina tradition," Scott says.

The precision, intelligence, preparation, and selflessness displayed by those late-1960s squads became utterly characteristic of Smith's program, which between the 1961–62 and 1996–97 seasons amassed 879 victories, at the time the second-highest career total among Division I men's basketball coaches. (Mike Krzyzewski now holds the NCAA record with 1,202 victories at Army and Duke.) Critics alleged that Smith's control was too great, reflected in only two NCAA titles despite the wealth of talent he brought to Chapel Hill.

It was only because Scott broke spectacularly free of Smith's meticulous mold that UNC won the 1969 ACC tournament, and with it the league's automatic bid to the NCAA tournament. Scott's 40 points in the conference tournament final, all but a dozen contributed after the Heels fell behind 43–34 at halftime, remain the highest scoring total in an ACC championship game and one of the great clutch performances in the tradition-rich conference.

A year prior to Scott's outburst against Duke at the Charlotte Coliseum, Smith, who believed a gaudy scoring leader was a sign of faulty teamwork, had insisted, "We could turn Charles loose and he'd score 40 points a night." A year later a Raleigh *News and Observer* headline declared "Scott Is Toughest in Tight Situations." Scott perpetually elicited paroxysms of praise, with one writer calling him a "sensitive magician"; another saying he exuded "electric reverberations" on the court; and a third declaring he had "more moves than North American Van Lines and more shots than a man drink [sic] somebody else's whiskey." "If Charlie Scott can't completely bedazzle, befuddle and bamboozle an opponent then he can't be bedazzled," exclaimed Bill Currie, then the radio voice of the Tar Heels, as quoted in the *North Carolina Anvil*.

"He was ahead of his time," Packer said of Scott. "He could play any position. He could just play basketball."

The 6-foot-6, 175-pound Scott is a direct link in a transcendent chain of midsize players that began with his boyhood hero, Elgin Baylor, "the first true master of air, space and time," according to Lyle Spencer, as quoted in *The Official NBA Encyclopedia*. Scott, in turn, proved a role model for an aerial marvel from Shelby, North Carolina, named David Thompson, who revolutionized the game as a two-time national Player of the Year at N.C. State in the mid-1970s. Thompson then inspired a youngster from Wilmington, North Carolina: Michael Jordan, whose superlative basketball career took flight after he hit the winning shot to earn Smith his first NCAA championship in 1982.

Scott's own breakout game occurred in the ACC tournament final on March 8, 1969, as he almost single-handedly rallied North Carolina to victory from a second-half deficit that reached 11 points with less than 17 minutes to go. Compounding the difficulties for the Tar Heels that Saturday night at the Charlotte Coliseum, Grubar went down for the season with a knee injury and starting big man Bill Chamberlain, the school's second African-American basketball player, was saddled with fouls.

That's when Scott, and the hyperbole that accompanied his exploits, ascended to new heights. "The man who peeled off the shroud was Charlie Scott," Mel Derrick wrote in the *Charlotte Observer* after North Carolina defeated Duke, 85–74. "That's 's' as in sensational, 'c' as in confident, 'o' as in oh-h-h, and 'tt' as in terrific twice."

Scott scored 28 points in the second half on 12-of-13 shooting. Overall, he missed but 6 of 23 shots in the game. His achievement was further burnished by the fact that the victim was Duke, emphatically eclipsed in Vic Bubas's last year as head coach, and that the circumstances were winner-take-all, given that only league champions could advance to the NCAA tournament in those days.

"From the backboards of one end of the court to the other he was a leaping, whirling, twisting ball of fire," Jim Morris wrote in the *Durham Sun*. "And, somehow, whether it was by a steal, an intercepted pass, or a fine rebound or play by a mate, Scott seemed to be constantly flying toward the basketball with the ball."

But the flight was painfully solo away from the court, even in his moments of greatest triumph. Scott's recollections of his years at North Carolina were marred by having felt lost amidst the multitude, isolated even as part of a team, untethered although playing for a caring coach whose religious convictions and social consciousness made him a stalwart supporter.

"You want to know what I did after I scored the 40 points?" Scott said of the 1969 conference tournament. "I was by myself. Who am I going to go out with? I was by myself after I did that. We had great fun in the locker room. After that we walked out of the locker room; everybody went one way, and I went another way. I had to celebrate it by myself. I had no one to celebrate it with, no one to tell me, 'Oh, that was great!' That's why sometimes the things that you do do not seem to be as significant to you as they are to other people. I didn't get to feel part of all of that."

Why that was the case is open to debate. Certainly Scott's exclusion was racially tinged. Especially in those early days of integration, race was a constant if unquantifiable factor that affected his interactions with individuals and institutions. Certainly Scott encountered unique pressures and demands, with scant precedent to guide him or those around him. "No matter what you did on the basketball court," he said, "after the game culturally you were still isolated."

Fans at home were supportive, but there was plenty of verbal abuse on the road, particularly at Clemson and South Carolina, where assistant coach Bill Guthridge chased one fan who followed Scott toward the locker room and called him a "big, black baboon." That was par for the course at Columbia, much to Grubar's amazement and disgust. "I'll tell you what," said Grubar, a commercial real estate broker in Greensboro, North Carolina following college. "The man put up with more than I think anybody could ever put up with. Just in terms of the racial taunts, the spit, the water, the N-word. It was horrible. It was *horrible*."

Scott appreciated his teammates' compassion in such circumstances. Upon reflection, however, he considered their concern inherently limited because society was built for and by whites. He believes that his playing companions had rarely, if ever, experienced similar abuse and were concerned only in an immediate, rather than a global, sense. "I never thought about it then, but half of my teammates probably called Blacks 'baboons' in their life at one time when they were growing up," Scott said. "I do believe compassion comes for the individual, not for the race. I think they felt compassion for me and not for the circumstances involved."

To some extent Scott's isolation was of his own making. By the summer of 1968, halfway through his college career, he was a married student living in Durham, not Chapel Hill. ("Do you ask a married guy to go with you to a party?" Grubar asked rhetorically.) And like Duke's C. B. Claiborne, Scott found refuge at North Carolina Central, the predominantly black university in Durham. The two ACC players spent considerable time during the off-season engaged in pickup basketball games at Central or at Durham's historically Black Hillside High, which soon produced John Lucas, the Maryland basketball and tennis star.

A striking number of pioneering Black basketball players were first married in college, a practice more prevalent in general during the 1960s than it is today. "It was a direct result of being alone so long, of really feeling alone," Scott said of his marriage. "My father died when I was young, and [before then] my mother and father had separated. I had no close family ties. I felt very lonely, and I thought marriage was the answer. It wasn't.

"The loneliness of individuality catches up with you. I don't know who said it: 'One is a lonely number.' One is a *very* lonely number. The need for companionship is very great for an individual that's going through that. I think having female companionship probably has more to do with the compassion [a woman can offer]—that's really what the athlete is looking for. You don't want to seem like a wimp to your male friends, but with your wife, you can sometimes let out your vulnerabilities. That might have a lot to do with why we all got married at a young time. To me, quite honestly—no offense to the young lady—it was a wrong reason for getting married. I was naive about what marriage meant. The only thing I was thinking about was that I'd never be lonely again."

Nor was Scott particularly close with other African-American students, including those he had known growing up in New York. "Scotty wasn't the most beloved brother because he talked, he ran his mouth so much," said Charlie Davis, a fellow Harlem product who came south to Wake Forest a year behind Scott. "If he wasn't on our front burner, then you know he wasn't on white folks' front burner."

It became evident that Scott was not on the all-white media's front burner when the choice for basketball's ACC Player of the Year was announced within days of his stellar performance in the 1969 ACC tournament. Scott, the top scorer (22.3 points per game) and most charismatic player on the league's best team, finished second in the balloting with 39 votes to 56 for South Carolina's John Roche, the first sophomore ever selected for the honor. "Charlie Scott got shafted," said Gilbert McGregor, a contemporary at Wake Forest.

To be fair, the Gamecocks finished one game behind the powerful Tar Heels after being picked for the ACC's second division. Overachievers have a persuasive charm. Roche was USC's floor leader and top scorer (23.6 points per game) in 1969 as Frank McGuire established a program that went undefeated in league play in 1970 and won its only conference championship in 1971.

"Basically the whole offense was thrust around the way Roche played," Billy Packer recalled. "So there was a difference between what he did to carry his team that year and what Charlie did at North Carolina. And I think it would be one of those things where you're saying, philosophically, where would South Carolina be without Roche? Where would North Carolina be without Scott? Both of whom were obviously very significant players. And I think that's where that vote would have come from.

"Is there somebody that could have been racist? There could have been. But as a basketball person, I definitely could have made a strong case for John Roche and what he did for his team."

Scott and Smith saw matters differently, particularly after five voters left Scott entirely off their 10-man all-conference ballots. "This is a frustrating thing when you go to the Olympics and represent your state, your country, your conference," Scott told the *Washington Post*. "They put a guy ahead of me because he's white."

Smith was convinced his player was mistreated. "That was extremely disappointing. There was no way he shouldn't have been Player of the Year. Charlie was really upset, and he had every right to be." Hurt and angry, Scott considered sitting out North Carolina's NCAA games. Instead, he participated with a vengeance, scoring 32 points to sink Davidson in the East Region final and advance the Tar Heels to the Final Four.

Charles "Lefty" Driesell, a fiery man and a voracious recruiter, once thought he had convinced Scott to attend Davidson, the Charlotte-area private school where Driesell was head coach. "I'd rather die than lose to Carolina again," Driesell declared before Scott beat the Wildcats on a jumper with two seconds remaining. The next day Driesell, eventually a Hall of Famer, announced that he had taken the job as head coach at the University of Maryland.

UNC was routed by Purdue in the 1969 NCAA semifinals, but the Tar Heels recovered to defeat Drake in the now-defunct consolation game, with Scott scoring 36 points. That same day, the *New York Times* ran a story on Scott entitled "Negro Basketball Star a Hero to Many North Carolina Whites."

The article asserted that Scott had "climbed one of the few ladders available to Negroes in the South" and was "accorded a public esteem traditionally reserved for Robert E. Lee, Jefferson Davis, George C. Wallace and other sons of the South." Academicians were laudatory, including an unidentified UNC faculty member who said, "I think that the more Charlie Scotts we have, the easier it will be for the South to change its mind about Negroes." Also quoted was a white public school superintendent in Charlotte who suggested that, to speed desegregation, all schools should "get themselves a colored big-shot star" to smooth the way.

The *Times* made no mention of the MVP voting that had rankled Scott and Smith. And the story quoted a fickle student improbably claiming that the Purdue loss "just proves 'niggers' choke in the clutch." Undeterred, journalist James T. Wooten noted, "If the faculty members are correct, Mr. Scott and Mr. Maloy [Mike, of Davidson] may be providing the same impetus for Southern intercollegiate athletics that Jackie Robinson, the first Negro in the major leagues, gave to organized baseball."

O

Baseball, in fact, had been Scott's first love growing up on 131st Street and Eighth Avenue in Harlem, a historically Black section of Manhattan. By the 1960s nearly half of the country's African-American population lived in the North, where, as Scott puts it, Black citizens faced "segregation by diplomacy. You didn't know it, but you were still segregated. Nothing had really changed; it's just that it wasn't talked about in the North. It was just a matter of where you lived."

Urban African Americans often worked either as domestics or as unskilled industrial laborers. "When you grow up in Harlem, I don't think you have professions at the top of your mind," Scott said. An NAACP investigation in 1960 reported that many craft unions, from plumbers to iron and steel workers, routinely excluded Black workers from apprenticeship training programs. "The Northern Negro was made painfully and constantly aware that he lived in a society dedicated to the doctrine of white supremacy and Negro inferiority," C. Vann Woodward wrote in 1966 in *The Strange Career of Jim Crow.*

Scott was the youngest of four children and the only boy in a low-income family that shattered when his mother left and remarried. He lived in the St. Nicholas project with his father, who died of cirrhosis of the liver when Scott was 14. "From the time I was 11, I basically took care of myself," Scott said. He picked up basketball on the streets, frequently playing 10 hours per day, and took cues from the NBA's Baylor because "he was artistic, he was creative, he was different." Later, writers fondly spiced stories on Scott with a mention of his having two front teeth knocked out during a playground game.

It wasn't only Scott's teeth that were disappearing. Friends such as Jimmy Walker, a future star at Providence College, were leaving the city for prep schools in the South. When Laurinburg Institute in North Carolina offered Scott a scholarship as part of its aggressive outreach to Black athletes, he took it. Accustomed to being on his own, he didn't worry about homesickness. His father died the first year Scott was at Laurinburg, completing his isolation.

"At that particular time, coming from New York, North Carolina wasn't that bad," he said. "There were things about North Carolina—the state itself—that I liked. I liked the idea of serenity, openness." Strangely, the fact that the area was just emerging from the throes of overt, institutionalized racism didn't enter strongly into Scott's thinking. "I knew about it. I knew it existed. It's like anything—when you're young, you don't think it's going to happen to you."

On one occasion Scott and two African-American friends were picked up by the sheriff while walking in Laurinburg, a town about 100 miles southeast of Charlotte, near the South Carolina border. The boys were driven several miles to a house where a white woman had been raped. They were brought before her at gunpoint, but the woman said none of them was her assailant, and they were permitted to leave.

"It's like culture shock," Scott said of a Black man going from an insular, ethnic urban setting to face the prejudice and segregation of rural North Carolina. "Here it was definitely right in front of you. You could not go in this movie here; you could not go in there. People were going to call you nigger here." Charlie Davis, who attended Wake Forest in Winston-Salem, North Carolina, recalls that he "cried for a month" upon arriving at Laurinburg from Manhattan. "I called my mother a number of times saying, 'I'll come home. I'll get a job. Just get me out of here.' You're down in a place where you see your first cross burning a mile or so down the road. People drive by firing shots into your campus. You're isolated. It was different."

Laurinburg Institute, named after the town and called by some "the black Andover of the South," was founded at the turn of the 20th century and run by African Americans for African Americans at a time when the area offered scant public education for Black children. The Institute's first prominent graduate to make it in sports was Sam Jones, class of 1952. He went on to stardom at N.C. Central and later with the NBA's Boston Celtics. He was followed by, among others, Walker, Davis, Mike Evans (Kansas State), and pro baseball player Wes Covington.

Frank McDuffie, president, basketball coach, and band director at Laurinburg, said that when Scott arrived, he "hadn't had a real meal in two months" and required a few attitude adjustments. "To be honest, he was a problem," McDuffie told Larry Keech of the *Greensboro Daily News.* "All he wanted to do was play basketball. He had no interest in his studies or his surroundings. He was a loner, a typical New York kid who didn't seem to like what he had heard about the South. He hated white people, for instance." Somewhat contradicting his assertion that he did not think much about race before heading to Laurinburg, Scott said, "I was probably under the impression that most whites hate Blacks, especially Southern whites."

By the end of his three years at Laurinburg, Scott was class valedictorian and had scored nearly 1,200 points (out of a possible 1,600) on the Scholastic Aptitude Test. He also was "the most complete player I've ever seen," McDuffie said. "He was determined to excel in everything he did. He even thought he could sing a little."

There were no sophisticated scouting services in those days, yet word of Scott's prowess spread quickly, drawing large crowds to Laurinburg's games and numerous recruiting inquiries from colleges around the country. Scott quickly settled on Davidson College, an all-male school located just north of Charlotte that Driesell, a Duke graduate, was building into a national basketball power.

The region's Black players were largely an untapped resource, and Davidson went after many of them. Terry Holland, a Davidson grad and Driesell assistant at the time, says this was more happenstance than strategy. "We were obviously aware of the difficulties of recruiting African Americans. In other words, they would need to fit in when they got to your campus. There might be some reaction from alumni, things like that. But coaches tend to be idealistic. If we're recruiting a great player who has some flaws, we always think we can fix those flaws. And the same thing with these other issues that were out there. We were vaguely aware of them, but we thought, 'We'll deal with them later, if it ever becomes necessary.'"

Holland vividly recalled his introduction to the Laurinburg star, who attended a Driesell summer basketball camp. "Charlie Scott is the first kid I remember going after hard," said Holland, head coach at the University of Virginia from 1975 to 1990 and later athletics director at East Carolina University. "But, again, I don't remember having any discussions about what [his enrollment at Davidson] would mean or anything. I thought, 'This guy is really good. God, I can't believe how fast he is.' I remember the first time I saw him play. I said, 'The court's too small for this guy. The court needs to be bigger so he can take advantage of his speed. He's going to run off the court.'"

Soon Scott was Davidson's regular (and legal) weekend guest at a downtown motel in Charlotte across from a movie theater at which the *The Sound of Music* had an extended run. "I think he saw *The Sound of Music* like 120 times," Holland said. "Something crazy. He loved that movie." Scott signed a nonbinding letter of intent to attend Davidson and proceeded to recruit other Black players, including Perry Wallace. "I met him there," Wallace said later. "I remember, he was the one who showed me around. We went to *The Sound of Music*."

But Scott did not have eyes only for Davidson. He often visited other schools in company with Laurinburg teammates, assuring Davidson's coaches of his fidelity all the while. Holland recalled Scott insisting, "I just want to be able to visit these other schools because it is the only way the other guys on the team will get pursued." The Davidson staff "sort of went along with it," Holland said, because "these trips were important to the economy of Laurinburg Institute."

Meanwhile, another rising program got wind of Scott, whom McDuffie said had cooled on Davidson. There had been a sour incident at the Coffee Cup, a greasy spoon in the town of Davidson, during which members of the McDuffie family were told to sit in the kitchen, rather than in a booth with Driesell and Holland. "The waitress came back and said, 'We don't serve Blacks on that side of the restaurant,'" Scott said, recalling that he was there as well. Holland said that Driesell and the waitress "got into a huge argument" and that McDuffie and his wife, Sammie, "didn't act like it was that big a deal at the time."

But the damage was done. Besides, Scott believed that Frank McDuffie, a Tar Heel fan, perceived a greater opportunity for Laurinburg in sending its star player to the University of North Carolina, the state's flagship public institution of higher education. "I think in the back of his mind, which I think was really smart, he wanted his player to be the first one to go," Scott said of McDuffie. "He understood the significance of going to the big state university. And I think he pushed me in that direction."

North Carolina assistant coaches John Lotz and Larry Brown vetted Scott's game and agreed that they preferred him to Rick Mount, another coveted recruit. (Mount later helped Purdue sink UNC in the 1969 Final Four.) Smith insisted on seeing a player in action before offering him a scholarship, so he drove to Laurinburg to see Scott play and to visit the McDuffies. To augment his recruiting pitch, the head coach brought with him two professors, including UNC law professor Dan Pollitt, and a Black medical student who attended Smith's church.

Pollitt was an informal advisor to President Lyndon Johnson (as mentioned in a copy of *Newsweek* that Smith brandished) and was an active legal and policy advisor for the UNC chapter of the NAACP. As for the med student, Smith brought him along not simply because of his race. "We'd heard that Charlie Scott wanted to be a doctor," Pollitt said. He recalled that when Scott visited the Chapel Hill campus, an apocryphal tale circulated that "they let him perform an appendectomy at the hospital. That was the story. Everybody went overboard—'He wants to be a doctor? Well, here, try it to see if you like it.'"

Duke was among the other schools Scott visited. He did not feel comfortable. "I felt like, if a pin dropped at one end of Duke's campus, you could hear it at the other end of Duke's campus," he said. "If I was going to be the first African-American player, I didn't want to be under so much scrutiny." Claiborne, Duke's first Black player, was assigned to be Scott's host. "He hung out with me for the whole weekend when he was there," Claiborne said. "We talked very honestly about schools and what it was like to go here. In the end I said, 'It sounds like you'd be better off going to Carolina.' He'd already made up his mind, but he wanted to see Duke."

Ultimately, Scott found Chapel Hill, which fancies itself the "Southern Part of Heaven," more cosmopolitan than Davidson. He visited on a concert weekend when the Temptations and Smokey Robinson and the Miracles played. He escaped the prepackaged aspect of his visit and comfortably strolled the sylvan grounds of the first state university chartered in the United States. "One afternoon he was going to take a nap, and we couldn't find him," Smith recalled. "He took a walk through campus. That shows how smart he was. He'd stop and ask questions, and the students were great to him."

Most schools assigned a senior to accompany a recruit. Smith saw to it that the escort was Grubar, a future teammate and "some salesman" for the school and program "because he loved it so much." Scott and Grubar, who still attends North Carolina basketball games, launched an enduring friendship that day. Grubar took him to fraternities and to a party. "We stayed out late, until 12:00 or 2:00 in the morning," Grubar said. "Really enjoyed each other, really enjoyed the camaraderie. And Coach Smith told us what a good player he was."

The issue of race—of Scott becoming the first African-American player on a campus of some 15,000 students, most of them white males—was not mentioned by either athlete.

McDuffie told a reporter his star player ultimately picked the "gentlemen" of the North Carolina coaching staff over "a violent, demanding coach" in Driesell. Asked upon his retirement in 2003 to cite the greatest recruiting disappointment of his career, Driesell immediately harkened to 1966 and to the player who stood, literally and figuratively, between him and a Final Four: "Charlie Scott signed with me, really, then he changed his mind."

"You know, sometimes you're just lucky," Scott said, looking back on his decision. "I think I made a great, lucky choice." A key reason was that no Southern coach more consciously sought an African-American player than

Dean Smith, whose father, Alfred, had been the first coach to integrate high school sports in Kansas. "For me, integrating basketball was an obvious thing to do," Smith said in his autobiography, *A Coach's Life.* "I did not see it as a political issue but primarily as an ethical one. It was the right and fair move to make."

The University of North Carolina and the town of Chapel Hill are known for progressive thinking, with considerable justification. "As a state university, it is uniquely successful, and almost every phase of enlightenment and progress in the state, and to some extent in the South, can trace its birth to this small town," wrote John Ehle in 1965 in *The Free Men.* Both town and school benefited especially from the presence and leadership of Frank Porter Graham, the university president known as one of the South's leading liberals during his tenure from 1930 through 1949. Under his leadership the North Carolina football team became the first in the South to play on the road against an integrated squad; Graham also ended the medical school's practice of automatically excluding Jews from its student body.

During the 1960s, when students and faculty joined Chapel Hill residents in protesting continued segregation of business facilities, one leading state Democrat declared, "The liberals are a red, festering sore on the body of a great university." Television commentator Jesse Helms, later the state's Republican U.S. senator, suggested putting a fence around Chapel Hill and designating it the state zoo. The setting was less hospitable for African Americans than one might expect, however. Chapel Hill was still part of the South, with its strictly segregated facilities and ingrained racial attitudes. "Negroes and whites were worlds apart here, just like everywhere else in Dixie," said Robert Seymour in *"Whites Only": A Pastor's Retrospective on Signs of the New South.*

Not many years before, the limits of tolerance in Chapel Hill had been starkly revealed when Black activist Bayard Rustin came to town. On their 1947 "Journey of Reconciliation," Rustin and others traveled the upper South by bus, testing adherence to a U.S. Supreme Court ban on segregation in interstate transportation. When Black passengers sat in the section reserved for whites as the bus prepared to leave Chapel Hill—reputedly "an enlightened oasis in the middle of the segregated South," according to Rustin biographer John D'Emilio—they and their associates were arrested. A bystander accosted one white participant for "coming down here to stir up the niggers."

Charlie Jones, a local minister, bailed the group out of jail. Angry white cabdrivers followed them and surrounded Jones's house, while callers threatened to lynch the Jones family and burn down their home. Sympathetic students and, finally, police, intervened, and Jones and the demonstrators left town. Rustin and a colleague later served 30 days on a road gang for violating the state's race segregation law and Rustin wrote an exposé about chain gangs.

UNC's first Black students, admitted in the early 1950s, won admittance via lawsuit. The law and medical schools were integrated in 1951, the undergraduate student body in 1955. African Americans initially were prohibited from sitting with other students at football games, relegated instead to a section reserved for Black employees and located behind a goalpost. Seymour, Smith's minister and fellow conspirator in pushing integration, noted that while Graham likened UNC to a lighthouse, "A lighthouse sends its strong beam into the far distance, but it can be very dark at the lighthouse base."

Pollitt remembered that "everything was segregated" when he arrived at the university in the fall of 1957, a semester after McGuire led the Tar Heels to their first NCAA championship. Soon an effort was made to desegregate the new university hospital, a matter brought before the governing Board of Visitors. Incredulous, one woman asked Pollitt, "[Does this mean that] even when people are sick, you're going to put them in a bed next to a Black person?" The hospital remained segregated well into the 1960s, adopting indirect and genteel tactics similar to those used to keep North Carolina's schoolchildren racially divided. Mixing was allowed in hospital rooms, but only in the unlikely event that both parties approved the arrangement.

Typical of the unapologetic racism of some in Chapel Hill was an elderly white woman's reaction to word that two African Americans had drowned in University Lake, the town's primary water supply at the time. "I could taste them for months whenever I drank water," she told Ehle.

Chapel Hill's segregated school system was sued in 1959—the same year Reverend John R. Manley became the first African American elected to the school board—by a Black teenager who was prevented from attending an all-white school. Some white citizens met the prospect of integration with a petition drive decrying the impact on property values. But by the fall of 1961, as Smith took the reins of the UNC basketball program, the public school system became the first in North Carolina and among the first in the South to activate a plan for total, voluntary integration.

In June 1963 the town council narrowly rejected an ordinance opening public accommodations to African Americans. Later that year, and extending into 1964, the town was beset by marches and sit-ins aimed at opening desegregated restaurants, a movie theater that lacked even a balcony to which to relegate Blacks, and other facilities. One demonstration involved blocking a road to prevent access to a Tar Heel basketball game.

Seymour pushed integration as a matter of faith long before the battle took to the streets of Chapel Hill. Olin T. Binkley Memorial Baptist Church, where Seymour presided, took the radical step of adding a young African-American theological student to its staff. Then Seymour enlisted Smith, an assistant basketball coach and Binkley congregation member, to accompany the pair to The Pines, a local restaurant conspicuously resistant to integration. Smith's job interview had included a visit with McGuire to The Pines, where the team traditionally ate its pregame meals.

"I of course agreed to go and did not really consider it a big deal," Smith said in his autobiography of the meal with Seymour and the Black theology student. "Years afterwards, some reports have made it sound like I personally integrated every restaurant in Chapel Hill! The truth is, I was just an assistant coach and hardly the most influential person in town, an unlikely standard-bearer for integration. But Bob knew that I knew the management and that they valued the business of the basketball team. My presence would make the point."

The trio was welcomed and seated without incident. "That was it," Smith concluded in *A Coach's Life*. "How ridiculous it all seems now!"

Not so ridiculous, countered Paul Hewitt, the ACC's second African-American head basketball coach when hired by Georgia Tech in 2000. "Dean Smith was a pioneer regardless of what he wants to tell you," Hewitt said. "It took a special person to do that. He may not want to admit it, but I'm sure that wasn't the easiest thing to do. Here's an assistant who I'm sure had some aspirations of being the head coach there one day. It wasn't the most popular thing to do if you want to be the head coach."

When McGuire departed a step ahead of an NCAA probation, the only such punishment in North Carolina program history, Smith was elevated to head coach at age 30. The heightened stature brought a demand from Seymour for further spiritual action. "Your church work is to go out and get a Black ballplayer," Smith recalled being told. "Obviously, I believed in that."

Later, Smith admitted, had he truly been courageous, he would have visited Black high school gyms throughout the state to find a suitable player, spreading word of his search as he went. Instead, he shopped selectively, and in his first season as head coach he almost landed Greensboro's Lou Hudson. But Hudson, a top student in his school, failed to qualify academically at North Carolina. Handicapped by the state's inferior educational system for African Americans, and facing self-imposed ACC standards higher than what the NCAA required, Hudson went instead to the University of Minnesota. He became a star and enjoyed a 13-year NBA career. Throughout his coaching tenure Smith remained a critic of using the SAT, with its cultural biases, as a basis for deciding college admission and eligibility.

Smith signed unsung Willie Cooper in 1964, two years after missing out on Hudson. "Back then, you felt like it was time if you were a basketball person," Donnie Walsh, then a UNC assistant, said of bringing in Black players. Cooper, the second-best member of a small-town high school team, came to Chapel Hill on an academic scholarship with the expectation that he would ease into the picture after a year on the freshman squad. He was "well accepted by the team" and by fans, Smith said. But the plan unraveled when Cooper, a business major, quit basketball to concentrate on his academics at the start of varsity practice for the 1965–66 season. (His daughter, Tonya, played guard on the 1994 UNC women's squad, which won the NCAA championship, and his son, Brent, played on the school's junior varsity in 1992.)

That left the icebreaker's role to Scott, who arrived on campus a year later and quickly became a fan favorite. "It is to the credit . . . of Carolina fans that Charlie Scott is not generally regarded as 'that Negro' but more as Charlie Scott, 'star,'" Joel Bulkley wrote in the *North Carolina Anvil*. "Carolina fans can forgive his being a Negro and dressed in blue, so long as he delivers the goods. An unfair statement, perhaps, but how else to explain the University's belated fielding of racially mixed teams."

The statement was fairer than one might think, according to Pollitt. "After Charlie Scott had been here two or three years, Wake Forest recruited a black or two," he recalled of Charlie Davis and fellow New Yorker Norwood Todmann. "Some Tar Heel fan says, 'Hey, ref! Hey, ref! Them Wake Forest niggers are after our colored boys!' Charlie Scott was now our colored boy."

Such a reception surprised neither Scott nor Smith. Scott, for all his self-proclaimed naivete, was sufficiently savvy after years in the South to understand that acceptance was often tinged with consciousness of, and gnawing discomfort with, his race. He believed he was welcome wherever he went in

Chapel Hill because basketball was king and he served the team well. "If I hadn't been a success from the beginning, I don't think anything else would have mattered," Scott said. "I think the thing that integrated things in Chapel Hill was success."

Scott also shared a sense, felt by many Black players, that he was required to meet a higher standard, toe a narrower line, and carry a heavier burden as he made the transition to a white world from a parallel Black universe. "I couldn't be just an ordinary basketball player," Scott told the *Daily Tar Heel*, the student newspaper. "I had to be better. I also had to be better academically—I couldn't just be an ordinary student."

Fortunately for Scott, his coach was aware of his predicament. Few pioneering African-American players had a coach who recognized that the barrier-breaker's role was unique, and that the pressures a Black player faced on, and especially off, the court during the tumultuous 1960s differed profoundly from those experienced by white teammates. Smith recognized these truths and planned accordingly, avoiding situations that might produce awkwardness or conflict.

Most coaches bragged that they treated their first Black athlete just like every other player, a statement as revealing of shortsightedness as of egalitarianism. Scott pointed to Smith's decision to have the team run into the locker room prior to the playing of the national anthem—a move that became characteristic of the North Carolina program and spread to other schools—as exemplary of the coach's forethought. Those were days of Black power and symbolic protest, and removing the team from public sight minimized the chance that Scott or another player might sit through the anthem, a common gesture at the time. (Smith denied this was his motivation.)

"My perception is, just from talking to Charlie and other people up there, that they were more sensitive to issues and they did more to make the transition easier," Duke's Claiborne said of North Carolina. "Then, too, Charlie Scott came along a couple of years later [in the integration process], so they had had more time to get ready, in one sense. But certainly his transition into that environment was more planned."

Smith and assistant Lotz were particularly receptive to Scott's need to talk through his difficulties. Lotz was often Scott's confidante, accompanying him for a burger or a chat. He was the best man at Scott's 1968 wedding. He drove around Washington, D.C., with Scott, after the conference MVP vote was announced in 1969. Smith was the father figure, the voice of authority, the public backstop when conflict arose.

By contrast, Grubar, a contemporary and among Scott's best friends on the UNC squad for three years, cannot recall ever discussing race with his teammate.

"They'd never been around a Black that much, and I'd never been around whites that much," Scott said of his fellow Tar Heels. "I don't begrudge anybody. It wasn't a talked-about thing. Coach Smith dealt with it when we had to. And rightly so, I think. If I would have kept it on my mind all the time, it would have been very hard."

Smith's courage and care in augmenting Scott's success did not go unnoticed. "When someone sticks their neck out like that, it serves them well for many years to come," said Duke's Ernie Jackson, who in 1971 became the first African American voted football's ACC Player of the Year. "He wound up getting a lot of great athletes. I think there was a good amount of loyalty among Black folks toward him for what he did. He was one of the few."

A simple litany of superior, in-state African-American players who subsequently cast their lot with Smith's program eloquently illustrates the point: Bob McAdoo, Phil Ford, Walter Davis, James Worthy, Michael Jordan, Brad Daugherty, Jerry Stackhouse, and Antawn Jamison.

The slender Scott certainly belongs in that elite company. He was quick, aggressive, high-flying. ("He can jump like a frog hit by lightning," one journalist offered.) His rainbow jumpers, launched going to his right after dribbling hard to his left, were a fearsome weapon. He often guarded the opponent's best player. He expressed as much satisfaction with a good pass as a score. He was explosive, a game-changer. "He has an elastic quality when he has the ball, either moving toward a shot or passing off, the kind of performer that fills up your vision," wrote Bruce Phillips in the *Raleigh Times*.

Kentucky coach Adolph Rupp, reaching a bit to make his point, said of Scott after one game, "He destroyed my man [Larry] Steele who was trying to guard him. Maybe we should send Scott to Viet Nam. He could terrorize the Viet Cong like he does everyone in this country."

Gene Corrigan, then a flack for the ACC and later the conference commissioner, wrote in a press release that Scott "has what is commonly known as IT. Charlie makes things happen." Good things, that is. "Nobody is greater than Charlie when the chips are down," said teammate Eddie Fogler. "Another thing that makes him great is his ability to block everything out of his mind but the game. He's moody off the court sometimes, and even in practice. Maybe something's bothering him and he's not feeling well. But in a game, watch him when he goes up for a shot. Watch his concentration. He blocks out everything but that moment, that shot."

Scott's scoring average increased annually, from 17.6 as a sophomore to 22.3 as a junior to 27.1 as a senior. His scoring average his senior year has not been matched since at North Carolina. Scott also led the team in assists in 1969 and was routinely among the squad's leading rebounders. Acutely aware of his stats, he habitually stopped by the UNC sports information office to check his shooting percentage, which was a solid 48 percent for his career.

Billy Packer, an ACC basketball habitue since the 1958–59 season, said Scott "was one of the best that's played in this league. Charlie was a tremendous defensive player. He had great anticipation; he had a lot of Michael Jordan's instincts in regard to that. Not a great shooter, but a great scorer. He had a good medium-range jump shot and was a great finisher on the break. Caused havoc. A terrific player. Played with a chip on his shoulder."

That "chip" did not win Scott many friends, and it may have proven costly when it came to votes for league honors. "He wasn't the most beloved individual," Wake's Charlie Davis said. "I can assure you that if Charles was arrogant in the way he tended to be back then but couldn't play as well, he wouldn't have spent four years at Carolina. They wouldn't have tolerated him. Coupled with his ability, you can tolerate a few more things from him."

Scott surely blended well with UNC's upperclassman-dominated squad in 1967–68, which opened with wins in 22 of its first 23 games en route to a 28–4 record. The sole loss during that stretch came at Vanderbilt against Perry Wallace's team. After the game Scott traveled into the black part of Nashville to visit friends at Tennessee A&I, a school he had considered attending because John McLendon coached there. Leaving A&I late that night, Scott couldn't find a cabdriver willing to return him to the white side of town; he had to phone Smith, who came and gave Scott a ride.

Several weeks later the Tar Heels played in Portland, Oregon, in the Far West Classic. They swept three games to win the title. Scott was voted the tournament MVP during the championship victory against Oregon State. But after teammate Larry Miller scored 27 points in the second half, the hierarchically oriented Smith prevailed upon voters to reconsider, and the award went to the senior captain instead. The coach explained the privileges of seniority to the jilted sophomore.

Later, Scott came to believe that Smith acted to preserve the team's psyche, out of fear that an African American's immediate success might disquiet the 14 white players. (Smith insists he did not think in racial terms.) "I don't say that begrudgingly, but it's easy if you're not the person dealing with the abuse, to say, 'Well, let's not make it an issue,'" Scott told interviewer Mark Briggs years later. "But it always was an issue with me, though. It's an issue with me today so it damn sure was an issue with me at that point in time. I understand what he was trying to do. He was right in saying, 'If I don't make it an issue, then it won't become an issue within my team.' The thing is, I had to live outside that team."

The Tar Heels never ranked lower than seventh in 1967–68 and lost only two ACC games, one in triple-overtime at Duke. They won the ACC tournament, then won the NCAA East Regional by defeating top-10 teams St. Bonaventure and Davidson. They advanced to the national championship game—one of five visits under Smith—only to lose by 23 points to UCLA. (Much to the reported chagrin of his players, Smith resorted to slowdown tactics, to no good effect.)

Twelve days after the NCAA title game, Martin Luther King Jr. was assassinated. Riots swept the country. Two months after that, Robert Kennedy was assassinated.

With militancy rising, Black athletes were encouraged to join a boycott of the upcoming 1968 Olympics in Mexico City. Rallying to the call of former athlete Harry Edwards, many college stars declined to play on the U.S. Olympic basketball squad in those days of strictly "amateur" participation. Among those who declined were Lew Alcindor (Kareem Abdul Jabbar), Mike Warren, and Lucius Allen of UCLA and Houston's Elvin Hayes.

Scott was invited to go and accepted. "People ask me why I played in the Olympics," Scott said. "Well, if you go to North Carolina and you turn around and boycott, you really defeat the purpose of why you went there. You go there to show you can integrate. If you boycott, what are you trying to show?"

On the eve of the Games, police in Mexico City massacred some 250 unarmed student demonstrators. The Olympics also were marked by a silent black power protest on the awards stand by U.S. sprinters Tommie Smith and John Carlos. Their black-gloved salute, fists raised and heads bowed during the playing of "The Star Spangled Banner," got the pair ejected from the Olympics and evoked a stormy reaction.

The U.S. basketball squad, led by 19-year-old Spencer Haywood, won the gold medal, a routine result for a country that had yet to lose a game in

Olympic basketball competition. Scott averaged 8.0 points, fifth-best on the team. "I was living Jackie Robinson's dream all over again," he said of the year in which he played in the Final Four and the Olympics. "Things were all jelling; I couldn't ask for any better things in life."

The Olympics took place in October, causing Scott to miss the first semester of the college year. He practiced and played with the Tar Heels but didn't go to class until January. By then Howard Lee had taken office in Chapel Hill, the first African American elected mayor in a predominantly white town in the South since Reconstruction.

Scott emerged quickly as the scoring leader and incontrovertible star on the 1968–69 team, which finished 27–5 overall, 12–2 in the ACC. "In college he was probably as good or better than Michael Jordan, in my opinion," says Fred Lind, a contemporary Duke player. "He could do it all." Wrote Frank Barrows in the *Charlotte Observer*, "He is the caliber of player about whom people talk, the third favorite topic of conversation in Chapel Hill, ranking behind only coeds and beer."

Such prominence made the aspiring lawyer and politician the perfect choice to carry the banner for the campus Black Student Movement. In December 1968 the BSM presented chancellor J. Carlyle Sitterson with a list of 23 demands, including an African-American curriculum for the school's Black undergrads, more aggressive recruitment of Black students, a more active role by the university in helping Chapel Hill's Black community, and better working conditions for nonacademic employees.

Overall, by the late 1960s student protests nationwide shifted from civil rights to the antiwar movement. But rising minority enrollments on campuses spawned groups that fought for the rights of Black students as well as for local African Americans stuck in chronically discriminatory circumstances. The visibility and relative acceptance of Black athletes made them ideal spokesmen (women were not offered athletic scholarships at ACC and SEC schools until years later) for causes identified by their campus brethren. "Rather than simply serving as symbols of African American achievement," Pamela Grundy asserted in *Learning to Win*, support grew for the notion that "Black athletes should use the prominence they had won to lead battles against other, more entrenched problems."

Given their capacity to embarrass the university and their dependence on athletic grants-in-aid, African-American players ran a considerable risk by stepping forward. University of Florida basketball player Steve Williams and track athlete Ron Coleman slipped out a side door, fearful of forfeiting their scholarships, when police came to remove occupying students from the president's office at their school in April 1971. Similarly chastened, Duke football player Ernie Jackson avoided the situation entirely when black students occupied his school's administration building in February 1969.

Wake's Davis was asked by "a number of our more militant brothers on campus" to boycott a game in support of a protest. "I had to point out, 'I've got a family, my mom and my dad. I have an opportunity to do something that can alter the lives of my family. Y'all are talking about me giving up something. What are y'all giving up?' Certainly those types of discussions went on during that period of time: How much can you really impact, and on whose shoulders is it? Who's supposed to make this sacrifice to make this impact?"

Protests arose at the University of North Carolina over working conditions for African Americans at the student dining hall, where Pollitt said "a plantation mentality" prevailed. The BSM presented distilled demands to Sitterson in late February 1969. Scott and Bill Chamberlain, a little-known freshman, publicly participated in a rally and negotiating session. Chamberlain declared, "If I'm going to represent this university on the basketball court, I think the university should go to bat for me and take some positive action soon." Smith insisted he encouraged Chamberlain and Scott to participate. "That was being part of the student body," he said.

The BSM publicly promised "revolutionary tactics" if the response from the school administration was unsatisfactory, and it hinted that Scott and Chamberlain would quit the team. Privately, Scott was asked to boycott a game. He went to speak with Smith, a man with a legendary memory. In a conversation the coach does not recall, the star player found himself out on a limb. "He said that I would put him in a position to choose between me and his family," Scott said. "If he chose to back me, it was possible that the school would not back him. . . . I understand what he meant by that. I think that's the only time that he really felt the pressure—that I was going to pressure him to respond to things. In his defense, I would say that, probably, if he thought it was the right thing to do, he would have backed it. But it was really a power move by the Black students."

When workers at the dining hall went on strike within days of the players' appearance, the school released a statement saying that Scott was not a member of the BSM and that he had spoken with Sitterson at Smith's suggestion. "Personally, I have been extremely happy at Carolina," Scott was quoted in the release. "Everything for me so far has been excellent. Coach Smith has always understood me and my problems. I would recommend him to any student-athlete. There are, of course, problems at all colleges and universities, but I would wholeheartedly recommend the University of North Carolina. My concern grew out of the situation in which Black students have found themselves at universities throughout the country."

Scott's measured pronouncements and decidedly nonconfrontational choices had limited impact on public perception. This was the South, where integration moved forward grudgingly and Republican Richard Nixon deftly exploited racial polarization to propel his run to the presidency. (Once in office, Nixon let his public facade slip after learning that members of a professional organization provided scholarships to African Americans. "Well, it's a good thing," the president said. "They are just down from the trees.")

Scott's visible alignment with protestors, however mild, earned him a reputation in some quarters as a Black militant. The label moved a Charlotte columnist to defend Scott as "a man in the middle" of a tough situation. "Charlie Scott is no trained seal," Mel Derrick wrote. "Neither is he a wild-eyed Black racist preaching hate and revolt. He's a sensitive 20-year-old with the weight of the ages on his shoulders."

This was the context in which ACC-area media members cast their ballots for the 1968–69 ACC Player of the Year. Regardless of what motivated them to select South Carolina's Roche, the result came as a "cold slap in the face" to Scott. "At that time nothing in my life was more bitter and more disappointing to me, and an outward sign of racism, than voting him as ACC Player of the Year," Scott conceded. "It took me a lot of years to get over that. I went from being an idealist to a skeptic."

Scott paced the ACC in scoring the following year as a senior. Despite substantial personnel losses, UNC tied for second in the conference in 1970 and finished 18–9. (Remarkably, the Tar Heels would not suffer another season with fewer than 20 wins until 2002, five seasons after Smith retired.) Dick McGuire, then chief scout for the New York Knicks, declared Scott "the most complete player in America." Nevertheless, Roche—the leading scorer on the league's best team with a 14-0 conference record—again was named ACC Player of the Year. "I thought that was a bad vote," Charlie Davis said. "I couldn't understand. I thought that Scotty was arguably the best player in the country. I thought it was generally acknowledged that he was the best player in the country."

As if to compensate, the Atlantic Coast Conference Sports Writers Association voted Scott the league's top all-around athlete for 1969–70.

Roche remained South Carolina's top scorer in 1971 as the Gamecocks finished second in the conference and won the ACC championship. This time, the Player of the Year award went to Davis, the league's top scorer and the first African American to be so honored. "I thought they were right the first year: Roche deserved it," Davis said. "They were wrong the second year: Scott deserved it. They were right the third year: I deserved it."

By then Scott was playing for the Virginia Squires in the American Basketball Association, where he was named the 1971 Co-Rookie of the Year along with Dan Issel of the Kentucky Colonels. Scott averaged 27.1 points, exactly his average output as a senior at North Carolina. He later played with four NBA teams and was a three-time all-star with Phoenix, where his 24.8-point career scoring average remains best in franchise history. He went to Boston in 1976 and helped the Celtics win the NBA title in six games over Phoenix. Scott's final season in pro ball was 1980, when Roche, of all people, was among his teammates at Denver.

Today, Scott's jersey is among the several dozen honored uniforms hanging from the rafters of the cavernous Dean E. Smith Student Activities Center, where the Tar Heels have played since January 1986. A drawing of a number 33 North Carolina jersey also adorns Scott's suburban home, where he lives with Trudy, his second wife, and children Simone, Shawn, and Shannon. (The number 33 eventually was retired at UNC, but not until Antawn Jamison wore it while winning national Player of the Year honors in 1998.)

Like most former Tar Heels, Scott maintains his connection with the program. Visiting Chapel Hill on the occasion of his freshman squad's 35th reunion at which placemats featured the team photo, Trudy Scott overheard two of her children scanning the youthful faces to locate their father. Given that he was the sole African American in the group, a simple sorting by skin pigmentation would have yielded a definitive result. Instead, the children employed a colorblind method that holds promise of better things to come. One of the boys asked his sister, "Which one's dad?"

"Oh, silly," she replied. "Don't you know? He's always the one wearing number 33."

CHAPTER 6

DOOR JAMB

Wendell Hudson, University of Alabama, 1969–73

A man can't ride your back unless it is bent.

Martin Luther King Jr.

In this case the intersection of symbol and history lay not at some abstract juncture susceptible to debate, but just south of University Boulevard between Sixth Avenue and Hackberry Lane on the Tuscaloosa campus of the University of Alabama.

Ruin ate at Foster Auditorium—at its peeling plaster, its loosening interior signs and ceiling panels, its flooded basement. Odd pieces of furniture lined disused hallways. Upper-level seating was cordoned with yellow caution tape, and access points were covered with plywood. Birds nested in light fixtures. Carpets as stained as the pride once defended at the building's door squatted in rolled heaps beside a dark curtain hiding stacks of folding tables.

For a quarter-century, until supplanted in 1968 by Coleman Coliseum, Foster hosted Crimson Tide basketball games, university assemblies and shows, and class registration. The brick and stone building, located a block from the university's gracious main quadrangle and within sight of the soaring football stadium, seated 5,400. But while the "Rocket Eight" generated excitement en route to an SEC title during the pre-integration 1950s, basketball rarely attracted a full house. "Alabama never tried to have a basketball program," noted Clyde Bolton in *The Basketball Tide*. As a newspaperman Bolton covered the Tide for almost 40 years beginning in the early 1960s. "It was just something you covered. It was about like college baseball now—an afterthought."

That all changed with the arrival of head coach Charles "C. M." Newton and a flood of Alabama-born African Americans, starting with Birmingham's Wendell Hudson in 1969–70. The Tide made its first postseason appearance during Hudson's senior season. By then, four of Alabama's five starters were Black.

Foster Auditorium achieved its greatest basketball distinction on a fluke shot by All-America George Linn, a star of the so-called Rocket Eight, named after a popular V-8 model of Oldsmobile. In a 1955 win over North Carolina, Linn rebounded a missed shot, turned, and, while standing beside his own backboard, successfully launched the ball through the basket at the other end of the court, 84 feet and 11 inches away. UNC coach Frank McGuire came off his bench to mark the spot where Linn stood. A permanent bronze *X* later was placed on the court to commemorate the record shot, at the time and for years afterward the longest made in a college game.

The building's real prominence was unrelated to basketball, however. Under the colonnade at the entrance of Foster Auditorium, Alabama governor George Wallace made his televised "stand in the schoolhouse door" in June 1963, defying federal orders to integrate the state's flagship university.

The first attempt to integrate the University of Alabama, made in 1956, had ended after three days of demonstrations, a riot, and the expulsion of the applicant, Autherine Lucy, ostensibly for her own safety. This second attempt, by Vivian Malone and James Hood, came less than a year after James Meredith's entrance into Ole Miss brought disorder, bloodshed, and two deaths.

President John Kennedy, anxious for a more salubrious outcome at Alabama, dispatched his brother, Attorney General Robert Kennedy, to Montgomery to meet privately with Wallace at the state capital. Lest the visitor sully with his tread the spot where Jefferson Davis had been sworn in as Confederate president in 1861, conscientious members of the United Daughters of the Confederacy anticipated the parlay by strategically laying a wreath upon the sacred site.

Wallace had ridden a wave of white animosity and a century of resentment against the federal government into the governor's mansion. "After the civil rights issue got so hot in Alabama the way to get elected was to holler 'nigger,'" said Alabama football legend Paul "Bear" Bryant in his 1974 autobiography *Bear*. Understandably, then, the Kennedys could not dissuade

Wallace from pursuing the course he had outlined barely six months earlier in his inaugural address as governor. "In the name of the greatest people that have ever trod this earth, I draw the line in the dust and toss the gauntlet before the feet of tyranny," Wallace had famously intoned, "and I say segregation now, segregation tomorrow, segregation forever." Later, Wallace warned state education leaders that "if you agree to integrate your schools, there won't be enough state troopers to protect you."

So Wallace stood at a lectern placed outside Foster—a building erected with federal funds by the Works Progress Administration on the eve of World War II—and ceremoniously blocked the 1963 enrollment of Malone and Hood. Adding to the volatility of the moment, Tuscaloosa was home to Robert Shelton, National Grand Wizard of the Knights of the Ku Klux Klan. Wallace did issue repeated pleas to vigilantes "to stay away and let the governor of your state handle this all-important matter as your representative." Still, the threat of violence hovered over the confrontation like a thunderstorm rumbling on the near horizon that sweltering day in mid-June, with state troopers much in evidence and police sharpshooters stationed on Foster's roof.

Wallace ultimately stepped aside, acquiescing when a general from the federalized Alabama National Guard formally requested that he do so. "The national press and most of Alabama's major dailies rushed to note that Wallace surrendered," wrote E. Culpepper Clark in *The Schoolhouse Door*. "But that was the way it was supposed to turn out. As a reenactment of Appomattox, the schoolhouse door fulfilled expectation—federal, force-induced surrender followed by a settled conviction that the real cause, white supremacy, was not, indeed, could not, be lost."

The incident helped launch Wallace's national political career and signaled the beginning of the end of the so-called Solid South as a Democratic voting bloc. The Foster facedown spurred President Kennedy to go on national television the same night to call for enactment of sweeping civil rights legislation. The United States was confronted with "primarily a moral issue," Kennedy said. "It is as old as the Scriptures and as clear as the American Constitution." He called upon Congress to "make a commitment it has not fully made in this century to the proposition that race has no place in American life or law." Underlining the stakes, shortly after Kennedy spoke a white assassin ambushed and murdered civil rights leader Medgar Evers in the driveway of his home in Jackson, Mississippi.

○

Laws changed and restrictions eased, but the image of Wallace's intransigence lingered. Certainly it came to mind when Mildred Hudson's only son told her in the spring of 1969 that he wished to attend the University of Alabama. "My mom was terrified," Wendell Hudson said. "You've got to understand the times. Wallace had just stood in the door there recently." Although a smattering of Black students had attended "the Capstone," as the university is called, none had been athletes.

"He broke the ice for the rest of them to go down there," Ms. Hudson said of her eldest child, a 6-foot-6 center who played at Birmingham's all-Black Parker High School. "Somebody had to break it, but sometimes I wonder why it had to be him."

Of all the barrier-breaking African-American basketball players throughout the Southeast, none speaks more positively of his experience, seemed more at peace with his former teammates, or enjoyed a more fulfilled playing career than Wendell Hudson. Hudson even returned to work at his alma mater, where he became an assistant athletics director in 2003. (Months earlier, Alabama had failed to hire another Black alumnus, Sylvester Croom, as its head coach in football. Croom went to Mississippi State instead and became the first African American to run an SEC football program.)

Only in retrospect can Hudson's arrival on the Alabama campus be seen as perfectly timed, although it most certainly was.

Hudson's senior year in high school, the Parker Thundering Herd, boasting several college prospects, captured the 1969 state high school championship. That was the first season in which Black and white Alabama teams competed for the same title. Parker, once billed as the world's largest Negro high school, went 33–1. The showing in mixed competition elevated the profile of a program that had won the 1964 Black high school championship against Nashville's Pearl High, the school where Perry Wallace and company similarly ran the table the first year Tennessee accepted all comers.

The 1969 state tournament allowed Hudson to shine on the state's biggest prep stage. "I stepped in and did some things that surprised even some of my teammates. They were like, 'Man, I didn't know you could do that!'" he said. Meanwhile, Newton, in his first year as Alabama's head basketball coach, endured a 4–20 season. The inauspicious debut was hardly reassuring for the little-known 38-year-old, who recalled being greeted at Tuscaloosa by a story headlined, "C. M. Who? Named 'Bama Coach."

Newton had Latin teammates while pitching in the New York Yankees' minor league baseball organization. At modest Transylvania College in Lexington, Kentucky, he had quietly integrated the basketball program as head coach and head of physical education. "Sometimes the sheer decency of the fellow startles you," Bolton wrote in the *Birmingham News*.

Newton, in short, was ready, both personally and professionally, to dive into the great stream of untapped talent that flowed through the formerly all-Black and all-ignored schools of Alabama. It helped that Bryant, Alabama's football coach and athletics director and a legendary figure in the state, was supportive, for reasons of his own.

"What I wanted to do was build a basketball program at Alabama," said Newton. "I had been there in 1964 working on a doctorate and had seen the high schools play, both Black and white. When they merged I saw a whole group of talent in that state that I felt could make the program competitive. The question I asked of Coach Bryant was, 'Are there any restrictions?' And his answer was, 'No, there are no restrictions. You've got to recruit legally and you've got to recruit guys that can finish school here, that can graduate and will graduate.' So, [race] was not an issue."

For his part, Bryant said he hired Newton, a calm pipe smoker rarely given to profanity, "because he's the only basketball coach I know who isn't crazy."

Bryant won six national titles at his alma mater between 1958 and 1982, went to 24 consecutive bowl games, and finished with a 232–46–9 record at Alabama. He insisted he was ready to sign African-American athletes during his coaching tenure at the University of Kentucky (1946–53) but said, "I didn't get anywhere." He believed that Alabama's lack of Black players, coupled with the state's racist image, cost his program a shot at a national title in 1966. Yet Bryant continued to steer Black players to other schools because "the time wasn't ripe."

Sounding much like Adolph Rupp, the influential basketball coach with whom he feuded at Kentucky, Bryant shifted the blame to others. "I said I wasn't worried a bit about our players, but we had to play two games in Mississippi, and for that and other reasons it might be too tough on the kid. I wanted him to be treated and to act like any other Alabama player." Then, perhaps getting to the crux of the matter, Bryant added, "And I damn sure wouldn't stand for him showing up with a bunch of photographers and some big-talking civil rights leader trying to get publicity."

Change soon overtook Bryant, in part due to a federal lawsuit filed against him and the school in July 1969 for failure to make adequate efforts to recruit African-American players. Alabama signed wingback Wilbur Jackson in December 1969, and he arrived on campus in time for the 1970–71 school year.

Then, on September 12, 1970, Southern California came to Tuscaloosa and won handily, 42–21, with African-American back Sam "Bam" Cunningham running roughshod over the Tide. Afterward, Cunningham's performance was said to have done "more for integration in the South in 60 minutes than Martin Luther King did in 20 years." The remark generally was attributed to Bryant, but he ascribed it instead to Jerry Claiborne, his assistant at the time and a future Hall of Fame coach. The remark, coupled with Cunningham's superior effort, gave rise to a legend that the USC game forever altered Bryant's thinking. Perhaps it did, but by then the process of adding Black athletes at Alabama was well under way.

Given Bryant's blessing, Newton made history at Alabama by signing Hudson, the school's first African-American scholarship athlete in any sport when he committed to enroll for the 1969–70 year. The signing—which took place at the all-state player's Birmingham home—was purposely low-key and "proved as undramatic as it was historic," according to an observer. Newton, following Bryant's advice, invited only a handful of photographers and reporters to share in the Kool-Aid and doughnuts set out by Ms. Hudson as 18-year-old Wendell cast his lot with the basketball program. The *Birmingham News* touted the signing in its April 26, 1969, "Dixie Edition," but widespread attention was fleeting. Hudson was not considered a major prospect, and this was only basketball, after all, in a state where football is "a way of life," as Bryant said.

"I've been asked, 'Why did you go to the University of Alabama?'" said Hudson, whose other scholarship offers came mostly from small schools. "Sometimes I think that when people ask that question, it's really 'Why did you think you should go?' Well, I never thought I *shouldn't* be there. I never felt like I was inferior. Somebody else did, evidently, but that was not something that was brought up in my house and in my family, the way we were raised."

As Bryant anticipated, the school's first Black athlete encountered difficulties on the road. There also was resentment in Birmingham's black community because Hudson had chosen to attend a white school. For the most part, though, the fearsome antagonisms championed by George Wallace and the secret resentments of others blew quietly past.

"I have talked to people before about going to Alabama. Unfortunately, people want to hear the horror stories more than they want to hear the good things," Hudson said. "I don't have the horror stories. I played for the right people. I probably went to what everybody thought was the worst place, after what all transpired there. But once Coach Bryant said everything was OK, everything was OK. Who was going to fight it? Too many people wanted to be a part of Coach Bryant's football program."

Hudson went on to an outstanding collegiate career. He set a freshman record at Alabama for rebounding, then recovered from a broken wrist his sophomore year to earn consecutive berths on the all-conference squad as an upperclassman. He was named SEC Player of the Year as a senior, the first Black athlete so honored. Hudson paced the league in rebounding in 1972 (13.1 per game) and in scoring in 1973 (20.7). His senior year the Crimson Tide reached the National Invitation Tournament, its first post-season appearance in 61 years of playing basketball.

Of the 11 Alabama players who took to the NIT court at New York's Madison Square Garden that year, 9 were Black. Hudson's signing had done for the University of Alabama what Perry Wallace's did for the SEC: opened a floodgate through which poured talented, homegrown African-American players. Raymond Odums and Ernest Odom came to Tuscaloosa a year after Hudson, followed in short order by Charles Cleveland, Leon Douglas, T. R. Dunn, and others.

Remarkably, within a decade of George Wallace's stand in the school-house door, Newton had built a successful program at Alabama's flagship university, a program so heavily reliant on Black players that some accused the coach of discriminating against whites.

"Looking back, the key to the whole thing at Alabama was Wendell," Newton said in his memoir, *Newton's Laws*. Echoing Dean Smith at North Carolina, he continued, "I've gotten a lot of credit over the years for integrating the Alabama program and the SEC. I've even been called courageous. But it didn't take any courage on my part. However, it took tremendous courage on Wendell's part."

All involved point to Hudson's calm, steady, unassuming but uncompromising manner as a crucial element in winning acceptance for African-American athletes. Teammate Paul Ellis says that "Hud," as he was called, had "great character. If he told you he was going to do something, he did it. His mother raised him correctly. . . . He just was Wendell. That's all he ever wanted to be, was Wendell. He just wanted to be treated like everybody else.

Maybe that was his distinguishing characteristic, that he just was himself. I don't think I could say anything better about him."

Farra Alford, another white teammate, likewise had high praise for Hudson: "If I was starting a team today, he'd probably be my first pick of all those great Alabama kids. He was just incredible. And you're never going to have a problem. He's just a class act."

Personality, of course, was not the sole or even the primary consideration in enlisting a Black athletic pioneer. And choosing to sign Hudson was not easy for Newton, who previously and unsuccessfully had pursued prominent African-American prospects Bud Stallworth (who went to Kansas), Henry Harris (Auburn), Tom Payne (Kentucky), and Artis Gilmore (Gardner-Webb). Of that group, all but Harris went on to a professional career.

Newton heard again and again, within basketball circles and beyond, that the first Black player at a Southern school had to be an immediate success, both to stifle bigotry and to fend off suspicions among African Americans that his presence was mere tokenism, appeasement. This apparently was coaching gospel; as late as 1970, nearly three of every four African Americans on integrated college basketball teams were starters. "You've got to get someone who's a superstar, high school All-American, that type of reputation, or they won't be accepted. Someone that's a can't-miss prospect, whatever that is," Newton said. "Wendell did not fit that bill coming out of high school."

Yet Newton saw ample raw material from which to fashion a star, and he believed Hudson could inject elements largely lacking in Alabama's program—indeed, lacking in most programs dominated by white players. "I think he gives us something we don't have," Newton said upon Hudson's signing, "that leaper, a guy who can get up and get the basketball. Another thing that has been impressive is his quickness."

Other, less tangible traits were equally important. "When I watched him, Parker [High School] not only won, and he was a big part of their winning, but it seemed like he got every rebound and he scored whenever they had to have a basket," Newton said. "But the thing that really endeared him to me was just his personal qualities." Hudson was an honor student and Boy Scout from a home in which hard work, devotion to family, and personal responsibility were stressed.

Leon Marlaire, a Birmingham businessman and member of the Rocket Eight, attended Parker games and helped woo Hudson. "Wendell was just one of these who knew how to act and react," he said. "He was just the class

Black athlete. You couldn't have gotten a better kid as far as a person, or as a good athlete, to start in a program, and C. M. knew that. And it wasn't because he was Black; the kid was a great athlete."

Yet there was ample evidence at the time of Hudson's recruitment that the Alabama staff's assessment relied dangerously upon wishful thinking. Colleagues were lukewarm at best to Hudson as a prospect. His only in-state scholarship offer came from Miles College, a small Black school in Birmingham. Auburn, Alabama's bitter in-state rival, suggested Hudson attend junior college, where he could strengthen a frame that carried approximately 175 pounds, the weight at which he was generously listed as a college freshman.

Hudson's game was not polished. He was not the leading scorer or the top prospect on his high school team. A lackluster shooter, he would finish his college career making a paltry 57.7 percent of his free throw attempts. Hudson also was undersized to play center. He possessed nowhere near the reputation or credentials of Parker teammate Alvin McGrew, who chose to play pro baseball, or of Ellis, a freckle-faced guard who had already signed with Alabama. Ellis was in fact a high school All-American who averaged 27.8 points his senior season in Selma.

North Carolina's Charles Scott appreciates the conundrum coaches faced when integrating their squads. "I do believe for a school's program, it's important for that first Black athlete to be great," Scott said. "How are you going to say somebody's going to be great when you get him? It's a tough call."

Newton's recruiting judgment was later ratified by Hudson's success and by four SEC Coach of the Year awards during a decade at Tuscaloosa. But signing Hudson was admittedly a leap of faith. "Nobody else is recruiting him. You're sitting there thinking, 'Damn, the guy can play.' Now, are you that crazy? Are you that far off base?" Newton said. "I finally told our staff, 'Look, we're 4–20 this year. I've got a four-year contract. They're going to fire me anyway if we don't get this thing straightened out. . . . Let's do it the way we want to do it, the way we think we ought to. We think Hudson can play. Let's sign him and move on.'"

Winning Mildred Hudson's approval was another matter.

"I'll never forget it. She said, 'Coach Newton, I'm entrusting you with my most precious thing, my son. What's it going to be like for him?'" Newton said. "And I told her, 'Ms. Hudson, I don't know. I'm kind of a middle-class white guy. I don't know what it's going to be like.' I said, 'The only thing that I know is that I can guarantee you I will not treat Wendell any differently than I'll treat anybody else. I will treat him exactly the same. If he needs fussing, I'm going to fuss at him. If he needs hugging, I'm going to hug him. I'm going to coach him the best I can. I'm going to make him go to class.'

"She said, 'That's good enough.'"

But it wasn't.

Mildred Hudson was born and raised in Birmingham and knew all too well Alabama's racial mores and passions. She knew where she could journey, and through which doors she might pass. She knew that the veneer of civility could be banished in an instant, as when singer Nat King Cole was beaten on stage when performing at Birmingham's Municipal Auditorium in April 1956. Four years later, Freedom Riders seeking to integrate interstate transportation pulled into Birmingham's bus station on Mother's Day and disembarked to a beating with baseball bats, lead pipes, and bicycle chains. Public Safety Commissioner Theophilus Eugene "Bull" Conner kept police at a distance so local Klansmen could operate with impunity. "Damn the law, we don't give a damn about the law," Conner declared. "Down here we make our own law."

Frequent bombings—some 50 between 1947 and 1963, more than in any other city in the country—earned Hudson's hometown the nickname "Bombingham." Explosions directed at African Americans in the Fountain Heights section (called "Dynamite Hill") provided frightening reminders of the limits of white tolerance. "We used to live right down the street, down the hill, and we could hear it," Ms. Hudson said. "We would cut the lights off and lay on the floor." Local pastor Fred Shuttleworth called Birmingham "very close to hell itself."

Birmingham, self-styled as "the Magic City," became the focus of direct action by civil rights leaders in the spring of 1963 after Martin Luther King Jr. deemed it "by far the worst big city in race relations in the United States." Determined to force downtown department stores to desegregate their facilities and to hire African-American clerks, Black protestors nonviolently marched through the city's streets, led by thousands of children who were beaten and arrested with singular savagery. "No American then alive is likely to forget the snarling police dogs and fire hoses that greeted thousands of schoolchildren when they marched, singing, into the city's central shopping district," said Harry Ashmore in *Civil Rights and Wrongs*.

Ms. Hudson witnessed the tumult but kept herself and her children at a remove from the action in the streets. She said it was a matter of being unable to adhere to Dr. King's principles: "That's why I said I couldn't march with them, because if [the police] hit me, I would hit them back."

Ms. Hudson defied considerable odds to raise her children successfully as a single parent. She gave birth to Wendell when she was 16, while living with her mother and attending high school. With no father or husband in the picture, Mildred Hudson began work in a downtown department store at age 20; she stayed until retirement 46 years later. She worked hard at raising Wendell and his sister, Vanessa, and providing for them as best she could.

"I remember sitting in a class as a freshman, and they were talking about the poverty level. At the time I thought, yeah, that was me," Wendell Hudson said. "I had to go to college to find out I was in poverty. Really, because I had food to eat. I was cared about. I had a clean house. Same with my clothes. We made it. You went to school and you were supposed to do things, and there was right and wrong and that kind of stuff."

The Hudson children were required to say a blessing at every meal, to attend church and Sunday school every week. Wendell and Vanessa joined their mother each morning for breakfast before she left for work. They were not allowed to go out to play, or to have friends in the house, until she returned. Supper was followed by chores, and then by reading. Once, as punishment, Mildred Hudson made the children listen to her read the Bible. They liked it so much that she finally had to beg off, pleading, "OK, we've read enough here."

Ms. Hudson allowed Wendell to remain on the basketball team at Parker with the understanding that his grades would not slip. Calm and patient, he also was responsible for minding his younger sister after school. "The only time I really had any trouble out of him, is one time I told him, 'Don't go nowhere,'" Ms. Hudson said. "And he carried his sister down to my mother's house and he went on to the school and started playing basketball."

Trouble of a more serious nature was exactly what she feared when her son confided his intention to attend Alabama. "You're going where?" she asked. She cried over the thought that her firstborn was leaving home and cried even more over his choice of school. "When Wallace wouldn't let the other two black people in, all of that ran across my mind when Wendell said he was going," Ms. Hudson said. "But so long as he was happy, I made myself satisfied."

Regulating children's conduct was a group effort in Birmingham, as it was in many communities. Wendell Hudson rarely missed the father he never knew because he had ample support from caring male teachers, coaches, relatives, and friends. But collective interest in his welfare was not entirely without cost. When his college selection departed from the norm, Hudson discovered, as did other African-American racial pioneers, that support for his freedom to choose—a right for which the civil rights movement struggled and suffered—sometimes was more abstract than real among fellow Blacks. Crossing the state's racial divide was criticized as a sellout, a betrayal of his own community.

That view did not deflect Hudson from his course, but he knew it took a toll on his mother. "When I signed at Alabama, I know in people's minds they thought, 'You're going to play in college now? At the University of Alabama? They're not going to let you play because you're Black and they just signed you for a token.' My mom was hearing this stuff, and it terrified her. She thought, 'Why are you going down there?' Taking me to Tuscaloosa was a sad trip for her. She worried about her son and what was going to happen."

Ms. Hudson heard nothing from her elder child for two weeks after he arrived on campus. Finally, almost beside herself with worry, her mind filled with the horrors that could befall a young Black man in Tuscaloosa—fears reinforced by people around her—she placed a telephone call to the athletic dorm at the University of Alabama and asked for Wendell Hudson. The phone was public, located at the end of the hall. When he picked up, teammates teased Hudson that the female caller was his girlfriend and otherwise laughed and carried on as college freshmen will. The ruckus, which Mildred Hudson overheard at a remove, confirmed her worst fears. Unable to contain herself any longer, she demanded, "Boy, what are those white boys doing to you?"

Those white boys were forging friendships and weaving the first tentative filaments that would bind them as a team. Many had not previously known an African American as someone other than a servant. To this day Newton teases Farra Alford, a real estate developer in Lexington, Kentucky, that he did not know a Black person other than his maid until arriving at Tuscaloosa. Alford, who attended an all-white prep school in Richmond, Virginia, insists his camaraderie with Hudson was unforced: "We had no racial anything, except we kidded each other about it."

Ellis, the freckled-faced shooting star from segregated Selma, first heard on the radio that Hudson was set to join his recruiting class. "I remember my father saying, 'What do you think about that?' I said, 'It doesn't matter to me. We're going up there to play basketball and have a good time.'" That proved to be the case. "Wendell and I, all of us—we never had a problem because we were there for the same reasons. Plus we were all good people. Wendell's mama was a wonderful person. And our [families] were just good, solid people."

Just as important as acceptance by his teammates was Hudson's reception from Alabama's large football contingent, overwhelmingly comprised of rural whites.

All scholarship athletes stayed in Bryant Hall and ate together. The first time Hudson entered the athletic dining hall alone for the evening meal, the reaction reminded him of Birmingham in the aftermath of the Sixteenth Street Baptist Church bombing that killed four young Black girls in 1963. "I can remember walking in that door and there was chatter, chatter, chatter; then it was like you could hear it calm down, calm down, calm down. There was just quiet. Absolute quiet."

Strangely, happily, Hudson did not think to fear being the only Black athlete in the entire dormitory. Nor did he feel apologetic for his presence. "I knew the looks that I was getting. But at the same time, I didn't ever think I shouldn't be there, because there was nothing to stop me from going to be a part of that. It was not a violent, militant, fist-in-the-air thing, but I thought, 'You're not going to bother me.'"

The statement made by his presence met with immediate approval when he passed around a corner to get his food. "The Black people serving were smiling from ear to ear," Hudson said. "Really, I had more food that I could eat on that plate." The next year, when he broke his wrist, Black food service workers cut up Hudson's steaks for him.

Later that semester, while players were in the dining hall for an evening snack of fruit, milk, and peanut butter and jelly or bologna sandwiches, Coach Bryant offered Hudson an unspoken but incontrovertible gesture of acceptance. The freshman had gone through the food line, trailed by three basketball teammates, and sat down alone. Suddenly Bryant, a large and fearsome man with what journalist Clyde Bolton described as "the temperament of a car alarm," entered the dining hall, cut to the head of the food line, and then headed toward Hudson. "He came to my table and he said, 'Can I sit here?' And I'm like, 'Uh, yes, sir.' *Bryant Hall.* Can you sit here? I said, 'Yes, sir, you can sit here.' That was the longest peanut butter and jelly sandwich I ever had. That peanut butter, I couldn't get it down because nobody else came to the table.

"Everybody saw it. Everybody. All the football guys. That was the talk the next day. 'Man, what were you and Coach Bryant talking about over there?' I was trying to eat that sandwich as fast as I could and get this thing out of the way. But when that happened, what did that tell everybody else?"

Apparently the message got through. Senior football players annually initiated freshmen athletes, basketball players included, with a paddling and other punishments. Hudson admitted the prospect "terrified" him after the treatment induced crying from John Hannah, an imposing offensive lineman subsequently inducted into both the college and pro football halls of fame. Summoned to the room of senior Danny Ford, later head football coach at Clemson and Arkansas, Hudson was ordered to bend over. As he awaited the paddle's sting that would usher him into the "A Club," Hudson contemplated bolting the room. Ford didn't make it easy. He tapped the frightened youngster lightly a few times on the rump, paused pregnantly, then smacked the bed as hard as he could. "I almost jumped out of the window," Hudson said. Mercifully, that was as tough as it got.

But tolerance differed from respect. Respect was earned on the basketball court, where fellowship in toil was a great equalizer. "I think a lot of racism is ignorance on both parts," Alford said. "If you don't know about somebody, you feel uneasy about them. But let me tell you something: When you sweat and work your ass off with somebody, knock heads with them every day all day, then [the uneasiness] goes away. You know them real well."

Hudson also earned his place by bringing to bear an extraordinary array of gifts and talents that translated into victory. For instance, though he was not a great shooter he became a superior scorer, increasing his average each year on the varsity. "He was very unselfish," Ellis said. "Wanted to win, wanted to do what it took to win. Very team-oriented. He just knew what to do on the floor, knew how to get open."

Hudson averaged 15.5 rebounds and 18.4 points as Alabama's freshman team finished first in the SEC in 1969–70. Teammates insisted, with some amusement, that Hudson successfully lobbied Newton for dispensation to simply go and get the ball during games, rather than bother with painstakingly boxing out to gain position. "He could just flat jump," Alford said. "I used to tease him, because I used to think I could score against anybody. C. M. said I couldn't guard anybody but I could score. I told Wendell, 'It's not fair. You don't have to have a move. All you have to do is turn around and jump.' That's what he did. He played a lot inside at 6-6. He was just something."

Freshman year also provided Hudson's white teammates with a crash course in bigotry. There were nasty scenes at Auburn, Mississippi State, and especially Ole Miss. Hudson recalls playing only a few minutes at Oxford before fouling out in questionable circumstances. That left the only Black athlete in the building within easy hearing distance of students for a prolonged period of time, and they let fly with a torrent of racist verbal abuse. "We were all ready to go in the stands," Alford said. "Hud could take all that crap. It made us madder than it made him. I'd never heard people talk like that to anybody for any reason." Hudson knew better than to react. "He just let it run off his back," Ellis said.

The next year, while sidelined with a broken wrist, Hudson accompanied the team everywhere except to the University of Mississippi. "After going to Ole Miss, when we're talking about bad, there were scales of 1 to 10. If you've been to 10, everything else just ain't that bad." Newton told the story of a ride home from Ole Miss on which Hudson asked the driver to stop once the bus crossed into Alabama. "I thought he was sick," the coach said. "Instead, he got out, got on his knees, and kissed the ground. 'I've never been so happy to be back in Alabama,' he said. Our players cracked up." Hudson could not corroborate the improbable story.

Hudson believes the freshman visit to Oxford, unpleasant as it was, had long-lasting benefits for him and his teammates. "It probably brought Paul [Ellis] and the rest of us together, because [the Ole Miss fans] called me every name in the book, and they started talking about Paul and them. All of a sudden, I think my teammates realized, 'You know, these people are really sick.' I can remember them turning around and they were like, 'Man! We're sorry. This is unbelievable.' I was like, 'I'm sorry for y'all. I've heard this stuff. They're throwing this at y'all now.'"

Hudson was acutely aware that Ellis hailed from Selma, as did classmate Glenn "Goober" Garrett. Selma was by some reckonings the heart of racial darkness in Alabama. Between 1882 and 1913, there were 19 lynchings in Dallas County, where Selma is the county seat. Whites burned down the town's first school for Black children in the 1890s. Selma was the center of the White Citizens' Council movement in the state during the 1950s and early 1960s. There were more than 15,000 African Americans of voting age in Dallas County in 1963, but fewer than 250 were registered to vote.

After the murder of a local Black activist involved in voter registration efforts, civil rights leaders gravitated to Selma to dramatize the plight of

African Americans seeking enfranchisement. They planned a 54-mile march from Selma to Montgomery, the state capital, to petition Governor Wallace for protection of those trying to exercise their democratic right to select public officials. The route would pass through Lowndes County, where, upon threat of death, to that point none of the 5,122 voting-age Black residents had attempted to register during the 20th century.

Similar disenfranchisement permeated the South. Rights granted after the Civil War were stripped beginning in the 1890s as "Black Codes" and Jim Crow segregation swept the region. The 1896 Supreme Court case of *Plessy v. Ferguson*—with the majority opinion written by Henry Billings Brown, a Yale graduate—affirmed the legality of a "separate but equal" delineation in society that often was enforced with brutal thoroughness. "Most of the American laws defining race are not to be compared with those once enforced by Nazi Germany, the latter being relatively more liberal," author Stetson Kennedy remarks bitterly in *Jim Crow Guide*.

By 1910 African Americans were disenfranchised in most Southern states. Poll taxes were a favorite tactic to discourage Black voting. All-white primaries and grandfather clauses that restricted voting to those whose relatives were eligible prior to the abolition of slavery further limited African-American participation. Literacy and interpretation tests (including near-impossible questions such as the number of windows in the White House) also were used to turn away Black would-be voters. But simple intimidation worked best, from evictions to loss of credit to fatal beatings. As future Georgia governor Eugene Talmadge declared in the late 1940s, "I done decided the best way to keep the niggers from voting is to let all the white folks vote, and then pass the word around that Mister Nigger is not wanted at the polls."

On March 7, 1965, some 600 interracial marchers approached Selma's humpbacked Edmund Pettus Bridge, on which rust bled mutely from the name spelled high above the four-lane travelway. The marchers' route across the Alabama River was blocked by state troopers dispatched by Wallace, along with local police and vigilantes organized for the occasion. Ordered to stop, the marchers were immediately set upon by mounted and dismounted men who gave a great Rebel yell and charged into the crowd leading dogs, firing tear gas, and swinging billy clubs, bullwhips, ropes, and rubber tubing wrapped in barbed wire. "Get those God-damned niggers!" shouted Sheriff Jim Clark. "And get those God-damned white niggers."

Alabama had once again inadvertently advanced the nation's civil rights agenda on what came to be called "Bloody Sunday." Over the ensuing hours all three national television networks repeatedly showed scenes from the grotesque melee, reaching some 48 million viewers. According to Dan Carter, author of *The Politics of Rage*, "No past incident, not even the Birmingham church bombing, prepared Wallace and his acolytes for the scathing attacks from the national media that followed the Pettus Bridge beatings."

The unprovoked attack galvanized national support for the Voting Rights Act, which became federal law within months. "Selma reflected the apex of a startlingly short-lived moment where the lines between good and evil, right and wrong, seemed as stark as the great bluffs above the Alabama River, and the prospects for shimmering, incandescent, healing change seemed just over the horizon," notes Peter Applebome in *Dixie Rising*.

Ellis returned to Selma in adulthood, selling insurance from an office on Broad Street, a wide thoroughfare piercing a vibrant downtown rich in historic structures and possessed of a timeless quality, with angled on-street parking, a drugstore that sells hot peanuts by the bag, and folks who look you in the eye and nod as they pass on the sidewalk. "We get a lot of bad press, but our relations here are real good from a racial standpoint," Ellis said. "Every time you pick up a newspaper out of town, they come down here to write bad articles about us. I'm sorry, but I call it the liberal press. This town doesn't have near the problems other towns have. Not even close."

Yet as recently as 2001, a controversy raged in Selma over the placement of a statue of Nathan Bedford Forrest, the noted Confederate general, slaughterer of black Union troops at Fort Pillow, defender of Selma in the Civil War's dying days, and founder of the Ku Klux Klan. (A 2001 story in the *Montgomery Advertiser* conceded only that Forrest was "accused" of ordering the massacre and "helping lead" the Klan.) Moving the five-ton statue to the edge of an integrated housing project already named for Forrest struck many African Americans as strikingly insensitive, whereas many whites saw it as inconsequential. "That's Selma," said angry native Mary Johnson, who worked in the Voting Rights Museum just around the corner from the Pettus Bridge. The city council eventually paid for the statue to be moved, and the publisher of the local newspaper bemoaned the incident in print as "another PR nightmare for Selma."

Back in 1970, Hudson wondered about Ellis as the two huddled together on the bench at Ole Miss beneath a barrage of racial invective. Civil rights became intimately personal that day for a teammate who had spent his life separated from African Americans in school, sports, and social activities. "I'm quite sure, knowing Paul was from Selma, that he didn't really know anybody who was that affected. It was always other people," Hudson said. "Well, now I'm your teammate. You get to know me. I'm a person like you, and I have feelings and we all sweat out here together. I'm not an abstract now. I'm really a person here with you. How is that going to affect me, and how is that going to affect you? Are we going to have any kind of relationship?"

Tellingly, the bonds forged in those years endured a lifetime. Alford, Ellis, Hudson, and Leon Douglas stay in touch. They can discuss racial issues with the sober weight of middle age, or slip easily into the teasing banter common within teams and other male circles. "We just had a great, great respect for each other and still do," Alford said. "Wendell Hudson is still one of my very best friends." During his interview for this book, Alford phoned Hudson to report that a writer was coming by to discuss their Alabama days, noting, "I was going to talk about this Black sonofabitch that I had to play basketball with."

Alford also laughingly recalled an incident when the racial tables were turned. Players from Stillman College, a Black junior college in Tuscaloosa, called Hudson and asked the Alabama star to bring some players to their gym for a pickup game. "So Wendell picked Leon Douglas, Charlie Cleveland, Ray Odom, and Paul Ellis and me. A kid from Selma, Alabama—a carrot top from Selma—and me. Of course we got in the car to ride over, and right away he said, 'You've got to get in the backseat.'"

Traveling in Tuscaloosa was not entirely safe for a young African-American male. Ronald Coleman, the first black scholarship athlete at the University of Florida, recalled his reception at a restaurant in Tuscaloosa as "the most obvious, the most blatant act of racism I was confronted with." In town for a track meet during the early 1970s, Coleman and teammates endured a rifle-wielding threat at the restaurant and a chase back to their motel by several cars filled with whites.

C. M. Newton's family also discovered the limits of Tuscaloosa tolerance. Abuse was heaped upon his eldest daughter, who was just entering high school when the family resettled in Alabama. "She didn't bring it home to me or to her mother, so I didn't know about it" at the time, Newton said. "Deb does not have very good feelings toward Tuscaloosa to this day." Newton insisted he was no pioneer and "wasn't trying to be a sociologist." Yet he remained steadfast while his family suffered and he received abusive letters from fans and opprobrium from colleagues.

Coaches who later recruited African Americans told him he would ruin the league. They also questioned the feasibility of disciplining Black players. "Everybody talked about that," Newton said. "I think if you're a coach and you're going to believe that kind of stuff, then you are probably going to coach that way. I never believed it. I believed players are players. They will pretty much do what's expected of them, provided they understand the expectations going in. That's true whether they're Black or white or green or whatever." Dick Davis, an assistant coach at Florida, told Newton, "You did the best job in this league recruiting [African-American athletes], disciplining them, and playing together."

Newton also carefully steered a course that protected members of the Crimson Tide from off-court incidents such as befell Florida's Coleman. "I never wanted my players to be put in embarrassing situations, bad situations," said Newton, who went on to coach at Vanderbilt and to serve as athletics director at Kentucky, where he hired Tubby Smith, the first Black basketball coach in school history. "I'd grown up in the South. I knew what it was like. I wasn't naive to the world around me. I wasn't going to be dictated to by that, either."

Alabama's travel arrangements were not left to the team trainer, an assistant coach, or an athletics department functionary, as is ordinarily the case. Rather, the head coach handled the team's affairs personally. He would phone ahead, identify himself, and then probe for potential trouble. "'We're going to be coming through Columbus, Mississippi, and we want to eat at your place,'" he said by way of example. "'We've got six Black players. Is that a problem for you?' And if it was a problem for them, I just thanked them and wrote them off."

Newton also closely monitored crowd behavior on the road, particularly the first season Hudson was at Alabama. The varsity and freshman teams traveled together. Assistant John Bostick coached the freshmen, which allowed Newton to sit behind the 'Bama bench before joining his squad at halftime. At Ole Miss and Auburn, where sizable football players led the verbal assault, he recalled going directly to the athletics directors to enlist assistance in halting "a hell of a lot of abuse."

Newton's sensitivity, attention to detail, and commitment to his players was not lost on Hudson. "I played for the right person," he said. "I think he was a special person at that time. I think he did think through a lot of things that a lot of other people didn't think through, and I think he was bound and determined to do it the right way himself if he was going to be a part of doing it. I think he wanted to win basketball games, and I think this was a way he thought he could. I think he asked himself, 'Now, what effect is this going to have on these young men that are going to come in here? How am I going to make sure that their experience can be as good as possible?' I don't think there's any question about that."

In turn, the coach credits Hudson with paving the way for integration at Alabama. "He helped a great deal, the experience he had. He's the one who made that experience. You can say it was a racially charged time, but Wendell just sailed through."

The Alabama varsity was 8–18 in 1969–70, Newton's second season, doubling the victory total of his debut effort. All but one win came at home. The low point came at archrival Auburn, where coach Bill Lynn let John Mengelt stay in the game to score 60 points in a 121–78 rout. The freshman squad offered hope for the future, finishing 15–9. Hudson led the group in rebounding and was second in scoring.

Hudson, Ellis, Alford, and company joined the varsity for the 1970–71 season. The team finished 10–16 but was 6–6 when Hudson, the leading scorer and rebounder, was lost for the year with a broken wrist he incurred while attempting to block a shot. Considering the school's predilection for football, it was inevitable that a basketball media guide later described the injury as pertaining to "the same bone that former Alabama quarterback Joe Namath broke last year while playing with the New York Jets."

With a healthy Hudson in 1971–72, Alabama achieved the first of nine consecutive winning seasons. The 1972 club finished third in the SEC and was 18–8, the most wins by the Tide since 1956, when Johnny Dee's Rocket Eight were SEC champions (and declined an NCAA bid lest they face an opponent with a Black player on the squad). Newton was voted the 1972 SEC Coach of the Year, an honor bestowed again in 1973, 1975, and 1976. The 1972 Alabama squad beat Kentucky, making Newton the only former Adolph Rupp player to direct a team to victory over his ex-mentor. The Tide also swept Auburn for the first time since 1956, a year the games were played on a neutral court in Montgomery.

Hudson was voted to the 1972 first team all-conference squad, an honor he duplicated in 1973. Through the 2021–22 season he still ranked seventh in Alabama history in field goal accuracy (53.4 percent), third in points per game (19.2), and second in rebound average (11.9).

Hudson's rebounding and shot-blocking (not a recorded statistic during his career) were special strengths that often left opponents and teammates marveling. It wasn't merely that Hudson jumped high. He had the ability to calibrate his leaps and to adjust, sometimes in midair, as the occasion demanded. "If he needed to get 20 inches off the ground to get it, that's all he'd do," Ellis said. "If he needed to get 36 inches, he always jumped as high as he had to. He'd go in for a shot inside, and no matter who was guarding him, he'd always just elevate a little higher. It was unbelievable."

Alford said the only collegiate player of a similar size who could jump like Hudson was North Carolina State's David Thompson, nicknamed "Skywalker." The guard remembered an instance in which Hudson jumped across the lane and snatched an opposing 7-footer's hook shot out of the air with both hands. Len Kosmalski, the 7-footer in question, certainly remembered. "He caught it about a foot above the basket," said the former Tennessee center. "He sure did."

Alford contended Hudson's most remarkable moment came at Auburn. "They had Henry Harris. Henry was on one side, and he stole the ball and was heading down to the basket this way, and Wendell was on the other side of the floor," Alford said. "Wendell jumped to block Henry's shot. He's 6-6. He hit his head so hard on the rim going up that it cut the top of his head. Knocked him on the ground."

That aerodynamic excellence, for all its occasional hazards, always thrilled Mildred Hudson. She loved to watch her son play at Parker High, and she and relatives from Birmingham drove regularly to Tuscaloosa to witness similar performances for the Crimson Tide. In the process, Hudson's mother quickly shifted from dread to enjoyment regarding the University of Alabama.

Her own experience was that "nobody was ever snarly. When I would go down there, they didn't look at it that I was colored." Often she sat with Ellis's parents. She also found peace because of Wendell's unwavering reaction to his surroundings. "I didn't ever hear him complain about the school, and that helped a whole lot," she said. "Maybe if I had heard him complain, 'Well, they're doing this to me, they're doing that,' I would have pulled him from down there. But I never did hear him groan the whole time he was down there."

Of course there are things a son will not tell his mother. Hudson kept largely to himself the burden of occasional snubs in the dormitory and of more frequent difficulties in the classroom. "I would say, if I was being militant it would be in the classroom because there were just some people that didn't want to admit that I was there. They wanted to talk about subjects and say things in a way they had been saying it for years. I'm sitting in there, and I'm thinking, 'Wait a minute, that's offensive to me. Hey, look here! I'm here!'"

For example, a history professor told a class that "'Nigras'—he didn't say niggers—'were better off in slavery.'" Hudson said. "I'm thinking, 'Hey, you're crazy! Absolutely.'" Hudson said he argued with professors over such remarks and refused to drop classes even when it was "blatant" that he was not wanted.

But not even ingrained racism could withstand the magnetic attraction of success and stardom that enveloped Hudson's career. His senior season, Alabama tied for second in the SEC and advanced to postseason play. Hudson was named an All-American and was voted 1973 SEC Player of the Year, the first African American so honored.

Several unusual supporters accompanied the team to New York for the 1973 NIT. Bear Bryant had become a regular at the end of the Alabama bench during road trips, and he postponed spring football practice in order to accompany the basketball squad. Mildred Hudson also went to the tournament. Her employer paid for the first airplane flight of her life as a gift, and her coworkers collected meal money for her. The basketball was good, but New York proved a bit of a disappointment. She expected "a beautiful place" but found danger instead. "They drive too fast, and there are too many cars on the road up there for me," Ms. Hudson said.

The racial composition of the Alabama squad was the early story in New York. Typical was a questioner who asked Newton, as he recalled, "How can you, coming from a state where George Wallace stood in the schoolhouse door, start four Black players? How is that?" Newton became irritated and declared that the real question ought to be how his homegrown team could possibly compete against Manhattan College, its first-round opponent, given that New York was, he said, "the mecca of high school basketball."

Then he rashly predicted the Tide would win, a result achieved only when Glenn Garrett hit a jumper at the horn for the final 87–86 margin. A win followed over a Minnesota squad Newton says was "one of the best college teams I had seen," featuring Jim Brewer and Dave Winfield. In the semifinals Virginia Tech ousted Alabama, 74–73. North Carolina topped the Tide decisively in the third-place game, and Hudson's college playing career was over.

An all-Black Alabama squad won the SEC title in 1974, the season after Hudson and his class graduated. The 1975 squad earned an NCAA berth,

Alabama's first. 'Bama went to the national tournament again in 1976 with what Newton considers his best unit in 34 years as a coach, but ran into undefeated Indiana in the Mideast Regional semifinal. All three seasons, the Tide won or tied Kentucky for first in the SEC race, a feat unmatched in school history.

Looking back on his days at Tuscaloosa, which concluded in 1980, Newton says he is proudest of building the program with in-state talent. The coach became close with several players from his early Alabama teams. When the recently widowed Newton was inducted into the Naismith Basketball Hall of Fame in 2000 as a "contributor," he invited Hudson and a few others to share in the moment.

Hudson was the 30th player chosen in the 1973 NBA draft, taken in the second round by the Chicago Bulls. He stuck only a year before injury ended his playing career. He then returned to Tuscaloosa to work for Newton as an assistant coach. Later Hudson served in a similar capacity at North Alabama, Ole Miss (no hard feelings), Rice, and Baylor before becoming the head women's basketball coach and golf coach at McLennan Community College in Waco, Texas. Eventually he advanced to director of athletics. After 18 years at the junior college, he took a job at his alma mater in November 2003.

That made it easier for Hudson to visit his mother who still lived in the West End neighborhood of Birmingham, where until it closed in 2011 the all-Black elementary school was named, despite local protest, for Robert E. Lee. (The KKK klavern in Birmingham also was named after the commander of the Confederate Army of Northern Virginia.) As of 2022, about three-quarters of the students in the city school system were Blacks, whites having fled integration en masse. That was the sixth-highest concentration of Blacks in an Alabama public school system; Selma ranked fourth. "Black children can grow up here without ever encountering white people except a teacher or someone waiting on you in a store," said Phyllis Hancock Cooper of the Birmingham Civil Rights Institute.

De facto segregation has outlived George Wallace, "a dark poltergeist" and classic demagogue, according to biographer Marshall Frady. Three years before he died, Wallace traveled to Selma to apologize to African Americans gathered to commemorate the 30th anniversary of Bloody Sunday. Calling his listeners "my friends," Wallace said, "Those were different days and we all in our own ways were different people."

Up the road at Tuscaloosa, Foster Auditorium, where Wallace first stepped onto the national stage, got a new plaque in 2004 commemorating "The Site of the Stand in the Schoolhouse Door." In 2005 the building was designated a National Historic Landmark. In 2006 it was sealed due to structural instability.

The hopeful view is that Wallace stood against an inexorable tide—within a decade Hudson and teammates used Foster for afternoon pickup games with Black players from Stillman College while the Crimson Tide played at 15,383-seat Coleman Coliseum.

CHAPTER 7
PIPE DREAM

Norwood Todmann, Wake Forest University, 1966–70

Being black is to watch whites look upon my natural hair, my mustache, my African garments, my black music and literature, my black community language, and my other symbols of black pride as being deviant.

F. D. Harper, *Journal of College Student Personnel*

Grown men cried when they spoke of Norwood Leroy Todmann.

They cried because he was the best of them, admired and followed, and now he is lost. "He's the guy who would set the tone for us as a group, even people who were older than Tod. He was a fighter, a unique guy, a smart man," says Gilbert McGregor, a younger Black teammate at Wake Forest. "That's why it hurts me so much to know what has happened to him, because he was a special guy."

They cried because he earned respect at an early age and seemingly transcended the limitations of a difficult Harlem upbringing, only to succumb to the gravitational pull of crack cocaine, according to his friends. "When I think of him as an individual, I lose it," said Ernie Morris, an older friend from New York. "One day you're rolling sevens; the next day you're crapping out. It brings tears to my eyes. He was a good guy."

They cried because he was a proud exemplar of traits that an increasingly self-conscious Black community sought to cultivate during the late 1960s, and now they said he was reduced to living on the streets of New York, haunting homeless shelters and washing auto windshields at traffic lights. Perhaps the demands of being the first African-American basketball player at Wake Forest took their toll on Todmann, as they did on other pioneering Black

147

athletes throughout the South. Certainly the dreams that brought Todmann to Winston-Salem did not bear the anticipated fruit. Not for him, anyway.

McGregor choked up as he recalled Todmann's house arrest in the mid-1980s, the time spent at halfway houses trying to shake a drug habit. "I just thought, 'Not Tod!' Because I looked up to him and his logic and his wisdom and his determination. Not Tod! But that's the one lesson, if anybody's going to learn—drugs don't respect your personality, don't respect your drive, and don't respect your wisdom. If you take them, they can take you. And I guess they took Tod, and that hurts me. I don't know how much the Wake Forest experience led to that."

Charlie Davis, who grew up a block from Todmann in the Harlem River housing projects, said his friend was a perverse victim of his own self-confidence. "He knew, as I knew, that we had never known anybody who messed with the [crack] pipe and came out all right. Now, one of the things about Tod is that he thought he was capable of doing things that others couldn't do. 'I know all about it, I understand, I can handle it.' And he couldn't."

Davis first encountered Todmann in a "biddy" youth basketball league, when the guard scored 73 points for an opposing team in a 32-minute game. Davis and Todmann became friends, measuring their games against each other at "the Pit" in their neighborhood and on other playgrounds around New York.

Davis, the first African American to be named basketball Player of the Year in the Atlantic Coast Conference, attended Wake Forest in part at his older friend's recommendation. "Ultimately, it was Tod who said, 'Charles, don't worry; you'll be fine down here,'" Davis said. "That just shows the level—where he was as compared to where I was. If Tod said it was OK, it was OK."

Neither player anticipated that Davis's presence would cost Todmann his place in the Demon Deacon lineup. At 6-foot-3, Todmann was 2 inches taller than Davis. Both were listed as 180-pound guards. Both were similarly limited defensively. But Davis possessed superior offensive skills—his 24.94-point career average and 51 points in a game against American University in 1969 remain Wake Forest standards. So Todmann became a bench-warmer by his senior season, his diminished role a lingering sore point among his African-American teammates.

Changes in court time apparently did not disrupt relationships away from basketball. Prior to Todmann's senior year, he hired Davis, McGregor, and other players from Wake Forest and traditionally Black Winston-Salem Teachers College (now Winston-Salem State University) to help run a summer basketball program for disadvantaged youths. "He wanted to promote pride in the communities of the poor and motivate those who had not been previously motivated," Davis said.

A grant proposal written by Todmann secured federal funding for "Athlete-to-Resident," modeled after New York's highly successful Rucker League. Holcomb Rucker, a New York Department of Parks employee, started his program in Harlem in 1946. According to Nelson George in *Elevating the Game,* Rucker believed that "sport was one of the quickest tickets out of the ghetto for African-Americans, and even lesser players would, through sport, learn positive lessons in life that would aid them in rejecting crime, alcohol, and drugs." Todmann directed the staff and competitions in Winston-Salem, overcoming resistance from some city functionaries along the way. He also managed to attend summer school at Wake Forest, passing two courses.

Then, on the eve of the program's championship game, Todmann's mother fell ill and quickly died. Her appendix had ruptured, reportedly after her ailments were misdiagnosed. Todmann insisted on fulfilling his responsibilities to the youngsters in the program, maintaining a facade of calm command that made a lasting impression on Davis and McGregor. "He handed trophies to all those kids, and then he went to bury his mother," McGregor offered. "I said, 'I don't know a man who is stronger than that.' I'd never seen anything that strong."

That Todmann demonstrated such inner strength and had so much else going for him, only to fall by the wayside in later years, remains a source of puzzlement to friends.

"If you asked me in the recruiting process who 30 years later would be at the head of the class, I would have said Norwood Todmann," said television analyst Billy Packer, who as a Wake assistant brought Todmann south from New York. "Considering his background, his creativity, his academic background as well as ability, his gift of gab, his social grace . . . If you said to me, 'Billy, which of these guys will be the most financially successful?'—and I don't just mean ACC guys—I would have said Norwood Todmann. He may have been one of those guys who had too much street smarts to blend it all together."

Street smarts were hardly the currency of exchange at Wake Forest, a small, coeducational, Baptist-affiliated school that struggled for years to come to terms with dancing among undergraduates and athletic contests on Sundays. For 122 years the college was located in the town of Wake Forest, off the beaten path north of Raleigh, the North Carolina state capital. So unimposing was the intimate campus that, according to legend, football coach D. C. "Peahead" Walker landed Bill George, the school's first All-American and a pro football Hall of Fame inductee, by taking him to Duke on his 1947 recruiting visit. "Wait a minute," George supposedly said upon arriving to enroll at Wake Forest. "This is not the place that the coach showed me." Walker reportedly replied, "I was showing you our west campus. This is the east campus; you go to school here two years, and then you move over to the other campus."

That assertion was less far-fetched than it might seem, for Wake Forest has occupied two campuses. Heirs to the Reynolds tobacco fortune successfully offered 325 acres on a former family estate and an annual contribution to entice the school to relocate in June 1956 to Winston-Salem, about 100 miles to the west. By 1967 Wake Forest was a full-fledged university. Later it dropped its religious affiliation.

College president Harold Tribble was charged with executing the move to the newly constructed campus, among the more impressive metamorphoses in the annals of modern American higher education. "The decision divided every constituency of the institution—students, faculty, alumni, trustees—and the only way it could be accomplished was by his unswerving determination," said Thomas Hearn, Wake Forest president from 1983 to 2005. "There were a lot of people made angry by a lot of things that he did, but to think that they could accomplish that, with all of the financial and cultural and religious and political issues involved, was remarkable." The transformation, executed to the accompaniment of a four-page spread in *Life* magazine, took years to plan and cost $19 million, more than triple the original estimate.

When Wake Forest was transplanted to the Triad, an area that includes Greensboro and High Point, Winston-Salem (the Moravian settlement of Salem joined with the town of Winston in 1913) was the state's second-largest city and leading industrial center, thanks to Hanes hosiery and Reynolds's Camel cigarettes. (The Winston-Salem metro area was fifth-most populous in the state in 2022.) The school's move coincided with rising campus debate over integration. A 1957 vote by the Wake student legislature rejected by a three-to-one margin a resolution calling for a color-blind admissions policy. A year later an editorial in the *Student,* a campus maga-

zine, drew statewide attention and echoed divinity students and faculty at
Duke by declaring that the school, "if it is to continue to call itself an intel-
lectual and Christian center for education, must integrate." The magazine's
stance was in keeping with a largely ignored 1955 resolution by the Baptist
State Convention of North Carolina calling for an end to racial discrimination in Baptist-affiliated colleges.

Integration gained immediacy in early 1960 as Wake Forest undergrads
joined Black college and high school students in lunch counter sit-ins. The
nonviolent movement, which within a few months spread to 54 cities in nine
states, was ignited on February 1 at the 66-seat, L-shaped Woolworth's
counter in Greensboro. By late February there was a sit-in at Woolworth's
in nearby Winston-Salem, and on May 25 that city became the first in
North Carolina in which local merchants signed an agreement desegregating lunch counters. The Wake students' actions in support of integration
brought celebrity status among campus peers and prompted a vote by the
Wake student legislature to endorse the acceptance of African-American
applicants. The stance was distinctly at odds with overall student body sentiment; in a poll taken that spring, Wake Forest undergraduates decisively
rejected integration.

The board of trustees voted in 1961 to accept Black students in summer
school and graduate programs, but they resisted opening the undergraduate
level. The trustees reversed field a year later, prodded by what Hearn called
a form of inspired blackmail. A group of students formed the African
Student Program, raised money to bring Edward Reynolds from Ghana to
North Carolina, and then pressured the college to live up to its ideals. As
Hearn summarized approvingly, the students demanded, "How could we be
sending missionaries around the world to convert people to Christianity and
then fail to open our doors to them?"

Wake's doors finally opened to undergraduate admission "regardless of
race" in late April 1962. According to Bynum Shaw, author of *The History
of Wake Forest College*, the school was the first major private college in the
South to integrate its student body. The open-door policy took effect about
a month after the basketball team's first (and to date only) visit to the Final
Four, with a squad led by All-ACC center Len Chappell and guards Billy
Packer and Dave Wiedeman. Packer, the son of a coach, came south from
Pennsylvania to play for Horace "Bones" McKinney and soon grew accustomed to seeing newspaper write-ups about his Demon Deacon squad, a
power in the ACC. The Deacons went to the conference tournament final

every year from 1960 through 1964, advancing to NCAA competition in 1961 and 1962.

Occasionally there were also modest stories in the Winston-Salem newspapers about another team in town, and about a player named Cleo Hill. "I didn't even know where Winston-Salem State was," said Packer, whose given name is Anthony William Paczkowski. "So I'm reading the box scores, and one time I picked up the paper, it was a Friday night, and I see Winston-Salem State's going to be playing against, I think it was Tennessee State. I said, 'I think I'll hitchhike over there and watch the game.' It wasn't to me like some breakthrough of racial relations between Wake Forest and Winston-Salem State."

Packer was naive. Whites and Blacks throughout the South still largely populated separate realms. That was certainly true in North Carolina, even with its reputation for racial moderation. "North Carolina's progressivism consisted primarily of its shrewdness in opposing racial change," argued William Chafe in *Civilities and Civil Rights*. "The idea of 'excellent race relations' revealed much about the psychological needs of white people . . . Most contact between whites and Blacks occurred in situations shaped by a gross power imbalance that made impossible any forthright exchange of views." Chafe's book focuses on Greensboro, the first city in the South to announce it would comply with the decision in *Brown v. Board of Education,* only to take 17 years to actually integrate its public schools.

Packer's innocent visit to a historically Black Triad campus defied that equation, much to the surprise of Clarence Gaines, the coach at Winston-Salem State. "I looked up, and there's Billy," recalled Gaines. "We didn't even have white dogs come to watch us play. I know the first time I saw him, I said, 'Here, boy, you come sit beside me here.'"

Gaines called Packer "the great sociologist," an appellation rejected by the veteran college basketball analyst, who said he simply obeyed an insatiable curiosity about the game and those who played it. The oddity of being the only white person in Winston-Salem State's crowded gym did strike Packer as he sat on the bench that night in the early 1960s. Yet his more lasting memory is of what he saw on the court.

"I was an all-conference player in the ACC, and I couldn't even play in this guy's league, against him," Packer said of Hill. "Cleo Hill was better than anybody in the ACC. There was nobody close to him. As a matter of fact, of the guys I've seen in this state, Cleo Hill was the forerunner of David

Thompson and Michael Jordan. The whole league had guys like that. Cleo and I became buddies, and we used to scrimmage against them."

Typical of a stunning number of white players from the era, Packer had not registered the fact that there were no African-American players in the ACC. "I never really thought about it. I just accepted that in the South that's the way it was." He was enlightened after overhearing a conversation between McKinney and Irwin Smallwood, a Greensboro journalist, about the ramifications and difficulties of recruiting Lou Hudson, a local African-American athlete. Hudson, also recruited by North Carolina, ultimately followed a route to basketball stardom in the Big Ten. "Things didn't move as fast as people might think," Smallwood said. "It wasn't just snapping your fingers."

McKinney contemplated recruiting Black players even before his school integrated, then pursued African-American prospects until his retirement in 1965. ACC recruiting lore has it that Lew Alcindor of New York's Power Memorial Academy narrowed his final college choices to Michigan and Wake Forest, along with eventual choice UCLA. Anticipating a campus visit, McKinney had a Wake alumnus construct a bed frame and mattress to accommodate the 7-footer. Alcindor never came; the unused bed reportedly remained in a campus closet for a quarter-century.

McKinney, a Baptist minister as well as a basketball coach, donated used equipment to Gaines's money-starved program and encouraged the informal basketball exchange that Packer precipitated with players from Winston-Salem State. "I went there all the time," Packer said. "We'd go over and practice against them, and I'd bring them over [to the Wake Forest campus]. Bones had no problem with that. We all played. We liked it. They were good competition." For years afterward, the schools scheduled unofficial scrimmages prior to the start of fall practice.

There was no trouble playing pickup ball at Winston-Salem State. The same could not be said for Wake Forest. "There were incidents," Packer said. "You've got to think of the times. That's where people were coming from in those days—not only *not* giving somebody a chance, but saying, 'You've got no business here.'" (A longtime Wake official says Packer provoked confrontations because he "rubbed a lot of people the wrong way." A second person with whom Packer worked at Wake Forest added somewhat fondly, "Billy, often wrong but never in doubt.") Soon after Packer graduated, Tribble announced that Wake Forest would actively recruit African-American athletes. The president reiterated that intention privately when the school hired Bill Tate, an assistant at Illinois, as its head football coach in January 1964. "We would like for you to recruit Black kids," Tate said he was told. "I said I had no problem with that. I planned to do it."

Few Southern schools recruited Black athletes at the time in football, basketball, or any other sport. Only Maryland, with Darryl Hill in 1963, preceded Wake Forest in employing an African-American football player.

(Hill transferred from the U.S. Naval Academy and sat out the 1962 season after signing with Maryland. An October 1963 visit to Wake's Bowman Gray Stadium proved one of Hill's most bittersweet experiences. Many of the 5,000 fans in attendance booed and ridiculed him prior to game time until Brian Piccolo, the Demon Deacons' All-ACC running back and the 1963 national rushing and scoring leader, made a point of standing visibly at Hill's side. That instantly quieted detractors. "He said he was embarrassed by the behavior of the fans," Hill said of Piccolo, whose later friendship with Chicago Bears teammate Gale Sayers, an African American, was the basis of the 1971 movie *Brian's Song.* "He said he admired what I was doing, and he and his teammates were going to play fairly.")

The struggling Wake Forest football program brought in African Americans Robert Grant and Butch Henry in 1965. The following season Kentucky had the SEC's first Black football players, Greg Page and Nat Northington.

Not until 1968 did another ACC or SEC school sign a Black football player. By then Freddie Summers, the first African-American quarterback at a historically white school in the South, was in his second season at Wake Forest. He would precede by five years the arrival of Tennessee's Condredge Holloway and Mississippi State's Melvin Barkum, the SEC's first Black quarterbacks. Such slowness was largely by design, according to the December 1966 issue of *Ebony*. "It was not stated openly, but the consensus of opinion was that tan players were not up to the mental duties demanded of a quarterback—the snap decisions, deft play-calling, and overall leadership," the magazine said.

"It's too bad Wake has not enjoyed the credit for being [almost] the first school to recruit Blacks," said Tate. "It's gone by the wayside, and people have lost sight of it. I think it's a major, major thing, and Wake Forest should claim credit for it." Two seasons after Tate was fired, a 1970 squad laden with his recruits won the school's first ACC title in football. The second came in 2006.

The path to integrating the football program was not smooth. Gene Hooks, then the school's athletics director, recalled visiting a Deacon Club in Raleigh with Tate shortly after the coach arrived. "Somebody asked Bill if he was going to recruit Black football players. He said, 'Yes, we're going to recruit them, and if the rest of the teams don't, we'll have a real good time.'" A Raleigh newspaper reported the comments, and according to Hooks subsequent Wake booster club meetings were either ill-attended or marred by dissention over the issue. Hate mail followed.

Wake Forest's integrated football squad had difficulty finding hotel accommodations on the road. Racial epithets also were hurled the players' way at several places. Bill Overton, an African-American linebacker and offensive tackle from Boston, said of a visit to South Carolina, "I remember people throwing liquor in my face when I left the field." There was also talk of death threats on a trip to Clemson. He used the circumstances to get even with a bullying team trainer, sitting conspicuously next to him on the bus. "He turned as red as a Christmas decoration," Overton said. "He was yelling and swearing at me to move."

Packer returned to Wake Forest prior to the 1965–66 season to assist McKinney, only to see his former coach resign due to substance abuse problems. Packer remained an assistant as two head coaching changes ensued. The turmoil at the top allowed Packer considerable freedom to develop his recruiting philosophy. He was keen to move his alma mater "from last to respectability" by landing the best players he could. Race, he insisted, was not a consideration.

"Wake primarily had not recruited in metropolitan areas. I said the first thing I'm going to do is go to the biggest cities. New York is the biggest city, so I get in my car and go to New York City. Power Memorial—everybody had heard of Power Memorial. It's no big research on my part. I go to the school, and I go right into the principal's office and say I want to see the transcripts of the five starters." There Packer discovered Todmann, a prolific scorer who eventually broke Alcindor's school career scoring record. Todmann was an exceptional young man with excellent grades, too. "He was a very, very articulate and very insightful kid, way beyond his age," Packer said. "He had two, three jobs in the summer. Very industrious."

Todmann looked after two younger siblings. He did not know his father, and his mother was largely occupied with feeding a drug habit. A coach said he watched Todmann's mother bring a man to the family's apartment and into her bedroom during a recruiting visit. "The thing about Tod that really set him apart from most guys was that he was a bit more mature than we were," Charlie Davis said. "In a lot of ways, even though he was only a year older, he was looked up to in the community. That's just the way he was."

Packer did not know he was recruiting Todmann to play for Jack McCloskey, who came to Wake Forest in 1966–67 after a decade as head coach at the University of Pennsylvania. He did know he had a big-time prospect from a high-powered program. "He was a shooter, a very good outside shooter. Could post up. He turned out not to be a good defender and never got stronger," Packer said of Todmann. "In this day and age, he would have been a McDonald's All-American who turned out to be just an average college player."

Both Davis and McGregor described Todmann as a smaller version of "the Big O," Cincinnati's great three-time national Player of the Year in the late 1950s. "Technically, he was a small Oscar Robertson," McGregor said. "He had a power game from the guard position. He was 6–3, which was a pretty big guard at the time. He would back you down. He would post you up. He'd shoot the little turnaround jumper."

Davis took it a step further. Todmann fancied himself "the reincarnation" of Robertson, he said. "He mimicked and attempted to do the things that the Big O would do. Tod was a good shooter who could become streaky-great. A decent ball handler. Remember, he was 6–3. He was a bit bigger than most guards, so he was able to post guys up, had lots of moves inside—head fakes, step under, layups. Good passer. He was a heck of a player. Could run the court. Prided himself on defense. Loved to be the guy that shut down people. And he understood the game."

McCloskey saw Todmann's predilections the way others do but has a less laudatory view of the result. "He liked to post up," McCloskey said. "He wasn't big enough to be in there, but he was not a good outside shooter, either. Defensively he had weaknesses."

Todmann was not a good fit for the program he joined according to Charles Scott, who knew Todmann from boyhood in Harlem. "Todmann was a little slow; he was a more methodical-type player," the North Carolina great said. "I don't think that fit Wake Forest's style, looking back on it now." Todmann's career nevertheless began on a highly promising note. He paced the 1966–67 Wake Forest freshmen with a 23.7-point average and scored in double figures in every game. The varsity, meanwhile, struggled to a 9–18 record in McCloskey's debut season, the school's third consecutive losing effort.

"He basically came down with a little swagger in his step," said Overton, the football player said of Todmann. "He was a great guy, absolutely a great guy. Tall, lanky, very focused as an athlete. Smart, intelligent. I would say he had strong convictions of what he wanted to do from a basketball perspective."

Todmann was described in the school's 1967–68 basketball media guide as "a good scorer, who will be tough to keep out of the starting lineup." He fulfilled that forecast upon joining the varsity. The sophomore became an immediate starter, finishing third on the Wake Forest squad with a 13.3-point average. He scored in double figures in nearly three-quarters of the Demon Deacons' games, and his 76.9 percent free throw accuracy ranked fifth in the ACC.

On the other side of the ledger, Todmann shot an execrable 37.4 percent from the floor and, testament to his weak defensive technique, paced the squad in fouls and was disqualified nine times. He also was thoroughly overshadowed by Scott, the other new African-American player from New York. While the Deacs plunged to 5–21 and last in the ACC in 1967–68, Scott finished among the ACC scoring leaders as North Carolina went 28–4 and reached the Final Four.

Wake Forest finished 18–9 and tied for third in the ACC the following season, the best showing of McCloskey's six-year tenure. Todmann appeared in all but one game, reducing his shot attempts and improving his field goal accuracy. Yet the shadows overtaking his career grew ever deeper. "Could improve on defense" in the 1968 media guide had become "needs to be tougher on defense" by 1969. His 11-point average was doubled by Davis, who finished fourth in ACC scoring (22.8), just ahead of Scott. Todmann's playing time waned toward the end of the season, culminating with a two-minute outing in an ACC tournament loss to the Tar Heels.

"Charlie Davis comes along, and Todmann was immediately pushed to the back because Charlie Davis is the player that they're building behind," said Scott, who had some epic shootouts with Davis in 1969 and 1970. "I think on Wake Forest's team, it wasn't meant to be for him. I don't think Todmann had the skills that would have made him stand out as much as necessary to be a star in the ACC."

Todmann was an afterthought by the 1969–70 season, appearing in 17 of 27 games as the Demon Deacons slipped to 14–13. He didn't play at all in half of the final 16 outings of the season. He scored 22 points over the last 18 games. Bighouse Gaines, who regularly harvested players like

Todmann from the ghettos of the Northeast, evinced no surprise at the holes in the Wake guard's game, particularly his offensive shortcomings. "My philosophy was, I knew the kids in the Midwest were much better shooters, and I knew the kids in New York were excellent ball handlers but couldn't hit the side of a damn barn by shooting."

This opinion did not prevent New Yorkers from counting themselves among the game's elite. "At that time, New York carried a connotation that you were the best," said Charlie Riley, a product of central Harlem who played for Gaines. "Our knowledge of the game was far-reaching. When you learn the game in New York City, you learn the fundamentals of the game. You learn to appreciate the game. There had to be others before us. We just thought it was a very simple game. It wasn't about who scored the most points or who got the most ink, because there wasn't any ink."

Packer ratified Riley's assessment, saying there was "no question" that New York City basketball was the best, creating a style molded by circumstances and exemplified by players such as Todmann. "You had to be great in the paint; you had to be creative because the court was small. The jump shot wasn't much of a factor, because a lot of times you played outside," Packer said.

Regional differences were a less compelling source of pride and prejudice than race, however. Racial tensions quickly surfaced in 1969 when Wake Forest started two African Americans in Davis and McGregor, and simmered below the surface as McCloskey failed to start a third in Todmann.

The issue of quotas remained heated as Black athletes filtered into previously segregated sports. Jerry Harkness, a member of the integrated Loyola squad that won the 1963 NCAA championship, told writer Frank Fitzpatrick, "There was an unwritten rule that you didn't take more than one or two Blacks on your team." A later rule of thumb, cited by George in *Elevating the Game,* supposedly dictated "two Blacks on court at home, three on the road, and four when behind." Former Florida coach Tommy Bartlett said he felt pressure to have three whites on the court during the late 1960s and early 1970s. In his autobiography Bill Russell asserted that in 1966, 16 years after the integration of pro basketball, "there was a quota in the NBA" dictating "that no team should have more than two Negroes— three at the most—because in the opinion of the owners it would be bad for a draw at the gate—and money, not heart, rules pro sports."

The relationship between money and race was not overlooked on college campuses, either. A 1961 Wake Forest faculty committee charged with studying "the practice of racial discrimination in college admissions" rec-ommended integration despite concluding that "the most disinterested and authoritative opinion heard by the Committee was that Wake Forest should realistically be prepared for some decline in financial support if Negroes are admitted." Sure enough, following President Tribble's 1963 announcement that Wake Forest would actively recruit Black athletes, an alumnus stated a preference for "no athletic program at all rather than an integrated one." McCloskey kept a letter he received years later from a woman "incensed that we had a couple of Black players on the floor representing Wake Forest. I couldn't believe that someone could be upset like that. It just was astound-ing to me."

Packer likewise was taken aback by an encounter with a head football coach from a conference school. The man, whom Packer would not name, approached the basketball assistant and said, "Hey, I hear you're going to a bowl next year." Packer knew the football team was struggling. "I said, 'Well, I didn't know that.' I was kind of surprised the guy would even know who I was. And I said, 'Gee, I don't know if they'll be that good, but they're improving.' And he said, 'Yeah, you're going to the Nigger Bowl.' Because he knew that I was helping to recruit Black athletes. And I thought to myself, 'How sick are you?'"

C. M. Newton certainly recognizes that his pursuit of African-American prospects went against the norms of college sports as the 1960s ended. "I think what stunned people was the fact that, not so much that we had a Black player or two Black players, but that we didn't have any quotas on how many we were going to have and how many we were going to play," he said. "That was not by design; it just so happened that the best players in our state coming along then were Black. They were interested in our program, they could do the schoolwork, and they were good people."

Unlike Newton, Packer was convinced that "the constituency that was at the universities and in the crowds" in the late 1960s would not accept a team dominated by African Americans. He therefore adopted what he calls "my own quota system" as a recruiter. "This was my own rule: I would never recruit a player and put him in a position—and I wasn't the head coach—and put him in a position where his minutes were determined by his race."

McCloskey denied having quotas in acquiring or using players, both as head coach at Wake Forest from 1967 through 1972 and in his long and highly successful career as a head coach and general manager in the NBA.

Race was not an issue, he said flatly. Recalling a 1969 conversation with a writer from Richmond, Virginia, McCloskey presents his lineup choices in a favorable (if inaccurate) historical light. "He called me and asked, 'How does it feel to start three Black players, the first time to start three Black players in the ACC?' And I said, 'Really? Who's that?' The guy said, 'Todmann and Gilbert McGregor and Charlie Davis.' I said, 'Oh, gosh, I guess you're right. I didn't notice.' That was the end of the conversation."

Davis and McGregor are less inclined to dismiss race as a consideration. "That was just the nature of the beast; that's where we were," Davis said. "They weren't ready for three Black players on the court at the same time. Jack took a lot of phone calls and got a lot of letters. I don't necessarily believe that he bowed to them, but I think he was well aware of just what was happening and wasn't ready for it. I think in some ways that colored what he chose to do. There was no way that we weren't going to be a better team if Tod had been playing rather than sitting on the bench. It didn't matter if you wanted to say that we'd get small with him out there or whatever—we were a better team with him playing. And we never could get that done."

McGregor blames everyone involved. "Norwood Todmann should have been in the backcourt with Charlie Davis," he says. "But just as I didn't step up, I don't think Charlie did, either. Because if Charlie Davis had said, 'I ain't playing unless Tod plays,' Tod would have played."

That McGregor thought in terms of ultimatum and rebellion reflects well the temper of the times. Assertions of equality gave rise to Black pride and Black power while the civil rights movement splintered in leadership, philosophy, and tactics. "Black Power," Chafe explained, "was revolutionary precisely to the extent that it rejected traditional white definitions of success, achievement, political dialogue, and social manners."

Todmann helped stimulate a sharper focus among the several dozen black men on Wake's campus. "He makes me think of Bill Russell, in that [he basically said], 'Don't worry about my appearance,'" Davis parroted Todmann, who tended to wear the same tight black shirt for days on end and to neglect combing his hair. "'Listen to what I'm saying. Look at what I'm doing, because that makes more of a statement about me than clothing. So what? I can wash up.' He measured himself in his thoughts and the things that he wanted to do more than his appearance. Tod was always really tied up in the educational thought process, the things that had to do with the mind as opposed to the outward things like clothes or material things. That wasn't what was important. Which, once again, is part of what made him seem more mature to us."

There were battles of liberation to be fought within one's own consciousness, on campus, and in the larger community. Sometimes they overlapped. The players lobbied in vain for Wake Forest to admit African-American women. "But the girls didn't bring in any money," McGregor said bitterly. "They didn't bring any Black females, and then they didn't want you to date the white girls." Both Davis and McGregor were convinced that a member of campus security followed Black players to monitor their dating habits and that a group of white girls were sent home from school for spending time with them.

Real or perceived, the treatment angered, embittered, and alienated. "They didn't care about us; they didn't care if we were special or not," McGregor said. "If we'd have been white guys with the same skills, abilities, and the same uniqueness of personalities, they'd have been all over that. That's the hurtful thing."

Wake's Black athletes fled campus with unusual enthusiasm, large young men stuffing themselves into a football player's Volkswagen and a very few other cars in search of a more familiar, welcoming world. The catchphrase following completion of classes and practice was an open-ended "If you're not there when the car cranks up . . ."

The destination of choice was Winston-Salem State. Gaines's program, a power in the all-Black Central Intercollegiate Athletic Association, relied heavily on players from the Northeast. Transporting youngsters to the segregated South might seem an unkind act, but Gaines, who grew up in Baltimore, said in fact that he offered refuge. "First of all, it was a better way of life. See, most of those kids you picked up out of the ghetto, they were living in cold-water flats. You had some kids that were not that poor, but the majority of them had no place else to go."

Then, too, the coach believed "there was more segregation in New Jersey and Pennsylvania and New York, and I don't think the kids were even conscious of it." From Newark to Baltimore to St. Louis to Las Vegas, Gaines personally endured treatment that underlined his second-class status as an African American. Others—such as Virgil Hawkins, who attempted to integrate the University of Florida law school during the mid-1950s—found prejudice among Northerners to be less overt, but in some ways more insidious. "I never knew where I was," Hawkins told journalist Al Burt of his days in Boston and elsewhere. "In the South, you always knew. It's just like walking on a carpet with a snake in it. I'd rather see the snake out there so I can hit him than to have him hiding in the carpet and I don't know when he's going to bite me."

Sometimes prejudice in the supposedly welcoming North was quite overt. White police went on strike in Detroit in 1959 when told they would have to ride in integrated squad cars. After a 1966 march for equal rights, Martin Luther King Jr. declared, "I've been in many demonstrations all across the South, but I can say that I have never seen—even in Mississippi and Alabama—mobs as hostile and hate-filled as I've seen in Chicago."

Forty percent of school children in America attended segregated schools at the time of the *Brown* decision, and change came with painful slowness that mocked the Supreme Court's admonition to proceed "with all deliberate speed." *Brown* was actually five cases rolled into one, including instances of discrimination from Kansas, Washington, D.C., and Delaware, where in 1950 the state university was forced to integrate under court order.

Once desegregation gained traction, the South reluctantly adapted. In 1968, Todmann's second year in Winston-Salem, 77.5 percent of black children in the South attended public schools that had greater than 90 percent minority enrollment. The proportion was 42.7 percent in the Northeast. By 1980 the South had only 24.6 percent of its African-American students in heavily minority schools, while in the Northeast the proportion of separated Black students *rose* to 48.7 percent in 1980 and to 49.9 percent by 1992. Those trends remain evident today.

Winston-Salem was sufficiently temperate in matters of race to elect a Black city council member in 1947, the same year Jackie Robinson broke the color barrier in Major League Baseball. Yet, never to be forgotten, law and custom demanded adherence to the dictates of a segregated society. "Many whites believed that a social contract existed between the races," Stewart Tolnay and E. M. Beck argued in *A Festival of Violence.* "That contract sharply defined the limits of acceptable behavior and permitted whites to punish transgressions of those limits."

Illustrative was what happened when a Villanova squad arrived in Winston-Salem to face Wake Forest in 1960. The Wildcats' two Black players boarded the elevator at the team hotel, only to have the operator throw their luggage back into the lobby. The hotel manager told coach Alexander Severance, "If we let those niggers stay here, no white person will ever stay in the hotel again." George Raveling and his teammate spent the night at

Winston-Salem State, where Gaines was little concerned with black and white.

Gaines readily welcomed Wake Forest players to campus, especially once Packer broke the ice. The hospitality was more encompassing for African-American players. Davis fondly recalled a pickup game early in his career during which Gaines, a huge man, approached and engulfed him with a comforting arm. "He lets me know, 'Hey, it's going to be all right. If you need anything, you come on by.' And he wasn't talking about me coming to play basketball. That was just part of where you were, what it was all about. I went to school at Wake Forest. I lived at Winston-Salem State. I lived in the black community of Winston-Salem." McGregor met his wife at Winston-Salem State.

Pickup games between players from Wake and Winston-Salem State became routine. Gaines cited the intensity of the crosstown rivalry in 1967, when Wake was led by All-ACC guard Paul Long and Winston-Salem State by Earl "the Pearl" Monroe. "Paul Long would have his little crowd, and Earl Monroe would have his. They played about every night of the week. No officials. I've never seen such clean and competitive basketball. It wasn't a matter of anybody slouching off. Earl was playing Paul, and Paul was playing Earl."

The 1967 Winston-Salem State squad became the first from a historically African-American school to win an NCAA championship. "We stayed at a Holiday Inn across the street, so we just went over there to watch the game and see Earl Monroe," Maryland's Gary Williams said of a visit to Winston-Salem as a player. "He had, like, 52 points. And I'd never seen a crowd like that, in terms of the enthusiasm. I never saw such a display—he had the spins and all that stuff that nobody that I played with did."

The electrifying Monroe, also nicknamed "Black Jesus," averaged 41.5 points for the Rams en route to the College Division title. He later enjoyed a stellar career with Baltimore and New York in the NBA. "They had great players," Williams said of Winston-Salem State in the Monroe era. "They could have, if not beaten, been just as good as most of the teams in the country."

While adventuresome whites such as Packer and Williams felt comfortable visiting the Black side of town, Charlie Riley, a Cleo Hill teammate, said African Americans were apt to stay within their community. "The first day I'm in Winston-Salem I step off the curb, and a car that's in the center lane comes all the way over and almost hits me," Riley said. "That was my introduction. I said, 'Oh, shit.' Understand where I'm coming from—there was nothing that I wanted from white people in Winston-Salem. I didn't want them to cook for me; I didn't want them to cut my hair. I definitely didn't want to date their girls, so I was harmless. I wasn't a threat in any area, and my teammates were basically the same way."

Riley also thought, "If you don't want me, I don't want you. The food is probably not that good, anyway." But Wake's Black athletes cast their lot in the world of whites, and for all their discomfort they were well-rewarded for that choice.

Davis started each day at Wake Forest by playing the song "To Be Young, Gifted and Black" by Nina Simone and Weldon Irvine Jr. His fortunes were so good that he felt twinges of guilt. In contrast with family members in Harlem, none of them high school graduates, he received a university education and had nice clothes, three square meals a day, and comfortable accommodations. His brother was hit in the leg during a drive-by shooting; Davis felt quite safe from random violence among Wake's 3,000 students. Regaled during games with chants of "C. D." from admiring fans, the Wake Forest star also received illegal monetary compensation, proffered not by school officials but by boosters. "You might shake somebody's hand and have your daddy's salary for a week in your hand," Davis said. "You might come to your room and there's an envelope under your door."

Still, for any highly skilled athlete, the ultimate compensation was and remains playing time. Allocation of opportunity is a prerogative of the coach, a primary tool in building a team work ethic and a code of individual conduct on and off the court. "Kids want to play," said Pete Gillen, former head coach at Providence, Xavier, and Virginia. "It's more important than anything. It's more important than winning."

As Todmann's career advanced and his playing time diminished, it became clear that he had fallen out of favor with McCloskey. Nothing personal, said the former coach. "I just didn't think he was an outstanding player. That's the only thing I had against Norwood Todmann."

Packer had already departed Wake Forest for a career in television and private business by Todmann's senior year. His take was that Todmann never developed the key qualities required by his demanding coach, a conclusion echoed by media guide comments about the player's defensive liabilities. "He and Jack never hit it off, I don't think," Packer said. "Jack McCloskey was a tough, excellent basketball man, a real student of the game. He was very tough physically himself and was very demanding as far as toughness was concerned. And I really don't think Jack wasn't going to change, and Todmann never did fit into where he was coming from. Jack was a lot like Mike Krzyzewski in terms of toughness. You can't envision somebody playing for Mike Krzyzewski that doesn't eventually develop a toughness, or naturally have it. Because if you don't, your playing time is going to go in the other direction. There's just certain guys like that, and McCloskey was a lot like that."

McCloskey's approach was evident when a prominent player from New Jersey came to Wake Forest on a recruiting visit. Tryouts were allowed in those days, so the two assistant coaches and McCloskey arranged a pickup game against the recruit and a pair of players from campus. McCloskey insisted on guarding the visitor and testing his toughness. As soon as the prospect drove to the basket, McCloskey cut his legs out from under him, sending the youngster crashing head first to the floor. Packer was aghast. His boss was satisfied when the prized recruit stood up and resumed playing. It was a Pyrrhic victory; the player chose to attend Notre Dame.

Disputing the assessments of their former coach, Todmann's admiring teammates insisted the guard's ball handling, aggressiveness, and leadership would have made a positive difference during what amounted to a breakeven 1969–70 season.

Davis and McGregor also heard an explanation from Todmann for his reduced role that fit their notions about their friend, their coach, and their sense of embattled isolation. "Tod was getting screamed at every day in practice by Coach McCloskey his senior year, my junior year," said McGregor, fourth among career per-game rebounders (10.6) in Wake history. "I don't know what it was; something had gone wrong with their relationship. Tod came to see me one day after practice. He said, 'I just went to see Jack. I told him, you know, if I'm playing that bad that you've got to scream and holler at me all the time, just bench me. And he told me that he would.'"

Here McGregor, a former television commentator on NBA and occasional ACC broadcasts, slowed to enunciate each word carefully and distinctly: "And he never played again."

Davis essentially told the same story. He later played for McCloskey with the expansion Portland franchise in the NBA. He claims to "love Jack to death," admiring him as "the best Xs and Os guy I've ever been around." But he said Todmann crossed a line and was punished for questioning the coach's authority. "You weren't allowed to challenge," Davis says. "Pretty much Tod said, 'If you've got to yell at me that much, don't play me,' and Jack didn't play him. And we lost. We lost."

McGregor, who once regarded Todmann as a surrogate big brother, was more blunt. "There's an expression about calling 'bullshit' on somebody—when they're sitting there and feeding you all this smoke, and they're telling you all this stuff and you're supposed to go along with it. And you call 'Bullshit' and they get angry. And I think Tod must have called bullshit on Jack."

McCloskey appeared genuinely puzzled by the players' interpretations. He recalled no confrontation with Todmann, although he conceded that one could have occurred. "If I did yell, I wanted him to be a better player," the coach said.

Todmann's senior year, McCloskey was a man of 46, with a stint in the military and 19 years of coaching under his belt. He was struggling professionally in the "very, very competitive" ACC. "It was like the Big Five in Philadelphia when you were an Ivy League school," he said. "You said, 'Geez, are we ever going to win a game, let alone a championship?'" McCloskey compiled a 70–89 record in six years at Wake Forest, enjoying three winning seasons, two first-division ACC finishes, and a single winning conference record.

Beyond the arena, and bleeding into it, unrest was rampant, particularly on campus. "It sometimes seemed that the entire country was under attack from young people who rejected the rules and values of middle-class white America," author Chafe wrote. The president of Wake Forest entered the 1969–70 academic year with a temporary restraining order in hand, particulars to be filled in as needed to thwart unruly students.

Authority for its own sake, unquestioned obedience to norms, and norms themselves were under challenge throughout American society. The disciplined ranks of sports were not immune, as the Black power protest at the 1968 Olympics amply demonstrated. Maryland football players voted to dump head coach Bob Ward in 1969, and they got their way. Virginia basketball players sought to oust head coach Bill Gibson but failed. Players at Duke rebelled against the tight control exerted by head coach Raymond "Bucky" Waters.

Black basketball players at Wake Forest threatened to boycott a game to protest the playing of "Dixie" at home contests (Packer dissuaded them). They chafed at McCloskey's unwillingness to allow them to affix black patches to their basketball uniforms to demonstrate support for an African-American football player they believed was unfairly accused of cheating. "I loved that period," Davis said. "It was stimulating. It was exciting. As an African American, you were beginning to feel good about who you were."

Perhaps it was inevitable that Todmann, with his heightened sense of pride and militancy, would clash with McCloskey and his traditional world-view. Perhaps a young man unaccustomed to failure embellished the coach's private response when recounting it, aware of how his friends would react. Perhaps the older man simply did not consider the incident to be as weighty a matter as Todmann did, or as worthy of his attention.

And perhaps, as in all things spanning the American racial divide, what one person took as common language, sensibility, and custom wasn't held in common at all.

"By and large, Tod did what you said, but he would have discussions with you," Davis said. "Even today, a whole lot of white folks do not like mature or somewhat aggressive African-American males who think and do based on what they believe, as opposed to what others would have them do or believe. Take that back to 1967, 1968: You've got a young, somewhat mature African-American male . . . This guy's going to think, and then he's going to express himself. It's not going to be, 'Duh, duh.' He's going to artic- ulate it and make some sense of what he's talking about. That doesn't endear him to a whole bunch of folk, especially if you're not the main man."

Todmann graduated from Wake Forest in five years. He attended grad school at New York University and became a hospital administrator but was derailed in 1986 by a federal conviction for conspiring to distribute cocaine to an undercover police officer. Todmann, who pleaded guilty with a codefendant, was sentenced to six months in a halfway house and five years' probation. His Wake associates saw no sign in college of drug use or possession.

Todmann recently was spotted washing auto windshields on Manhattan streets in a scramble for spare change, and he sometimes wandered near a park on 145th Street where he once dazzled with a basketball. "We've all been trying to search for him, reach out to him," said Artie Georges, a long- time friend in New York. "He has separated himself from everybody."

Unfortunately, for Todmann and pioneering contemporaries such as Auburn's Henry Harris, separation proved destructive, mocking promise that once burned bright.

CHAPTER 8
PRISONER OF CHOICE

Tom Payne Jr., University of Kentucky, 1969–71

Until the lion writes his own story, the tale of the hunt will always glorify the hunter.

African proverb

There was a homey, nostalgic flavor to Central City, Kentucky, with its drive-in restaurant selling "coneys and tots," railroad tracks bisecting a main business artery, a large enamel tooth announcing the presence of a dentist's office, and a busy three-chair barber shop directly across from a downtown cafe that served good, inexpensive food. Similarly out of step with the times was the town's primary claim to fame as the home of Don and Phil Everly of the Everly Brothers, a singing group that had its heyday in the late 1950s with popular songs such as "Wake Up Little Susie," "Bye Bye Love," and "All I Have to Do Is Dream."

Unhappy truths often lurk beneath the most charming of facades, and Central City was no exception. Education rates and incomes there were below average for Kentucky, and the population of approximately 5,800 reflected a decline since the 2000 census. Don Everly was actually born in nearby Brownie, which no longer exists, and Phil is a Chicago native. Other than the annual Everly Brothers Homecoming, held from 1988 through 2001, the area's claim to fame was a lynching in Livermore in 1911. A mob there grabbed Will Porter, a Black man who had shot a white resident in self-defense, and took him from the jail to the local opera house. Admission was charged to witness his agonizing death, with customers in pricey orchestra seats repeatedly shooting at his dangling body.

Nearly half of Kentucky's lynchings occurred here in the western part of the state, where African Americans were most numerous. To its credit, nine years after Porter's death Kentucky became the first Southern state to pass anti-lynching legislation.

Modern punishment is more orderly and civilized, and a source of needed economic development. Nearly 1,000 prisoners could be housed at the $34 million Green River Correctional Complex, built in 1994 out River Road in the countryside just beyond Central City. The low buildings of the medium-security campus are girded by formidable double fencing, topped by ribbons of coiled razor wire that gleam brightly when sunlight hits just right, lending an illusion of warmth and motion at odds with the confined circumstances.

Tom Payne Jr., who wore inmate number 031259 at Green River, had spent more than half his life locked in similar facilities in three different states; he was past retirement age when the State of Kentucky finally releases him in 2018 from his current home, Little Sandy Correctional Complex in Sandy Hook. His was the voice of experience when he spoke of survival within prison as "an art," requiring skills more basic than anything he learned or employed as a briefly shining star on the basketball court.

"I've met all kinds of men, from the very worst that'd kill you at a heartbeat to some men that, you might not believe this, but are very noble," Payne said. "They're in prison and they've changed their lives. They're special human beings, but they just continue to be punished for whatever they did in the past." Clearly Payne, a footnote figure in a debate on race that continues to divide Kentuckians, counted himself in this category of the reformed but misunderstood. "Then you have, like I said, the opposite end of the spectrum where you have some of the most vicious, coldest, insensitive, coarse, callous—whatever you want to say—human beings that you could ever imagine. And you have to know how to walk around them and to learn to read people so you don't give them any kind of tracks that could lead them where you end up having your life took, or where you're forced to defend yourself."

The 7-foot-2 Payne retained an athlete's physique, cutting a neat, narrow-waisted figure in his prison-issue khaki uniform. He was in prison because he sexually assaulted a number of women. He thereby not only violated laws in Kentucky, Georgia, and California—committing crimes in the latter two states while on probation from a life sentence in Kentucky—but as a Black man stirred some of the South's most persistent passions. All of his victims were white.

Perhaps as compelling in some quarters, Payne's behavior embarrassed and dishonored the University of Kentucky, where he was the first African-

American basketball player. That is no small matter in a state where basket-ball is so pervasive an obsession that an obstetrician and major Wildcat booster allegedly made a habit of branding "UK" into women's uteruses before removing them during hysterectomies.

Payne, having endured many of the alienating experiences common to the game's racial pioneers, told at least one journalist that the racism he encountered at UK caused him to hate whites, producing the aggression he directed at women. "My whole life took a turn going to UK and getting damaged so much," he told Brian Bennett in an April 2001 interview in the Louisville *Courier-Journal*. "My anger and hatred toward white society came up, and I lashed out. It was never about sex or violence with me."

Payne later retreated from that statement, though not entirely. "You never hear any person apologize for racism," he said. "A lot of people are really trying to justify that there was no racism, that Kentucky wasn't racist. And it's a historical fact that Kentucky was racist and there was racism."

Adding fuel to the fire, Payne's comments and conduct reflected badly upon Adolph Rupp, his legendary coach. Rupp, nicknamed "the Man in the Brown Suit" because he always wore the same color-coordinated ensemble on the sidelines, won four national titles, 27 Southeastern Conference cham-pionships, and 876 games in 42 years directing the Wildcats. But in history's glare he became a figure of controversy, as widely remembered for his apparent resistance to integrating his powerful program as for his success on the court.

"It's like messing with an icon like Abraham Lincoln," Chester Grundy, director of multicultural student programming at UK, said of undermining Rupp's legacy. "It's comparable when you understand the importance that basketball has in the life and culture of Kentucky, and that importance in my mind is a religious kind of importance. I don't think I'm overstating it. In terms of that culture, and the kind of allure that surrounds the basketball tradition in Kentucky, Rupp is the central icon."

Members of Payne's family believe that, because his transgressions and comments offended Kentucky basketball adherents, he was punished for more than his crimes. "You don't do something to an institution like that and muddy its name," said Darrell Payne, a younger brother and former prosecutor, parole officer, and public defender. "He would be out today but for Kentucky and its grudge. If he wasn't Tom Payne, the first Black at the University of Kentucky, he'd have been out . . . I say this will all my heart. I'm no dummy. I've been around in the system."

Grundy did not go that far. But the UK graduate questioned the effort and understanding that went into selecting and supporting Payne. He insisted Payne's failure was preordained in the absence of sustained care. "If you didn't have a supportive environment here, then the prospects of being able to survive and deal with all the pressures that come with playing in the SEC at that time, that's unreal," Grundy said. "I think, had Rupp bought into the idea of it and supported Payne in all the ways he could have, then it could have been a different outcome here. I don't know if Payne was the guy to do it, but given a situation where you've got a good prospect, a good, solid student, and a solid athlete to do this, had there been a supportive environment it could have turned out different."

Payne made an immediate mark in his single varsity season at UK, becoming the first Black player voted first team all-conference at any school in the SEC. Then he turned professional, to the dismay of fans and coaches, and began a spiral that landed him in prison. For decades he was stuck in institutional amber, a forgotten man, or rather a man whom others would just as soon forget.

Oscar Combs, founder of *Cats Pause,* a publication on Kentucky basketball, derided Payne's protestations as just so many excuses meant to justify the unjustifiable. "Tom Payne, well, you know he was ahead of his time," Combs said. "Tom Payne would have fit in perfectly today because it was always 'Everybody else and not me, and if I finally got caught doing something wrong, well, it's because of the environment I came up on,' or because of this or that. It was never him. All those rapes, he wasn't guilty of any of them."

Actually, by the time Payne finished serving half of a 28-year sentence in California, he had quit denying his guilt, more or less. Eligibility for parole involved admission of his crime and undergoing counseling that included group therapy with women who had been sexually assaulted.

Only Payne's mother, Elaine, persisted in asserting her eldest child's innocence on charges of rape and attempted rape that dogged him virtually since the day he signed a professional basketball contract with the Atlanta Hawks in September 1971. And even she did so with diminishing vigor, the weight of evidence compiled in sexual assaults in three states too overwhelming to dismiss. "I believe that some things that caused him to do, maybe, some of the things that he may have done, I think was because there was a lot of pressure on him," Ms. Payne said. "I never believed he did it because . . . he was never destructive in any way. Never hit a kid. Showed no personality of being a bully. He was very compassionate and loving and very unselfish. He was the most unselfish person in the world."

Payne first earned his way as an adult playing basketball, with Atlanta and then with the minor league Louisville Catbirds. He later moved to California, where he worked variously as a bodyguard, bouncer, boxer, and actor. His greatest assets were an obedient, likable manner and a well-muscled, towering frame; his mother said his height made it easy for him to stand outside the family home and wash ground-floor windows without using a ladder. "He was built like a champ—huge, handsome, gorgeous," said a Hollywood associate quoted in the *Los Angeles Daily News*. "Women just went crazy over him."

But Payne was ill-cast for the leading role he first assumed in high school, which took him in six years from project to prodigy to pioneer to prisoner. Today, a top high school player is bombarded with information, ratings, outside advice, and a range of opportunities that create a worldliness unknown in Payne's era. He and his parents were painfully unsophisticated, with scant understanding of the demands and expectations that flowed from his choices—from Payne's embrace of the sport that catapulted him to fame and riches to his decision to become the first Black player under Rupp at Kentucky.

Complicating life in the limelight, Payne was notably shy. Yet he could not avoid drawing attention because at an early age he towered over his parents, siblings, and contemporaries. He stood 6-foot-4 by the sixth grade, 6-foot-10 by his sophomore year in high school. The growth was "like he was jumping up overnight," his mother said, causing his parents to have doctors monitor his health closely. "Tommy probably got whuppings because my father was trying to keep him under control," Darrell Payne said. "He was so big that I think that might have intimidated my father a little bit."

Corporal punishment, or the threat of it, remained the order of the day when the family moved from a military base into a five-bedroom home across West Broadway from Shawnee Park in Louisville. "My father, he had that house under control," Darrell Payne said. "When you came home in the evening, you could drop a nickel and you could hear it from the third floor. That house was clean and in order."

Thomas Payne Sr. found stability as a first sergeant in the U.S. Army, where a Black man had the rare opportunity to earn advancement in a career other than teaching or the ministry. Sergeant Payne also learned the importance of discipline, and he drummed, sometimes beat, obedience into his nine children. "He had a distant personality," Mrs. Payne said of her husband. "He was a very sweet man. He was very sweet to the children and me, but he had that personality. People would tell me, 'Your husband looks so mean.' He just didn't play. He took things very seriously."

Originally from Middleton, Ohio, the elder Payne was among the army's first African-American paratroopers. He served one tour in Korea, then he and his wife lived on bases around the United States. Of their children only Tom Jr. was not born on a military installation.

Harry Truman desegregated the armed forces in July 1948 by Executive Order 9981. Growing up within the military's embrace meant the Payne family enjoyed freedom from racial separation and overt prejudice long before that became the norm in society at large. "There's all races mixed together there," Ms. Payne recalled of life on base. She held a degree in biology from the University of Louisville and got Army jobs as a hostess and a librarian. "Most of my children had never been exposed to the negative side of life. We shielded them."

From about age 5 to 15, Tom Jr. prospered. There were chores to be done on-base, and he earned money by cleaning floors and by shining shoes for GIs in basic training. But as part of a happy pack of "free kids running around," Payne also "messed around with all kinds of sports." In that era prior to sports saturation and multimillion-dollar contracts, Payne said that despite his size, participation in athletics "never was thrust upon me." He played Little League baseball and football, and tasted success on a football team that won a title at Fort Knox.

Unfortunately, the Kentucky into which the family emerged from its military chrysalis leaned toward the mores and customs of the South, despite having remained in the Union during the Civil War. "When they first came to Louisville, it was sort of traumatic," Ms. Payne says of her children.

Kentucky fervently enforced the separation of church and state during its infancy as a state, not so much for reasons of religious liberty as because the clergy had the bad taste to repeatedly attack the institution of slavery. "For separation of church and state, then, read separation of morality and state," Wendell Berry suggested in *The Hidden Wound*. (South Carolina's legislature similarly hesitated to charter religious colleges, in part for "fear that religious organizations would preach the abolition of slavery," Louis Wright explained in his bicentennial history of that state.) Berry, a native

Kentuckian, also recalling a telling rhyme from his childhood: "A naught's a naught and a figger's a figger. All for the white man, none for the nigger."

Abraham Lincoln's birth state was, along with Delaware, the last to abolish slavery following what some still call the "War of Northern Aggression." Kentucky also emulated its southerly neighbors by embracing Jim Crow, though later and less universally. The state's infamous Day Law, aimed specifically at integrated Berea College, a liberal private school, banned interracial education in 1904. Kentucky was less adept at actually providing a quality public education, ranking last in the nation at the conclusion of World War II in the percent of its adult population holding high school diplomas. Segregation infected even the state's signature sporting event: African American jockeys had ridden 15 of the first 28 winners in the Kentucky Derby at Louisville's Churchill Downs, but they were prohibited from participating after 1911.

Kentucky also joined 40 other states (at various points in history) in outlawing marriage between "a white person and a negro or mulatto." Segregation and the undergirding race theories had a strong sexual subtext. Consequently, author Harry Ashmore contended, "the Victorian concept of female chastity as a safeguard of ethnic purity" came to the fore among white segregationists. That theme echoed from the early days of slavery well into the era of school desegregation. Supporting the mythology was a view of African Americans as "sexually precocious, libidinous and lubricious," as historian Adam Fairclough put it. Black males in particular were viewed as "sexually driven 'brutes' with a special affinity for white women," according to Stewart Tolnay and E. M. Beck, authors of *A Festival of Violence.*

Assaults on white women, alleged and otherwise, were the most frequently cited reason for lynchings across the South although they were the actual cause in only one in five documented cases. "Many white people—particularly in the open country—assume that Negroes are prone to crimes against women and that unless a Negro is lynched now and then the women on the solitary farms are in danger," Arthur Raper wrote in his 1933 book, *The Tragedy of Lynching.* Summarily dispatching the offender protected a violated white woman from the indignity of having to testify in court to the sordid details of her assault. (No such protection was extended to African-American women.)

The justification for such organized violence was self-apparent to many whites.

"Neither crazed fiend nor the dregs of white society, the bulk of the lynchers tended to be ordinary and respectable people," said Leon Litwack in *Trouble in Mind*, "animated by a self-righteousness that justified their atrocities in the name of maintaining the social and racial order and the purity of the Anglo-Saxon race." Newspapers advertised lynchings; one included the headline "Negro Jerky and Sullen as Burning Hour Nears." Excursion trains were run to the site of the action, employees released early from work, children excused from school. Postcards celebrated the gory outcome.

Summarizing the attitudes of Southern whites, South Carolina's Ben Tillman declared on the floor of the U.S. Senate in 1907 that "our brains reel" and "we revert to the original savage" upon hearing that a white woman was raped by an African American. "I have three daughters, but so help me God I would rather find either one of them killed by a tiger or a bear and gather up her bones and bury them, conscious that she died in the purity of her maidenhood, than to have her crawl to me and tell me the horrid story that she had been robbed of the jewel of her womanhood by a Black fiend."

Tom Payne was fortunate, then, to be born in the second half of the 20th century, when the practice of lynching Black men for raping and assaulting white women had virtually ceased outside the Deep South.

Payne was equally fortunate to spend his high school years in Louisville, by 1960 a metropolis of nearly 400,000 and in many respects Kentucky's most racially progressive city. Louisville hired African Americans as police officers and firefighters in the 1920s, preceding most Southern communities by decades. (Atlanta, Georgia, for example, proud of its racial tolerance, hired its first Black firefighters in 1963.) By the early 1950s Louisville had African-American elected officials and integrated libraries, pools, parks, amphitheaters, and drugstore lunch counters.

The undergraduate student body was integrated by 1951 at the University of Louisville, the first white Southern institution of higher education to hire a Black faculty member. And when the Supreme Court handed down its decision in *Brown*, the Louisville public school superintendent quickly announced an integration plan. Schools containing nearly three-quarters of Louisville's students integrated without incident in the fall of 1956, prompting a *New York Times* reporter to declare, "Segregation died quietly here today."

Yet, as historian George Wright noted, "for the most part, Blacks in that city and Lexington—not to mention the smaller towns of the state—remained as segregated as Blacks in the Deep South throughout the 1950s." Louisville's integration plan was less inclusive than it appeared, since it allowed for voluntary student transfers. By the 1964–65 school year, more than 95 percent of Kentucky school districts had integrated, and the state became a national model for school integration. Louisville, however, moved in the opposite direction. In 1968, when Payne began his senior year in high school, the student bodies at many Louisville public schools were virtually single-race, prompting this newspaper headline: "Schools Move Back Toward Segregation."

The city on the banks of the Ohio River also was a hotbed for basketball within a state that, like Indiana and North Carolina, embraced the sport above all others.

Farra Alford, an Alabama teammate of Wendell Hudson, vividly recalled hitchhiking across Lexington with a friend during the mid-1960s to see a team from Louisville's Male High School play at Dunbar High School. Competition for the state basketball title was integrated, although society at large was not. "We watched one of the greatest high school games you've ever seen," Alford said of the Dunbar win in overtime. "They were ranked one and two in the state. We didn't think anything of it. We were just basketball people, and we went down to the gym. Well, I walked in this gym with my fellow skinny white guy, and that gym was rocking—unlike any gym I'd ever been in before. We were the only two shiny faces in that gym. And you couldn't have gotten out of there if your life depended on it. The fire marshal wasn't anywhere in sight, there were so many people in there to watch this great high school game."

By the time Payne enrolled at Shawnee High School in 1966, the University of Louisville basketball team already had been integrated for four years, boasting players such as Wade Houston, Eddie Whitehead, and Wes Unseld, the first black player to whom Rupp offered a basketball scholarship.

When the Shawnee basketball coach saw a towering stranger walking the school's halls at the start of the academic year, he immediately invited the new student to join the varsity. Payne had not previously played organized basketball, yet he dutifully accepted the coach's invitation. He quickly found his immersion in athletics "an eye-opening experience, because sports was almost everything in this state, especially basketball."

Surely a youngster from Kentucky, of all places, was not entirely oblivious to basketball's lure and luster. "We would produce many more great football players in the state of Kentucky if they didn't all want to play basketball," Alford said. Both Payne and his mother were born in Louisville, and the family had been stationed at Fort Knox and Fort Campbell, both within the Bluegrass State.

Nor does it seem quite credible to expect Payne, "a really intelligent guy" according to his admiring younger brother, to fail to recognize that a 7-foot American athlete could translate his skills into a free college education, if not more.

Yet Darrell Payne is convinced that stepping into a cauldron of excitement and expectation was not necessarily the best thing for his brother. "I think he got fished into it because he was big," Darrell Payne said. "It was a way for him to cope with people teasing him about his height, being so big, so noticeable. I don't think he would have done it if he had it to do over again. Never had no interest in it. All of a sudden he just picked up a ball [because] someone told him he could play."

Gangly and clumsy as a sophomore in high school, Payne worked hard and was a star by his junior season. College offers poured in. Recruiters "promised everything, but we didn't go for that," Payne's mother said. "My husband didn't want to depend on anyone. In fact, they were scared to approach my husband about anything like that."

Like many players of the era, including Chicagoan Mike Krzyzewski, the future Duke coach, Payne had his heart set on attending Bradley University in Peoria, Illinois. Krzyzewski's parents insisted he attend the U.S. Military Academy instead, an especial honor for the son of Polish immigrants. Payne's father decided his namesake would break racial barriers at Kentucky, one of the nation's great basketball programs. "He wanted him to be a pioneer, to set the stage for other African Americans," Darrell Payne said. "He thought it would make Tommy a tougher person, coming out of that school playing under Adolph Rupp."

Attending Kentucky additionally kept Payne close to home, where his family could see him play. "We were naive," Ms. Payne said. "I didn't know nothing about UK and basketball and football and that atmosphere down there. I should have let him go to the school of his choice."

In those early days of collegiate athletic integration, the pitfalls were numerous and often hidden, and not everyone had the wherewithal to successfully navigate America's racial divide. "I wasn't prepared to be a pioneer," Payne said. "Jackie Robinson was prepared to be a pioneer. A lot of guys had been prepared. They had been raised in certain environmental influences that allowed them to understand racism. They knew what they were going through . . . [Robinson] was a lieutenant in the army, a second lieutenant when he went into the army. A graduate of UCLA. He was prepared. He played in the Negro Leagues before entering the major leagues. . . . I was just a big, old, green, tall, naive kid who had been in the army all his life. Think about it: I had only three years off the army base before that. I was not prepared socially for any of this."

But Sergeant Payne's opinion carried the day. His father's power was further illustrated when Tom Jr. finished high school and was essentially ordered to get married. Faced with family restrictions on dating, Payne had not gone out with girls until he was a junior in high school. Teammates helped break the ice, and soon Payne was enraptured with a girl. She became pregnant. They would have a daughter, get divorced, remarry, and divorce again. Taking care of his family and playing basketball without the benefit of a steady income became a consideration when Payne decided to cut short his college career.

"The truth about Tom being raised in the army is, his father was always telling him, 'You've got responsibilities, and you've got to stand on your own feet," Elaine said. "His father brought him up like that. He said, 'You're not going to run around here with a lot of children with my name and not be married.'"

Instead, Payne's name was forever married with that of Rupp, the "Baron of the Bluegrass." Rupp, born in Kansas in 1901 and known as "Dolph" to his family, learned basketball by shooting a rounded sack filled with hay into a metal rim affixed to a barn. He could shoot and pass, he recalled, "but that ball wasn't much for dribbling." He tasted victory at the University of Kansas, serving as a little-used guard on 1922 and 1923 national championship squads coached by Forrest "Phog" Allen. Dean Smith, the North Carolina coach who would later surpass Rupp's career victory total, also played at Kansas for Allen in the early 1950s.

Unlike Smith, for Rupp "basketball was not a game—it was a life-or-death proposition," according to a history of the Kentucky basketball program by Bert Nelli and Steve Nelli. As coaches Allen, Rupp, and Smith combined for 2,501 wins and nine national titles. Rupp had the fewest losses (190) although he coached the longest, from 1930 through 1972. His teams dominated the football-oriented SEC, making 20 NCAA appearances in his 42 seasons at Lexington. From January 4, 1943, until they were beaten by Georgia Tech on January 8, 1955, the Wildcats won 129 consecutive home games, the longest such streak in NCAA history. Rupp's teams finished atop the final wire service polls on six occasions, and he coached 23 All-Americans.

UK went undefeated in 1954, a year after its schedule was cancelled and the program placed on probation. A New York judge hearing cases related to a nationwide gambling scandal in college sports had found Kentucky "the acme of commercialism and over-emphasis," and was particularly critical of Rupp's failure "to observe the amateur rules, to build character and protect the morals and health of his charges." NCAA probation followed, but an internal university investigation predictably exonerated Rupp as "an honorable man who did not knowingly violate the athletic rules."

Boosters were less scrupulous. Opponents often complained that UK supporters promised recruits more lucrative summer jobs and larger payments for complementary game tickets than did fans at other schools. While common, neither practice was strictly legal under NCAA rules. But, then, Kentucky was the standard of measure in many respects. The Wildcats had the most touted players, the best resources, the SEC's nicest arena, numerous and vociferous fans, and a coach widely admired by his peers. "Rupp had such a great reputation; everybody wanted to go to play for Rupp," said Ray Mears, head basketball coach at the University of Tennessee from 1963 to 1977. "He made the South what it was," said former Florida assistant Dick Davis. Rupp won on the court with a set offense and man-to-man defense. He was an early proponent of the fast break, easier to employ with the talent and depth UK secured through numerous scholarships and a superior support system.

Rupp's personality could be similarly overpowering. Bear Bryant encountered his basketball counterpart's "abrasive way of talking and dealing with people" during eight years as head football coach at the University of Kentucky following World War II. "You either liked Rupp or you hated him. There didn't seem to be a middle ground," Bryant says in his autobiography. He became a Rupp fan later in life but chafed in Rupp's shadow at UK after receiving a cigarette lighter for winning the 1950 SEC football title while the basketball coach got "a great big blue Cadillac with white-wall tires."

Players found Rupp tough and demanding. "Some day I'm going to write a book on how not to play basketball, and I'm going to devote the first two hundred pages to you!" he shouted at one player. He did write a book, *Rupp's Championship Basketball,* in which he insisted, "Championships are not won by wishing and by hope. They are won by hard work and a willingness on the part of the boys to sacrifice some of the normal phases of college life."

The coach relied primarily on eight players, calling the remainder of the roster his "turd squad." Fear, sarcasm, and verbal abuse were the order of the day, according to C. M. Newton (who played under Rupp and later returned to his alma mater as director of athletics) and others. "Rupp was unique," Bill Spivey, a consensus All-American at UK in 1951, told Dave Kindred of the Louisville *Courier-Journal*. "He wanted everybody to hate him—and he succeeded. He called us names some of us never heard before." Vernon Hatton, a UK All-American as a senior in 1958, added, "It takes six or eight years to get over playing for Coach Rupp. Once you get over it you get to like him."

Dominating his surroundings as he did, Rupp "set records for vanity that will not soon be surpassed," Kindred opined. Following Rupp's death in 1977, five years after he was forced to retire, Joe Kemp described a visit to "Uncle Adolph's" office for the *Kentucky Kernel*, the University of Kentucky student newspaper. Trophies crowded the walls and floor and were under and on the desk. "There's no room on the walls," Rupp said. "I have won every award in coaching and you can look it up."

Rupp also confided to Kemp "one reason why we lost" the most historic game of his career, an attitude which brought the coach's racial attitudes and record to national consciousness and remains a source of rancor and debate in Lexington. According to Kemp, Rupp said with a wink, "They had some niggers on their team and we didn't." He added, "Hell, every time the referees called a foul on Texas Western, the boys on that bench yelled, 'Discrimination, discrimination.'"

The contest occurred in 1966, when Kentucky's heavily favored and top-rated squad was upset in the NCAA title game by Texas Western. Nicknamed "Rupp's Runts," the 27–1 Wildcats boasted the likes of Louie Dampier, Larry Conley, and Pat Riley. But they were beaten 72–65 by coach Don Haskins's team. The result was notable because the Miners were the first major-college national champion that started five Black players, and because they confounded stereotypes by winning with tough defense and disciplined offense. Their triumph on the game's biggest stage, and against so prominent a program, forever shattered prejudices about how African Americans played the game.

The Texas Western win was sweeter to many because it came against Kentucky and Rupp, who had conspicuously failed to sign an African-

American player. Upon becoming president of the university in 1963, John Oswald pushed Rupp to integrate his program, to no avail. "Adolph would come back from talking with Oswald and say, 'That son of a bitch is going to drive me crazy,'" recalled longtime assistant Harry Lancaster, as quoted by Frank Fitzpatrick. "'He's unreasonable.'"

Rupp was widely known for publicly commenting that the reason Blacks were so athletic was that the slowest ones had been eaten by lions back in Africa. Fitzpatrick calls Rupp "the snarling epitome of an unyielding establishment" and made a good case for the argument in *And the Walls Came Tumbling Down*, a book about the 1966 national championship game and the two programs involved. "Nothing I ever saw or heard of [Rupp] contradicted my impression that he was one of the more devout racists in sports," Bill Russell told a reporter. "He was known for the delight he took in making nasty remarks about niggers and Jews, and for his determination never to have Black players at the University of Kentucky."

Former associates like Newton and Joe B. Hall, a Kentucky player and assistant who succeeded Rupp as head coach in 1972, insist Rupp was no racist. Three themes are usually struck to defend the coaching great. The first is that Rupp was "a product of his time," as Newton asserts. This simplified explanation had universal application in a country where African Americans were treated respectfully, up to a point. The experience of a native son (who wishes to remain anonymous) from a supposedly progressive Southern city is instructive in that regard. He expresses amazement at his own father's ability to nurture an African-American housekeeper and her mentally handicapped son for 40 years, yet to think nothing of pushing a Black woman off a seat when she had the temerity to sit beside him on a bus.

The second theme is that Kentucky could not add an African American to its roster because the SEC simply was not ready for it. The University of Kentucky, like most Southern universities, was forced to integrate under compulsion of a federal court, but the barriers to its graduate and professional programs fell in 1949, prior to what is regarded as the civil rights era. (The same year, the cornerstone was laid for 11,500-seat Memorial Coliseum, a $4 million colossus at the edge of campus. The Wildcats played in the building from 1950 through 1976, losing a mere 38 of 344 games there.)

Bryant claims that he advocated signing Black players once UK integrated, but that Rupp was opposed. Newton, who smashed racial barriers at

Alabama during the late 1960s, says he understood Rupp's hesitance. "It would have been a very difficult thing for a coach at that time, the 1950s and even the early 1960s, perhaps, to integrate a program in the South—just because of what the player would face going into the Deep South. Even if it worked, say, at Kentucky, going to Baton Rouge or Starkville or Oxford or Tuscaloosa or Auburn would have been a very difficult thing to do."

As early as 1961 UK president Frank G. Dickey said it was "inevitable" that African Americans would play for the school, but he argued that "the most effective method of bringing about integration would be through a joint movement of the SEC universities." Dickey wrote privately to other SEC presidents in May 1963. While assuring them, "We have not recruited any Negro players nor do we have any immediate plans to do so," he cited "external and internal pressures" that were forcing the university's hand. Wishing neither to leave the conference nor to "embarrass any of our fellow members," Dickey inquired how colleagues would react if the Wildcats signed a Black athlete.

Rupp claimed the SEC "prohibited" the use of Black players but, Newton said, took a more nuanced view in private. "I know the times I talked to him about it, he said, 'Everybody wants me to recruit a Black player, but I cannot in good conscience. We've got to get out of the Southeastern Conference if I do.' Maybe that was a copout. I don't think so. I think he was probably reading the climate of that time pretty well."

Perhaps. Then again, Kentucky football coach Charlie Bradshaw added a pair of African-American recruits in 1965, four years before Rupp signed Tom Payne. When Nat Northington signed at his Louisville home, both UK president John Oswald and Kentucky governor Ned Breathitt were on hand to be photographed. The following year Breathitt stood at the base of a statue of Lincoln in the capitol rotunda and signed a state antidiscrimination act, the first in the South.

Northington became the first African-American athlete to compete in the SEC when he appeared for the UK varsity on September 30, 1967, in a game against Ole Miss. Barely two months later, Vanderbilt's Perry Wallace broke the league's varsity basketball color barrier. By then the relative handful of Black students on the Kentucky campus had been picketing Memorial Coliseum, signs in hand, for several years.

The third defense of Rupp's reputation employs what might be called the interchangeability argument. A plaintive Hall favored this theme, a Lexington favorite, claiming Rupp was victimized by coincidence.

Had all-white Duke beaten Kentucky in the 1966 semifinals and advanced to lose to Texas Western, there would be no talk of Rupp's racial attitudes, Hall said. (The Blue Devils did have C. B. Claiborne on their freshman squad that year.) "Would that onus have been on Vic Bubas as it was on Rupp? I say, yeah. Nobody would be thinking of Coach Rupp as a racist. It was very unfortunate that the time that we went to the NCAA and played an all-Black team, we were an all-white team. That became a great cause to get behind, and to emphasize the injustices. Coach Rupp was just a victim of that."

Rupp as victim certainly was at odds with the perception in the Black community. John McLendon, the Hall of Fame coach, recalled a special sweetness to the celebration among African Americans because Rupp was the loser against Texas Western. Kentucky was so unpopular with the state's Black populace that, unlike ordinary college students, Chester Grundy and friends avoided wearing their school's paraphernalia off campus. That was particularly true in Lexington's predominantly Black business district along Dewey Street, an area later destroyed inevitably, by urban renewal. "It was a liability to say you were at UK," Grundy said. "It might be taken that you were some kind of sellout or something, because there was that kind of hostility."

The hostility was not without basis, judging by the reception St. John's received when it came to Lexington in December 1951. The New York squad coached by Frank McGuire included Solly Walker, the school's first Black player. UK folks remembered Rupp publicly working to create a welcoming atmosphere for Walker. McGuire adherents were equally insistent that Rupp privately lobbied to have Walker stay home.

Walker made the trip. He encountered colored and white water fountains and the like, and at mealtime was banished to the kitchen at the team's Lexington hotel. McGuire and several others kept him company. "He was with me all the way," Walker recalled of his coach. (When the Boston Celtics came to Lexington for an exhibition game a decade later, the team's Black players were refused food service in their hotel. Led by Bill Russell, they chartered a plane and left town without playing the game. Similar treatment during the 1964 state high school basketball tournament in Lexington was cited by Wes Unseld as a factor in his decision to reject Kentucky's recruiting overtures.)

Second-ranked St. John's jumped ahead in the game as Walker did most of the early scoring, but No.1 Kentucky won in a rout, 81–40. The teams met again in the 1952 NCAA East Regional finals at Raleigh, with St. John's prevailing. McGuire's squad reached the national championship game, only to lose decisively to Kansas. Riding the KU bench was guard Dean Smith, who later worked for and succeeded McGuire at North Carolina.

The Wildcats were led in Lexington by Cliff Hagan, described in a wire service account as "a leaping, twisting whirlwind." The Associated Press story said that "the crowd treated Walker, the first Negro to play in the Coliseum, like any other player and he got a big hand when he went out for a rest in the second period." Walker's memory of the game differed significantly from the newspaper version. He says the reception was antagonistic from the start and he was booed repeatedly. "That was the way the crowds were—the crowds were hostile," Walker, a retired school principal, said of playing at Southern venues. "On the court the games were physical but nothing out of the ordinary." McGuire later cited the Lexington experience as a reason he hesitated to recruit African-American players at North Carolina and South Carolina.

Fifteen years after Walker came and went, life at UK still was not all that great for African-American students. Black undergraduates were afraid to traverse sections of the Kentucky campus, especially at night. Any walk along fraternity row was likely to occasion verbal abuse, if not worse. "It was a rule of thumb for us that you don't go out by yourself at night around here," Grundy said. "Particularly on weekends, when the fraternity boys would be drinking and got a little bold."

A mid-1960s game at Memorial Coliseum proved similarly alienating, with Rebel flags waving, the band playing "Dixie" to rally fan support, and racial epithets hurled at Black players on the opposing team. "It was one of those kind of things where you look around and say, 'Is this my school? These are my classmates!'" Grundy said. "It was really an eye-opener. That wasn't an unusual night. That was just a night when you saw it, when it was in your face."

When Kentucky and Texas Western met in the NCAA finals, a group of UK's Black students went off to watch the game in isolation. They locked themselves in a dorm room and stuffed pillows under the door to dampen the noise of their cheering "because we knew who we were going to be rooting for," Grundy said, laughing at the memory. "It was just an incredible, incredible evening watching Kentucky get beat like that. It was just one of these things where it was just 'Wow! Wow!' It was vindication.

"And then you had to collect yourself before you walked out into the hallway. Like, 'Damn, we got beat!'" Grundy laughed again. "We couldn't have asked for greater vindication. Here we had been pushing this team to desegregate, and look who they get beat by. So that was a very powerful moment."

The Texas Western game also captured the attention of a teenage Tubby Smith, starting him on a path that led 31 years later to his becoming Kentucky's first Black head coach. "Growing up in southern Maryland, the first time I knew or even followed basketball was after the 1966 game that was held at Cole Field House at Maryland," he said.

The shift in the game's tectonics was not appreciated in all corners, as demonstrated by the Lexington sports editor who crowed at Kentucky's 1966 team banquet that "at least we're still the best white team in the country." This strain of thought persisted. The Lexington Country Club was not integrated until 1993, when former Wildcat Sam Bowie was admitted. Upon Tubby Smith's hiring in 1997, *Lexington Herald-Leader* columnist Merlene Davis was moved to warn the new coach, "We cling to the lie that everything, race-wise, is just fine" in Lexington. "I sincerely fear for your safety and the safety of your family," she wrote.

During the 1960s, a period of intense civil rights consciousness, the University of Kentucky's reputation, if not Rupp's actual reluctance to sign black players, became an increasing impediment to basketball competitiveness. The Wildcats struggled to acquire a superior center, even as Unseld went to Louisville and Jim McDaniels chose Western Kentucky. Both native sons became consensus All-Americans, as did Western's Clem Haskins. Heading into his final season, Rupp signed another all-white class, prompting a Kentucky newspaper to run an analysis under the headline "UK an also-ran in Negro recruiting." Older African Americans in Lexington discouraged Black players from attending Kentucky. So did assistant coaches from other schools for more than the usual reasons.

Hall insisted, "We were a typical school, not biased in any way, not prejudiced." Instead, he said, Kentucky was singled out "because people were tired of Coach Rupp dominating." Chief among UK's tormentors on the recruiting circuit was Villanova assistant coach George Raveling. Hall recalled a high school all-star game at which Raveling "got on us, got on me, for not having Black players at Kentucky." Hall took umbrage, listing all the Black players he was recruiting. Raveling turned to his briefcase and, according to Hall, said, "'Well, you'll never recruit a Black player as long as I've got this satchel.' He had collected articles claiming that Rupp was a racist and that Black players wouldn't go to Kentucky. . . . So I said to George, 'George, if you're going to criticize us for not having Black players, why are you fighting to keep us from getting Black players? That doesn't make sense.'" Raveling now admits, "That sounds like me at that time."

Into this vortex of hostility, disappointment, and expectation stepped Tom Payne.

"He was constantly under the gun," Darrell Payne said. "Black people didn't like him because he went to Kentucky. White people didn't want him there. He was right in the middle, 18 years old, getting it on both sides."

Payne, uncommonly strong and filled out at 220 pounds, was named a prep All-American his senior year in high school. That season the center averaged 25 points and 29 rebounds, scoring 40 points in one game. "He played on a team that didn't throw him the ball much until they got in trouble, and then they would give him the ball and he would shine," Hall said. "He was a blooming star."

But Payne had a marginal academic profile, as reflected in press estimates that as many as a quarter of the schools showing interest were junior colleges. "He didn't push himself," Darrell Payne said. "As a matter of fact, of the nine brothers and sisters, Tommy and my sister Margie, who is a doctor, are probably the most intelligent." Only Tom failed to graduate college among the family's children; most of his siblings hold postgraduate degrees as well.

Payne visited the Kentucky campus and expressed pleasant surprise to a reporter "that some of the stuff I had heard wasn't true." Hall and Rupp visited the Payne home in Louisville's West End, bestowing personalized attention that reportedly was lacking in previous Kentucky recruiting efforts aimed at Black prospects. "Coach Rupp always tried to have a relationship with us," Elaine Payne said. "I don't think there's any question he was a racist, but he did a lot of good things for Tom, too."

Newspaper photographers were at the Payne home to capture his historic signing with Kentucky. The Payne men and the university coaches all wore ties and jackets. In one photo the 6-foot-1 Rupp measures his hand against Payne's. Gazing at the camera, the player has a far-off look. Rupp's fleshy face, with its big ears and pronounced nose and chin, is lit by a smile. Payne "has as great a future as Lew Alcindor ever thought of having," the coach pronounced. "I think he's a better prospect than Bill Spivey, and Spivey made All-American for us as a junior."

Race was no factor in the signing, Rupp said. Competitive necessity was. "We're just so happy to at last get the big boy we've wanted for so long," he said. As journalist Dave Kindred noted in 1976, "The eternal verity in Rupp's personality was his love of victory."

Whether Payne was the right person to break the color barrier at Kentucky is open to debate. His subsequent failures as a person stand as persuasive evidence that he was not. How much trouble Rupp could have anticipated is also questionable, considering there was nothing overt in Payne's background to indicate the difficulties that lay ahead. Those who distrust Rupp's motives wonder if Payne's post-college depredations served as silent vindication of the coach's hesitation to recruit African-American players. Others doubt that the Hall of Famer gave much thought to picking the right person to break the UK color line. "If Rupp's going to pick one, he wouldn't care whether he was a good guy or not, [so long as] he could play basketball," said Jimmy Davy, a Nashville journalist who covered SEC athletics for nearly a half-century.

Grundy agreed. "I compare Payne to the man who was picked to desegregate the UK grad school, Lyman Johnson. This guy was the model—did undergraduate work at Michigan, was heavily involved in civil rights activity in Louisville. So he was much like Rosa Parks. This was not somebody out of the blue that sat down one day. These people were groomed for this, fully aware of what they were going into and the consequences to career and to their personal lives. So there could have been that kind of engineering, but I think the Payne situation was kind of arbitrary. He was a 7-footer."

Payne failed to score adequately on the ACT—a standardized examination used for college admissions and for determining intercollegiate eligibility—and was unable to join Kentucky's freshman squad. His parents paid for his education while he competed on a Lexington Amateur Athletic Union team, leading the league with 22 points and 15 rebounds per game. Early on, the AAU squad played the UK freshmen and beat them handily, with Payne outperforming big man Jim Andrews, a prized recruit. "This is what happened," Payne said, lowering his voice. "I believe undercover they didn't want a Black, and I believe undercover that they wanted to show people that he couldn't make it. But what happened was God, Providence. I became so good that I totally devastated the UK freshmen."

Payne said Rupp, a realist, then recognized that the young center could help Kentucky. His AAU performance led Kentucky coaches to arrange for people to take correspondence courses in Payne's name to ensure his eligibility as a sophomore, as Payne later told reporter Brian Bennett of the *Courier-Journal*. Payne's single season on the varsity, 1970–71, the Wildcats finished 22–6, first in the SEC with a 16–2 mark, and 10th in the polls. Payne was the team's top rebounder (10.1) and second-leading scorer (16.9). "He played some marvelous basketball for us," Rupp said.

"I think he was very quick," said Dick Toth, an opposing frontline player at Georgia. "Surprisingly strong, even though he looked on the slender side. He was very good around the basket, he really was." Toth's teammate, Tim Bassett, said of Payne, "On any given night he could play like Wilt Chamberlain." Bassett also said Payne "gave off an air that scared some people," a trait reminiscent of his father and hardly helpful in making a good impression on fans and other strangers.

Rupp missed a stretch late in the 1970–71 season due to illness. Hall was designated to run the team in his absence, presaging his eventual assignment as permanent successor. Hall coached the Wildcats for 13 years (1972–85), during which Kentucky won nearly three-quarters of its games, made three appearances in the Final Four, and captured the 1978 NCAA title. Hall said Payne "really came on" toward the end of that lone season with the varsity. "He really was playing very well. Great athlete. Great physique. Gosh, he was strong and aggressive and could run."

Among those who came to watch Payne in action was Dirk Minnifield, who would later attend UK and briefly play with Payne in the pros. "All of us Black kids were aware of Tom because he was the first Black player at Kentucky. We all looked up to him," Minnifield, who grew up in Lexington, told a newspaper reporter. As an adult, he said, Payne taught him "about being faithful to my wife and how to avoid the pressures of being an athlete. He was this great-big lovable guy. A normal guy."

Hall, the assistant, was the coach closest to the young player, in the manner of basketball programs everywhere. Payne was a guest once at his home. Perhaps that is why Hall refused to directly criticize Payne or to refute many of the younger man's assertions, now made as a repeat felon of compromised integrity.

Certainly that link seemed important to Payne. Speaking from prison confinement he repeatedly, almost longingly, looked to Hall for a measure of understanding, for a kind word that he was not all bad, even if he had gone wrong. "To be totally honest with you," Payne said, employing a characteristic turn of phrase that might indicate a need to look askance at other statements, "the one thing I would like to see out of all this is that there come some kind of reconciliation. That's all I would really like to see. If Joe Hall or any of them, if they could ever meet me or see me just so we could have a hug and say, 'It's all right,' it's a reconciliation. Not who was right and who was wrong and everything else."

Yet the analysis of Payne's Kentucky experience advanced by him and his family does not lend itself to mending fences. They speak of unequal treatment in receiving off-the-court benefits, legal and otherwise, particularly galling for a young man with a wife and child to feed. Payne and his brother recalled in vivid detail a time he was booed when the Wildcats lost in their own UK Invitational Tournament, a reception at odds with Hall's recollection. Family members said the tires on Payne's car were slashed at least four times.

And there was the persistent and enduring theme of race. "When I went to Kentucky, they should have embraced me and loved me just like they loved any of the other ballplayers. But this"—Payne rubbed his skin—"got in the way." Like Grundy, and like Perry Wallace at Vanderbilt, he said life on campus was fraught with insult, if not peril. "You might go through the students and the white students won't even speak to you. They see the other ballplayers and they speak. Little things like that. Guys looking down on you because you're Black. Having disdain towards you."

Temporary escape, if not deliverance, came in the form of a bidding war between the National Basketball Association and the upstart American Basketball Association. It was the dawn of the big-money era in professional sports, and the leagues held a so-called "hardship draft" that allowed college students to turn pro if they had an arguable financial need. "We're helpless in the face of the vandalism the professionals are using on the colleges," Rupp said. "And you can use that word. Vandalism is the only way to describe it."

The loophole enabled big man Spencer Haywood, once committed to attend the University of Tennessee as its first African-American player, to leave college early as pro ball's initial hardship case in 1969. Payne likewise succumbed to the lure of the money. Represented by agent Sonny Vaccaro, later to become famous as a purveyor of athletic shoes and then a critic of athlete exploitation, Payne signed a five-year deal with the Atlanta Hawks on September 10, 1971, for $800,000, a whopping sum at the time.

The early departure sparked Kentucky fans to flood the Payne family home in Louisville with angry phone calls. More vandalism struck Tom

Payne's property in Lexington. Rupp wished Payne well but said the player was not ready for the pros. Worse from the perspective of the Kentucky faithful, the coach said the loss of Payne would "murder us" in the season about to commence. (Kentucky finished 21–7 and repeated as SEC champion.) Payne fired a few parting shots, including claims that the coaching staff ignored him over the summer. Rupp said he tried to phone 25 times without success. The debate seemed a bit irrelevant when Payne was issued an August speeding ticket while driving a new Cadillac registered in his name and bearing Pennsylvania plates, hardly a sign he intended to maintain his amateur status.

Rupp doubted publicly whether any pro team would offer Payne a contract at his level of development "unless they ship him to the Eastern League or maybe to Italy." Atlanta coach Richie Guerin admitted he initially thought it would take Payne two years to get up to speed, but he was far more optimistic after working with the young player for less than a month. "I think Payne is going to be a very, very influential defensive player some day," Guerin said. "The guy might be our center for ten years."

The Hawks carried three centers during the 1971–72 season: Payne, Bob Christian, and Walt Bellamy. Payne appeared in about a third of Atlanta's 88 games, averaging approximately eight minutes per outing.

Gilbert McGregor, who played a year for the Cincinnati Royals, remembered commiserating about playing time with his fellow rookie. He found Payne a bit off-kilter. "When Tom was talking to me, he was talking very, very quickly about how things weren't going right, about how people weren't treating him right," McGregor said. "His getting into trouble afterwards, I could see that maybe things weren't well with his situation, if not with him."

The trouble arrived shortly after Payne completed his first pro season. Arrested in Atlanta, he was convicted on two counts of rape and one of aggravated sodomy (he was acquitted on two other counts of rape). The Georgia sentence was for 15 years, but he was paroled after 5. His father died of cancer soon after he was imprisoned. While incarcerated, Payne was extradited to Kentucky in 1977 and convicted on one count of rape and two counts of attempted rape stemming from incidents in Louisville in 1971. The Kentucky sentence was life, but Payne was paroled after six years.

Payne briefly returned to pro ball in 1983 with the Louisville Catbirds of the Continental Basketball Association. His coach, Ron Ekker, spoke highly of the ex-convict, praising his "creative mind" and "deep reading" and his care in avoiding any situation that might lead to allegations of impropriety.

Soon Payne moved to California. He took a shot at boxing; his trainer for a time was Archie Moore, the former light heavyweight with a pro record 141 knockouts to his credit. Payne had more success as an actor with his chiseled body and an oval face featuring high, smooth cheekbones. He appeared in the television movie *Stingray* and the television series *Night Court*, in a McDonald's hamburger commercial, and in a music video. A police detective called him "a black Arnold Schwarzenegger." Payne was contemplating a career in professional wrestling when he was arrested again in February 1986 in Los Angeles, this time for a raping a woman who stood 4-foot-11. "In all honesty, he could have made a million dollars this year," his agent said.

Payne spent the next 14 years in California's penal system. When paroled, he expected to move into a Cincinnati house with his brother Darrell. Instead, Kentucky laid claim to him as a parole violator and ensconced him first at Green River, then at Little Sandy Correctional Complex. His main activities as a prisoner were reading, working out, and going to church. He said he was eager to help younger inmates and anxious to get out of prison in time to help raise his daughter by his third marriage.

Family members spoke of flaws and inconsistencies in the rape cases that went against him, but Payne steered clear of discussing his crimes, even with his brother. "Tommy's always said, 'I can't get those years back. What does it matter? I've got to look forward now.' That's how he responded when I used to ask him," Darrell Payne said.

Tom Payne does grant that "there's no excuses" and said he has "grieved" over what he did, especially in California. "I have prayed for the people involved in this situation, not only in my own family but the victim's family. I prayed that there would be some kind of healing that would transpire between all of us." Healing the rift with members of the Kentucky basketball community appeared comparably important to Payne. "If I am a symbol, let it be a symbol of redemption," said the long, lean prisoner with a gray-flecked mustache.

Instead he remained largely forgotten. Despite his historic spot in UK annals, Payne's family could not even find his photo when visiting a Lexington museum celebrating the basketball program. Tubby Smith embraced the school's racial pioneers and native black Kentuckians like Big House Gaines during a decade as head coach, but his reach did not extend to Sandy Hook or Little Sandy. Payne was no credit to the program, even if he had reformed, as he insisted.

"It's just a tragic story, a very tragic story. He really wasn't the guy to do this," Grundy said of Payne's groundbreaking role. One can argue whether Payne was set up to fail. None can argue that he most assuredly did.

CHAPTER 9
FRIENDLY BOUNCE

Al Heartley, North Carolina State University, 1967–71

The drama of heroism raises above all the issue of physical and moral courage: Does the hero have, in extreme circumstances, the courage to obey—to perform the task, the sacrifice, the resistance, the pilgrimage that he is called on to perform?

Wendell Berry, *The Gift of Good Land*

Luck may be the residue of design, as baseball executive Branch Rickey famously and aptly stated. And sometimes the ball simply takes a friendly bounce.

Surely the North Carolina State basketball program would have integrated eventually, if for no other reason than remaining competitive always requires adjustment to changed circumstances. When Everett Case built a dominant power at NC State, winning nine Southern Conference and ACC titles within a 10-year span from 1947 through 1956, neighbors made competitive adjustments to avoid being left behind. North Carolina, loser of 15 straight to Case, hired Frank McGuire away from St. John's University in New York in 1952. Wake Forest went with Bones McKinney, a former professional player and Demon Deacon assistant, in 1957. Duke, more noted for its football prowess, hired ex–Case assistant Vic Bubas in 1959. Now the state ranks with basketball bastions Indiana and Kentucky in its fascination with the sport. "Basketball is the one common denominator in North Carolina that I think is truly loved by everybody," Charles Scott, the UNC pioneer, said.

Yet if NC State administrators felt a compulsion to match their in-state neighbors in signing Black players, the marching orders were not communicated to head coach Norman Sloan, at least not that he could remember a quarter-century later.

Al Heartley's presence on the Wolfpack basketball squad was not, then, the result of a grand design on the part of school or coaching staff. Nor was his barrier-breaking role at the Raleigh university the product of extensive efforts seeking African Americans at a time when the state's high schools were bursting with talented Black players. Instead, Heartley just showed up, unrecruited and unknown, and set an enviable example.

Sloan, a former Case player in his second year coaching at his alma mater, was seated in his office in the fall of 1967 when he noticed "this slender Black kid is standing in the door. And I remember thinking, 'This is a kid from a small school. He's going to tell me he played forward in high school and he wants to come out for the freshman team.'" Actually, the 6-foot-1 Heartley had played guard. But otherwise Sloan's recollection, retold in newspaper stories about Heartley until it became a minor feel-good legend, was accurate. He informed the freshman that tryouts would be advertised in the school newspaper and gave the matter no further thought.

Sam Esposito, a 10-year Major League Baseball veteran and multisport schoolboy star from Chicago, coached the freshman squad. When preseason practice began, Esposito conducted the tryouts in one part of the school's practice gym while Sloan worked nearby with the varsity. "About halfway through practice he came and said, 'Skip, come here. I want you to watch something,'" Sloan recalled. "Al Heartley was eating everybody's lunch. He just whipped them every way you could whip them. He said, 'Am I seeing what this kid's doing? He's just been beating everybody over here.'"

Heartley, in school on a partial academic grant-in-aid, made the freshman squad. He started at forward, where he beat out a scholarship player, and finished third on the team in scoring and rebounding. The next season he won a full athletic scholarship, shared sixth-man chores on the varsity, and established a reputation as a defensive standout. As a junior Heartley became a starter, appearing in all but one game for a squad that won the 1970 ACC tournament and with it the official conference title. His senior year Heartley enjoyed a day dedicated in his honor in his nearby hometown of Clayton and received the 1971 Alumni Athletic Trophy, awarded to NC State's top senior athlete. He also made the 1970 ACC All-Academic squad while majoring in applied mathematics and was frequently on the dean's list.

The fact that Heartley had arrived at his basketball tryout wearing tennis sneakers was aptly symbolic. Heartley unknowingly followed the pioneering path taken at NC State by Irwin Holmes, the first Black varsity athlete in ACC history. Like Holmes, Heartley was a walk-on. Like Holmes, Heartley had a black teammate as a freshman who left after one year. Like

Holmes, Heartley was an in-state student with an interest in engineering. Like Holmes, a tennis player who in 1960 became the first African-American undergraduate to earn a degree at NC State, Heartley finished his collegiate career as a vital member of his squad, serving as team captain.

Where Heartley's role differed from Holmes's was in its enduring impact.

Holmes played what was regarded as a minor sport, one in which no scholarships were awarded, crowds were minimal, and scant media attention was paid. Few ACC followers even know his name today, or that he made history on February 9, 1957, when he and Manuel Crockett appeared for the Wolfpack in an indoor track meet against the University of North Carolina.

Heartley performed as a scholarship athlete on a big stage, and while two other Black players came to NC State during his career, neither lasted. "What I am really proud of from an NC State standpoint is not necessarily that I broke the barrier," Heartley said, "but that next, after me, came David Thompson. And David came into a situation where he was more comfortable. I don't know that David would have been a pioneer because David was not that kind of personality. But David was a great player. He's from North Carolina, the first great player from North Carolina to play in the ACC. And then other great players came. After David there were Phil Ford, John Lucas . . ."

Thompson, a shy youth from Shelby in western North Carolina, led NC State to an undefeated season as a sophomore in 1972–73 and to its first NCAA championship in 1974. The spectacular wing was a national Player of the Year and is generally regarded as the greatest basketball player in ACC history. Ford, a guard from Rocky Mount in eastern North Carolina, was ACC Player of the Year in 1978 and ran the Four Corners delay to perfection for Dean Smith. Lucas, a guard from the same Hillside High School in Durham that produced Irwin Holmes, departed Lefty Driesell's Maryland program as the top selection in the 1976 NBA draft.

"There was a lot of truth to what he said about paving the way for David Thompson," Sloan said of Heartley. "I don't know how David would have felt if we hadn't already had a Black player in the program. It was a strange thing, the pressure you feel as a coach. I had Al, who was outstanding; he was a class student, an honor student. No other Black kids. Then we got David. Then we had Phil Spence.

"I remember talking to those guys and I guess you would call it apologizing for the fact that we didn't have more Black kids in the program.

"David was wonderful. 'No problem, Coach. You don't need to do this.' I said, 'I want you to know, I'm sensitive to it.' And I said there's no reason for it other than the fact I just haven't been able to recruit enough quality players that are Black to be in the program.'"

Some would say Sloan's difficulties were not surprising given that NC State drew much of its student body from eastern North Carolina. "In North Carolina, after you got past Raleigh that was a different world," said Winston-Salem State's Big House Gaines. "You almost needed a passport to go over there and understand the attitudes and life patterns." The region supplied steady political support throughout the 30-year United States Senate career of Jesse Helms, an intractable opponent of civil rights initiatives, including recognition of a Martin Luther King holiday. "Eastern North Carolina, a rural area with large numbers of Blacks, has traditionally been viewed as the most racist area of the state," William Chafe said in *Civilities and Civil Rights*. "It was there that the Wilmington Race Riot of 1898 occurred, overthrowing a biracial coalition government there and leading to statewide disenfranchisement of Blacks in 1900. The area has been seen as being more like the Deep South than the rest of the state."

Smithfield, where Heartley was an honorable mention all-state player at Johnston Central High School, long had a billboard at the edge of town that proclaimed, "Welcome to KKK Country." Speaking in Raleigh in 2001, Harvey Heartley, Al's older brother, said, "If you leave here right now and go down 20 miles, you've got the Klan. It's always been there." (In his book on Southern politics and race in the 1950s, Numan Bartley tells an improbably heartwarming story about the North Carolina Knights of the Ku Klux Klan. Eager to teach Lumbee Indians in a southeastern county the proper respect for white supremacy, the Klan burned a cross and held a large rally near the town of Maxton in January 1958. "None of the local people showed up for the rally, except for the thousand or so gun-toting Indians, some of them wearing warpaint, who surrounded the Klan meeting," Bartley said. "Encouraged perhaps by the bullets being fired into the air by the encroaching ring of redskins, the Klansmen reached a quick consensus that discretion was surely the better alternative, and white-sheeted people were soon fleeing panic-stricken in all directions.")

The Heartleys came up, as the country expression goes, when segregation was still very much in evidence in rural North Carolina. The Klan was a force, but the Hartley parents, both schoolteachers, "never talked too much about it or too much against it," said Harvey, the eldest of three sons. "It was just sort of knowing that, well, white people got their stuff and you've got your stuff. They don't want you over there, so don't you be trying to be over there."

Blacks and whites went their separate ways in most respects. The oldest Heartley sibling recalled spending considerable time in Raleigh's Black business district, some 15 miles distant from the family's Clayton home. As late as 1959, among the 46 Black-owned businesses squeezed into several blocks downtown were movie houses that catered to African Americans, nightclubs, drugstores, restaurants, newspapers, and a full gamut of services. "If you were in the know, you didn't have a bad life," Harvey Heartley said.

In white Raleigh, Blacks could not so much as try on dry goods or use a bathroom.

Solly Walker, visiting for a game with his St. John's squad during the early 1950s, learned the harsh reality of segregation when he boarded a Raleigh bus and took a seat. The bus did not move. Finally, the driver turned to the New Yorker and said, "Man, can you please get to the back so this bus can move?" Walker said, "So I got off the bus and walked back to the campus."

There were far fewer restrictions and much more cross-pollination in the fields, with Black and white farmers helping each other plant and tend tobacco, the main cash crop in the sandy soils of the east. Out in the country, children could mix without thought or consequence, according to Chip Connor. The white former Virginia player and assistant coach was raised in a setting similar to the Heartleys', on a tobacco farm just above the state line in South Boston, Virginia. "The kids who were my age, we just played together just like any two kids would," Connor said. "I'd been around Blacks my whole life. I had enormous exposure, but it was all in the tobacco fields—pulling tobacco, working in the tobacco fields."

Harvey Heartley said such intimacy came to an abrupt halt in the presence of other whites. "Those same people that you would work with, if you came to town they would turn their head or go to the other side of the street because they didn't want people to know that they knew you. It was crazy; it was insane what would happen." Echoing the experiences of African Americans who ventured onto the South's historically white university campuses, he continued, "Or, you would see them in an area where they would see their white friends, and they would ignore you or they wouldn't say things. . . . Those things still happen today. Oh, yeah."

Public separation by race applied to athletics. The older Heartley said he and his friends played baseball against white boys, engaging in fistfights after each game and coming back the next day for more. African Americans in the area also went to the whites' gym in Smithfield to play basketball; the basketball games were routinely broken up by the police.

Al Heartley, 14 years younger than Harvey, recalled "only a few occasions" during the summers when he and his friends faced whites in baseball. "We'd come over to their park and play, and they'd come over to our park and play. We were told to stop that, that you should not do that. In fact, we were told not to go across the proverbial tracks."

Separation remained very much in force in the school system as well. Harvey, born in 1934, never attended an integrated school. Neither did his youngest brother, born in 1948, until college. Despite entering public school shortly after the *Brown* ruling, in a state noted for its racial moderation, Al Heartley did not even have the opportunity to enter an integrated educational setting until he reached high school.

Historians regard the leaders of North Carolina in the 1950s as masters at sabotaging integration while avoiding the appearance of extremism. "We're just like Georgia and Alabama except we do it in a tuxedo and they wear suspenders," summarized a white North Carolina attorney. Or, as Chafe put it, "Never before had the rhetoric of moderation been used so effectively to implement a politics of reaction."

Governor William Umstead pronounced himself "terribly disappointed" in the *Brown* decision but vowed fealty to the law of the land and set about achieving compliance. Unbowed, within a year of the ruling the North Carolina General Assembly resolved that "the mixing of the races in the public schools . . . cannot be accomplished and should not be attempted." Within two years a regional tide of resistance produced a "Declaration of Southern Principles," also known as the Southern Manifesto, signed by 101 U.S. congressmen. Drafted first by South Carolina's Strom Thurmond, the document called the *Brown* decision "a clear abuse of judicial power" and commended "the motives of those States which have declared the intention to resist forced integration by any lawful means." Three North Carolina representatives refused to sign; only one managed to win reelection in the fall of 1956, and he survived by campaigning as the more virulent racist.

Meanwhile, Umstead had died in office and was replaced by Luther Hodges, a moderate in name more than deed. "Containing the highest percentage of Negroes to total population of any state outside the Deep South,

Perry Wallace recounted
the pain of his Vanderbilt
experience, and was
shunned after graduation.
Vanderbilt Media Relations

Henry Harris's Auburn
career never rose to
expectations.
Auburn Sports
Information Office

North Carolina's Charles Scott was the only ACC pioneer to make all-conference.
UNC Athletics

Wendell Hudson (front row, third from right) soon bonded with Alabama teammates. University of Alabama Photo

Norwood Todmann
fell by the wayside
at Wake Forest.
Wake Forest Media
Relations Office

Tom Payne Jr. (left)
and Kentucky assistant
Joe B. Hall, Adolph
Rupp's successor as
head coach.
Collegiate Images

Al Heartley, from walk-on to team captain at N. C. State.
N. C. State
Media Relations
Office

Ronnie Hogue scored frequently at the University of Georgia.
UGA Sports
Communications

Craig Mobley and parents look a bit wary upon signing with Clemson.
Clemson University Sports Information Office

Casey Manning was
a fan favorite at the
University of South
Carolina.
USC Sports
Information Office

His sister cried when Collis Temple Jr., chose to attend Louisiana State.
LSU Sports Information Department

Coolidge Ball felt surprisingly comfortable at Ole Miss.
University of Mississippi Athletics Media Relations

Larry Robinson (center) inspired younger players on his University of Tennessee squad. University of Tennessee Sports Information

Steve Williams
fled a campus sit-in
at Florida rather
than risk losing his
scholarship.
UF Sports Information
Office

Larry Fry
purposefully broke
racial barriers at
Mississippi State.
Mississippi State
Athletic Media Relations

Jerry Jenkins
remains among
the top scorers in
Mississippi State
history.
Mississippi State Athletic
Media Relations

North Carolina was potentially one of the most volatile of upper South states," Bartley said. "Hodges protected himself by announcing his intention to call a special legislative session to enact anti-integration measures and by defending segregation almost to the point of massive resistance."

Hodges advocated the removal of state control over education, placing decision-making with local school boards in the name of voluntary compliance. The "Pearsall Plan" allowed "enough reasons for school assignment that were not explicitly racial to guarantee that no Black would ever go to a white school," Chafe said. "In the end the Pearsall Plan . . . postponed meaningful desegregation in North Carolina for more than a decade— longer than in some states where massive resistance was practiced."

In 1959 only 53 of 225 requests for transfer by African-American students were granted in the entire state of North Carolina. Most were the children of military personnel in a single district. Few Black parents chose to "brave threats and bureaucratic gauntlets for the privilege of sending their children in twos and threes to hostile white classes," Robert Weisbrot said in *Freedom Bound*, a history of America's civil rights movement. Of course this was exactly the idea. "Why, if we could be half as successful as you have been," an Arkansas official wrote admiringly of North Carolinians, "we could keep this thing to a minimum for the next fifty years."

Raleigh, for instance, integrated its schools in 1960, but only marginally. Substantial integration did not occur in Raleigh until 1970, after the sham of "freedom of choice" was ended by a U.S. Supreme Court ruling that said such plans were invalid if they failed to yield successful integration. By then Al Heartley was an undergraduate at NC State.

Heartley's sophomore year in high school, local resistance loosened, and volunteers were sought to desegregate the white school. Several classmates chose to go. Heartley, like many athletes at Johnston Central, did not, content instead to stick with friends, teammates, and a setting with which he was familiar and in which he thrived. "We needed pioneers in those days, and I didn't want to be a pioneer at that level," he said. "I played basketball; I played baseball. I was in the band. I was president of my class. So I wanted to stay."

Heartley finished as valedictorian of his class but never quite realized his goal of winning the state 3A title in basketball. In each of his varsity seasons, Durham's Merrick Moore High School beat the team from Smithfield in the district finals. "They went on three years in a row to win the state championship, so each year was going to be the year we won. We never did win. So that kept me coming back," Heartley said.

His reluctance to become a teenage pioneer was shared by many African-American students of the era. "When the Black students left Central High," Boyce Quinn wrote in 1968 in the *North Carolina Anvil*, describing a school in a nearby county, "they also left their school traditions and loyalties, rivalries, school songs and legends; and even more important-ly, their positions of power and influence—the Black student who would have been school or class president would now be nothing; the faces of the students who would address the assembly, edit the yearbook, sway opinion, decide the date of the prom—those faces would be white."

Martin Luther King Jr. and other civil rights advocates fought for the right of any person to partake in broader society, but in many respects the insular world to which African Americans were relegated, whether in Nashville, Tennessee, or Clayton, North Carolina, was both comfortable and nurturing. The extended Heartley family looked out for one another. They owned farms, stores, and rental properties. The boys' grandfather had a truck farm and owned automobiles back in the days of the Model A and Model T. "We were by no means rich, but we lived a good life," Harvey Heartley said.

Basketball was a valued component of that good life. Black high school teams barnstormed through the Southeast, playing weekend tournaments. Games matching prominent in-state Black high schools drew large crowds. "There wasn't nowhere else to go," Harvey Heartley said. "So you played ball." Some Black gymnasia in eastern North Carolina still had outhouses in the second half of the 20th century. Others, such as the gym at Johnston Central High in Smithfield, were heated by a potbellied wood stove. Having the stove proximate to the playing floor "was hazardous to your health, especially if somebody pushed you," Harvey Heartley said. "It would be cherry red. You just didn't go to those corners. You shot jumpers at the foul line, extended." Years later, his youngest brother still played with the wood stove in the corner and visited gyms where a player inbounding the ball couldn't run the baseline because he had to stand between two-by-fours framing the structure.

The pinnacle of African-American basketball in the state was the Central (originally Colored) Intercollegiate Athletic Association, composed primarily of colleges from Virginia and North Carolina. (Schools such as West Virginia State, Morgan State, Howard, Lincoln, Hampton, Norfolk

State, Winston-Salem State, and N. C. Central dropped out over the years.) Despite scant coverage by white newspapers, youngsters across the region followed favorite teams and players, their interest peaking in early March with the league tournament.

The CIAA's postseason tournament, established in 1946 by John McLendon and others, was the second-oldest in college ball, surpassed only by the Southern Conference, and brought together many of eastern basketball's best players, black or otherwise. Some—such as Central's Sam Jones, Winston-Salem's Earl Monroe, Hampton's Ricky Mahorn, Norfolk State's Bob Dandridge, and Virginia Union's Charles Oakley—went on to fame in the NBA. Others remained stars in a smaller universe but dazzled nonetheless. "That was the best basketball we could see at the time," Al Heartley said.

Duke's C. B. Claiborne played for a CIAA alum, Hank Allen, in high school in Danville, Virginia. He fondly recalled Allen taking the entire basketball squad annually to North Carolina to opening-day games at the tournament. Heartley had the same experience, courtesy of his high school coach, Reginald Ennis, known as "the Hawk" when he played for McLendon at N.C. Central.

"He'd take the basketball team and say, 'Hey, you need to see more than what's in Smithfield, N.C.'—small town, tobacco, KKK sign, and all that," Al Heartley said. "Then we'd see the first round of the CIAA Tournament. That's when all the schools came from Virginia, and the North Carolina teams, and they'd have on their beautiful warm-ups and the cheerleaders would be there. All of that pageantry you saw, but you saw it in an all-Black context."

Al Heartley said he wondered how the CIAA stars would compete if they met the ACC players he saw on television. But his brother, who played for McLendon at North Carolina College and later coached for 23 seasons at another CIAA school, St. Augustine's College in Raleigh, had no doubts. "We knew we were better than they were. If you look at it now, if you look at the natural progression of things, if you take all of the Black players out of the ACC and put them in the CIAA, and then play . . ."

That "natural progression" included a style of play marked by up-tempo offense and defense and a commitment to entertain as well as compete.

Cal Irvin, who coached for many years at North Carolina A&T State University in Greensboro, once gave a speech entitled "Our Game" at a national coaches' convention. (The border-state hotel where the coaches met attempted to block Irvin from entering the building, but he, Gaines, McLendon, and others persevered.) "Our game wasn't different, but we had more speed and it was not quite as patterned," Irvin said. "We were more freelancing, with a more provocative, open game. That's why black basketball was so popular. It was entertaining. Maybe it wasn't the best defense, but it was some defense."

Contemplating contemporary college basketball—with its pressure defenses, flowing attacks, and one-on-one moves—Harvey Heartley saw a familiar game, one now dominated by African-American athletes. "What they're playing now, we played then," he said. Describing a style christened "Forty Minutes of Hell" when Nolan Richardson used it at Arkansas from 1986 to 2002, Harvey Heartley added, "We have always played 94–40, smoke and smother. What that meant was we were going to come after you from baseline to baseline for 40 minutes. When you shot and missed, there was going to be smoke going down to the other end, and then once we scored we were going to smother on defense."

This was the context in which Al Heartley learned the game from his brother, from Ennis, and, by extension, from McLendon, whom Irvin called "a brilliant coach, a brilliant tactician, a brilliant mind." The Johnston Central varsity was a combined 53–15 during Al Heartley's varsity career. His senior season, when the playmaker averaged about 14 points per game, the team was 22–4. Recruiters scarcely noticed. "Nobody much talked to me about college ball," Heartley said.

When it came time to choose a school, Heartley's oldest brother wanted him to attend what had become North Carolina Central University. Middle brother Matthew had gone to North Carolina A&T. But his parents preferred NC State, believing a degree from a predominantly white university would open more doors in society at large. "It was a dilemma at that time for good Black [students] whether to go to a predominantly white school or to a good Black school," Al Heartley said.

NC State was noted for its engineering and technical schools, where Heartley's interest lay. He also wanted to take a path that differed from his brothers, an option supported by a high school guidance counselor who urged him to break new racial ground. "You're the kind of person we would like to see go to a school like NC State or Carolina or Wake Forest or something like that," the counselor said. "You've got the academic credentials. You've been involved in athletics. We'd like to see you go."

An added inducement was the Wolfpack's underdog basketball status. Duke was riding high under Vic Bubas when the youngest Heartley approvingly watched "the cow college, as they called it," upset the Blue Devils to win the 1965 ACC tournament.

Two years later, Heartley was an NC State freshman studying mathematics. His academic focus did not rule out basketball entirely; he avidly participated in campus pickup games. Among the competitors was Willis "Breeze" Cooper, a scholarship freshman from Raleigh's all-Black Ligon High School. There he led a team coached by Harvey Heartley to a state title. Al Heartley knew he could compete with Cooper, and NC State's other freshman guards were not overwhelmingly impressive, either. Looking for confirmation prior to approaching Sloan, Heartley consulted his brother and mentor. Harvey Heartley told him, "Well, I've seen them all, and you're as good as any of them out there. If you can play in Smithfield under Coach Ennis, you can play anywhere in the world."

The first day of tryouts, Heartley immediately caught the eye of Esposito, also NC State's baseball coach. Esposito was always on the lookout for quick hands, mental alertness, and athleticism. Heartley possessed all three, as well as an unusual aptitude for basketball. "He is one of the quickest learners I've ever had," Sloan later told a reporter. "He has an amazing ability to pick up something we explain, not forget it, and put it into operation immediately."

The freshman squad already had four guards on scholarship, so the 163-pound walk-on was moved to forward, where he was sometimes matched against players more than a half-foot taller. "But I played, and that was the key," Heartley said. "I played, and as I played my confidence grew because I saw, 'Hey, I can play with these guys.'" He started all but the first game, finishing with averages of 8.3 points and 7 rebounds.

Heartley's defensive prowess immediately came to the fore, much to the chagrin of Billy Packer, a Wake Forest assistant coach. "It was my second group of recruits," Packer said. "Charlie Davis is a freshman. So I'm sitting right behind Norm Sloan, whose teams I'd played against at Florida. Fiery kind of guy. So Wake's playing State, and this guy from State is doing a good job on Charlie Davis, and I'm bitching at the referee.

"Sloan turned around to me and he said, 'You're going to find out down the road that my man is a pretty good defender.' Sort of like, 'Why don't you just shut your mouth, OK?' Pissed me off. But he's a head coach and I just keep my mouth shut. Sloan taught me a hell of a lesson that night. Forget about bitching. Just because you're so involved in your guy, you're not really watching the game. And the defender was Al Heartley."

Not until midway through the 1967–68 season did Sloan learn that Heartley was related to the coach at Ligon High. "Harvey called to ask how his kid brother was doing," Sloan wrote in *Confessions of a Coach*. "That was the first time I realized the connection." Sloan had sufficient respect for the elder Heartley that he later offered him a job as an assistant coach at NC State.

The following season, Al Heartley became the first African American to play varsity basketball for the Wolfpack. More significant to Heartley at the time, he was awarded a scholarship that became available when Cooper and another guard transferred. Between seasons, however, Heartley received a sobering reminder of the racial realities on NC State's campus, and beyond.

Irwin Holmes had enjoyed a positive experience nearly a decade earlier, marred only by a racist instructor and a bigoted intramural captain. Once, when the tennis squad stopped at a Durham restaurant and Holmes was refused service, the entire team walked out. "For a bunch of Southern boys, that was really special," Holmes said. Heartley, too, spoke fondly of his four years at NC State. But he was unquestionably scared the night of April 4, 1968, after Martin Luther King Jr. was assassinated in Memphis.

Angry African Americans took to the streets in downtown Raleigh, among them students from Shaw University, where the Student Nonviolent Coordinating Committee had been founded in 1960. Soon, as in more than 100 cities across the United States, rioting broke out in North Carolina's capital. "You could see the red glow in the sky from the fires," Al Heartley said. "And I'm sitting over there on State's campus with 10,000 students"— 10,835 including graduate students—"and there were only about 100 Blacks. That was kind of frightening because I didn't know what was going to happen. Nobody knew what was going to happen."

White students packed the quadrangle outside the dormitories inhabited by Heartley and about a half-dozen other African Americans. The Black students gathered in a single room, locked the door, and listened to radio descriptions of turmoil in downtown Raleigh and elsewhere. Occasional glances outside brought sight of National Guardsmen and a swarm of yelling students. "They were our classmates," Heartley said of the throng. "They knew there were Black students in those dorms. But we were never attacked. It was all just a lot of racial slurs. . . . That's what's scary about a mass of people, because you don't know who's doing it. There's not a face; there's just a voice. And it was at night, so while you saw people, there was not a lot of light. There were campus lights. There weren't individual faces [such that you could say] the guy down the hall was out there." Heartley laughed without glee. "You couldn't tell that, but we weren't going to go out there to see."

The roomful of isolated students skipped class the day after King's assassination, wary of the reception they might receive. When they finally ventured out, the campus atmosphere was sorrowful. Most white students said nothing and averted their gaze. "If I have a memory outside of basketball, when that [anniversary] comes up every April, I think about it," Heartley said.

His basketball memories are positive, particularly within the team. Heartley reported that he received no special treatment, good or bad, due to his race. He was simply accepted as another player.

Treatment from fans was more mixed, at home and on the road. A freshman visit to tiny Louisburg College northeast of Raleigh was particularly rough.

Wolfpack fans were not averse to expressing their prejudices, either. An NC State fan from the eastern part of the state wrote Sloan to complain about Esposito and either Cooper or Heartley. "You've been on the job a little over a year and you've made two significant contributions," the booster wrote. "You've hired a dago as an assistant coach and brought the first nigger into the program." Sloan said that when his team won the 1974 NCAA title, "this same jerk . . . was one of the first ones down on the floor to grab my hand." Sloan found it ironic that, after explaining his program's dearth of Black players to David Thompson, "I would be explaining to boosters why we had a scarcity of white players. I felt compelled to do that because people made ridiculous charges and allegations." Sloan also expressed embarrassment at the way some Wolfpack fans treated the parents of Thurl Bailey, a Black player at NC State from 1979 to 1983, during games at Reynolds Coliseum.

"They were handled pretty well," Harvey Heartley said of African-American players under Sloan. "Norm was a good coach. He knew what the deal was. He knew what the South was."

Sloan's successor, New Yorker Jim Valvano, started five African Americans in 1983, Bailey among them, en route to a surprise NCAA title. (Sidney Lowe, the point guard on that squad, became the school's first Black head basketball coach in 2006.) When the team struggled at midseason, Valvano admitted he was taken aback to receive a steady stream of letters criticizing him for employing an all-Black lineup.

Casey Manning, the first Black basketball player at the University of South Carolina, said this acute, uneasy awareness of race was consistent with his impression of NC State. He recounted making a telephone call to the university athletic department to confirm his memory that Al Heartley broke the Wolfpack's color barrier. "The lady wasn't mean or vicious or anything. She just said, 'Yeah, it was Al Heartley. He was the first nigger captain at NC State.' Now, this was 1984. It's a true story."

In recent years students in Raleigh greeted a North Carolina center with a sign equating his appearance with that of a Neanderthal and a Clemson forward with a sign proclaiming 10" VERTICAL JUMP 20" LIPS. These racial slurs were perhaps unintentional, but were slurs nonetheless.

Black players such as Solly Walker performed in Raleigh long before the ACC color line was broken, thanks to the vision of Everett Case, a consummate promoter whose teams averaged 26 wins and 6 losses at the height of their prowess, 1947 to 1956. The Indiana native and his "Hoosier Hotshots" brought fast-break basketball to North Carolina and then showcased it in 12,400-seat Reynolds Coliseum, the largest basketball arena in the Southeast when it opened in December 1949. For a decade N.C. State led the nation's colleges in attendance. "When we came here, people in this part of the country were basketball illiterates," Sloan, among Case's first recruits, told writer Tim Peeler.

Reynolds, an on-campus facility modeled after Duke (later Cameron) Indoor Stadium, also hosted NCAA tournament regional games; the ACC tournament once that league commenced play during the 1953–54 school year; and the Dixie Classic, a three-day post-Christmas tournament. These riches moved Raleigh leaders to proclaim their city the "world capital of basketball." In those days of television's infancy, the Dixie Classic provided a rare glimpse of many of the nation's top teams, which came to Raleigh to face Duke University, the University of North Carolina, North Carolina State College, and Wake Forest College. "It was the Sugar Bowl and the Rose Bowl rolled into one," said William Friday, then president of the University of North Carolina system, of which NC State remains a part. Friday would command the demise of the Dixie Classic after a national betting scandal engulfed NC State and North Carolina in 1961.

The Dixie, a Case creation, reached a competitive peak in 1958 when half of the teams in the field ranked in the top 10 in the polls. Among the visitors was Cincinnati, led by Oscar Robertson, the national Player of the Year from 1958 to 1960. Robertson was from Indianapolis, Indiana, where

Sloan had spent part of his youth sneaking into Hickle Fieldhouse to play pickup games. Sloan also occasionally ventured to Indianapolis's so-called Dust Bowl, where Robertson and other players from Crispus Attucks High School held court. "When you got to feeling your oats, why, you'd kind of go down there and see how good you were, and go back home with your tail between your legs," Sloan said.

Second-ranked Cincinnati beat Wake Forest but lost to NC State and North Carolina. Robertson scored 29 points in each of the three games, leading Case to comment, "I know a lot of Southern coaches who would like to pull a Branch Rickey with that boy." Case himself steered Black prospects to Northern schools for most of his career. "He didn't say not to get any," said Howard Garfinkel, who informally recruited for N.C. State from 1955 through 1960. "We just didn't. That's a great question. Never mentioned. Nobody ever said anything. It wasn't an issue. Not down there. Those were the days of the White Citizens' Councils."

Robertson, a 6-foot-5 guard, was not one to shrink from anything, including the hostility of the overwhelmingly white crowd at Reynolds Coliseum. "That became a legendary story," said Raveling, then a player at Villanova. "There weren't people, Black guys, playing basketball at that time that hadn't heard that story."

Robertson's reception, and how onlookers remember it, presents a striking example of the parallel and contradictory realities often experienced by Blacks and whites in the segregated South.

Virginia's Connor, who attended the Dixie Classic as a wide-eyed high school kid, heard no booing or abuse. Neither did Friday, a longtime advocate for reform in college sports who grew up in North Carolina and attended Wake Forest and NC State (he graduated from the latter in 1941). He recalled that Robertson, Michigan State's "Jumping Johnny" Green, and other Black athletes visiting Raleigh in late 1958 were positively received. Friday took it as a sign of better things to come. "I knew that sport was going to be the way that people would get to understand what integration really means," he said.

Packer, a Pennsylvania native and Wake freshman, heard the boos and witnessed something far less encouraging. "Oscar's treatment was obviously not good at that time—not only the way people played against him but people's attitudes about it," Packer said. Garfinkel was similarly bothered. "They didn't treat Oscar very well. That turned me off a little bit to those great North Carolina fans."

Harvey Heartley heard and saw the abuse but emerged with a different perspective. Watching from his vantage point in a section reserved for African Americans at the south end of the building, he saw Robertson actively taunt the crowd that taunted him. "Oscar was arrogant, too," Heartley said. "See, he was out of Indiana. Indiana and the Midwest, they had a macho attitude, almost like the Marlboro Man."

Local newspaper coverage was similarly varied when Robertson and Wake Forest's Dave Budd, a notoriously rough player, engaged in a scuffle during the Bearcats' opening-round victory over the Demon Deacons. Raleigh's *News and Observer* focused on the details of their fight for a rebound and on bland denials that the extracurricular activity went beyond the norm, even though Budd stood over Robertson with fists clenched and the Bearcat junior suffered a scratch on his neck and a cut on his forehead. Dick Herbert wrote that "both boos and applause—with the applause clearly in the majority—greeted Robertson's return to the game." Nowhere in its extensive coverage did the Raleigh newspaper mention Robertson's race.

By contrast the *Durham Morning Herald* repeatedly noted that Robertson was a "Negro star." Nearly a decade later it would regularly apply "Negro" as an adjective in its mentions of Claiborne, Duke's first African-American player. The *Herald*'s Jack Horner noted that Budd and Robertson were "hot-headed individuals" who were "elbowing each other frequently" prior to the entanglement that sent them crashing to the floor. Horner reported that, earlier in the game, Budd had been heard to say, "Black boy, everywhere you go today I'm going to be right there." When Budd went to the bench with his third foul midway through the first half, Robertson was said to inquire, "Where are you going, white boy?"

Robertson's "general court manners got the Bearcats in hot water with the paying customers and they rooted hard against Cincinnati," Horner wrote. As to the scrap, the *Herald* quoted Budd saying he did not hit Robertson because "I happened to think about his race and knew if I hit him, it would cause a lot of trouble. If it had been any other player, no one would have thought too much about it. But because of his race, I guess it will look bad for this section."

Was race relevant to the discussion? Current sensibilities indicate otherwise, but in the context of the segregated South, a lack of attention was significant.

"To know that period of the South is to know that it was frozen in silence," Eugene Patterson, editor of the *Atlanta Constitution* from 1960 to

1967, told Howell Raines for *My Soul Is Rested*, an oral history of the civil rights movement in the Deep South. "People were not discussing the issue. Neighbor and neighbor were afraid of each other. Conformity was established by precedent . . . Getting the silence broken and getting a public dialogue started was the beginning of the end of segregation."

When the civil rights movement gained traction, many newspapers tried to dampen the effect. For example, the publisher of Kentucky's *Herald-Leader* "ordered his editors to either ignore the Watts riots [during the 1960s] or downplay the story significantly" said author Billy Reed in *Transition Game*. "His theory was that if Lexington's Blacks didn't know what was happening in L.A., they wouldn't be inclined to riot." The newspaper also declined to cover student demonstrators protesting the failure of the UK basketball program to recruit Black players. The *Herald-Leader* apologized to its readers in 2004 for its previous bias and failures of coverage, announcing, "It has come to the editor's attention that the *Herald-Leader* neglected to cover the Civil Rights Movement. We regret the omission."

Much had changed by the time Al Heartley arrived on the scene in Raleigh. Still, his ACC playing days, particularly as a freshman, were accompanied by a muted version of the treatment accorded Robertson. Fans even tossed ice at Heartley (the same slight that sent Indiana Pacer Ron Artest racing into the stands seeking retribution during a late 2004 NBA game against the Detroit Pistons). Sloan admitted there was discomfort, if not friction, within his team as well. Some white players did not want to room with Black players on the road. The coach also had yet to learn to quit calling all of his players "boys" and to drop the expression "calling a spade a spade," a racial faux pas later pointed out by Thompson.

"I would not say it was uneventful," Heartley said of his reception as a Black male. "But I didn't hear as many racial comments as you would think we would have heard." Immersion in competition left him largely deaf to verbal abuse, except at Duke, where students routinely mocked NC State players for their major courses of study. "The guys who were in physical ed, they kind of laughed at them, taunted them. That was always good for me because my major was applied math, so they didn't know what to do. 'Applied math? Uh, oh. This guy must be pretty smart.'"

Certainly Heartley showed intelligence on defense, where young players infrequently excel. "I didn't score much in high school," he told Mary Garber of the *Winston-Salem Sentinel*. "But our team worked hard on defense.

We pressed all the time and we never played a zone."

Heartley quickly became known as a defensive stopper, his reputation secured by the thoroughness with which he dogged Charlie Davis, the similarly sized prolific Wake guard. "The only thing closer to Charlie than Heartley was Davis' mustache," wrote Bruce Phillips in the *Raleigh Times*. The duo faced off repeatedly over their college careers, and Heartley never ceased to prove a wet blanket for the combustible New Yorker. "He has the quickness to really give you a hard time, and he did a good job guarding me," Davis said in 1971 after being held to 14 points, half of his average. "I don't like to play against him."

Perhaps the highlight of Heartley's first varsity season came at Madison Square Garden, where the Wolfpack defeated New York University in early December. He made all his shots, scored 5 points, and had 4 assists. Phil Pepe of the *New York Daily News* praised Sloan's club, particularly "a sophomore named Al Heartley, who comes from Clayton, N.C., but played like he is out of a Brooklyn schoolyard." Garber later felt compelled to facetiously explain to Winston-Salem readers that being likened to a New Yorker was a compliment.

The trip to Manhattan was Heartley's first, as was the airplane ride. The self-described "little kid from Clayton" so savored the moment when the Garden's public address announcer said, "Two points by Heartley" that he momentarily froze in place. "I stopped because I couldn't believe it. 'They've got my name up there!'" he thought. "And Norm said, 'Go on, go on, go on!'"

Heartley, described by one writer as "slippery" and "cobra quick," finished the 1968–69 season averaging 4.6 points; he appeared in all but two games on the 15–10 squad. He also had the highest grade point average on the team. A Charlotte sportswriter touted him as "undoubtedly the Cinderella player of the ACC." But the glass slipper Heartley sought was a spot in the starting lineup, a status he could not achieve unless he and Sloan came to an accommodation about playing style.

Later in his career, the volatile Sloan—nicknamed "Stormin' Norman" by a local media contingent he unlovingly dubbed the "Worm Brigade"— employed a more free-flowing offense. But not during Heartley's years. Sloan was not averse to fast-break basketball, having played in Case's system. His half-court sets were more old-school, though, emulating the frontline-oriented "center opposite" approach perfected by Tony Hinkle, the Butler coach. Guards had little role in that offense except on a break. Sloan's resistance to one-on-one moves by guards, the very habit that put him in Case's doghouse, led to confrontations with Monte Towe, the Indiana spark-plug who directed the 1972–73 and 1973–74 squads to a combined record of 57–1, still best in ACC history. Sloan also was prone to using a two-three zone defense.

Initially, then, Heartley was not a good fit for Sloan's style. "I was not used to playing the controlled, methodical offense like so many teams during that time," Heartley said. "That just wasn't my style, and I had to adjust at State. Among the adjustments I had to make to play point guard was to starting running plays and being patient and running the half-court offense. We just didn't do much of that in high school. We were pressure defense. You had the open shot, you took it. [At N.C. State] everybody went to the boards except the point guard."

N.C. State was set at four positions at the start of the 1969–70 season. The exception was at playmaker, where there were two solid, safe options and Heartley. Sloan gave each an equal chance, and Heartley moved to the fore. "He wasn't a great player, a great recruit, but solid," Packer said. "Team-oriented, defensive-oriented. He made good, heady plays. Smart."

Heartley brought quickness to the lineup, particularly teamed in the backcourt with roommate Ed Leftwich, the program's other African-American player. (Leftwich played in 1970 and 1971, then left.) Heartley was unselfish with the ball, which teammates liked. By midseason a school press release declared he had "earned a starter's role with sound defense and a knack for running State's offense. Once a questionable ball-handler, he's settled to the point that pressure defenses don't worry him." Oddly, given Sloan's reservations about assertive guards, the major knock on Heartley's game was that he did not shoot enough.

The junior appeared in all but one of NC State's games in a 23–7 season, and the Wolfpack tied with North Carolina for second place in the league. The 1969–70 record, the best under Sloan until Thompson joined the varsity, culminated with the coach's only league title until the 1972–73 season.

Yet the most significant aspect of Heartley's emergence has gone largely unremarked over the years. His was the mind that became an on-court extension of his coach's will, the hand that steered the Wolfpack's course. "He's the closest thing to a quarterback we have in that he assesses the situation on the court, takes charge and runs the offense," Sloan said. "His approach to the game, as it is to his studies, is a mental approach. He's

always taking notes and looking at films, making up for his lack of real physical size by seeking that opponent's flaw that he can exploit."

At a time when African Americans struggled to establish themselves in a
desegregated setting, overcoming stereotypes that kept them from decision-
making positions in all walks of life, this was no small matter. "Point guard
was a position we weren't supposed to be able to play," Jerry Harkness, a
Black All-American on Loyola's 1963 NCAA championship team, told an
interviewer.

A season would pass before the ACC honored a Black man as Player of
the Year in football, Duke's Ernie Jackson, or in basketball, Wake's Davis
(both in 1971). Two years would pass before the SEC had its first African-
American quarterbacks. Three seasons would pass before every varsity basketball program in both conferences was integrated. Thirteen years would
pass before the majority of ACC players were Black. Heartley arrived on the
scene relatively early in the process. And, of all the barrier-breaking basketball players in the SEC and ACC, only he commanded the responsibilities
of floor generalship.

Except, that is, in the most important game of his career.

NC State entered the 1970 ACC tournament in Charlotte as the number three seed. South Carolina, the third team in league history to play
through the regular season without a conference loss, was heavily favored to
win the tournament. Led by John Roche, the two-time conference Player of
the Year, Frank McGuire's Gamecocks predictably advanced to the final.
Meanwhile, Heartley started in the Wolfpack's opening-round win, then
took a backseat to teammate Joe Dunning, who scored 14 points in a 67–66
semifinal victory that lifted NC State to the championship contest.

Dunning, who made 41.9 percent of his shots on the year to Heartley's
37.3 percent, started against South Carolina and played every minute. Not
just every minute during regulation, but through a first overtime, and then a
second. NC State used five players for all 50 minutes, an enduring record for
the event. McGuire played just six men as the Wolfpack slowed the tempo.
"Joe Dunning took my place, simply because Norm had decided that we could
not play our normal game and run with South Carolina," Heartley said.
"That was not the style that I grew up with, the style that I could play. So my
biggest disappointment is, while it was great to win an ACC championship, it
was the only game my junior year that I didn't play in. Didn't play at all."

Bottom seed Clemson almost eliminated South Carolina in the opener
with a delay, a tactic familiar to Sloan in those pre–shot clock days. He had

secured great notoriety, and a stunning upset, by employing a deep, deep freeze to win 12–10 in the 1968 ACC tournament semifinals. The victim was a talented Duke team coached by Bubas, who years earlier had beaten out Sloan for a spot in Case's backcourt. During one stretch in the first half of the low-scoring game—which UNC announcer Bill Currie said on-air was "as exciting as artificial insemination"—Pack center Bill Kretzer dribbled the ball unmolested for 14 minutes.

NC State quickly fell behind South Carolina in the 1970 final. With his starters in foul trouble, Sloan went to a delay. Playing McGuire's squad straight-up had not worked during the regular season, anyway. This time Roche was hampered by a severe ankle sprain. Just as with Bubas in 1968, Sloan found McGuire too proud or too stubborn to force the action with a superior squad. McGuire was so disdainful that he twirled his finger by his temple to indicate craziness and pointed to his NC State counterpart. The unorthodox strategy even moved Joan Sloan to send her son to the bench to ask her husband what he was doing.

Heartley sat beside Sloan as the game unfolded, the coach repeatedly patting the guard's leg and asking if he was ready. Heartley kept saying yes, aching to take the court. Sloan kept patting, yet stood pat without his primary playmaker. Finally, Leftwich stole the ball from South Carolina's Bobby Cremins with 22 seconds remaining in the second extra period and drove for the decisive basket in a 42–39 win. Dunning had 8 points, double his season average. The victory earned NC State the league's sole bid to the NCAA tournament and muted critics whom Sloan said "were starting to mumble and rumble" about his coaching.

"Much as I've talked about that game, I haven't thought about Al and the sacrifice he had to make," Sloan said decades later. "That shows you what caliber young man he was, and is. He figured it out. He knew, but he didn't like it, I'm sure. I wouldn't have liked it."

Employing analytical coolness, Heartley confirmed Sloan's assessment in every respect, declining to inject a racial or personal component into the equation. "As I look back on it, he made the right move. I don't have any problems with his decision because Joe was a better outside shooter," Heartley said. "He won't be high in the stats, but he hit some key shots. Looking back on it, yeah, he would have done a better job of that than I would have. I don't know that I would have taken those shots, because that wasn't my style."

The following season, Heartley's last, the defending ACC champions got off to an 8–5 start. Gone were forwards Rick Anheuser and Vann Williford, the Most Valuable Player of the 1970 tournament and a two-time All-ACC performer. Looking for leadership, Sloan designated the hardworking Heartley as team captain. "The students loved me," Heartley said. "I got a lot of cheers because they felt, hey, here's an example of a guy who can come to a school, walk on, play, do well, and end up his senior year as captain."

Heartley remained popular with local journalists as well. For them he was an improbable hero of human proportion. "Nobody could ever picture him as the Wolfpack captain," A. J. Carr wrote in Raleigh's *News and Observer*. "No more than they could picture Tiny Tim as president, Joe Namath as mayor of New York, or Ed Sullivan as an astronaut. But the lean Heartley seems to defy the laws of probability."

Heartley appeared in every game in 1970–71 as NC State fell to 13–14, the last losing season of Sloan's 14-year career in Raleigh (1967–80). The starting point guard increased his scoring by half, to 6 points per game, and improved his accuracy, assertiveness, and confidence. He forced numerous turnovers, scored a career-high 16 points, and hit a pair of pressure free throws in the waning seconds of a victory at Duke. "I wouldn't trade him for any guard in this league," Sloan said.

Heartley graduated on time with a degree in mathematics. He got a management job with Southern Bell in North Carolina and advanced to general manager of BellSouth (later AT&T) in Atlanta. Basketball paid the way and allowed him to live the dream of many a North Carolina schoolboy, Black and white, a dream fanned by Everett Case, Frank McGuire and John McLendon in the aftermath of World War II. "Norm gave me an opportunity to play, something I will always thank him for," Heartley said. "Everybody criticized him, said he was a rough coach. My comment is, 'The man gave me a chance, so I'll always love him.'"

CHAPTER 10

PENN PALL

Ronnie Hogue, University of Georgia, 1969–73

Hereditary bondsmen! know you not,
Who would be free, themselves must strike the blow?
Lord Byron, "Childe Harold's Pilgrimage"

Ronnie Hogue, like many members of the African-American community in Washington, D.C., vividly recalled the fate of Lemuel Penn, a cautious adult who knew better than to stop, even for a sandwich, in rural Georgia. Penn was 49 years old, a man who had taught in the D.C. school system for 20 years before rising to assistant superintendent in charge of vocational and adult education. He was active in the Boy Scouts and the Methodist Church. He was married with three children.

On July 11, 1964, Penn was on his way home from Fort Benning on the Georgia–Alabama border, where he spent two weeks fulfilling his obligations as a lieutenant colonel in the U.S. Army Reserve. He had stayed on base the entire time in order to avoid any "racial unpleasantness," he told his wife. Less than a month earlier, three civil rights workers—James Chaney, Andrew Goodman, and Michael Schwerner—had been murdered in Mississippi.

Hogue was a few months shy of his 14th birthday when Penn, driving with two other Black reserve officers in a Chevrolet sedan bearing D.C. plates, was transformed into yet another casualty of white intransigence. For all the great changes afoot in the region's racial landscape, the pitfalls did not differ all that much from those in 1945, when Richard Wright wrote in *Black Boy* that "the problem of living as a Negro was cold and hard. What was it that made the hate of whites for Blacks so steady, seemingly so woven into the texture of things?"

Penn and his traveling companions drove 65 miles northeast from Atlanta, where unfinished Interstate 85 ended, to Athens, where they paused a few feet from the aged, ornate arch that is the gateway to the University of Georgia campus. Penn took the wheel, and the trio departed the town of 30,000 residents on lonely two-lane roads, shadowed by a cream-colored Chevy station wagon bearing three passengers.

"For most of the 1950s and 1960s, Athens, Georgia, was a hotbed of Klan activity," Robert Pratt explained in a book on the desegregation of the University of Georgia. "Underneath the facade of gentility—in this college town of oak-lined residential streets and stately antebellum homes that gave the appearance of culture and refinement—existed a class of poorly paid white workers who labored in the city's textile mills and whose socioeconomic status was only marginally better than that of Athens's Black population." The rising tide of change created by the civil rights movement, embodied in the 1961 integration of UGA, created a new reality for these laborers. "Simply being white would no longer be enough to give them status and a feeling of superiority over all black men and women," Bill Shipp said in *Murder at Broad River Bridge.*

The Ku Klux Klan had been reborn in Georgia in 1915, and in Athens, the self-described "Classic City of the South," Clarke County Klavern No. 244 was active, belligerent, and on the prowl the night Penn and company passed through town. Shortly after Penn turned onto Georgia Highway 172 and started down a long hill toward the Broad River, the trailing Chevy wagon accelerated and pulled alongside the out-of-state vehicle. A shotgun blast took off the side of Penn's face, killing him.

Typical of Deep South justice, an all-white Georgia jury did not convict the men accused of Penn's murder. The night after the acquittal, the Imperial Wizard of the National Knights of the KKK told a rally at Stone Mountain outside Atlanta, "You'll never be able to convict a white man that killed a nigger that encroaches on the white race in the South." Later, two men charged as Penn's assailants were found guilty in federal court of violating his civil rights; they spent several years in prison for the crime.

So, when Georgia basketball recruiters came calling five years after Penn's death, seeking Ronnie Hogue's services both as a guard and as the school's first prominent African-American athlete, the D.C. resident was understandably hesitant. "I didn't want to go to Georgia because of that," Hogue recalled. "I didn't want to go down to Georgia because I thought, 'See that, they like to shoot Black folks.'"

Ultimately, Hogue relented. Hometown acquaintances warned the highly recruited guard that there also were racial problems at New York's Syracuse University, a school he was seriously considering. He liked and trusted John Guthrie, the assistant coach making the primary pitch on behalf of Georgia head coach Ken Rosemond. And Hogue saw potential in a program that seemed committed to escaping Kentucky's near-stranglehold on SEC basketball, and to emerging from the shadow of a football tradition so strong Adolph Rupp said Georgia fans believed a field goal counted three points year-round. "For years," Jesse Outlar wrote in the *Atlanta Constitution*, "they've been hoping on Ag Hill that some day Georgia would field a basketball team the football team could be proud of."

Hogue also felt wanted at Georgia. "It was really nice because the Blacks down there in Athens really wanted a ballplayer, a Black athlete, to come down there. The whites, too. So both of them wanted me."

The choice did have its drawbacks. Hogue faced a local lawman's loaded weapon during his time in Athens, nearly blundered into a Klan rally, was attacked during a postgame melee, was wrongfully accused of drug use by his coach, and played for two losing teams in three seasons on the varsity. "I think I was lucky I didn't get scarred or hurt by those times," he said. Yet Hogue "never regretted" his choice of schools, largely because he found whites on campus far more tolerant, and tolerable, than the general populace. "It was a very open university," he said. "The University of Georgia—people might get mad at me—is not really *south* South. You have a lot of northern people down there. . . . The University of Georgia didn't take in the lower-class whites; it had mostly middle-class and upper-class whites, who had very good respect for other people."

Happily, Hogue's perception indicated a distinct improvement over undergraduate attitudes gleaned in a classroom survey shortly after a riot marked the court-ordered integration of the university in 1961. Historian Robert Cohen said "the fact that college students, among the state's best educated youths, expressed with such seriousness absurd ideas about Black skull size, jungle rhythm, and shiftlessness should give us pause to consider the sources of these ideas and the nature of Georgian and southern education—or more precisely miseducation—about race."

To this day the University of Georgia struggles with low enrollment by African-American students—about 7.5 percent of the student body in 2020, in a state where nearly a third of the population is Black. Racially exclusionary policies by Greek organizations on campus exacerbate racial divides, as they do at many other universities in the South. Black students at Georgia boycotted homecoming in 1994 due to their exclusion from the ranks of judges and beauty contest finalists. UGA also has twice endured scandals regarding academic chicanery geared toward maintaining the eligibility of student-athletes, many of whom were African American, at the expense of genuine education.

The university has, on the other hand, gone to court to defend its right to consider race in admissions in order to achieve a more diverse student body. The Holmes/Hunter Lecture Series was established to annually explore race relations, aspects of higher education with implications for race relations, or Black history. And in January 2001, on the 40th anniversary of the integration of UGA, the school unveiled a plaque on the Holmes/Hunter Academic Building, hard by the campus entry arch, commemorating "the courage and fortitude" of academic pioneers Charlayne Hunter and Hamilton Holmes and their families "in paving the way for others to follow."

Georgia also broke new ground in December 2003 when it hired former Bulldog football letterman Damon Evans as director of athletics. He was the first African American to hold such a position in the Southeastern Conference. That breakthrough would have been difficult to foresee as the 1960s ended. Then, it was considered a bold move merely to recruit Ronnie Hogue.

Guthrie insisted his superiors, Rosemond in particular, were enthusiastic about bringing in Black athletes. At the time, Vanderbilt and Auburn were the only schools in the SEC that had integrated their basketball programs. "Georgia was very interested in breaking the barriers," said Guthrie, later supervisor of officials for the SEC. "They were very receptive about it and very sincere about it, and Ronnie realized that." Hogue was equally interested in a pioneering role, prompted by a Boy's Club coach who worked for the U.S. Department of Labor. "Bill Butler talked to him a lot about being the first, about paving the way and opening up doors," Guthrie said. "And Ronnie was very sincere about that. That was his way of knocking down some barriers, rather than doing it the protest way, or whatever."

Of course coaches focus first and foremost on winning, the preeminent requirement for retaining their jobs. Rosemond and Guthrie, newly hired at Georgia after a stint as an assistant coach at George Washington University, were no exception. Rosemond relied heavily on players from the Northeast, as did both Frank McGuire and Dean Smith. Rosemond had worked for the latter as an assistant and freshman coach at North Carolina. The former Tar

Heel, a member of the school's 1957 national championship squad, was still in search of a guard when he hired Guthrie, a close observer of D.C. prep basketball.

Guthrie, a native Georgian, was quite familiar with Hogue's talented McKinley Technical High School squads, which won consecutive Interhigh League championships in 1968 and 1969. Both years Hogue made the Interhigh East first team, as well as second team All-Metropolitan as chosen by the *Washington Post*. Half a dozen players from those McKinley squads were recruited to attend college. "We crushed everybody that we played," said Tim Bassett, eventually a seven-year pro. Bassett said he was considered the fifth-best player at McKinley, if that. "My high school team was the best team I ever played on. It was just that good."

Interhigh rivalries, and the violent extracurricular action that accompanied the games, were so heated that the contests were played in the afternoon rather than under cover of darkness. "People loved their teams," Hogue said. "You couldn't beat somebody and walk down the court and brag about it." When the McKinley Trainers hosted the Cardoza Clerks for the Interhigh title in 1968, the *Post* noted that "only students from participating schools" were allowed to attend.

Bassett recalled a stunning rally at Springarn High School that left McKinley comfortably ahead with little time remaining. The gym was so overcrowded that students pressed onto one end of the court each time the action moved to the other end. "We knew something was going to happen because the rivalry was that fierce," Bassett said. "When our crowd started chanting, 'What's the matter, Springarn? Why are you so quiet? Boom, boom,' I said, 'Oh, God, we're in trouble. We need to win this game and get out of here.'"

Before they could do that, a fan came out of the stands, "threatening to shoot Ronnie if he scored again," Bassett said. Guthrie, often the only white person in the stands at Interhigh games, believed Hogue could handle the pressures of breaking Georgia's athletic color barrier after watching him confront the gun-wielding gambler at Springarn. "This guy came running out there down at the end," the recruiter recounted. "He said, 'You make another shot, and I'm going to shoot your ass,' or something like that. And Hogie came right back down and jumped up and stuck it, and just turned and laughed at the guy."

Guthrie also knew that Hogue was not academically qualified for admission to George Washington, as was the case with Bassett, who later joined the Georgia program. "And I said, 'Well, there's a great one here in

D.C. that we're not recruiting at G.W.,'" Guthrie said. "The barrier thing was a side movement, to be honest with you. They wanted a good person who was a good player. That was the main thrust. We were looking for a guard. Ken Rosemond didn't say, 'Get me a guard who's Black.'"

That is what Georgia got, however. Hogue became the first African-American athlete in a prominent sport at the university, the first Black athlete at UGA to earn a full scholarship in any sport, and the first to live in McWhorter Hall. "The Mac," named after the school's first football All-American, was the athletic dormitory. Guthrie helped Hogue move into his quarters there. "The night I left him, it really kind of settled on me that, gee, this is really something," Guthrie said. "This guy's got to be strong, because it was 1969."

Maxie Foster, an Athens native, had become the first African-American athlete at UGA a year earlier. But he was a track athlete on a partial, "performance" scholarship and lived at home. "I admired Ronnie," Foster said. "I thought he was an excellent athlete. I thought he could have done a lot better had he not come into what we called a one-finger system, where you held up a finger and ran one play."

Hogue nevertheless fared quite well. Soon enough, the Bulldogs were running plays for him. "He was the main focus of the offense, I know that," Dick Toth, a frontcourt teammate, said. Hogue proved a tough defender, an exceptional scorer in the clutch, and a remarkable jump shooter, particularly from the corners. Consequently, he started all three years on the UGA varsity and remains among the top career scorers in school history with a 17.8-point average.

"He was a sweet, great kid, but a fierce competitor," Guthrie said. "When you put the switch on to start the game, he got in a different gear. Sitting around talking to you, he was the most social person in the world and the most likable guy. It wasn't that he was nasty when he played, but he jumped into a different gear, which all great players do."

Hogue was named to the SEC's All-Sophomore team in 1971 (along with Kentucky's Tom Payne) and to the all-conference squad in 1972. He led the Bulldogs in scoring both of those years. His 46 points against Louisiana State in December 1971 remains the single-game modern scoring record at Georgia, surpassing performances by All-Americans Dominique Wilkins, Bob Lienhard, Vern Fleming, Alec Kessler, and exotically named Zippy Morocco. Remarkably, the left-handed shooter managed his scoring feat in an era prior to the three-point field goal.

"Ronnie was tough," said Gino Gianfrancesco, the team's point guard and the co-captain with Hogue their senior year. "He was physically strong, even though he looked thin. He was just street smart and basketball smart. He could get off a shot when he needed to. He could jump an extra inch if he had to to get off a shot. He just had that kind of ability. He made me look good."

Halfway through his varsity career, Hogue was lauded in the Athens *Banner-Herald* as "very possibly the best basketball player to ever don the red and black of Georgia." At the conclusion of the 1971 season, the sophomore was awarded both the Tommy Reeder Scholarship and the Joe Jordan Memorial Trophy, high honors given in memory of former Georgia players. "I played basketball because I loved basketball. Basketball was my girlfriend," Hogue said.

"He was a little bit of a jokester, but when he got on the basketball court, I'll tell you one thing, he was almost like a miniature Michael Jordan," Toth said. "He could just stop on a dime and go up and take the jumper. Unbelievable quickness. Wanted the ball if there was ever a close game, which there weren't too many of back in those days."

Rosemond was fired after the 1972–73 season, concluding an eight-year tenure with a 92–111 record. His final season ended with nine straight losses, a 10–16 record, and a brawl at Georgia Tech that left Hogue swinging a chair to keep attackers at bay and the 6-foot-8 Bassett "afraid for his life."

The intensity of the rivalry between Georgia and Georgia Tech is typical of many states, matching the prominent liberal arts university against its younger, more technically oriented sister school. As with Virginia and Virginia Tech, North Carolina and North Carolina State, South Carolina and Clemson, Florida and Florida State, Alabama and Auburn, Mississippi and Mississippi State, the Bulldogs and Yellow Jackets still face off at least once annually, regardless of whether they are in the same league. (Atlanta's Georgia Institute of Technology was a member of the SEC for 32 years, from 1933 through 1964, winning the league title in 1938. Even after withdrawing from the SEC, Georgia Tech played Georgia twice a year in basketball until the mid-1980s.)

The Yellow Jackets were coached from 1952 through 1973 by John "Whack" Hyder, a Georgia native and Tech alumnus. Hyder's program was best known for breaking Kentucky's record home-court winning streak in 1955. His retirement had been announced prior to Georgia's March 1973 visit and was marked by a pregame ceremony that involved Georgia governor Jimmy Carter. Meanwhile, rumors regarding Rosemond's imminent firing swirled around the Bulldog program. Ominously, Joel Eaves, the UGA athletics director and former head basketball coach at Auburn, would say only the standard, "When the schedule is completed, we will go through an evaluation of our basketball program."

Eaves ultimately hired James Harrison "Babe" McCarthy, the former coach at Mississippi State, as Rosemond's replacement. But McCarthy left before ever coaching a game for Georgia, and the job went to Guthrie, who lasted five seasons without posting a winning record.

The 1973 game with Tech, matching squads with losing marks, was closely contested. Georgia rallied to within 4 points (56–52) after trailing by a dozen midway through the second half, but reserve Tommy Hyder, the coach's son, scored a pivotal layup as the Jackets pulled away to a 77–67 victory. "I don't guess I've ever wanted a game more than this one," the elder Hyder said. "This is the most tremendous win I've ever been associated with."

The loss was the eighth straight in Atlanta for the Bulldogs, a span encompassing Rosemond's entire tenure. The game is best remembered, though, for ending with a bang, as fans from the crowd of 4,879 at half-empty Alexander Memorial Coliseum streamed onto the court to join a brawl that seemed to focus on Ronnie Hogue.

Tech's Steve Post said the Georgia senior "blind-sided" him as the game concluded. After the contest Whack Hyder similarly pinned the blame on Hogue. Speaking long after the fact, however, Hyder identified a different Hogue victim. "Just before the last whistle blew and all that, the ball was coming down, and the guard popped my son in the mouth," Hyder said. "Knocked a tooth out. Boy, we had at it for a while." The coach insisted Hogue was suitably roughed up and that the Georgia player subsequently sought him out and apologized.

Not surprisingly, the Georgia version of the fight differed significantly.

Guthrie said game tape clearly showed that the hostilities commenced after a Georgia Tech player landed an elbow to the face of a Bulldog. "And then something else happened, and a guy runs at Bassett, actually like he's going to hit him." What Guthrie called "a typical free-for-all" ensued, with football players spilling from their seats under one basket, their enthusiasm stoked, he said, by "enjoying some spirits before they got in the game."

Georgia's Gianfrancesco thought he had precipitated the fight. Watching from the bench, he had seen that a Yellow Jacket veteran "kept punching"

Georgia freshman David Lucey. "I was mad. So, when I got in the next time and we were going down the court, the officials were ahead of us, and I just elbowed the crap out of that senior. . . . Nobody saw it but the fans, and nothing happened right away. Then, all of a sudden, something happened underneath the basket and the Tech football players came on the court. That was it. That whole court filled up with people. But I remember nobody coming after me. They went toward Hogue and Bassett. They gravitated toward them, especially the football players."

That's what Dick Toth saw too. "At the buzzer I thought they had won the SEC championship, even though they weren't in the SEC. They just all came out of the stands, but I guess they were just all going after Ronnie."

Hogue and Bassett viewed these developments with alarm. They were, after all, the only African Americans on the court, if not inside the building. With no security personnel in evidence, voices raised in shouts of "Get that nigger!" and a crowd converging, the experience was apparently more bracing than it appeared to the *Constitution*'s Mickey McCarthy. "As fights go, well, it wasn't much of a fight," he wrote. "Hogue ended up being thrown over the press table. Tech people were there to meet him."

The black Georgia teammates, veterans of Interhigh warfare, began swinging fists and chairs. Hogue and Bassett, asked about the origins of the incident decades later, tell virtually identical stories. They believe the underlying cause was that officials let too much go unchecked in their eagerness for the likable Hyder to go out a winner.

"This guy had been baiting Hogue the whole game," Bassett said. "Not only was he baiting him, but he was physically trying to abuse Ronnie Hogue. And Hogue at one point had come up the court and said to me, 'Tim, if this guy hits me again, I'm going to take his head off.' I said, 'What are you talking about?' He said, 'Man, I'm sick of it. He's hitting on me. He's calling me a nigger; he's calling me every name in the book."

Hogue, like LSU's Collis Temple and several others in the second, early-1970s wave of pioneering Black players, was not inclined to turn the other cheek. Gianfrancesco says Hogue did not appear to be a good ball handler, for instance, "but if you can't take the ball from him, he's pretty good. And if you tried to take the ball from Ronnie, your nose would have an elbow in it." That approach, learned in rugged D.C. competition, had little to do with race, although Hogue describes himself by comparing a pacifist civil rights leader with a more militant figure. "I wasn't like a Martin Luther King guy; I was more like Malcolm X. If you know how to fight back, people give you respect."

Hogue emphatically denied apologizing to Whack Hyder after the fight. "They hit me, and I got a lot of people back. You can't cry to the coach. You just do what you have to do."

Reports of such assertiveness were almost breathtaking to Vanderbilt's Perry Wallace, who believed he was in no position to retaliate while touring the SEC from 1966 to 1970. Perhaps it was a mark of the evolving acceptance of African Americans that Hogue felt no compunction about defending himself, even at the risk of precipitating a brawl. "He was real lucky that he came after I did, because if he had tried that same stuff when I was playing, that would have been it," Wallace said. "Especially in some of the places like Mississippi State, Ole Miss, Auburn, Alabama . . . a number of those places. They would have just killed him."

Hogue could not be too sanguine about his 1973 prospects in Atlanta, either.

"I heard the crowd go, 'Ooh!'" Bassett said. "And when I turned around, it just appeared that everybody was sweeping Ronnie Hogue over to the scorer's table. He was fighting." Bassett started fighting, too, as adults joined the football players. "I had to get on a table and fight my way out of that place," Hogue said. "It's like a fire. You don't have time to stop and wait and think."

According to Toth, the team required a police escort out of town. The next day, Eaves decried the lack of crowd control and said, "The incident following the game at Tech was the worst I have ever seen in college basketball."

Oddly, another ugly episode at a Georgia–Georgia Tech basketball game had helped stoke the fires of intolerance in 1961, the day after Charlayne Hunter and Hamilton Holmes integrated UGA, the oldest chartered public university in the United States. (The University of North Carolina claims to be first state university because it accepted its initial student in 1795, while Georgia was sited and opened its doors in 1801.)

The state of Georgia had a long history of hostility to Black aspirations long before Holmes and Hunter stepped onto the Athens campus. According to authors Stewart Tolnay and E. M. Beck, the sentiment expressed in 1876 by the "principal keeper" of the Georgia Penitentiary was common as Reconstruction ended: "The only difference existing between colored convicts and the colored people at large consists in the fact that the former have been caught in the commission of a crime, tried and convicted, while the latter have not," the man said. "The entire race is destitute of character." Given that worldview, it is no wonder that from 1889 through 1940, Georgia was the nation's lynching capital. An average of nearly one African American per month was lynched in Georgia over that span.

Black veterans were not accepting of such circumstances. During the Spanish-American War, a Black regiment stationed in south Georgia vigorously objected to the racial status quo. Told that a nearby persimmon was known as the hanging tree, members of the Sixth Virginia Infantry cut it down and chopped the tree into firewood. The soldiers learned the most recent lynching victim had been hanged, shot, and castrated, his testicles displayed in a jar of alcohol in a local white saloon. Infuriated, they went to Macon, where they tore down a park sign that said NO DOGS AND NIGGERS ALLOWED and demanded service in white-only restaurants and bars. Military authorities quickly herded regiment members back to base, where they were disarmed and placed under arrest for 20 days. (Half a century later, a primary reason cited for the rise of the civil rights movement was the unwillingness of African-American World War II veterans, who had fought German and Japanese racial prejudice, to accept similar attitudes in the United States.)

For a time it appeared lynching might be overcome through political means. In *The Strange Career of Jim Crow*, C. Vann Woodward argued that the rise of Populism toward the end of the 19th century marked a concerted effort to combat the racial prejudice that "ran highest and strongest among the very white elements to which the Populist appeal was especially addressed—the depressed lower economic classes." As late as 1896, two years before the Spanish-American war, the Populist platform in Georgia contained a plank that denounced what was called "lynch law."

The state's Tom Watson, Populist candidate for U.S. president in 1904, told whites and Blacks, "You are made to hate each other because upon that hatred is rested the keystone of the arch of financial despotism which enslaves you both." Watson later changed his tune entirely, culminating his political career with election to the U.S. Senate as a Democrat in 1920. By then he was noted for virulent attacks on African Americans, Catholics, Jews, and socialists. "Lynch law is a good sign," he said. "It shows that a sense of justice yet lives among the people."

Keeping African Americans in a subordinate role was systematically accomplished through less violent means. Education had been forbidden for slaves, and segregated and unequal facilities were the modern equivalent of ensured subservience. Leon Litwack wrote that limited schooling and other repressive measures worked to "contain Black political and social ambitions" as well as "help whites maintain an adequate source of cheap labor."

Litwack told an illustrative story of a Northern visitor at a Southern railroad depot who was shocked when his companion kicked a Black man reading a newspaper rather than another who was sleeping. "'Would you please explain that?' the Northerner asked. 'I don't understand it. I would think that if you were going to kick one you would kick the lazy one who's sleeping.' The white Southerner replied, 'That's not the one we're worried about.'" In 1940 African Americans had access to accredited four-year public high schools in only 48 of Georgia's 159 counties (30.2 percent). The state invested $142 for each white child compared to $35 for each Black student. Eugene Talmadge, elected governor of Georgia in 1932, 1934, 1940, and 1946, observed, "I like the nigger, but I like him in his place, and his place is at the back door with his hat in his hand."

Whack Hyder grew up in rural Lula and Clermont, northwest of Athens. "It was segregated completely," he said. "[White] people had Black people working in their homes. They called them maids and all that, and they could look after their children, but they couldn't sit down to the table with people and eat, stuff like that. What a shame."

A shame, perhaps, but a way of life white leaders deemed worthy of vigorous defense, by law if not by rope. Federal movement toward desegregation spurred state legislators to approve a 1953 amendment to the Georgia constitution relieving the state of its obligation to provide for public education. By the time voters ratified the amendment in November 1954, the U.S. Supreme Court had struck down separate but equal education. Georgia promptly became a leader in the massive resistance movement. A flood of new state laws attempted to negate the effect of the *Brown* ruling, which the legislature resolved was "null, void and of no force or effect" in the state of Georgia. Typical was a statute making it a felony for any official to spend tax money for a public school in which the races were mixed.

One candidate for governor in 1954 wanted children to state under oath whether they preferred desegregated schools, with those choosing integration assigned to mental institutions since they were obviously "diseased." The winning candidate, Marvin Griffin, said, "The meddlers, demagogues, race baiters and Communists are determined to destroy every vestige of states' rights." He vowed to prevent it "come hell or high water."

Griffin's administration was corrupt, avidly segregationist, and heavy-handed in combating criticism from the urban press, according to Numan

Bartley, author of *The Rise of Massive Resistance*. Yet what evoked perhaps the stiffest adverse reaction was Griffin's meddling with sports.

Georgia Tech was invited to play in the 1956 Sugar Bowl in New Orleans, where it would face Pittsburgh, which had only one Black player, fullback Bobby Grier. As with most Southern states, segregation in Georgia extended to athletic competition. But restrictions on games played outside the state had loosened a bit over the years. Tech football coach Bobby Dodd privately secured the governor's permission for his team to appear in the game. Then came the backlash. Georgia Tech leaders stood fast, pointing out they had already faced teams with Black players. On December 2, 1955, less than a month before the bowl, Griffin announced his opposition to Yellow Jacket participation. "We cannot make the slightest concession to the enemy in this dark and lamentable hour of struggle," he said. "There is no more difference in compromising the integrity of race on the playing field than in doing so in the classroom. One break in the dike and the relentless seas will rush in and destroy us."

Messing with a Georgian's football is serious business. Georgia Tech students immediately hanged and burned an effigy of the governor, then marched to the state capitol, nearly 2,000 strong, and burned him in effigy again. In an improbable display of solidarity, more than 500 students marched in Athens, displaying a banner that read THIS TIME WE'RE FOR TECH. Eventually, the university's board of regents approved the New Orleans trip and Griffin relented, reassured by the stipulation that respect for local "laws, customs, and traditions" would require continued segregation within Georgia, even if it did not in other states. The decision also accommodated a lucrative football visit by UGA to the University of Michigan during the 1956 season.

Actual integration of university sports programs within Georgia was still more than a decade away. Historian Charles Martin, as quoted by Pratt, notes that "The shift to a policy of integrated competition outside the state demonstrated that by the mid-1950s the state's college athletic establishment placed a greater emphasis on the pursuit of athletic glory than on the maintenance of total racial exclusion."

Making the medicine go down more easily, Georgia Tech beat Pittsburgh, 7–0, for its fifth consecutive bowl victory. Pitt's Grier was the game's leading rusher.

Barely a month after that Sugar Bowl, Autherine Lucy was admitted to attend classes as the first African-American student at the University of Alabama. Her arrival precipitated a riot. Lucy was soon removed from the school and then permanently expelled, purportedly as a matter of public safety. The drumbeat of confrontation continued in 1957, when President Dwight Eisenhower, publicly ambivalent and privately skeptical about the *Brown* ruling, used federal troops to enforce court-ordered integration of Central High School in Little Rock, Arkansas. Voters in Arkansas overwhelmingly approved a referendum the following year that supported Governor Orval Faubus in closing Little Rock's public schools rather than allowing them to be integrated. (A Gallup Poll in December 1958 named Faubus among the 10 most admired men in the world, along with the president, Sir Winston Churchill, and doctors Albert Schweitzer and Jonas Salk.)

Integration similarly lagged in Georgia, where public schools remained totally segregated as the 1950s ended. Leaders in Atlanta, the so-called "City Too Busy to Hate," saw commerce suffer in Little Rock and realized that their city's economic well-being was at stake. Almost simultaneously, a group of parents advocated keeping public schools open even if integrated. Daily newspapers and business leaders joined Mayor William B. Hartsfield and other local politicians in demanding that the home city of Martin Luther King Jr. be permitted to run its schools without state interference.

Atlantans were on a collision course with newly elected Ernest Vandiver, who as a candidate had pledged, "When I am your governor, neither my three children, nor any child of yours, will ever attend a racially mixed school in the state of Georgia. No, not one." The issue was forced not by Atlanta, but by federal Judge W. A. Bootle, who upheld a legal challenge to segregation and ordered the University of Georgia to admit two Black undergraduates in January 1961. (African American Horace Ward, later a federal judge, had previously failed in a six-year court battle to gain admission to the law school.)

While lawyers sparred and the governor announced a likely cutoff of funds in conformity with state law, Atlantans Hunter (later Hunter-Gault) and Holmes arrived at UGA. Hunter resided on campus, a stipulation for all female students under the age of 23. Holmes spent his undergraduate career living with a Black Athens family, taking meals off campus, going to Atlanta each weekend, and otherwise minimizing contact with whites. A good athlete, Holmes expressed interest in joining the football team, but a dean said he would be risking his life if he tried. Holmes became a frequent visitor at the local YMCA, the primary athletic outlet for Blacks in Athens.

"He would come over and play basketball, and I would watch him and watch how he would interact with other guys," Maxie Foster recalled. Foster was impressed with Holmes's unpretentious manner. Today, he thinks of Holmes's presence as a form of "divine intervention" that encouraged him, the son of an Athens maid, to become a racial pioneer.

Both Hunter and Holmes, who later became an orthopedic surgeon, attended classes their first day without incident. According to Thomas Dyer, author of a bicentennial history of the university, "The vast majority of the student body regarded the new students coolly and dispassionately." Hunter moved into a single room at Myers Hall. That night, Dyer said, groups of students stood outside "shouting anti-integration slogans."

The following day, four students protested Hunter's presence by walking out of a course she attended on ethics and principles in journalism. (Hunter-Gault went on to a distinguished career in journalism, domestically and overseas.) Other students greeted her with a chant of "Dogmeat! Dogmeat!"— a term commonly directed at opponents during Bulldog football games—as she entered a building. Another shouted, "You may be in school, but you're still a nigger."

That night Georgia Tech, led by All-America Roger Kaiser, came to intimate Woodruff Hall for a basketball game. The Bulldogs apparently had the contest won, but in the final two seconds their archrivals somehow got the ball to Kaiser at midcourt, who threw up a one-handed shot that went in as the buzzer sounded. Suddenly the crowd, which a reporter said had been "filled with joy" when Georgia took a late lead, "went into an uproar." Students rushed the scorer's table in protest of the clock management, as did Georgia coach Harbin "Red" Lawson. Fifteen minutes passed before order was restored. The Yellow Jackets proceeded to win handily, outscoring the Dogs 14–5 in overtime.

"The crowd as it poured out of Woodruff Hall was angry," continued the story in the *Marietta Daily Journal*. "'Let's demonstrate! Let's demonstrate!' many of the younger ones began to yell. 'On to Myers Central' roared several others. The riot was beginning."

Apparently the demonstration was far less spontaneous than it appeared. A television reporter from Atlanta told Dyer, the historian, "That afternoon, we had all kinds of information and tips that there was going to be a riot after the basketball game. Everybody, everybody, including university officials, knew there was going to be a riot."

Approximately 2,000 people, Klansmen among them, gathered outside Hunter's dorm. They hurled bricks through her window, assailed her with racial slurs and obscenities, lit fires, and waved a banner that said NIGGER GO HOME. Thirty-nine officers, the entire Athens police department, were dispatched to Myers Hall, where tear gas and bursts from fire hoses kept the rioters at bay. No one was seriously injured, but 60 window panes were broken in the building, 10 in Hunter's room.

A call to state police, some stationed in Athens, failed to bring help for several hours due to a supposed "procedural misunderstanding." State officers arrived after the crowd had dispersed and escorted Hunter and Holmes back to Atlanta. The Black students were suspended for their own safety, mirroring Lucy's treatment at Alabama. Aware of the precedent, the next day a majority of UGA's faculty signed a petition calling for Holmes and Hunter to be reinstated immediately. Within days both were back in class.

The university hardly rushed to desegregate, particularly in athletics. As late as 1967, when other SEC schools had African-American athletes, Georgia's retiring president chastised the Georgia Athletic Association for its resistance to integration.

Change was comparably slow in the town of Athens, where racial separation was ubiquitous. The public schools were minimally desegregated in 1963, when four Black girls went to a white school under "freedom of choice." Maxie Foster followed a similar course two years later, enrolling at previously all-white Athens High School. Complete integration was not achieved until 1970.

Foster's pioneering move left him in social limbo. Some African Americans disdained him as an Uncle Tom, while whites unused to meeting Blacks on an equal footing were openly hostile at what had been "their" school. "The aggression and hostility were so bad that we couldn't eat in the cafeteria or use the restrooms, couldn't drink water in the halls," Foster said of the handful of Black students at Athens High. "It was just a really bad experience when we first got over there."

Foster found himself similarly isolated at Georgia. "It was a challenge just to go there, let alone to try to be successful," he said. The reception from other athletes was sometimes nasty. The track team dressed for practice in the same arena hallway where football players met prior to practice sessions. "They wouldn't let me walk down the hall," Foster said. "I was afraid of those guys." The harassment caused Foster to be late for practice several times; he was assigned to run punishment laps. Finally, he reported the incidents to his coach, Forrest "Spec" Towns, a gold medalist in the hurdles at the 1936 Olympics and a Georgia alum. Towns, who had been on the same U.S. squad as black sprinter Jesse Owens, set the football players straight.

The coach "went beyond the call of duty, because he would actually take me home," Foster said. Whites did not ordinarily visit Black Athens. Towns also gave Foster "a dollar or two" every few days, an NCAA violation fairly common among caring coaches with players from modest means. "I didn't understand it at the time, but it was a way for him to make me feel accepted and let me know that I had his confidence. So I really appreciated what he did," Foster said.

Foster played basketball in high school, enduring a road game in which his presence made the Athens High squad so unwelcome that fans rocked the bus on which the players were forced to dress. The sprinter said he tried out for the Bullpups, Georgia's freshman basketball squad, but after a few days was told he "couldn't play anymore because the alumni had a problem with it." Foster said the next year football coach Vince Dooley approached him about returning punts and kickoffs. He demurred, as did Hogue when a similar offer was extended several years later.

Hogue had played football and basketball in a recreation program and on the streets of southeast Washington, D.C. He always preferred basketball, even after being cut from the junior high school team because he was too short. "I just played every day. I used to shovel the snow off the court when it snowed to play basketball. My hands turned pink," he said, laughing.

His Georgetown neighborhood, which presidents drove through on their way to Washington Senators baseball games, was racially mixed. His high school, McKinley Tech, by contrast, was almost exclusively Black. Still, "I didn't realize segregation existed until I went to the South," Hogue said. "I read about it in my high school books, but I really had no idea what they were talking about."

There were 14 children in the Hogue family, 11 of them boys. Ronnie was the eighth child and shared clothes, toys, and a bedroom with his brothers. His father, James Albert Hogue, cut glass for submarines at the Navy Yard, then worked as a bookbinder at the government printing office. His mother, Lucille, was a nurse at Georgetown Hospital. Mrs. Hogue worked nights and Mr. Hogue worked days, so there was always parental supervision. "We were never on welfare, and I never saw a babysitter," Hogue said. "They never wanted us to live in projects, so we always had a house. That's what they worked for. Growing up, we always went to church."

Gaylord, an older brother, played basketball at Dunbar High in the Intercity League and earned a scholarship to Boise State. Ronnie surpassed him playing at McKinley Tech, where the District's first integrated basketball games were played in 1955. The fleet left-hander averaged 22.1 points and 7 rebounds as a high school junior, 17.8 points and 8 rebounds as a senior. Grown to 6-foot-2, he was flooded with recruiting letters.

John Guthrie stood out among those expressing an interest. "We got to know him, and he was more interested in me as a person," Hogue said. "I was asking people [about him], everybody said something real nice about him, like 'One of the nicest people I ever met in my life.'" Then Guthrie, the newly minted Georgia assistant, made an unlikely proposal. "He asked me if I would come on down there and check it out. I said, 'What? *Georgia?* No way, man!'" Guthrie recalled that among Hogue's "big concerns" was the fate of Lemuel Penn. "He asked me about it, and we talked about it. My explanation was, there's crazy people everywhere but that's not the norm."

Eventually Hogue accepted the invitation to visit Athens. He liked what he saw and how he was treated. Among the inducements was Stegeman Coliseum, the largest arena in the SEC when it opened in 1964 with seating for 11,000 spectators. Clair Bee, the Hall of Fame coach from Long Island University, came to Athens at Rosemond's request to analyze his Georgia squad and pronounced Stegeman, with its diagonal parabolic arches, fan-shaped columns, and honeycombed ceiling, "the prettiest coliseum I've ever seen."

Hogue also reconsidered his aversion to the University of Georgia when his mother, a Virginian, challenged his view that "all the bad people were in the South," he said. "My mother made me realize I had to learn to relate to the mass of white people, because I would have to deal with them eventually in the business world."

Georgia, however, had a seeming aversion to basketball. Football dominated the state, and Adolph Rupp's Kentucky Wildcats dominated UGA's basketball horizons. Rosemond celebrated as a sign of basketball's progress the mere fact he was asked to write a guest column for the *Gwinnett Daily News* in Lawrenceville, Georgia, prior to the 1968–69 season.

Rosemond was a relative youngster when hired at age 34 in March 1965. A year later, columnist Horace Crowd of the *Marietta Daily Journal* described the North Carolinian as "ambitious, displays keen enthusiasm about the game of basketball, [and] has all the earmarks of being a fine young gentleman. It's easy to see why he is adjudged one of the finest basketball recruiters in the south." Among the players Rosemond had helped recruit to North Carolina was Bob Lewis, twice voted first team All-ACC during the mid-1960s as Dean Smith's program gained traction. At Georgia Rosemond pursued in-state prospects such as highly regarded Joby Wright but for the most part looked north.

Recruiting homegrown players was difficult, particularly if they were products of the separate but equal school system. "When I got to Georgia in 1969, I went out and spoke at some places, and to be honest with you, it was way, way behind," Guthrie said. "Even though Ronnie was an inner-city type kid from Washington, the educational opportunities there were extensive."

Rosemond instead mined powerhouse programs in New York for players such as Lienhard, a 6-foot-11 product of Rice High School, and Toth, from Archbishop Molloy High School. Toth had played for Jack Curran, a former McGuire player at St. John's. According to Pat Stephens, Georgia's freshman team coach from 1966 to 1970, that made Toth an especially desirable recruit since Rosemond's "role model and idol was Frank McGuire."

"Eastern kids have the flair," Rosemond explained at a 1966 luncheon at Mama Leone's restaurant in New York. "They're better dribblers and ball handlers. Georgia boys can shoot and run but don't have the same savvy. To bring finesse down there I figure I need at least three Eastern boys."

Consistent with basketball's low profile at the university, Hogue's 1969 signing was not big news. "U.Ga. Signs Fourth Cager" read the headline in the Athens *Banner-Herald*. Rosemond praised him as "a versatile athlete" with leadership skills demonstrated by his captaincy of a championship squad at McKinley Tech. The story eventually mentioned that "Hogue thus becomes the second Negro athlete on scholarship at Georgia."

Hogue quickly earned a reputation among teammates as an upbeat presence and a superior player, said Gianfrancesco, who came from Pittsburgh, Pennsylvania. "He smiled all the time. He just loved life. He just loved to play basketball. He was a great guy to be around. He made everybody feel comfortable around him. And he was a heck of a player."

The fast-talking Hogue was noted for other interests besides basketball. Female companionship was a constant in his life; former teammates said Hogue's affinity for women was nearly as consuming as his passion for basketball. "Ronnie was a ladies' man beyond a shadow of a doubt," Tim Bassett said. "He had all the ladies at Georgia, and if he didn't, he sure tried." Gianfrancesco said Hogue often had women in his room 15 minutes prior to practice, yet he showed no signs of fatigue. "He liked the girls and all that, but never would you know it on the court or in practice. He had tremendous stamina. We were all a little wild back then."

Hogue devised a signal system with Steve Zilko, a white roommate he regarded as "a soul brother," to indicate he had female company. As a result Zilko frequently found himself seated in the hallway outside his own room, or sleeping on the floor of the room shared by Bassett and Gianfrancesco. Hogue was not averse to discussing his conquests, either, until even his friends tired of the subject. "One night, we were bound and determined to keep him from talking about sex," Bassett said laughing. So he and Gianfrancesco steered the conversation to math, history, politics—anything they could think of. The strategy worked, but only for a while. "I liked John F. Kennedy, too," Bassett said Hogue commented, "But, God, did you see his wife? I'd like to have her."

Dating whites was an issue for many African-American athletes stuck on campuses where there were few Black women. Bassett contends that if Hogue did not date white women, it was because "he didn't have time." But Hogue said he was mindful of the impression he made on young African-American boys and consciously decided to set an example through his dating habits. "If Black kids said, 'I want to be like Ronnie Hogue,' I didn't want them to see me dating a white woman and then think a white woman is better than their sister or their mother. When they see you, they want to be inspired by you. When they see you wearing a hat, they wear that kind of hat. When they see you with a white girl, they like a white girl. I think that was the wrong thing, at that time, to give out the signal for."

The era often required careful consideration of social issues beyond dating. Hogue was attuned to those as well. "I was real concerned about how Blacks were treated on campus," he says. Hogue was involved in successful efforts to rid the school of gratuitous racist symbolism such as Old South Day, when white students dressed in antebellum costumes that glorified the slavery era. "They would parade down the streets of Athens and celebrate those 'great' days. We stopped that. They were some exciting years, some interesting years."

Hogue was active in the Black student organization on campus and frequented the corner in the student center reserved by and for African-American students. "The atmosphere was so homey . . . that was the place we'd play cards, we'd congregate and talk and study," Maxie Foster said.

"We didn't have another place to do that. You could actually leave your wallet, your purse, your books, your backpack, whatever, go to class and come back, and that stuff would still be there."

That sense of safety and belonging, along with Hogue's own fears, kept him mostly on campus. "I used to be homesick," he said. "One of the worst pictures I saw, one that used to scare me, was with Peter Fonda and Dennis Hopper *Easy Rider* [1969]. There was a scene where, I think it was Jack Nicholson, he was riding and he gave a finger to a guy and the guy blew him away. Well, I used to walk by myself on the dark streets, and I used to worry about that."

For good reason. Once, during a civil disturbance in Athens, Hogue was in a car stopped by police. They "jumped out and held shotguns on us," Hogue says. "Told us, 'Don't move.' If somebody had done something, it would have been over with. That just stuck with me: You're all right on campus, but you walk out on that street, and you get your head busted open." Driving to Atlanta on another occasion, he encountered a hooded man standing in the road, waving people over to a KKK rally. "I just kept going because he didn't want me in there," Hogue said.

Despite his wariness, the self-described city boy, who felt compelled to periodically "get to Atlanta and breathe the dirty air," was quick to wander when the team visited Nashville during his first season on the varsity. Hogue was among a group of players who broke curfew and sneaked out after a loss to Vanderbilt. He disappeared, returning the following morning with an injured eye. The next night at Tuscaloosa, he showed no ill effects of his experience. "That was a perfect example of how he was," Gianfrancesco said. "He stayed up all night, somehow burned his eye. He tells the coaches it was his contacts, puts the eyepatch on, and beats Alabama by 1 at the buzzer."

Coaches apparently were aware that Hogue was "quite a character," as Gianfrancesco put it. So, when Rosemond found a marijuana joint on the floor following a tough loss, he accused his star guard in a tirade before the entire team. Hogue was so furious at being accused—falsely, he says—that he returned to McWhorter Hall and began packing. He told Rosemond, "I'm going home, and I'm taking my big man with me." This was news to Bassett, who was eager to use his Georgia career as a springboard to the pros.

Fortunately for all concerned, late that night Rosemond came by the dormitory bearing hamburgers as a peace offering. "Kenny had the courage as a head coach to go and apologize," Guthrie said. "Kenny was like any good coach: He had strict rules. He was a disciplinarian. He was concerned about his players."

So was Guthrie, who stopped by McWhorter later that same evening to further smooth any ruffled feathers. Guthrie believed it important to lend an ear to all his players, but particularly Bassett and Hogue, whom he knew encountered race-related challenges none of the others faced. "We talked about it all the time," Guthrie said. He characterized as "hogwash" the proud insistence of some coaches that they treated all their players alike. "You can't do that," he said. "Your sensitivity to the situation is the key to it."

Guthrie and Hogue, his prized recruit, had arrived in Athens as the Bulldog program seemed ascendant. Rosemond's 1967–68 squad, his third, had finished 17–8, the most wins at the school since 1949. Consecutive 13–12 records followed in 1968–69 and 1969–70, with victories on every conference court except at Kentucky and Tennessee, and over every SEC rival except Rupp's Wildcats. The run was the best at UGA in two decades. "I thought Georgia could be the UCLA of the Southeast," Hogue said. "It had the facilities, it had the money, the backing, everything. It was first-class all the way. A lot of people in college that I talked to didn't have that kind of financial backing."

The reality was a bit different from a coach's perspective. Tommy Bartlett, who reportedly turned down the Georgia job before it went to Rosemond, rues that athletics director Joel Eaves did not offer adequate monetary support. "I really respected him as a person, but he wanted everybody to do like he did, operate on a nickel and a dime," said Bartlett, who went on to coach at Florida. Former Georgia assistant coach Pat Stephens agreed the Bulldogs were financially outmatched against the powers of the SEC. "We brought good talent in there. But back in those days, there was just not the financial commitment at the University of Georgia for basketball to compete with the teams we had to compete with." Basketball sometimes took a backseat even in its own arena, with the playing floor being removed after the season in favor of dirt used for a rodeo and other agriculture-related purposes.

Hogue did his part to elevate the program, leading Georgia squads in scoring his first three seasons at Athens. "I felt I should have been all-SEC all the time," he said. "When it came to one-on-one, nobody touched me." He paced the 1969–70 Bullpups with 19.1 points per game. Considered by some the SEC's premier sophomore, Hogue was again the team's leading scorer (16.2 points) in 1970–71. But the varsity slid to 6–19, the school's worst record since 1956, and finished last in the league. The tone was set for the season when Georgia dropped its opener against Rollins, a team from a lower division of play.

The addition of Bassett, a first-team junior college All-American at the College of South Idaho, helped UGA rebound to 14–12 in 1971–72.

A highlight of Hogue's junior season was a win over Kentucky, only the second in a 37-game span against the Wildcats. The McKinley Tech team-mates led the way. Bassett, playing out of position at center, finished second in the SEC in rebounding, trailing only Alabama's Wendell Hudson. Hogue averaged a team-best 20.5 points, third in the conference, and made the All-SEC squad. "Ronnie has impressed me with his great quickness, good basketball sense, and poise under pressure," said C. M. Newton, the Alabama coach.

Hogue moved to forward in 1972–73. Both he and team struggled. His scoring average dropped to 16.2, the lowest of his career, and Georgia finished 10–16. "It like to burned me up," he said of his anger at the move to the frontcourt. After the season, the Capital (previously Baltimore) Bullets took Hogue in the seventh round of the NBA draft, the 116th pick overall. He was cut a week prior to the start of the 1973–74 season. He played for a year in the semi-pro Eastern League, then retired.

Academic success proved comparably elusive. Guthrie prodded Hogue to pursue his studies throughout college, with limited success. He even wrote a letter to the player's parents, warning, "I am anxious for Ronnie to pick up his academic pace." The amiable Hogue now admitted he was "more of a social person" than was probably desirable. "I had so much fun at Georgia. I think I had more fun than anybody. I learned about a lot more than basketball." Unfortunately, he finished well short of graduating with his class.

He and Guthrie remained friends—in a handwritten note Hogue admonished the new Georgia head coach in 1973, "You take it easy and go light on the food." The next year Guthrie arranged for Hogue to return to Georgia as an assistant coach long enough to complete work toward a degree in business management. "Ronnie has his degree at Georgia," Guthrie said proudly. Hogue eventually returned to Maryland.

Hogue did not give much thought during his college days to the pioneering role he played, and in retrospect claimed only modest impact. Others were more impressed. "I want to thank you for being the first Black basketball player at the University of Georgia. It was a tremendous responsibility and obviously you handled it extremely well," wrote Tubby Smith in December 1995, within months of becoming the school's first African-American basketball coach. "You paved the way for me and others like me, and we do appreciate that."

CHAPTER 11

FORBIDDEN TERRITORY

Craig Mobley, Clemson University, 1969–71
Casey Manning, University of South Carolina, 1969–73

A Negro was forever on trial . . . In a country where individual freedom was most idealized, he was charged not only with his own performance but with that of every other person of color of whatever character, ability or station.

Pauli Murray, *Proud Shoes*

Three gallons of gasoline cost $1. The environmental movement, fears of energy shortages, and demand for smaller, fuel-efficient automobiles were in their infancy. Thus the cars driven directly at Black students as they walked to classes on the isolated Clemson University campus or strolled the streets of the small, adjacent town of Clemson were almost without exception large and potentially lethal at almost any speed. "There is general fear and complete panic on the part of the Black students certain as we are that our physical being is in danger," wrote the president of the Student League for Black Identity. His letter to Clemson president Robert C. Edwards explained why, in one of the more unique incidents in the history of college integration, virtually every African-American undergraduate fled the South Carolina campus on October 26, 1969.

"The university administration knows no reason why Clemson students of any race should have fear for their personal safety," Edwards wrote in response. "To the best of our information, there have been during the fall semester no incidents involving racial connotations."

That difference in perceptions of conditions at the state university unquestionably stoked the fears of black students. If, as SLBI president Joseph Grant believed, "the majority of white students are restrained from abusing Black students only by the administration," then officials' failure to perceive any danger was anything but reassuring.

"I don't think anybody would have thought it was real until somebody got hurt," Craig Mobley said. "There were people they actually assaulted with vehicles. Nobody got hurt, but it got to the point like, 'We'll drive fast toward this person.' It got to the point where it was like imminent stuff hanging over the campus."

Mobley, the first African-American basketball player at Clemson, had been on campus barely a month when matters reached a boil. Like many students in those times of turmoil, he was confronted with the choice of either joining his contemporaries in taking unsanctioned direct action or acquiescing in a status quo perceived to be unjust. Mobley, in contrast with many athletes, chose to stand with his fellow Black students. "I'm walking down the street and it's dark at night; nobody's going to care if I'm a basketball player or not," he thought at the time. "That's the way I reconciled it. I said, 'I'm as Black as any other person on this campus.' It wasn't an issue for me to figure out whether I played ball. I'm Black. Bottom line."

But another bottom line had been articulated less than two weeks earlier in a letter to all Clemson athletes from Frank Howard, the athletics director and head football coach. A Vietnam War protest was scheduled for midweek, and Howard admonished athletes to "not take part in any demonstrations around the Clemson campus. The demonstrations will not stop the war in Vietnam and we have a very tough game against Wake Forest this Saturday afternoon in Death Valley. It is homecoming and we have to beat Wake Forest! This should be the upmost thing in your mind."

To this day Mobley wonders if his decision to join the student walkout ultimately shortened his playing career with the Tigers, which lasted only through his sophomore season. "Here's one of the things I'm asking myself: Did that have an effect on me playing ball down there? That's one of the things I don't know. I want to think it didn't, but it may have," he said. "Was I stupid or not? The point was, it was what I felt was the right thing to do."

Tensions were high on campus that fall of 1969. Protests against the Vietnam War were ongoing, unsettling university administrators at Clemson, as elsewhere. One demonstration was met with curses and tossed tomatoes and cherry bombs. Earlier in the year, president Edwards had requested that state police record the names and license plates of those attending an antiwar "talk-in" at Clemson House. Later, the school proudly staved off an attempt to have Clemson host a regional Vietnam moratorium meeting, a decision that was challenged unsuccessfully in U.S. District Court.

But the most burning issues revolved around race, that constant of life in South Carolina, "a white supremacy state par excellence," according to author John Gunther.

Here was the home of secession and the first shots fired in the Civil War. Here race-baiting politician "Pitchfork Ben" Tillman declared in the 1890s, "Governor as I am, I would lead a mob to lynch the negro who ravishes a white woman." Here occurred the events fictionalized in D. W. Griffith's 1915 film *Birth of a Nation*, which glorified the Ku Klux Klan and moved some unsophisticated South Carolina moviegoers to fire pistols at the screen "to save white womanhood from Black Radicals," according to historian Lewis Jones. Here rose to power Strom Thurmond, the longest-serving senator in U.S. history, 1948 presidential candidate on a white supremacist platform, and a stunning hypocrite who preached racial separation while fathering a child with a Black maid. Miscegenation, or interracial sexual relations, was a bugaboo so abhorred by segregationists that *Proud Shoes*, a revealing family history written by Pauli Murray, a North Carolinian of mixed blood, was banned in the South when published during the mid-1950s.

South Carolina's populace was predominantly Black through the first quarter of the 20th century. Outnumbered whites enforced their control with every tool from repression to derision. As late as 1957 the state supreme court ruled that to call a white person a Negro was inherently libelous and a basis upon which to sue for damages. When outmigration by Blacks shifted South Carolina's racial balance to a white majority during the mid-1920s, a report by the state department of agriculture exulted, "This means a new freedom for South Carolina. It is the removal of a vague but always present shadow. South Carolina at last has become a white state."

Racial separation was so pervasive in South Carolina that when World War II ended, the city of Greenville held distinct celebrations for Blacks and whites. Not until 1998 did the state end a legal ban on interracial marriage. Greenville residents still opposed celebrating a Martin Luther King Jr. holiday in 2003.

"It seems to me that the average [white] South Carolinian is so afraid that the negro will get ahead that he is willing to sacrifice his own rights just to make sure that the negro won't have any," a soldier wrote to Columbia's *State* newspaper in 1944. Confirming that assessment, and despite the fact that nearly 20 percent of South Carolina's white population was illiterate (the percentage was higher for Blacks), the state defied the *Brown v. Board of Education* ruling by adopting the usual constitutional amendment to close public schools rather than countenance desegregation. State parks were shuttered to avoid integration, and it became a crime for any public employee to hold membership in the National Association for the Advancement of Colored People. "Anyone who did not agree with the *Brown* decision was automatically assumed to be in favor of communism, atheism, and mongrelization," Walter Edgar said in *South Carolina: A History.*

South Carolina was among the last states to integrate its public schools, along with Alabama and Mississippi. In keeping with the credo of recalcitrance, it took a federal court order to force the Clemson Agricultural College of South Carolina to accept Harvey Gantt as its first African-American student in January 1963. Alabama governor George Wallace, anticipating his stand in the schoolhouse door, blasted South Carolina for accepting desegregation. Virtue nevertheless was found in succumbing peacefully to the inevitable. One in-state newspaper received Gantt's enrollment with the headline, "First in Secession—Last in Desegregation," and a historical marker entitled "Integration with Dignity, 1963" eventually was erected at Clemson University (the name was changed in 1964). Integration followed a similarly nonviolent course in September 1963 at the University of South Carolina, the last flagship university in the South to open its doors to Black students.

The pragmatic acceptance of campus integration by South Carolina's institutions of higher learning was celebrated, particularly in contrast with Alabama, Arkansas, Georgia, and Mississippi. Why was the Palmetto State comparatively receptive? "Part of the answer lies in the firm stand taken by state [and most local] officials on law and order," Edgar explained. "Another part lies in Harvey Gantt's often quoted remark, 'If you can't appeal to the morals of a South Carolinian, you can appeal to his manners.' Most white South Carolinians rejected mob violence in the 1960s just as they had rejected the Klan in the 1920s."

Of course a rejection of violence was far from certain during the 1960s; when Gantt enrolled at Clemson, state police were stationed at every town within 30 miles. Moreover, one could argue that a rosy view of South Carolina's acceptance of racial equality is not altogether warranted. Almost immediately after Gantt filed a lawsuit to enter Clemson, the South Carolina General Assembly signaled its defiance by voting to place the Confederate flag atop the State House. The flag flew atop the dome of the state capitol at Columbia into the 21st century. Under boycott pressure from the NAACP and other groups, and confronted by an NCAA ban on championship events within the state, the banner was moved to another site on the capitol grounds. Finally, in 2015, after nine Black people were murdered while attending church in Charleston, the Confederate battle flag was removed altogether.

Bob Cole, a longtime sportswriter for the *State*, said he heard "racist comments all the time" in Columbia but still found the debate over the flag "an eye-opening experience. Some people will never let it go." Such defiance came as no surprise to Cleveland Sellers, the longtime civil rights activist and academic. "We pretended, and to some extent we avoided. So now we are going around trying to figure out, well, where did this hatred and this whole thing come from about the Confederate flag?" Sellers advanced the minority view, literally and figuratively, that the perceived lack of racial violence in South Carolina is a "misnomer"; he cites as examples of enduring turmoil the fatal shooting of civil rights demonstrators in Orangeburg in 1968, an attack with chains and ax handles on a school bus carrying Black children in Lamar in 1969, and church burnings across the state during the 1990s.

History records the tragic low point of the nation's campus protest era as the May 1970 killing of four students and the wounding of nine others by National Guard troops during an antiwar demonstration at Ohio's Kent State University. But South Carolina had its own unfortunate and largely unsung shootings, as Sellers knew from bitter experience. He was an undergraduate at South Carolina State when three fellow students were shot to death and several dozen were wounded by highway patrolmen during a protest at a segregated bowling alley just off campus. Edgar stated that after the incident at the all-Black school, "The beliefs of a number of Black Carolinians in the moderation of South Carolina were shaken."

Orangeburg surely was on the minds of African-American students as racial frictions, and fears, escalated at Clemson a year after the shootings. The initial sources of conflict were "Dixie" and the Confederate flag—symbolic to some, symptomatic to others, and almost universally a problem as increasing numbers of Black students challenged emblems of school spirit at previously all-white high schools and colleges across the South.

Confederate flags were not prominent at basketball games, sparing controversy. Then again, basketball was an afterthought at Clemson. The basketball program posted losing records in 13 of its 16 ACC seasons prior to Mobley's arrival on campus and did not go to an NCAA tournament until 1980. A newspaper preview of the 1968–69 Tigers said succinctly, they "have no height, no speed, no experience and no depth." The team finished 6–19 and tied for last in the conference. Until the fall of 1968, Clemson played in Fike Fieldhouse, which seated 4,500 fans and was so dark that Duke player Joe Belmont went through warm-ups wearing a miner's helmet with lamp attached. "You just wondered if they were just using lights from the outside, it was so dark and dingy," Dick Grubar, a former North Carolina player, recalled. Pat Conroy, in *My Losing Season*, his autobiographical account of playing for The Citadel, described Fike as having "the feel of a place designed by a testy little man who had flunked all his engineering courses and hated basketball players with a passion."

Football was the beloved sport, reenacting warfare in which one might mentally substitute the young men in orange and white for the boys in butternut and gray. Calling football players "Saturday's soldiers," Tony Barnhart, author of *Southern Fried Football,* argued, "While other sports inspire excitement, enthusiasm, anger, and happiness, in the South, college football is the only sport that generates an emotional attachment that comes from the very core of who we are." That version of the South begins at South Carolina.

Football first captivated Clemson with the 1900 arrival of coach John Heisman, namesake of the premier award honoring college football's best player. The pioneer of the forward pass, the "flea flicker," and the center snap went on to establish winning programs at Georgia Tech and Auburn. Among his Clemson successors was Howard, a teammate of Bear Bryant under Wallace Wade at Alabama. Howard was the Tigers' head coach for 30 years. He retired after the 1969 season, letting it be known that the advent of Black athletes in big-time football played into his decision. The Hall of Famer's teams posted a 165–118–12 record with six ACC titles, six bowl appearances, and six top-20 finishes in the polls. A window to Howard's orientation was found in his dismissive comment on the 17-member Southern Conference, from which the ACC broke away in 1953. "It was so big," he said, "I felt like a member of the Rotary Club and the Ku Klux Klan."

On Saturdays Clemson's Memorial Stadium became more populous than all but a handful of cities in South Carolina. Howard and his players helped clear the site on which the stadium was built, with the coach placing plugs of chewing tobacco in the corners for good luck. Memorial, which opened in 1942, was later nicknamed "Death Valley" by the coach at Presbyterian College, whose team visited annually in the role of early-season whipping boy. Key to spectacle and spirit were the Confederate flags that fans routinely waved and the 20-foot version of the flag Tiger cheer-leaders customarily carried across the field at halftime. And of course the student band played "Dixie."

Whites tended to regard song and flag as inspiring symbols of a noble lost cause—the so-called War for Southern Independence—embodying what author Marshall Frady describes as "the Southern romance of an unvanquished and intransigent spirit in the face of utter, desolate defeat."

"No wonder the Confederates fought like madmen," pamphleteer John Tillery Lewis wrote in the early 1900s. "The martial music by which they stepped was almost enough to thrill the soul of a dead man." Describing NC State's basketball arena during the 1950s, one writer commented, "Reynolds also had the largest model Hammond organ available, which North Carolina coach Frank McGuire once said was worth 10 extra points to NC State each time the organist played 'Dixie.'"

The song is more than a wistful evocation of old times south of the Mason-Dixon Line. Often rendered in dialect, the song recalled what histori-an John Hope Franklin said white Southerners considered a "perfect" ante-bellum social and economic order predicated on the enslavement of African Americans. Even the song's origins are sullied. Composer Daniel Decatur Emmett, a white Ohioan, made his living prior to the Civil War as a "Negro minstrel." A big hit in the Northeast and England, "Uncle Dan" entertained by "blacking his face and hands with burnt cork and interspersing his coon songs with jokes," according to C. A. Browne, author of *The Story of Our National Ballads*.

As for the Confederate flag, the version most often used at games was the battle flag. First embraced by segregationist Dixiecrats in 1948, it was quickly adopted regionwide post-*Brown* as a symbol of defiance of federal authority to force integration. From the early days of the civil rights move-ment, when students staged sit-ins in Greensboro, North Carolina, coun-terdemonstrators waved Confederate flags. Upon becoming Alabama's governor in 1963, George Wallace had the helmets and cars of the state police affixed with Confederate flags.

"I know the Confederate flag," said Sellers, a native South Carolinian whose campus office for years was around the corner from a Confederate museum. "I know it by the state troopers at Selma beating people down with the Confederate flag on the side of their helmets. That's where I know the Confederate flag. When the Ku Klux Klan was rallying, the Confederate flag was there. When they came to burn you up in Mississippi or to blow you up in Mississippi, to shoot you in Alabama, they had the Confederate flag with them. That's the context in which I know the Confederate flag. The Confederates said absolutely nothing when the flag was being used as a symbol for the racial violence and oppression and resistance. They did absolutely nothing."

Not surprisingly, then, many early African-American students on Southern campuses made it their business to rid athletic events of "Dixie" and the Confederate flag.

Clemson's Black students first raised the issue of playing "Dixie" in April 1968. "We find the song 'Dixie' to be insulting and very embarrassing when used at rallies, games, etc.," the Student League for Black Identity wrote. "How can we 'legally' do away with this?" Discussions continued, with administrators reserving the right to choose whether flag and song were used. Reflective of interest in the issue, the 1969 student yearbook had four pictures of the Confederate flag in the first 27 pages, including the table of contents. "We don't stop them their singing, which is so sickening, we shall overcome. So keep on singing Dixie, don't give in," said a handwritten, syntactically challenged letter from "Some Dixie Friends" to university president Edwards. "Always [Black people] want more and more, no matter what you try to do for them, they don't appriciate [sic] any way, just hating the white people."

Given such sentiments voiced from beyond campus, and vocal support for the symbols of the Confederacy by white Clemson students, the school's African-American undergraduates experienced "a feeling of euphoria," according to the SLBI faculty advisor, when "Dixie" was played but once and the flag was absent entirely at the first home football game in 1969. The euphoria was short-lived. Even as Howard warned athletes against involvement in demonstrations, controversy erupted over a blackface skit scheduled for Tigerama, a Homecoming show meant to boost school spirit. The skit was cleansed of its racist connotations, but that weekend "Dixie" and the Confederate flag returned as the Tigers beat overmatched Wake Forest by two touchdowns.

"The black students on Clemson campus are fed up with the outward show of bigotry and the fallacy of white supremacy," SBLI president Grant wrote to the student newspaper. The *Tiger* editorially supported the Black students. Amid rancor over the Vietnam War and the derision of protestors as traitors, the paper chided Confederate partisans, "That 'glorious civil war' would be called treason today."

The Edwards administration soon changed its tune, saying publicly and privately that use of the flag and the playing of "Dixie" were matters for students to decide. The undergrad Central Spirit Committee duly voted to ban both, starting the following football season. Backlash was swift and included the formation of an unofficial campus group called SPONGE, an acronym for the Society for the Prevention of Niggers Getting Everything. Edwards continued to run onto the field with the football team prior to their games, as he did for all but one contest during his presidency.

(Edwards was not unsympathetic toward African Americans, at least individually. When Maryland's Darryl Hill, the ACC's first Black football player, came to Clemson in 1963, his mother was barred from entering the stadium despite holding tickets. The Clemson president not only intervened to invite Palestine Hill to his personal box to watch the game, but also gave her lodging for the night at his home.)

When Alabama visited Death Valley for a game on October 25, the campus was awash with Confederate flags. SPONGE banners were evident in the stands, from which great cheers arose when the Alabama and then the Clemson band struck up "Dixie." But when Tiger cheerleaders carried an American flag onto the field they were greeted with boos and jeers. The next day, citing ongoing harassment, 60 Black students staged their one-day walkout.

"Today I say, 'What the hell was I thinking then?'" Mobley admitted. "If it was a matter of playing ball or getting a degree, walking off campus was a sure way not to do either one." During the Black students' daylong hiatus from campus, Mobley returned to Chester, a small mill town 109 miles away in the north-central part of the state near Charlotte, North Carolina. His family traced its roots there to a great-grandmother brought from Africa as a slave. "My world was living in Chester," said Mobley.

In subsequent years Mobley continued to visit his parents' home, which had an old grass basketball court in the backyard. But he also made a place for himself in the Black community near Clemson, consciously trying to bridge a gulf between students on campus and African Americans in the surrounding countryside. He joined the Ebenezer Baptist Church in Seneca, where he started a Boy Scout troop and played piano and organ, just as he had done in Chester.

The town of Clemson itself remained hostile territory. "I couldn't go anywhere in Clemson and get a haircut," Mobley said. "I couldn't go anywhere in Clemson and eat. You didn't venture into downtown Clemson." The KKK also was a presence, with an annual parade in nearby Anderson.

○

When Mobley grew up in Chester, life seemed safe. A young Black boy could ride his bicycle most anywhere without direct supervision as long as he followed a simple rule of thumb: no contact with whites. Mobley recalls being warned to not cross the railroad tracks. The only time he mingled with white people was during the family's summer visits to New Jersey, where he was born. "If the only people you're always seeing are Black, how do you know if it's segregated or not? I had some awareness that there were more people [beyond Chester], but I never saw a Hispanic, I never saw an Asian, I never saw anyone from anywhere else."

Only once did Mobley directly encounter racial violence before heading to college, although the potential was omnipresent in Chester, according to David Sanders, a boyhood friend. "The Klan was very alive and vibrant in our town," Sanders said. He witnessed crosses burned in relatives' yards. "They used to meet on Sunday afternoons in an open field across from the hospital, so those issues weren't very subtle."

Mobley was among a group of Black youngsters accosted by white teenagers while taking a shortcut through off-limits "Mill Hill" on their way home from the Chester's segregated movie theater. Mobley, age eight, ran home at the urging of an older brother. A friend was injured. The white boys were apprehended and taken to the police station. Mobley said his mother, an elementary school cafeteria worker, and his father, a high school janitor with a peacemaker's reputation, helped place the incident in proper perspective. "What it taught me is that good people will do the right thing at the right time," he said. "It left a memory, but not a scar. The scar would have been, I should have hated a lot of people. What I think I found out, out of that, is what I think I've always known: It's always, who is the individual?"

In 1965 "freedom of choice" presented Mobley with the opportunity to attend previously all-white Chester High School. Curious to see what the white world was like, and eager to embrace what he regarded as "a challenge," Mobley took the plunge and prospered. He lettered in baseball, basketball, and junior varsity football. He was sports editor of the Chester High yearbook. He was president of the National Honor Society. Mobley had the twelfth-best grade point average in a class of 192, and his SAT score was above 1000. He was a sufficiently outstanding student to merit an appointment to the U.S. Military Academy, which he declined. (Military life did have its appeal; after college Mobley made a career in the U.S. Air Force. He eventually retired as a major and started a construction business in Los Angeles.)

Crossing the divide at Chester High brought familiar dilemmas. "I remember not standing when they played 'Dixie,'" said Sanders, who was a member of the school band. "That was the pep song for the school. They'd wave the flag and play 'Dixie' when we scored and at pep rallies. It was a big issue."

Mobley, a 6-foot guard, was serenaded frequently. He was a perennial starter under three different basketball coaches, averaging 10.8 points as a sophomore, 21.5 as a junior, and 20.3 as a senior in 1968–69. He also led the Cyclones in rebounding his last season. Mobley was named the conference's Most Valuable Player his senior year and led the league in scoring his final two seasons at Chester High School. Looking back with the eyes of a former high school and junior college coach, as well as a high school game official, Mobley observed, "I knew I had some quickness. I did have some transition speed. I just wish I had some more smarts."

He did work on his game, his parents pinching pennies so he could attend summer basketball camps at NC State and North Carolina. Mobley was highly impressed with Tar Heel coach Dean Smith, and the two began a sporadic correspondence that continued for years. But UNC offered only a partial scholarship and modest basketball interest. Besides, Mobley was intent on majoring in engineering, not a strength of the liberal arts institution in Chapel Hill. Recruited by Davidson, Newberry, Southern Illinois, and South Carolina, Mobley opted for Clemson and genial coach Bobby Roberts. "When you consider his academic record and his athletic ability," Roberts said in a 1969 press release, "we think that Craig will make a big contribution to the Clemson way of life in the next four years. His ideals would be an asset to any institution."

Only later did Mobley realize he was Clemson's first Black scholarship athlete.

For Mobley, basketball already was an invaluable asset in bridging the gap between Black and white. "How can you be yourself when you've got two worlds pulling against you?" he asked rhetorically. "I survived Chester, and the survival part was how to get the two groups together. That basketball game was a way of reconciling two groups for me. I'm in one world, but I'm still going to need the other one."

Mobley was the sixth signee in a recruiting class hailed as a way out of the doldrums for Clemson basketball. His signing was heralded in the *Greenville News* under the oddly descriptive headline "Tigers Ink First Negro." The *State* touted "the first Negro signed to an athletic grant by

Clemson" as "a smooth guard" with "a great shooting touch and catlike moves." The Anderson paper misidentified him as *Greg* Mobley.

The same day Mobley's signing was announced, so was the all-state high school basketball team. Seven-footer David Angel, another Clemson signee, was a unanimous pick. So was guard Casey Manning, who roomed with Mobley that August in Columbia for the North-South All-Star basketball game.

Casey Manning and Craig Mobley shared more than initials. Both were South Carolinians from county seats of about 6,000 residents. Both were outstanding students. Both were among the first to take advantage of "freedom of choice" by attending previously all-white high schools. Both were quick guards lacking topnotch jump-shooting and playmaking skills. Both wound up as reserves during their college playing careers. Both became home crowd favorites in the manner of hustling benchwarmers everywhere. Both graduated and enjoyed successful careers geared to public service. And both were the first African-American basketball players at their respective schools.

Manning came from Dillon, a manufacturing and agricultural community near the North Carolina border where his family had lived for generations. The family name was prominent among Blacks and whites in Dillon County, where one of the seven townships is named Manning.

Casey Manning, one of six children and the youngest of four boys, describes Dillon as "a typical Southern small town. You'll find similar small towns in Virginia, Maryland, all over the country." Dillon was a more tolerant place than most. Manning recalls segregation but no instances of racial violence, and he said he played basketball with whites throughout his youth. "Basically everybody grew up with everybody. They knew everybody. They fished in the same river. The population of Dillon was maybe 60–40: 60 percent white, 40 Black. There wasn't a white family in Dillon that didn't know a Black family, a Black family that didn't know a white family."

Dillon County also was a marriage mecca for much of the 20th century. The flood tide was highest during World War II, when thousands of soldiers stationed at Fort Bragg, 70 miles north, took advantage of South Carolina laws less restrictive than those in North Carolina. (Getting *out* of a marriage was not so easy in South Carolina, which did not legalize divorce until 1948.) In his history of Dillon County, Durward Stokes reported that nearly 7,000 marriage licenses were issued as late as fiscal year 1975, "representing a respectable amount of county revenue."

What further differentiated Dillon County then, as now, was a kitschy tourist attraction along Interstate 95, the main route from New York to Florida. "South of the Border," described by roadsideamerica.com as "a unique amalgam of Dixie and Old Mexico," is a $40 million complex seven miles north of Dillon that draws more than three million visitors annually. "S.O.B." is known for a string of "Pedro"-themed, pun-filled billboards that bestride the interstate for hundreds of miles, leading to a giant sombrero-topped observation tower overlooking 135 neon-encrusted acres of shops, restaurants, motels, and amusements. The founder and owner, Alan Schafer, a Baltimore transplant, became a major power in South Carolina's Democratic party. He was a friend of Frank McGuire, the South Carolina basketball coach, and of Manning, a star player at Dillon High School.

Manning averaged 31.8 points on a team that finished 18–2 and won the area championship his junior year. *State* sportswriter Cole declared that the young athlete's forte was "an uncanny knack for shooting," and Manning proved him right by averaging 34 points on a 23–3 squad that won the 1969 Class AAA state title. He scored 62 points in one game and 27 in the state championship contest. His tallest teammate was 6-foot-3; an inch shorter, Manning was used at every position except center. "I could run, I could jump, I could shoot," said Manning, who was named to the all-state team as a senior.

Recruiting letters began arriving his sophomore prep year. His family always pushed education, so "basketball sort of got in the way as to where I went to school, to a certain extent," Manning said. Early overtures came from Ivy League schools, Johns Hopkins, and similar institutions. His first choice was Davidson, a private, Presbyterian college he recalled as "proba-bly more [socially] liberal than the University of North Carolina in those days." But after Davidson basketball coach Lefty Driesell departed for Maryland in 1969, Manning reconsidered.

The choice came down to Clemson or South Carolina. Manning says "a combination of a lot of things" swayed him to choose the latter. "Carolina's a state university. Got a good basketball team. You can major in anything you want. Clemson is a fine institution, too, academically, but I'm not going to go to school in Pickens County for four years. Culture had something to do with it. Columbia is the capital city. It's got other Black institutions there. You've got a Black population there. You're not isolated. You've even got radio stations to listen to. It's close to home."

Moreover, McGuire's program was familiar. Prior to each season, the Gamecocks visited South of the Border for a meal and a public workout, according to Donnie Walsh, McGuire's top assistant. "We met Casey up there during those times, so it was pretty well in our minds that when Casey graduated, we wanted him to come—and that's more or less what happened." When Manning did sign, it was at a South of the Border restaurant. As a gift to his mother, a millworker, Manning signed with the Gamecocks on her birthday.

"Casey truthfully wasn't good enough to play in the ACC," said Bobby Cremins, an older teammate from New York and later head coach at Appalachian State University, Georgia Tech, and College of Charleston. "He scored a lot of points, but he was a little bit over his head with the New York guys. But he was a great, great person and a brilliant kid. We loved Casey. People easily accepted Casey. Easily."

Brian Winters, a younger teammate from New York and later an NBA head coach, had a similar but more positive recollection of Manning's game. "He was a good athlete. He was very fast and quick, and he was a good defender. He wasn't a great offensive player. He could make shots. He was a decent perimeter shooter. He could get to the goal because of his quickness. He didn't have a lot of skill off the dribble, scoring, etcetera. But he was a good player."

Walsh said Manning's deficiencies as a player were less telling than the fact that he was a bad fit for McGuire's conservative system. McGuire's players had freedom, but within a scheme in which they walked the ball upcourt, employed a two-three zone defensive alignment against quality opponents, and otherwise slowed the pace. "Frank's style was a lot of freelance and not set plays," Walsh said. "I think Casey could have been a good college player, but in the system Frank had, Casey was expected to make plays that his ball-handling might not have allowed him to."

McGuire also was not one to substitute, so bench players had scant opportunity to prove themselves during games. McGuire put his best players on the court and, barring foul trouble, let them play. "He always coached from a confidence standpoint, and he would say, 'What do you think I recruited you for?'" said Dean Smith, who assisted McGuire for three years at North Carolina before succeeding him as head coach.

The McGuire approach secured 549 victories from 1948 through 1980 and landed him in the Basketball Hall of Fame. He also spawned highly successful coaching protégés, most prominently Smith, Cremins, Al McGuire (Marquette [no relation]), Lou Carnesecca (St. John's), the NBA's Doug Moe (Denver), and Larry Brown, the only coach with titles in both the NCAA

(Kansas in 1988) and NBA (Detroit in 2004). "When we won the national championship, we won in it Kansas City, where [Frank McGuire] won his in '57," Brown said of Kansas University. "He was probably more happy for me than I was."

McGuire, a former St. John's player and coach, considered New Yorkers the best high school players in the country; he initiated a reverse "Underground Railroad," as the media put it, that brought South a parade of talents that included Len Rosenbluth, Pete Brennan, Tommy Kearns, York Larese, Billy Cunningham, Brown, Moe, and Walsh at North Carolina and Cremins, Winters, John Roche, Tom Owens, Tom Riker, Kevin Joyce, and Mike Dunleavy at South Carolina. "I don't think it's fair to say he wouldn't play them unless they were from New York," Smith said of McGuire's players. "That's true, but it's a terrible thing to say." The starters on UNC's 1957 national championship squad all hailed from the New York metropolitan area, as did four of five starters on South Carolina's 1971 ACC championship team.

McGuire left North Carolina after the 1960–61 season, the school's sole NCAA probation clouding the horizon. Three years later he popped up at South Carolina. He soon had the Fighting Gamecocks on probation. But McGuire always bounced back. He was a larger-than-life character, a tough product of a Manhattan settlement house who balanced a quick temper with charm and a taste for first-class living. He could win over a recruit's mother by taking her out for dinner and dancing, or shoot invective at an official even as he characteristically tugged at his starched shirt cuffs and adjusted his tie. "He had great magnetism" that ineluctably drew players and others to him, Walsh said. "At one time or another he won over two states. He could have been elected governor."

South Carolina only twice managed a winning record in 11 ACC seasons prior to McGuire's arrival. The major highlight during those years was the 1957 scoring performance by Grady Wallace, one of just two ACC players to lead the nation in scoring (along with Virginia Tech's Erick Green in 2013). "The program was in shambles," recalled Tom Price, a historian of USC athletics.

Within three years of McGuire's arrival, the Gamecocks were 16–7 and third in the ACC. The dark, cozy arena he inherited, University Field House, seated at best 4,000 spectators. The playing floor was sunken 3 feet below street level. "The gym was like a swimming pool," said Bucky Waters, the former Duke head coach. By the start of the 1968–69 season, USC was ensconced in gaudy, $9 million Carolina Coliseum, capacity 12,121, and players inhabited a plush dormitory called "the Roost."

The relentlessly competitive McGuire also made matters interesting off the court, where he thrived on conflict. "He was never happy unless he was involved in controversy," Price said. "Talk show hosts are like that now." McGuire was a perennial critic of the ACC tournament as a means of deciding a champion. Matters between league members USC and Duke grew so heated off the court that their season series was canceled in 1967. Once settled in Columbia, McGuire struck another enduring theme by claiming the conference was dominated by the interests of its four North Carolina members. "We're fighting for respect," he said of USC. "I was on the other side of the fence at North Carolina and know what these people think of South Carolina. But we're making progress and we will not be patsies anymore."

South Carolina's institutional angst extended to academic admissions standards, which in the ACC were voluntarily higher than those in other conferences. Athletic officials at USC, Clemson, and Maryland argued they were at a recruiting disadvantage against schools from the SEC, whose teams defeated ACC opponents 23 consecutive times on the football field. Agitating for relaxed standards did not stop Clemson's Frank Howard from calling the SEC "the knucklehead league."

Paul Dietzel, South Carolina's athletics director and head football coach, led the way in advocating change. Dietzel had made his reputation at Louisiana State, where he and his "Chinese Bandits" won the 1958 national title after defeating Clemson 7–0 in the Sugar Bowl. Yet, for all his concern about expanding the available talent pool, the South Carolina coach continued to pass on African-American prospects from his own backyard. One player he considered inferior went to Purdue. Dietzel told another, Columbia-area product Ernie Jackson, that he was too small. Jackson went to Duke and became an All-American. "They said that, but Dickie Harris, who was a guy who went there and got All-America honors, was about the same size as me," Jackson pointed out. "So that did not hold any water."

Meanwhile, ACC members Maryland and Wake Forest came to town with African Americans on their football squads, including quarterback Freddie Summers at Wake. South Carolina fans were not welcoming. Wake lineman Bill Overton had whiskey and racial taunts hurled his way as he left the field at Columbia, a city where KKK robes were produced at Heritage Garment Works through at least 1965. Other Black pioneers identified USC as the least friendly basketball venue in the ACC. "The University of South Carolina was by far the worst place I played," said Duke's C. B. Claiborne, who also visited Clemson and Alabama. "They would be talking—out on the court you could hear all kinds of 'motherfuckers' and 'your mamas.' Foul-mouth language, especially in a public place. I had never been exposed to that kind of foul-mouth language playing basketball." North Carolina's Charles Scott remembered a similar reception.

The school's conspicuous slowness in accepting African-American athletes only added to Black hatred of South Carolina, according to Harold White. A native of Columbia, he worked for more than 30 years in the Gamecock athletics department. "We just couldn't attach ourselves to this university," White said. "Those of us who grew up in this city or the state at that time felt unwanted. We felt denied, and we felt that the hard core of that segregation was directed towards us. So those of us who enjoyed athletics . . . took it out on this university. I don't care who we were playing— the other school didn't have any Black players, either, but we wanted the other school to win."

Reticence to integrate the athletic program was symptomatic of a more profound estrangement between the university and African Americans.

South Carolina College, located only two blocks from the State House, was founded in 1801 "to provide higher education for potential leaders who, by getting their learning within the state, could thus escape being contaminated with alien ideas," explained historian Louis B. Wright. "Young men from the barbarous Up Country would come to Columbia, fraternize with their betters from the planter class, and become advocates of that culture." An international faculty, the first separate college library building in the country, and the favor of the state government enabled the school to maintain a virtual monopoly on higher education in South Carolina for much of the 19th century. Of course the college remained segregated, with the notable exception of the Reconstruction era, when Blacks accounted for 90 percent of the student body and whites called South Carolina College "Radical University" or "the School for the Deaf and Blind."

A racist status quo soon returned, remaining in effect until the 1960s. Efforts to desegregate were battled vigorously in the courts. An attempt by a Black World War II veteran to attend USC Law School led to the creation of a law facility at all-Black South Carolina State as a means of satisfying the requirements of equal if separate education. The concept was a farce, particularly in the Palmetto State. For instance, in 1930 Southern spending for white education exceeded that for African Americans by nearly 3 to 1. In South Carolina the ratio was 10 to 1. (As late as 1940 the ratio in Alabama was 16 to 1.)

The political and legal vulnerability created by such blatant unfairness was not lost on segregationist Jimmy Byrnes. The oldest man ever elected governor of South Carolina, Byrnes was a former U.S. Supreme Court justice, congressman, and leader of the war effort under President Franklin Roosevelt as director of the Office of War Mobilization. He then served for two years as Secretary of State under President Harry Truman, over whom he had nearly been chosen as FDR's vice president in 1944. Upon taking office as governor in 1951, the 68-year-old Byrnes declared, "It is our duty to provide for the races substantial equality in school facilities." He pushed through the state's first sales tax to address the problem. Between 1951 and 1956 two-thirds of the monies allocated for education in South Carolina went to schools for African Americans in an attempt to stave off federal action. Reversing roles, white parents complained the newest facilities were going to Black students.

The futility of efforts to obscure systematic, historic, and pervasive inequality were highlighted in *Brown*, an amalgam of lawsuits in which the only case from the so-called Deep South, *Briggs v. Elliott*, originated in Clarendon County, South Carolina. Discrepancies there between Black and white school spending, teacher pay, and facilities were prodigious and egregious. Thirty buses were devoted to transporting 2,375 white students, whereas there were no buses for the 6,531 African-American pupils. Some Black children walked 9 miles to a school heated by a wood stove, lighted by kerosene lamps, and lacking indoor plumbing and running water. When Black citizens petitioned him for buses, the chair of the local school board replied articulately, "We ain't got no money to buy a bus for your nigger children."

Whether in rural Clarendon County, where Manning, the county seat, lies about an hour's drive southeast of Columbia, or in the state capital itself, racial tensions were never far from the surface. Neither were certain givens of racial etiquette, such as the unwritten rule that kept African Americans from setting foot on the University of South Carolina campus. "Those kind of things my parents warned us of often. 'Don't walk across the university campus!'" said Harold White, now retired from his position as the school's associate athletics director for academic support and student services. "'I heard many stories where people who lived on [the other] side of town would have to circle way out of their way not to come here."

Harry Lesesne, a historian of the University of South Carolina, had a similar recollection. "I actually heard a Black Columbian refer to this campus as the Forbidden City. You just didn't come here. You didn't come on the campus, even though it was your state university and you supported it."

South Carolina remained at the forefront of massive resistance to federal racial edicts in the years following the *Brown* verdict, to the extent that the dean of the USC School of Education was dismissed in 1955 because he dared concede the inevitability of desegregation. But as the 1960s dawned, and both the futility and the price of defending segregation became manifest, South Carolina leaders quietly altered course.

The region's duplicative spending on separate public facilities and its repression of the Black workforce were a drain on resources and an impediment to progress. A 1940 Alabama educational study made the indirect argument that treating African Americans as second-class citizens was fiscal foolishness, noting that "an acre of land wasted by a Negro is no more nor less a loss to society than is one wasted by a white man." The study also stated that "the higher the percentage of skilled workers in the total group the greater the opportunities for all." The costs of segregation were sometimes quite tangible. A bus company executive in Florida estimated that a terminal with segregated facilities increased the cost of the building by 50 percent. Clemson was forced to reject a sizable grant from the Atomic Energy Commission during the 1950s because federal funding barred discrimination based on race, color, creed, or religion. As the dean of the University of South Carolina Law School told a legislative committee inquiring why it cost more to educate Black law students compared to whites: "The price of prejudice is very high."

South Carolina business leaders rebalanced the ledgers of resistance once federal courts began forcing compliance with desegregation orders. The fate of Little Rock, Arkansas, was particularly instructive. After confrontations at Central High School were televised nationally, four years passed before another outside corporation was willing to invest in the city. South Carolina averaged 106 new plant openings per year during the 1950s, worth at least $67 million annually.

Pragmatism had already begun shifting Birmingham, Alabama, toward desegregation in keeping with "the New South doctrine of business progressivism, which held that what was good for business was automatically good for the community," explained Diane McWhorter in *Carry Me Home.* Atlanta was similarly moved by economic considerations, thanks in part to Coca-Cola chairman Robert Woodruff, reputedly the richest man in the South, who declared that "Coca-Cola cannot operate from a city that is reviled."

When Charleston native Harvey Gantt sued in 1962 to transfer to Clemson from Iowa State University, politicians, business leaders, and organizations—as well as Clemson president Edwards—began laying the groundwork to accept integration.

Riots at the University of Georgia in 1961 and at the University of Mississippi in 1962 also galvanized South Carolina's elite. "Governors in South Carolina, and South Carolina in general, I think, never wanted to be Mississippi or Alabama," Lesesne said. "That didn't mean they weren't just as opposed to integration as Mississippi or Alabama, but South Carolinians considered themselves too good to be George Wallace. They would be Jimmy Byrnes and be statesmanlike about it, but go about doing the same thing. The end would be the same."

South Carolina law enforcement officials were dispatched to Oxford, Mississippi, to learn how they might avert Ole Miss–style violence. Those lessons were applied when Gantt arrived at Clemson in late January 1963. More than 100 officers virtually sealed off the campus; students were required to carry identification cards at all times. Media witnesses were numerous and omnipresent.

Five days after Gantt enrolled, Wake Forest arrived for a basketball game. As the Demon Deacons reached their motel, coach Bones McKinney cautioned his squad to lay low. "Bones had told all of the players that it was a very serious situation there at Clemson, that all them were to 'Go in that door and pick up your key at the desk. Go right to your room. Don't say any-thing to anybody,'" longtime Wake publicist Marvin "Skeeter" Francis recalled. "Then, when he opened the door and walked in, he says, 'Hey, what's going on? Convention of the highway patrol?'"

There were no major incidents at Clemson, a matter of encouragement and challenge when the University of South Carolina prepared to admit three African Americans who sued to gain admission for the fall semester in 1963.

"They set about doing what they had done at Clemson, which was to do a whole lot of preparation," Lesesne said. "Controlling the media. Controlling access. The place was ringed with state law enforcement division officers. The National Guard was on standby. . . . The university was really ready for anything." To this day, a vestige of those concerns mutely faces Sumter Street and the James F. Byrnes Building in downtown Columbia. USC officials intent on slowing any attempts by whites to storm the university ordered the erection of a handsome black wrought-iron fence across the open end of the Horseshoe, a central feature of the old campus where gracious walkways and venerable buildings are shaded by stately oaks.

The avoidance of violence was not only cost effective but also consistent with the character of South Carolinians observed by Gunnar Myrdal, an attorney and political economist whose acclaimed book *An American Dilemma: The Negro Problem and Modern Democracy* was published in 1944. "It was not only that they considered the overt display of racism unseemly; they also viewed it as unnecessary, and likely to arouse the violent reaction of poor whites that disturbed the tranquility they cherished as the hallmark of gentility," Myrdal wrote.

There was also the matter of pride. "The mind-set here was, well, if Clemson can do it, we can do it," Lesesne said. Antagonism between the two schools dated to Clemson's founding in 1893 on land bequeathed by John Calhoun, the antebellum states' rights champion. Ben Tillman, perpetual critic of the educational institution in Columbia and the elite to which it supposedly catered, vigorously promoted the agricultural and mechanical college. "It's time the citizens of South Carolina had a state college they can be proud of," Tillman declared. (To which one legislator replied, "The farmers of this state need a college education like they need a telegraph line to the moon.")

Once integrated, neither university rushed to add African Americans to its rolls. Clemson had 134 Black students among approximately 8,000 undergraduates in 1971, while at the University of South Carolina Manning reported that he could go an entire day and not see another Black student on campus. Slow as they were to change admissions policies in a state where 34 percent of the residents were African American, the two universities were even slower to seek Black athletes. The absence was increasingly a source of contention in Columbia, where the expanding university heightened local tensions by swallowing adjacent neighborhoods, Black and white. Not until 1969 did South Carolina add its first Black athletes in football, track, and basketball.

McGuire was hesitant to recruit African Americans. He told associates the ill treatment accorded Solly Walker at Lexington, Kentucky, in the early

1950s proved the region was not ready. "He wanted to make sure the time was right," said Walsh, his chief recruiter at Columbia.

Still, there were attempts to recruit Black players prior to Manning. Among the targets was Henry Wilmore, a New Yorker whom Cremins recalls shepherding around Columbia. "We went on campus, and things went great. The students were fabulous. We had the best time." Not even a testy reception at a local after-hours joint, where giving a $20 bill to the doorman bought 15 minutes of racial tolerance, dampened the visitor's enthusiasm for USC. "The next day I believe he committed, but the 800 rule was still in effect, and he didn't have the SAT requirement," Cremins said. Wilmore went instead to Michigan, a Big Ten school, and became an All-American in 1971 and 1972.

Gilbert McGregor, a high school senior in 1967, was another African-American prospect wooed by South Carolina. McGregor, who ultimately attended Wake Forest, had never seen a Cadillac Eldorado until McGuire and Walsh pulled up to his house in Raeford, North Carolina, on a recruiting visit. "McGuire told me that the University of South Carolina was ready for its first Black athlete and that it should be me. That two years previously he didn't think they were ready for Lew Alcindor, that he could have gotten Alcindor because of his relationship with [Wilt] Chamberlain," McGregor said.

"Now, I might be from Raeford, and I might be a high school guy, but I'm saying, 'They ain't getting that ready in two years, from Alcindor to me. Two years isn't long enough for them to be ready. No, I don't think I want to go. Who you fooling, coach?' He told me they were ready, and I was chicken."

McGuire had coached the NBA's Philadelphia Warriors for a year immediately after leaving North Carolina. Chamberlain, the team's star center, averaged a record 50.4 points per game, including an unmatched 100-point effort against the New York Knicks at Hershey, Pennsylvania. The Warriors lost to Boston in the 1962 NBA finals, then moved to San Francisco. McGuire chose not to relocate but remained on friendly terms with Chamberlain, a bond that bought "some acceptance" in the Black community, Harold White said. In the mid-1960s McGuire also spoke at the first clinic held by the state's Black basketball coaches. "And then of course when Casey signed, that broke it," White said.

Well, almost. McGuire's slowness to add African-American players remained an issue three years later, when Columbia's Alex English, the most highly sought prospect from the state to that point, committed to South Carolina. "I had something I want to prove," English, one of five players whose jersey number has been retired by the school, said in March 1972. "A lot of people told me a Black player couldn't play for Coach McGuire. I didn't believe this, and I wanted to prove these people are wrong. I know Wilt Chamberlain is one of Coach McGuire's closest friends."

Still, it was Manning's signing that broke the ice. "It was a big thing, maybe just because Casey was a local player that everyone knew about," Walsh said. To the coaches "it was more like, 'We got a good basketball player' than basically he was the first Afro-American player."

To the local African-American community, it was much more. "He was the pioneer," White said. "He was an excellent person to serve as a role model, or one that could be put in that kind of position. Most of the Black kids who were placed in those early days had to be a special kind of kid."

Manning's pioneering role created a minimal stir in the sports world at large. "I don't recall that much hoopla about the circumstances of his signing," said Cole of the *State*. "It turns out he was a great kid. Everyone loved him." Manning, a long-serving Richland County Circuit judge in Columbia, felt accepted and appreciated on and off the court. "People felt they knew me, I guess, in a way. I might have been Black, but I was one of their Blacks, if you want to put it that way," he says. "It wasn't like I was a Black kid from New York coming down to play. When I got to the university, there were kids from my high school there. I was the local boy who went to the state university."

Manning might have been overlooked in part because he arrived during the most tumultuous, and successful, period of Gamecock basketball history. South Carolina was the nation's top-rated team prior to the 1969–70 season. While Manning averaged 16.3 points for Walsh's Biddies, third best on the freshman squad, the varsity finished the regular season 23–2. There was talk of building a dynasty to supplant John Wooden's UCLA Bruins.

The Gamecocks were undefeated against league rivals during the 1969–70 regular season, but needed to win the ACC tournament to earn the league's sole bid to the NCAAs. The regional was slated for their Columbia home court, and two victories there would secure a trip to the Final Four. "That championship that year was their birthright," Cole said. But John Roche, USC's star guard, hurt his ankle in the ACC tournament semifinals. In a move still second-guessed, McGuire and staff stuck with a hobbled Roche and fell victim to an NC State slowdown in double overtime.

Afterward Cremins and teammate Corkey Carnevale fled to a cabin in the North Carolina mountains for a week to lick their psychic wounds. For years Cremins half-jokingly called Norm Sloan a "son of a bitch" every time he saw the NC State coach.

"We were one of the top two or three teams in the country, and we had nowhere to go," said Walsh, now retired from a long career as an NBA front office executive, mostly with the Indiana Pacers. Back then, a team hosting an NCAA regional was barred from the NIT. "So, yeah, I think there was a sense that we had lost a great opportunity, because we had everything that year. We really had a great team. I can remember it was a devastating loss."

Against a backdrop of escalating agitation over possible withdrawal from the ACC, a bitter McGuire and an essentially unchanged squad battled their way through the conference in 1970–71 to finish a game behind North Carolina in the standings. The already-physical Gamecocks played with chips on their shoulders and were met with hostility wherever they went. There were frequent fights and near-violent incidents, including a brawl at Columbia in which, as photos showed, South Carolina players held and punched Maryland's Lefty Driesell. Despite the evidence, McGuire insisted his fellow coach punched himself.

The team's bitterness "magnified after that loss to State," Cole said. "That last year, it just reached a high-water mark because everywhere they went, there would be comments in the paper. McGuire still was living with that loss. . . . It was kind of ridiculous. And the players picked up on it, and by the time they got to Winston or wherever they were playing, the fans would be ready for them." Such treatment, although courted by McGuire, shocked some Gamecocks. "In the ACC, you're playing hatred," said Rick Mousa, a freshman in 1971. "It's hard to believe that fans can hate you just because you play for the other team."

South Carolina announced during the 1971 ACC tournament that it would officially withdraw from the conference in time for the 1971–72 academic year. (Struggling to recruit as an independent, the Gamecocks joined the Metro Conference 12 years later. They were admitted to the SEC, their current league, in 1991.) The ACC exit came on a positive note as South Carolina outscored North Carolina 52–51 to win the ACC tournament championship. The key basket came off a jump ball on which 6-foot-2 sophomore Kevin Joyce outleapt UNC's 6-foot-10 Lee Dedmon in the final seconds.

Unlike Joyce, a classmate and 1972 Olympian whose jersey number was retired, Manning did not get off the bench in the 1971 ACC tournament.

He played sparingly throughout his first varsity season, appearing in 18 games. He took 18 shots and scored a dozen points to accompany 13 rebounds.

Fond of sarcasm and of laying traps for the credulous listener, he told an interviewer he did not give much thought to being the program's first Black player. "I look at it like I'm the first guy from Dillon to play on the USC team," Manning said. In fact, Manning knew he was being watched, his actions measured, his fate translated into greater meaning even as he competed for playing time and pursued his degree in political science. "I was keenly aware of everything," he will admit. "I'm not dumb. You can't let it affect getting up in the morning and going to do what you have to do." He and his white roommate discussed racial issues. "Casey was very, very political and mature for his age," Dennis Powell said.

During Manning's junior year, South Carolina's first as an independent, he said "Frank went out of his way to put 'ACC Champions' on our warm-ups to piss everybody off. He enjoyed that." The 1971–72 season differed little from 1970–71 as far as Manning was concerned. McGuire praised his maturity, but Manning, slowed by a hernia operation prior to the season, again played sparingly. He appeared in 15 of the team's 29 games, took 25 shots, and scored 25 points.

Manning's lack of on-court opportunity engendered considerable grumbling in Columbia's Black community. "He handled that well," White said. "He never came out and said, 'Oh, I ought to be playing.' His disposition was one which I think transcended into the community; he understood and appreciated that he was part of the team."

Manning did start now and again his senior year; otherwise he was a valued substitute off the bench as he averaged 3.9 points, more than triple his output the previous two seasons. His first career start came in a victory over Utah in December 1972 in which he scored 16 points. He had 13 points in his final game, an NCAA consolation contest against Southwestern Louisiana.

Further salving wounded feelings, Manning became a favorite of the Carolina Coliseum crowd. The fondness went beyond the fact that he was a local product. White says Manning was the "guy who, when he gets in the game, becomes the darling of the crowd because he very seldom gets in. And they always want him to shoot, and, boy, if he ever makes one, it's really something. So Casey became a special kind of person not just because he was Black."

Manning's journey through the conference was not without racial incident, although his low profile as a player minimized the attention he drew. The most egregious situation arose at Clemson late in his junior year. By then the Tigers had a new coach, disciplinarian Taylor "Tates" Locke, and two Black players, neither of whom was Craig Mobley.

Bobby Roberts, the coach who recruited Mobley, was forced out at the conclusion of the 1969–70 season. Roberts had enjoyed initial success, including triumphs during an eight-day span in 1967 over all four ACC schools from North Carolina, earning him honors from the South Carolina General Assembly. But Roberts followed with 58 losses from 1968 to 1970, even as McGuire built the archrival Gamecocks into a national power. Clemson's move in November 1968 into Littlejohn Coliseum, a $3.6 million facility that seated 10,000 spectators, only intensified the pressure.

Roberts was replaced by Locke, at age 33 a self-described "realist and a pessimist." Clemson was, and remains, the toughest job in the basketball-oriented ACC. "Nobody really cared about basketball down here until Frank McGuire came down and embarrassed everybody," Frank Howard told Locke, who was highly recommended by Kentucky's Adolph Rupp.

Locke consulted Bucky Waters when first offered the Clemson job. The Duke coach advised Locke, then at Miami of Ohio, "If you cheat and don't get caught, you'll do well. If you cheat and get caught, you'll get fired. If you don't cheat, you'll get fired." Locke lasted five seasons. His final two years the Tigers posted winning records and brought in talents such as center Wayne "Tree" Rollins and guard Skip Wise. Locke resigned in 1975 after his program was accused of 41 NCAA recruiting violations. "I didn't cheat because the Joneses did or because it made me a big man," Locke admitted. "I did it because I was tired of losing."

Locke had arrived making promises of discipline and improvement. Eventually. "I think Clemson is destined to stay on the bottom of the league for another year," he declared. Lest anyone entertain unrealistic expectations, Locke said prior to the 1970–71 season, "We have nothing to look forward to this year except our opener."

The new coach proceeded to rid the program of three returning players, including several of Mobley's best friends on the squad. Among the survivors was Mobley, who still bears scars around both eyes from collisions during practice and games under hard-nosed freshman coach Art Musselman. Mobley was popular with fans but hardly the most promising sophomore on the team. "I can bet you the student body got me in most of the games that I played my freshman year," said Mobley, the fifth-best scorer on Musselman's weak squad. "As a matter of fact, I was more shocked than anybody else that the student body caused me to play."

The start of the 1970–71 academic year saw significant changes in Clemson athletics beyond basketball. Cecil "Hootie" Ingram replaced Howard as head football coach. On the heels of the controversy over Confederate symbols, Ingram "wanted to change the image, try something new," said Bill McLellan, a longtime Clemson athletics administrator. The school hired an advertising firm to devise a new emblem, and the Tiger paw became the accepted symbol of Clemson athletic teams, appearing on uniforms, flags, and other gear.

Come basketball season, Mobley was barely mentioned in forecasts for an inexperienced 1971 Tiger unit in desperate need of help. "Take four of the top five players away from the weakest basketball team in the Atlantic Coast Conference, and what do you have left?" asked Harry Lloyd in the *Charlotte Observer*. "An impossible situation for new Clemson coach Tates Locke, that's what." Clemson finished 9–17, last in the ACC. "There's certainly no winning tradition at this school," Locke said.

Mobley sat despite the coach's continued complaints of a dearth of depth. He appeared in fewer than half of Clemson's games, his playing time dwindling as the season progressed. A single member of the roster saw less action. "It works on your psyche and ego a lot, unless you don't really worry about having a psyche and an ego," Mobley said. He did manage one notable, if dubious, statistical achievement, missing all 13 of his field goal attempts in 1970–71. Mobley, as most players who ride the bench, felt he should have played more. "Tates said a few times, 'You could have played in this game,'" Mobley recalled. "That's like after the game was over with. That's great solace. The answer was that I just took it and moved on."

Mobley shelved his basketball aspirations in much the manner he forswore his boyhood dreams of flying a jet and becoming an astronaut, thwarted in the Air Force by a hereditary trait for sickle-cell anemia. "Pride had something to do with it, that much I can tell you," he said of his departure from the basketball program. "Nobody said, 'Don't play.' That I don't remember hearing. But choice-wise, some choices are made for you whether you say it or not." Later, Mobley kept his distance from his alma mater but remained deeply involved in sports. He served as chair and as a board member for the Watts Summer Games in Los Angeles, an athletic festival that promotes understanding among teams and athletes from throughout California.

Mobley's junior year, his primary extracurricular activities were serving as a disc jockey on the campus radio station and reaching out to the local Black community. He was thus not on the Clemson bench when the Gamecocks came to Littlejohn and were accorded a reception so mean that McGuire ended the series for five seasons.

Members of the crowd taunted McGuire about his son, Frank Jr., who had cerebral palsy. Moreover, someone tied a cord to the leg of the coach's chair and yanked it when he attempted to sit down. Even with several policemen stationed behind the South Carolina bench, verbal abuse rained down on Manning, who recalled that the situation got "real bad." McGuire said, "I don't mind them calling me names so much, but why did they have to say what they did about Casey?"

McGuire soon drew the bulk of the hecklers' attention, probably by choice. "He wasn't a shy guy," said Walsh, his former assistant. Derision focused on McGuire's Catholic heritage, a favorite topic around the league, according to Walsh. Yet this was different. "It's the worst I've ever heard in all my years of coaching, including the pros," McGuire said of that night in February 1972. "They even cursed the pope. Why? Don't ask me. I don't even know the pope's name."

By the time the series between the archrivals resumed in 1978, Manning had graduated from the University of South Carolina Law School. He has spent most of his adult life in Columbia, and in 1994 the basketball reserve took his seat on a more magisterial bench in the capital city. He maintained his connection with the basketball program, lending his deep, rich voice to radio broadcasts of Gamecock basketball as a color analyst. The program has yet to regain the heights of the early 1970s, when McGuire plied New York for talent and Manning broke the color barrier. "Somebody's got to bridge the gap," Manning said, looking back on his role as a pioneer. "You can't help the times you're born in; you've just got to live them out."

CHAPTER 12
ALL IN THE FAMILY

Collis Temple Jr., Louisiana State University, 1970–74

That sky was bluest when I could beat my mates at examination-time, or beat them at a foot-race, or even beat their stringy heads. Alas, with the years all this fine contempt began to fade; for the worlds I longed for, and all their dazzling opportunities, were theirs, not mine. . . . Why did God make me an outcast and a stranger in mine own house?

W. E. B. Du Bois, *The Souls of Black Folk*

A visit by the governor to a prospect's home was not uncommon when Louisiana State University sought a top in-state athlete. The maneuver was meant to impress, and the Temples likely were pleased when John McKeithen came to Kentwood in 1970. Yet the recruitment of Collis Temple Jr. as LSU's first Black basketball player doubtless brought his parents more pleasure than most. Seeing their son courted by the very institution that had arbitrarily rejected his father more than a decade earlier, with the state's chief executive making a pilgrimage to plead the case, provided a satisfying measure of vindication.

The earlier rejection lingered with the proud Temples, remaining a benchmark event in family history. Later, LSU could not seem to get enough of the Temple clan, signing three descendants to basketball grants-in-aid.

Collis Benton Temple had worked hard to raise six children and to serve his community. He and wife Shirley were educators and the offspring of educators. Both had grown up in Louisiana, paying their taxes and their dues. When Temple, a fortyish graduate of Southern University, sought to pursue a master's degree in supervision and education administration, he decided to stay near his home and work. So he applied to the Louisiana State University and Agricultural and Mechanical College, about an hour's drive down the road in Baton Rouge. Unfortunately, the high school principal possessed a characteristic that automatically disqualified him from consideration for admission, according to LSU. He was Black.

That the American Dream came with strings attached was no surprise to Temple. You could not be an adult African American in the mid-20th century, let alone in a small town in rural Louisiana, and not know limitations defined by edict and ordinance, by custom and habit, rules written and rules unspoken, rules enforced by duly sworn officers of the law and rules imposed by white people as a matter of racial privilege.

Limits for Black citizens were as integral to the state's landscape as Spanish moss, bayous, alligators, and nutrias, as the *Shreveport Times* succinctly reminded readers. "We venture to say that full ninety per cent of all the race troubles in the South are the result of the Negro forgetting his place," the newspaper declared in 1919, a year after World War I concluded. "If the black man will stay where he belongs, act like a Negro should act, work like a Negro should work, talk like a Negro should talk, and study like a Negro should study, there will be very few riots, fights, or clashes."

The circumscribed place to which the newspaper referred was not defined with the consent of the Temples or their forebears. By the time C. B. Temple was born in 1911, his democratic right to vote had been stripped by constitutional fiat. Restrictions embedded within the state constitution of 1898 reduced the number of African-American voters in Louisiana from more than 130,000 to a mere 1,342 by 1904, the most thorough racial cleansing of voter rolls achieved in the South. The number bottomed out at 598 statewide in 1922, stood at a still-paltry 866 on the eve of World War II, and would not increase significantly until the war ended.

Fear and terror were the inevitable companions of voicelessness.

Barely a decade prior to C. B. Temple's birth, four African-American men were lynched in his home parish after being accused of robbery; the stated purpose of this punishment was to "teach the worthless Blacks in town a lesson," as reported in a New Orleans newspaper. And Tangipahoa was a parish (the Louisiana equivalent of a county) considered "relatively liberal" by the state's standards, according to historian Adam Fairclough.

Brenda Temple Tull, the youngest of the Temples' five daughters, said her father always carried a pistol when he drove. "I grew up thinking that the glove compartment of the car was the place for 'the father's handgun,'" she said. Her father once explained that, while he was a boarding student at the Tangipahoa Parish Training School for Colored Children, he witnessed whites storming on campus, dragging a fellow student from his dorm room and then beating and lynching him. "I think C. B. had no intentions of being jumped by white folks, or anybody, without a hard fight," Tull said.

The family patriarch grew up in Amite and Greenburg, east of the bend in the L-shaped state, then moved to nearby Kentwood to pursue professional opportunities after his third daughter was born. "There are no perfect places, but I was always sensitive that there were these external entities, these external forces that you had to be very careful of," Tull said. "Kentwood was just a sleepy little town, and people had to be careful and cautious."

Black people, that is. "The nickname of the parish when I grew up was 'Bloody Tangipahoa Parish,'" recalled Temple Jr., "because people used to get beaten and lynched and everything else. That didn't go on a lot in the 1960s, but it was pretty bad. A pretty tough place." The youngest child and only boy, Collis Jr. had been born just across the state line in Magnolia, Mississippi. The border between the Deep South states was close to Kentwood and no barrier to shared attitudes and dangers. Some of the South's most rabid and tightly intertwined Klan chapters operated in the area.

"The tales of what could happen to Black men, women, and children were not the kind that made colored children squeal to fatigued parents, 'More, more! Tell us more,'" Jordana Y. Shakoor, a Mississippian, stated in her memoir, *Civil Rights Childhood*. "These stories were relayed to Black children not for bedtime pleasure but as a way of cautioning them to be careful, to stay in their places and never sass a white man or woman. . . . When colored children like my father heard the horrible but factual tales, they understood what their mothers, fathers, aunts, uncles, grandmothers, and grandfathers actually were telling them was that 'if they come to get you, we cannot help you. We cannot safeguard you, child, if the white men in sheets come to get you, because we can't even protect ourselves.'"

Determined to protect their children, Shirley and C. B. Temple wrapped them in a cocoon of school, church, and home and taught them to expect success despite whatever life threw at them. "My dad believed that everything happened for a reason and that because we had family support and inner reserves, and we had right on our side, we could go beyond," said Sandra Hall, another daughter.

The Temples steered their children away from danger and insult. They forbade ventures into the white part of town without parental accompaniment and instructed their children "to conduct ourselves with confidence and great caution around white folk," Tull said, as if describing a walk among unfamiliar dogs that might attack at the scent of fear.

"We spent a lot of time together as a family because we were not allowed to do things that exposed us to segregation," Hall said. "My parents were very strict about that." The Temple children were neither treated by the local doctor or dentist, nor allowed to visit the side door of the local ice cream stand or to sit in the Kentwood movie theater's segregated balcony, known as the "buzzard's roost." The family sought medical treatment in Baton Rouge or New Orleans so care could come at the hands of a Black professional in an office entered through the front door. They viewed movies at a drive-in theater 30 miles from home. And they purchased ice cream and milk shakes in Baton Rouge—until going into the business themselves, building an ice cream stand adjacent to their house across the street from all-Black Dillon High School, where C. B. Temple was principal. (Dillon High also served as an entertainment venue, hosting performers from Fats Domino to the Clara Ward Singers to a renowned theater group from Louisiana's Grambling State University.)

"My mom and dad basically kept me from being exposed to heavy, heavy racism at an early age so I wouldn't become indoctrinated by having to act and feel a certain way and be inhibited about dealing with people," Temple Jr. said. "Most of my friends had this thing about being afraid to communicate with [white] people and look them in the eye when talking to them."

The Temples took their children on summer trips throughout the country, yet so thoroughly insulated them at home that Brenda, four years older than her brother, recalled little contact with white people. "It's an amazing perspective that you have as a little kid," she said before proceeding to turn an enduring prejudice on its head. "One of the things I can remember is wondering how white people could tell the difference between each other, because I felt they all looked so much alike. I can remember being amazed and wondering how they did this with each other. And that shows how much difference there was between the communities."

Caution did not equate to being cowed, however. Because an annual, government-supported amusement fair in Amite restricted Black attendance to the event's final day, C. B. Temple helped to start the competing Tri-Parish Fair, which catered to African Americans from a larger area. When Freedom Riders came through the South in the early 1960s, he considered offering them shelter if they reached Louisiana. "Daddy seemed sometimes to enjoy the mental jousting with white folks as he figured out ways to outwit them, ways to negotiate this racist system, ways to think outside the box and sometimes accomplish what Black folk needed," Tull said.

Certainly the Temple children were not shy to assert themselves once they left Kentwood. Sandra and especially Brenda became active protestors in college. "A person was an activist if you lobbied to get someone other than the Beach Boys to come to campus," Tull said sarcastically of LSU.

Her brother stood up to a professor and a teammate at LSU who subjected him to their prejudices. The 6-foot-8 forward also was noted for his physical play and occasional bellicosity on the court. "Collis was a tough guy to play against," said Tim Bassett, the Georgia big man. "He would bang you." Temple was a proficient shot blocker before that statistic was recorded, and he led LSU in rebounding his junior and senior seasons.

Temple, whom coaches sometimes found too excitable for his own good, was involved in fights every year of his college career, often in response to racial slurs. He recalled, "I got into it at Tulane, got into it at LSU, got into it at Houston. A guy from Auburn. Got into it my freshman year at Tennessee." He was reprimanded but not suspended by the SEC after coming off the bench to engage in a brawl with Vanderbilt players in January 1974. "The fact that Temple is a senior, has compiled a very good academic record and enjoys an excellent personal reputation with his teammates, coaches and other officials at his school mitigated strongly in his behalf," stated league commissioner Boyd McWhorter in announcing the mild punishment.

Temple's on-court persona was consistent with another edict from his father: Outwork everybody and do the right thing. Besides running a high school and an ice cream stand, C. B. Temple raised cattle and hogs and bought and sold property, books, and timber. He made a point of inculcating similar skills and interests in his son. "I was really a project for my dad," said Temple Jr. "I tell people that every day of my life as a kid, the first person that I saw every morning was my dad. Seven days a week. Before five o'clock." His sisters spoke without rancor of the attentions lavished on their brother, of their father's "indoctrination" of his son from an early age.

The training took. Temple Jr. was and remained an avid entrepreneur. A man in constant motion, he sped through life, driving 15 or 20 miles per hour over any speed limit. As a youth he raised, showed, and sold livestock. By the time he went to LSU, he had accumulated enough money to purchase a rental house within sight of campus. The school's track coach was the renter, never dreaming the identity of the landlord. At one time Temple Jr. and two of his sisters, including Hall, employed several hundred people at a school in Baton Rouge and at a string of more than two dozen group homes there and in other towns—for foster children, youthful offenders, the mentally retarded, the mentally ill, seniors, [and] recovering alcoholics and drug addicts. "If you don't want to work, don't get around Collis Temple," said an employee during a feverish 2001 conversion of an old motel into an assisted-living facility.

The younger Temple believed he could have been elected to public office in Baton Rouge, where he settled after his playing days and remains recognizable and well liked. That, too, would have fulfilled a goal that eluded his father, who ran unsuccessfully for the state legislature. Instead, Temple Jr. serves his community by working to assist its least powerful residents; he also coached AAU basketball and brought home young men who needed a father figure and a loving hand. One of his AAU protégés, Brandon Bass, was the 2005 SEC Player of the Year and 2004 SEC Rookie of the Year for LSU. "He just takes in strays like they're little animals," Hall said of her brother. "My dad was like that."

As with many pioneering Black players, Temple Jr. is aware others thought he should have been more militant, bitter, angry. "Let me tell you about being visible and being militant," he said in his characteristically dry manner. "You know what being militant is? Being militant is taking care of your ass. That's being militant. Being militant is taking a boy and teaching him to become a man and a responsible person. That's as militant as you need to be, because all this other stuff is bullshit. You're taking people and making a difference and making something happen. . . . If you can't do something worthwhile yourself, and you can't empower other people to do something for themselves, then it really doesn't matter. It doesn't matter who calls you nigger, who hates you, who loves you. Don't none of it matter. If you can't make a difference, it doesn't matter."

Temple Jr.'s association with LSU proved helpful in his business life. That was why his father, similarly cognizant of the power of education and of networking opportunities, attempted to pursue a postgraduate degree at the university. "Daddy applied like everybody else to get his master's because he wanted to go to school in Louisiana," Hall said. "He loved Louisiana."

But the timing was not propitious, the affection not requited.

Once the NAACP decided to use court challenges to fight for integration rather than for equalization of funding, it took decades to formally dismantle segregated education. Separate but equal, first affirmed by the U.S.

Supreme Court in 1896 in the Louisiana case *Plessy v. Ferguson*, was never more than legalistic camouflage for discrimination, as evidenced by spending on education during the late 1940s in the 17 states that required segregated schools. Combined, they spent $86 million on higher education for white students, compared to $5 million for black students. This inherent inequality in opportunity spurred the Supreme Court to rule in favor of Black plaintiffs seeking to enter previously all-white graduate schools in Texas and Oklahoma. A court case similarly led LSU to become the first public university in the Deep South to integrate when it admitted Roy S. Wilson to its law school in 1950.

But lowering the wall of exclusion, no matter how minimally, did not sit well with General Troy H. Middleton, a committed segregationist who became president of LSU after Wilson's admittance. Under Middleton's leadership the tone set during the 1950s, a decade bisected by the *Brown* verdict, was one of "fighting integration every step of the way in the courts and doing little to make LSU's few Black students feel welcome," according to historian Fairclough. The first Black undergraduate entered LSU in 1953 under compulsion of law, but Alexander Pierre Tureaud Jr. lasted a single, unhappy semester before transferring.

Meanwhile, the state legislature busily wove together the usual skein of laws to defend and strengthen segregation. A creative departure was a 1956 act that barred interracial athletic competition or integrated seating at public sports and other events within Louisiana. The U.S. Supreme Court declared Legislative Act 579 unconstitutional three years later. The atmosphere at LSU and in the state capital remained so hostile to lowering racial barriers that Waldo F. McNeir, a professor of English, was forced to resign in 1960 after writing that "segregation is wrong" and chastising state politicians for blocking integration, a move he called "a disgrace and a national scandal."

Paying for African-American students to go to northern schools was a routine alternative for states intent on maintaining segregation but unable or unwilling to provide substantially equivalent educational facilities. Harvey Gantt attended Iowa State University at South Carolina's expense under such a program prior to returning home to become the first Black undergraduate at Clemson. Florida began an Out-of-State Scholarship Aid to Negroes program in 1953 that still had a $40,000 budget as late as the 1964–65 school year. Similarly, LSU rejected C. B. Temple during the mid-1950s but willingly paid his tuition at Michigan State University. Temple reluctantly pursued his education in exile, snatching chunks of time until finally compelled to move his wife and all but the youngest children to East Lansing while finishing his degree requirements.

Brenda, age eight, and Collis Jr. resided with their paternal grandparents that summer. "All he wanted to do was eat," she said of her brother. She, on the other hand, remembered "longing" for the rest of her family and feeling hurt and "abandoned" by her parents. "I was devastated to wake up at Grandma Ida B's in Amite and realize that my folks and the four older kids had left Collis and me behind," she said. "This is a small, little thing, but it is an example of what this whole, entire system did to human beings and their lives."

C. B. Temple earned his master's degree from Michigan State in 1956 and lived long enough to see his son receive two degrees from LSU. The elder Temple died in 1996, but his wife witnessed one of their grandsons, Collis Temple III, play basketball for LSU and earn his undergraduate and graduate degrees there, too. "I realized that there was a legacy to be carried on," Collis III, twice Academic All-SEC, said of his decision to become a Tiger rather than establish himself at another school. Shortly before their grandmother died, Garrett Temple, brother of Collis III, became a Tiger, too. He was a freshman in 2004–05 and starred defensively in LSU's Final Four run of 2006.

The story of C. B. Temple's admissions ordeal became a family legend, the same words echoing from telling to retelling. "He tried to come here; they wouldn't let him come here," said Collis Temple III. "He had to go to Michigan State for grad school. Then, in an ironic twist, the governor of the state of Louisiana came to my father's house—it wasn't illegal at that time—and asked my grandfather to let my father come to LSU. And my grandfather was wholeheartedly behind that, and the rest is history."

C. B. Temple wanted his son to attend LSU for much the same reasons he had attempted to enroll there. Like Kentucky's Tom Payne, Temple Jr. did his father's bidding. "I thought that whatever my dad told me was the right thing," Temple said. "And so, if he said this is what I should do, then I felt that's just how it was." Quality of education and closeness to home were considerations as well.

"They were unbelievably gallant to do what they did," Dale Brown, Temple's second coach at LSU, said of the player's parents. "If you're talking about integrating against racists sitting in the background, you couldn't have picked a finer, stronger family than them."

By the time Temple committed to Louisiana State, the majority of other schools in the SEC had integrated their basketball programs. "In signing Temple," a newspaper said, "the LSU athletic department finally admitted what they and everybody else connected with sports have known for a long time now, that you don't win consistently in big time college basketball any more without the good Black athlete."

Temple insisted pleasing his father was a far more prominent consideration than the fact that he was undertaking a role as a racial pioneer at LSU. Only later did his pioneering status come to the fore.

Tull did think a great deal about the decision's racial component, and she objected strenuously to her brother's choice. "I really was very, very, very, very worried about his going," she said. "He was raised to think that he was very important—which is great; that's the way everybody ought to raise their kid—that he was very valuable and valued. And then to send him someplace where he was going to be greeted not only like just another number, but greeted and treated like a nigger in many instances, I didn't know if he could handle it. It wasn't easy for me. I thought I was important, and I was only a girl and I wasn't an athlete."

LSU accepted its first group of African-American undergraduates a decade after its abortive, grudging 1953 experience with Tureaud Jr. The welcome mat was not unfurled the second time, either. Within a year campus barbers walked off the job when told they had to cut the hair of African Americans. Tull enrolled in 1966. "It was a challenging experience," she said of her four years at Louisiana's premier public university. "Those crackers loved LSU—LS and U, they called it."

The school was founded as the Seminary of Learning of the State of Louisiana in 1860, on the eve of the Civil War. In keeping with the military component of an LSU education, which continued until 1968, the first institution president was William Tecumseh Sherman, a West Point graduate and a retired colonel in the U.S. Army. Among those advancing the Ohioan's selection were Louisiana friends Braxton Bragg, Richard Taylor, and Pierre Beauregard, future Confederate generals. Sherman reluctantly resigned his presidency at the war's outbreak; as a Union general he became despised in the South for his scorched-earth march from Georgia to North Carolina in the last months of the war. (One of the more bizarre advertising slogans ever conceived was briefly floated in 1970 in Columbia, South Carolina. Most of that city burned to the ground when Sherman's troops came through in 1865, yet the chamber of commerce asked cheerily:

"General Sherman visited here . . . why don't you?") Civil War notwith-standing, Sherman retained close, fond ties with LSU throughout his life.

During the 1930s Louisiana State, otherwise known as the "Ole War Skule," gained patronage and notoriety as the pet of Huey Long, the most powerful, charismatic, and controversial figure ever produced in a state that has seen more than its share of colorful and frequently corrupt politicians. "Huey used to buy the legislature like a sack of potatoes," said his brother Earl, who himself served as governor for one partial and two full terms (1939–40, 1948–52, and 1956–60). "Hell, I never bought one in my life. I just rented them. It's cheaper that way."

Huey Long was so distinctive a character that he became the subject of a pair of Pulitzer Prize–winning books by LSU professors, a biography by T. Harry Williams, and a novel, *All the King's Men,* by Robert Penn Warren. Long "not only revolutionized Louisiana, but also became America's fore-most radical politician," contended historian Mark Carleton. "At home, Long's power and influence derived from his performance—paving roads, providing free textbooks to schoolchildren, upgrading public education and state hospitals, and generally bettering the lives of Louisiana's humbler cit-izens. Nationally, Long attracted a large following by promoting a scheme called 'Share Our Wealth,' which would have taxed the super-rich to pro-vide a free college education for all qualified students, guaranteed family incomes, and similar controversial benefits." Long also bullied, bought, berated, and bedazzled to get his way.

Among the most enduring monuments to Long's tenure as governor (1928–32) is the phallic 34-story capitol building, tallest in the country, in which he was assassinated in September 1935. Long lingered, mortally wounded, for two days. He was buried within sight of the capitol amid wide-spread but not universal lamentation. In *River Capital,* a history of Baton Rouge, Carleton revealed that Long was so unpopular within the corporate-oriented city, a center for the nation's powerful and wealthy petroleum industry, that churches "filled with people praying that he would die."

In his heyday Long viewed LSU, upon which he lavished support and attention, "as his personal property," said Thomas Cutrer in *Parnassus on the Mississippi.* Long's handpicked university president oversaw a great campus building boom before going to prison for embezzling university funds. The Huey P. Long Field House, constructed in 1932, contained the basketball arena, administrative offices, and what was at the time the world's largest outdoor pool. The state's premier politician was involved in hiring a new head football coach and a new band director, lured from a New Orleans hotel. He pressured a railroad to arrange low train fares for students to attend a road football game. He and the band director composed songs such as "Darling of LSU" and "Touchdown for LSU" (the latter still played at home football games). He sent in plays to the Tigers' bench and during one game conferred with officials on the field, reputedly instructing them not to call penalties on LSU near the goal line.

Late in 1934, Long, then a U.S. senator, rushed back from Washington, D.C., to lead a football pep rally and capriciously appointed an underage Tiger halfback from Mississippi to the Louisiana state senate. "It was the Roman emperor touch, the next thing to Caligula's appointing his horse a consul," Cutrer observed. When Long learned the student newspaper had run a letter denouncing his action, he ordered state police to seize and destroy all 4,000 copies of the *Reveille*. "That's my university and I'll fire any student that dares to say a word against Huey Long," the senator declared. The censorship brought protests, student expulsions, and embarrassment for the LSU journalism school. The incident underscored President Franklin Roosevelt's view that the heavy-handed Long was one of the two most dangerous men in America (along with General Douglas MacArthur). Photos of the "Kingfish" marching at the head of "his" LSU cadets raised chilling parallels in some minds with German dictator Adolph Hitler and his Brown Shirts.

Long's love of Fighting Tigers football was anything but controversial. Demand for seats at Tiger Stadium, built in 1924, caused capacity to expand over the years to 102,321, making it the fifth-largest on-campus football facility in the country in 2022. *Sport* magazine pronounced the stadium—which shares the nickname "Death Valley" with Clemson Memorial Stadium— "the most feared road playing site in America." The LSU football program boasts three unofficial national championships (a fourth playoff-era title in 2019); 12 SEC titles; 54 bowl appearances; and Heisman Trophy winners in halfback Billy Cannon in 1959 and quarterback Joe Burrow in 2019.

"Especially for the white folks in Baton Rouge, the LSU football game on Saturday night was indeed the center of culture, of social cohesion," said Ferrell Guillory, a former journalist who grew up in the state capital. "It is hard to put into words the intensity of feeling around town for an LSU home game." As for African Americans, they had their own section in the stands, to which Black spectators still gravitate. Temple says Black students in his day called it "Brothers' Roost," an obvious takeoff on less complimentary nicknames for segregated sections at other venues.

Basketball remained deep in football's shadow until Temple's playing career was over. "LSU is now, always has been, and always will be a football school," he said. "It was unbelievable then, one-sided, when Dale came." That was in March 1972, after Temple's sophomore season.

Bruce Hunter's book *Don't Count Me Out* chronicled Brown's tenure and an athletic hierarchy in which basketball had all the status of an African American in a segregated society. "Basketball players lived in the same dorm and ate in the same cafeteria with football players, but it was an accepted rule that they stepped aside and let football players go to the front of the meal line," Hunter said. Louisiana State was the ambitious Brown's first head coaching job, yet friends urged him not to take it. "'This is about the worst job you could get,'" he was told.

Football's stranglehold on the affections of LSU fans was broken briefly during Brenda Tull's undergraduate days, which coincided with the playing career of "Pistol Pete" Maravich, a three-time All-American (1968–1970), the 1970 national Player of the Year, and the greatest showman in SEC or most any league's history. Until his arrival the bright spot in Louisiana State basketball traced to 1953, when a squad led by All-America Bob Pettit reached the NCAA Final Four.

Maravich remains the top career scorer (3,667 points) and single-season scorer (1,381 points in 1970) in major-college competition. He notched three of the top nine single-game scoring efforts in Division I basketball history. His scoring averages from his varsity seasons are unparalleled: 44.5 in 1969–70, 44.2 in 1968–69, and 43.8 in 1967–68. Pat Stephens, detailed to scout opponents during his tenure as an assistant coach at Georgia, was mesmerized by Maravich. Stephens managed to see him play 30 to 40 times by planning his scouting trips so he could see LSU against whomever the Bulldogs would face. Arenas routinely sold out when the Tigers came to town.

Maravich, a slender, floppy-haired 6-foot-5 guard, arrived at Baton Rouge from Raleigh, North Carolina, as part of a package deal with his father. Press Maravich had coached at Clemson before replacing a terminally ill Everett Case at NC State early in the 1965 season. He directed the Wolfpack to a surprise ACC title, won conference Coach of the Year honors, and then headed south when his son did not qualify academically for ACC competition.

Pistol Pete wound up playing his entire LSU career in the John M. Parker Agricultural Center. Known as the "Cow Palace," the building seated 12,000 but was better suited to rodeos and animal shows than to basketball. Young Maravich drew full houses anyway. Captivated fans filled the building just to see his freshman team, leaving before the 3–23 varsity took the portable, elevated court. "It's a well-known fact that the Maravich era, between Press and Pete, revitalized basketball not only in Louisiana but in the Deep South," asserted former LSU athletics director Carl Maddox. "Both of them made an indelible impression on basketball in the South."

Indelible, perhaps, but only surface deep. The Tigers essentially broke even in wins and losses during Pete Maravich's first two varsity seasons. They did reach the NIT Final Four in 1970, his senior year. The 1969–70 squad won 22 games, most at the school since 1954, when LSU was the SEC champion. But "Poppa Press," as some called him, did not do enough to capitalize on the basketball program's sudden popularity, and he was fired two years after his son's departure. Press Maravich's overall LSU record was 76–86. "After Pete left, it was like the program crashed and burned," Temple said.

The state was awash with talented African-American players during that period. Press Maravich was quoted in 1968 saying he hoped to sign "a Black athlete who would help the team and who was also a good student," according to *Fighting Tigers Basketball* by Bruce Hunter and Joe Planas. Those efforts took several years to bear fruit. "We just kept trying," said Greg Bernbrock, who served as a Maravich assistant.

"If the right guy with the right mindset had come to LSU and taken the people from 1960 to 1970, man!" Temple mused. "There were a lot of great players that came out of Louisiana that should have gone, could have gone, to LSU, that were far better players than I was. I could rattle off three or four guys: Elvin Hayes would have been a hell of a player at LSU. Willis Reed would have been a hell of a player at LSU. And Bill Russell would have been a hell of a player at LSU. Don Chaney would have been a hell of a player at LSU. I can go on about other guys. Bob Love would have been a hell of a player at LSU. These guys didn't even consider going to LSU. It wasn't in the deal. Shit, LSU could have been national champions 10 times over."

Hayes and Chaney went to the University of Houston. Reed attended Grambling State. Love went to Southern University. Russell, who played college ball before Temple Jr. entered elementary school, moved to California and attended the University of San Francisco, leading the Dons to NCAA titles in 1955 and 1956. After an unparalled playing and coaching career, the NBA retired Russell's No. 6 jersey leaguewide upon his death in 2022.

Halfway through Press Maravich's tenure, he did successfully recruit Temple, an all-state big man. "He had so much athletic ability," Bernbrock said. "That's what you really look for in 17- or 18-year-old kids. He had the speed and the quickness." Temple also was an outstanding student from a solid family; he made first team Academic All-SEC as a junior in 1972–73. "Coach Maravich was very big on that, graduating 100 percent of his players," Bernbrock said.

Unlike other Black prospects the coaching staff approached, Temple appeared to feel comfortable with breaking the school's color barrier. Tull did all she could to change that, short of throwing herself upon the railroad tracks of her brother's aspirations. She cried when she failed.

"Of course you don't go in the bathroom in the morning and brush your teeth and say, 'Oh, God, I'm Black! What's going to happen to me today?'" she said. "But just all of the responsibilities, the stress, the pressure—I was just very, very concerned that it could break Collis because it broke the best of people." Tull angrily told anyone who would listen—coaches, administrators, relatives—that LSU was not a welcoming place for African Americans. "She let the chancellor know that, she let the dean of students know that, she let them all know it," her brother recalled. "She sure did."

Tull seethed when the school band played "Dixie" in celebratory moments; when a professor hailed for his Chaucer scholarship shared "racist cracker rantings" in her class, including his hatred for civil rights demonstrators; and when the school, like many others in the region, sanctioned an annual tribute to the past that included whites dressing up as Confederate soldiers and Southern belles. "I'm still speechless," Tull said decades later. "It's just incredible. People get upset now about the Confederate flag on somebody's hat. This was a whole production; it was a serious production. I thought, 'Let me get my Black behind away from here.' It's like a German organization having a replay of the Holocaust or something."

Football players were particularly unfriendly, Tull said. "I had seen instances when LSU's football team members purposely injured Black students who had gone out for the team. Many Black students, my friends and associates who traversed the campus, avoided passing dorms where athletes lived because the athletes were such animals that they would ambush Black students when we passed their dorm—verbally, and throwing things at Black students from their dorm windows."

But, try as she might, Tull knew she was fighting a losing battle the day she and the men of her family visited vast Tiger Stadium. "Daddy seemed to be impressed with the magnitude of it all—LSU and Collis. We were entering the hallowed stadium rotunda of the very school that had rejected Daddy as a graduate student," she said. "I felt inadequate to convince Daddy that, as attractive as this courtship was, these were dangerous waters."

In retrospect, Tull said her brother was the right man to navigate those waters, while Temple admitted he sailed into a worse situation than he realized at the time. "LSU was not really up to the task," he said. "They didn't like basketball, and they weren't particularly crazy about recruiting Black players."

Going to Louisiana State, let alone playing basketball, was far from Temple's mind as a youngster. He started for the football varsity as an eighth grader and dreamed of playing quarterback at Southern, which called itself the largest Black university in the country. His father had played football for the Jaguars, and both loved the sport.

Temple was not very good at basketball, but his mother indirectly helped to change that. Shirley Temple was a guidance counselor, and at the end of her son's ninth grade year, she insisted that he apply for admission to a half-dozen college summer enrichment programs. He was accepted into the University of Kansas science camp, where he took chemistry and human physiology courses for 10 weeks. Temple's classes ended by late morning, leaving him time to visit the gym to play basketball every day. There he ran into a pair of outstanding Kansas players, Joseph "Jo Jo" White and Bud Stallworth. White, on the verge of an All-America season, soon had the youngster shagging balls, then passing to him for shots. "It went from there," Temple said. "I must have been 6–2, 6–3. Fairly clumsy, fairly awkward. I spent that summer playing Jo Jo White one-on-one basketball, and it just caught on."

Temple spent the next two summers as an invitee to Ted Owens's basketball camp at KU. "That's why I got recruited so heavily," he said. Interest was particularly ardent from schools in what was then the Big Eight Conference. "I was a pretty good defender," Temple said. "I played hard. I was a pretty skilled player coming out of high school, for my size. I could have played guard in college. Had I gone to the right basketball situation, I would have been able to come in and play a two-guard." Thirty years later, his 6-foot-7 son, Collis III, played guard at LSU. (Collis III wore jersey number 41, as did his father. Younger brother Garrett, a 6-foot-5 guard, chose number 14, inverting the numeral worn by family predecessors.)

Bolstering Temple's appeal, he was capable of outstanding performances; in one high school game he scored 35 points and had 36 rebounds. He was versatile and athletic, lettering in basketball, football, and track in high school. His senior year, he moved to integrated Kentwood High and played on a team that won the state high school football championship. (Dillon High, where his father was principal, became an elementary school.) After college Temple was in uncommon demand, drafted by three pro basketball leagues and by the Detroit Lions of the National Football League. He appeared in 24 games for the San Antonio Spurs of the ABA and for a time played pro ball in Europe.

Strangely, perhaps, Temple did not rely heavily on his own assessment of the coaching staff's qualities when he decided to attend Louisiana State. His memories of Press Maravich are pleasant but fall short of enthusiasm. "I liked coach Maravich all right," Temple said. "He was a nice enough guy. He made an attempt to be pleasant to me, and he had a genuine interest in my welfare as a person. I appreciated that. I recognized it, and I appreciated it. He was an all right coach. The game had probably gotten past him at that time, but he was a pretty good coach."

Maravich was quick to stand up for his player when Temple got a racist reception from the team trainer. The athletic training room was immaculate, and those entering the all-male bastion were expected to wear nothing but gym shorts or a jockstrap. Temple, an unknowing freshman, went for whirlpool treatment clad in a gift from his girlfriend: a homemade terrycloth robe with black and gold designs. The trainer "looked at me and said, 'Boy, what in the hell are you doing in my goddamn training room looking like a goddamn nigger in that getup you've got on?' I looked at him. I think I told him I was just coming to get some treatment on my ankle. And he said, 'You'd better get your Black ass out of my training room in that damn getup you've got on.'"

Temple went straight to his coach's office to report what had happened. Maravich and the trainer got into a shouting match, and Temple subsequently was treated with more civility.

That was not the end of the matter, however. Temple found himself in the trainer's class on anatomy the following semester. The first day, spying Temple seated with several football players, the trainer/professor dragged a desk to the front of the room and ordered the freshman to sit in it. Every Friday there was a pop quiz. When Temple aced the first one, he got a 6:30 a.m. phone call from the trainer, who neglected to identify himself before demanding, "Who did you cheat off of on my test?" As a motivational method, the trainer's bigotry and rancorous distrust proved effective. Temple worked hard to earn an A in the class "because he called me a nigger."

Twice Temple had confrontations with teammates. One called him a nigger to his face, immediately precipitating a fight. Another teammate, a point guard from Indiana, slipped a long note under his dorm room door that "told me to stay out of his way and what he was going to do, and that they lynch people where he's from," Temple said. "He was one of those guys that didn't like Jewish people, didn't like Black people. It's so unfortunate, too, because life is so short. It's such a waste of time."

The note was not signed, but Temple knew who wrote it. He braced the guard and warned him to stay out of his way. Brown's version of the incident goes further. Known to embellish a story now and again, the coach claimed he saw the note being slipped under Temple's door, intercepted it, and read it at home that night. The language was brutal, "something to do with, 'You know you're not wanted. Why don't you leave school?' I'm not positive if it said, 'Go back to Kentwood, nigger.'"

Brown recalled summoning the offending sophomore into his office the next day. He said he offered three choices: "to knock you right through this plate glass window behind my desk with one punch, kick you off the team, or sit down and talk to you and see if I can communicate with a human being." According to Brown the player soon apologized, requested forgiveness, and became friends with Temple.

Conflict with opponents was more common. Racist treatment was not the exclusive province of whites, either. One of the worst instances of abuse came in a 1971 loss against an all-Black squad at the University of Houston. "I didn't get called a nigger; I got called an Uncle Tom-ass nigger by some of my friends, some of the guys that I knew," Temple said. "They beat the hell out of us, beat us 100–66, and they taunted us and talked about us. It was a bad, bad experience. They were racist."

Most often, however, whites dished out the abuse. Sandra Hall and her husband saw Temple in action; she remembered feeling "crushed" by the treatment her brother received in games at Tennessee and at LSU. In his mind, Kentucky ranks with Mississippi State as the worst places he played.

Considering Hall's impression of Tennessee—and the fact that Temple was subject to a halftime death threat at Vanderbilt, necessitating a police guard even at the team hotel—that is saying something.

"I've never really shared this with anybody, because nobody's ever really asked me where were the toughest places for me to play," Temple said. "But I almost felt like I was violating those people when I played at Kentucky. I just really felt unwelcome. And I think it probably had to do with Tom Payne and his experience, their experience with Tom Payne. I could just feel this almost aristocratic, blueblood resentment."

The Wildcat players were not much better, in Temple's estimation. One ugly, if brief, incident with a UK big man stuck in his mind as characteristic of the group. "We were elbowing and shoving each other running down the court," he said of a game at Baton Rouge his sophomore year. "The ball was out front. We were both running behind the ball. The referees were going down the court, and we were coming behind everything. And it was after I had made a shot. [The Kentucky player] was running beside me, and he said, 'Nigger, you're not going to make no more points today.'" The response was vintage Temple. "I just slapped him. People in the stands saw it. The refs looked around, but they didn't see anything other than him stumbling."

Louisiana State won the televised contest, 88–71, ending a 16-game losing streak against Kentucky. By then the Tigers had moved into the new 14,164-seat LSU Assembly Center. The arena was designed to accommodate the enthusiastic crowds sparked by Pete Maravich's play, but construction was delayed until long after the star was gone. Two seasons later, with Press Maravich's job on the line, LSU was forced to play its first six games on the road while the $11.5 million facility was finished. (The building was renamed the Pete Maravich Assembly Center in 1988 upon the player's death at age 40. These days it is called the PMAC or simply the "Deaf Dome.")

Making conditions more difficult for the 1971–72 team, Al "Apple" Sanders, one of the top rebounders in school history, was recovering from a broken ankle and Bill "Fig" Newton suffered a broken nose. Temple was the fifth option on the fruitless offense, and the coaches told him to concentrate on rebounding and defense. "Coach Maravich told me I couldn't shoot, kept telling me I had to rebuild my confidence," he said. Temple was one of three members of the 1971–72 squad to appear in every game, averaging 6.2 points and 6.7 rebounds as LSU finished 10–16. Life away from the court presented plenty of challenges, too. Older teammates took Temple to several hangouts near campus his freshman year. The group was tossed from each because a Black person was not welcome. Temple quit going. "I was very proud of how Collis handled all of the challenges, and I was very relieved and really amused every time he would write to us and describe the different kind of incidents and fights that he had," Tull said.

Temple's personal habits kept trouble at a remove. He was not much for partying or drinking. When seven Louisiana State players broke curfew and thus were benched in 1974 at Starkville, Mississippi, he was among the five who had obeyed the rules and got to play.

Temple also took care in dating, avoiding white women even though there were few African-American coeds at LSU. "I went to Southern University, which was 7 miles away," he said. "It was all Black girls, and that's where I dated; that's where I spent my social time." When Temple was a sophomore, his father bought him a car to make the crosstown journey easier. "The other [siblings] said, 'Why did you buy him a car and not us?'" Hall recalled. "Daddy said Collis needed to drive over to Southern to meet some girls."

Temple claimed that LSU boosters offered him a car and other benefits—the same things they provided for his teammates—but he declined. Such gifts were and remain against NCAA rules. "I couldn't take anything—no money, no nothing," he said. "I was trained and raised to get what you earn and earn what you get. And if somebody gives you something and it's the right thing, you show appreciation. If it's the wrong thing, you don't take it. That's just the deal. It's a pride thing."

Pride can be problematic when not grounded in reality, as LSU athletic officials discovered. Nearly two months before Press Maravich was fired, they began sounding out many of the most prominent coaches in college basketball, only to discover that virtually none was interested in taking over the Tiger program.

The search then turned to assistant coaches. Brown, an assistant at Washington State and a practitioner of positive thinking, came away from his interview feeling good about his chances. "Dale, man alive!" his wife said. "You'd have had a better chance if you'd been a Kamikaze pilot in Japan's air force. There's no way you're going to get that job." A week later, the master motivator was hired. He would remain LSU's head coach for a quarter-century, taking the program to Final Fours in 1981 and 1986, winning four SEC titles and 448 games, and bringing in consensus All-Americans Shaquille O'Neal and Chris Jackson (later Mahmoud Abdul-Rauf). For a time Louisiana State was the top program in the SEC. "I like to take the credit of saying I raised Dale," Temple said.

The taming was mutual. Among Brown's first orders of business was reining in his best athlete, who did not play under control. "Collis was so effervescent that he wanted to do everything at once," Brown said. "He kind of reminded me of a molecule. You know how molecules bounce off things—off your forehead and off the lamp, off the ceiling? That's how Collis was. He was all over the place. Quicker than heck. Could jump. They called him the Kentwood Kangaroo."

When Temple did not stay within Brown's scheme, he was benched and began to pout. That brought a phone call and a visit from C. B. Temple. The father sat down with Collis and the coach, asking what his son could do to earn more playing time. Hearing the explanation, "his dad backhanded him across the chest. I'll never forget it. Whap!" Brown said. "He said, 'Stand up!' And Collis stood up. 'You apologize to your coach right now!'" Temple Sr. dubbed the head coach a surrogate father in matters involving basketball, and "from that day on, Collis Temple was a model, perfect guy."

With or without the obedient big man, LSU was picked to finish last in the SEC in 1972–73. The team presented contradictory evidence in its season opener, a 94–81 upset of third-ranked Memphis State, which would go on to earn a Final Four berth. Touted as "the Hustlers," LSU's Fighting Tigers finished a surprising 14–10 and .500 in the SEC. "This team wasn't supposed to win a single game in our conference," Brown told Steve Wilson of the *Salt Lake Tribune* after a win in Utah over Weber State. "But I have a very gallant bunch of kids, and I'm extremely proud of them."

Brown was not above a bit of legerdemain to give his team an edge, according to some former Georgia players and coaches. They allege that he slightly altered the height of the rims at Baton Rouge to throw off their shooting, infuriating Bulldogs coach Ken Rosemond. Accusations notwithstanding, Brown was voted the 1973 SEC Coach of the Year. Temple, the tallest player on the squad even without his large Afro, paced the team in rebounding (6.9 per game) and field goal accuracy (.567).

The Tigers fell to 12–14 in 1973–74, Temple's senior year. They started strong, defeating top-10 teams Vanderbilt and Kentucky, only to fade to the finish. Temple was a leader throughout, notching varsity highs in average scoring (15.0 points), average rebounds (10.5), and accuracy from the floor

(.579) and free throw line (.570). Forced into service at center, he enjoyed the most productive scoring effort of his career with 28 points in a loss at Nevada-Reno.

Temple made the SEC coaches' All-Defensive team and the All-SEC third team. "He played his heart out," Brown said. "He loved the game. He wasn't really big enough for a center, and he really wasn't a good enough outside shooter. But he'd guard anybody; he'd take on any challenge." Temple's personal attributes were as important in his coach's estimation as his basketball achievements. "He broke down the racial barriers here that everybody said couldn't be done," Brown said. "Had anybody lesser than him come in, they might have never gotten this program off the ground for years. He really opened the way."

The barriers fell slowly. Temple recalled the futility of trying to convince other prominent Black players from Louisiana to join him with the Fighting Tigers. "They were afraid to come," he said. So Temple was content with making the most of his opportunity, both for himself and others. Sounding what might be the family motto, the son of C. B. and Shirley Temple explained, "You make your deal work. You don't let anybody rain on your parade."

CHAPTER 13

SHOOTING THE HOOP

Coolidge Ball, University of Mississippi, 1970–74

What do the cotton fields say when the green leaves are gone, and the square and the blossom and the boll? What do they say, when only the stalks remain, like skinny black girls in ragged dresses of white?

Do they say, Shouldn't our ancient suffering be more fruitful by now?

Lewis Nordan, *Wolf Whistle*

The reception accorded Coolidge Ball on a February night in 1970 subtly signaled the approaching end of white domination on the basketball court, at least at the University of Mississippi.

Away from the playing floor, public schools across the South grudgingly consented meaningful integration. Acceptance did not necessarily follow. Mississippi whites responded by enrolling in droves in private academies; many public schools quickly drained of white students, a problem that lingered into this century. Desegregation was similarly slow to reach the basketball court. The SEC color line had been broken years earlier, yet as Ole Miss hosted Kentucky in 1970, African Americans had played at the varsity level at only two league schools.

The 1970 All-SEC first team would be the last that was exclusively white; by 1975 a majority of All-SEC first-teamers were African American. A run of high-scoring, white guards with unruly hair reached a climax in 1970, led by LSU's Pete Maravich and Auburn's John Mengelt. Mississippi's Johnny Neumann, then starring on the freshman squad, would set school scoring records in 1970–71, leading the SEC with a Maravich-like 40.1 points per game before jumping to the Memphis Tams of the American Basketball Association.

Spectators at Ole Miss's Tad Smith Coliseum, "the Tad Pad," had savaged Vanderbilt's Perry Wallace, the first Black player in the SEC, only two years prior to Ball's official recruiting visit to Oxford. "Ole Miss was the worst place," Wallace said in a February 1970 interview. "The crowds there are naturally boisterous and enthusiastic and they made a big thing about getting on a player. They really gave me a hard time and I guess they figured they could best get to me on a racial basis." Ole Miss also was less than eight years removed from James Meredith's enrollment, an event called an "echo of the Civil War's last battle" by writer Willie Morris (as quoted in David Sansing's history of the university). Meredith's arrival on campus sparked a riot that left two dead and hundreds injured, resulting in the deployment of approximately 23,000 federal troops to ensure his safety until he graduated.

Ball witnessed Meredith's ordeal from a televised remove. He knew little of Perry Wallace. He considered attending Ole Miss because he felt comfortable that "a lot of change had been made" since its violent reaction to court-ordered desegregation. Key to that comfort level were members of the basketball program. "If I'd get along with the coaches and the players, I wouldn't worry about anybody else because you're around your teammates and coaches 90 percent of the time, anyway," Ball said. "So I wasn't worried about anything else. And at the time when I came, it was a different era—a different time, anyway, than 1962 when James Meredith came."

Yet Ball paid close attention to the crowd's reaction on his February visit and frequently cited it as a factor in his choice of colleges. A belated choice at that, since he initially committed to New Mexico State University before ultimately becoming the first African-American scholarship athlete at the University of Mississippi.

The NCAA allowed recruits to be introduced to the home fans in those days, a practice since prohibited but easily circumvented by tipping students to a prospect's presence and having them do the honors. The 6-foot-4 Ball was brought out at halftime alongside another recruit, a taller player from Louisiana. "I was glad there was a white player right next to me so I could make that comparison," Ball says. "They introduced him, and he got nice applause. They introduced me from the Magnolia State, and I got nice applause, an ovation. I thought that was pretty nice."

Ball played before the same fans for the next four years. He led the Rebel freshmen in scoring in 1970–71. He made All-SEC each year on the Ole Miss varsity and helped the school record three consecutive winning seasons from 1972 to 1974, a run unequaled since the late 1930s. He also met his wife during his college career. "I think Ole Miss was the place for me. If I had to do it all over again, I would be right back here," Ball said.

"I think God put me here. I enjoyed it. Now I'm living right back here in Oxford."

Fred Cox, Ball's roommate their junior year, said Ole Miss was lucky to have his teammate as its racial pioneer. "They just couldn't have picked a better person to fill the shoes," Cox said. "There's just nobody anyplace any better, any bigger-hearted, any more honest, any more sincere, than Coolidge Ball. And I'm not bragging on him."

By Ball's senior season there were two other African Americans on the squad.

One cannot truly appreciate Ball's success and acceptance without understanding Mississippi's devotion to a castelike social and racial order that sentenced African Americans to enduring threat and limitation.

Ball's family made their living from the rich, loamy soil of Sunflower County in the great alluvial wash of the Mississippi River. They certainly did not belong to the ruling elite that sent its children to Ole Miss. Lush as the land was in the Mississippi Delta, the area was known for its crushing poverty, enforced by a tenant system that left the Balls and many like them who worked "from kin to kain't," or sunrise to sunset, at the mercy of a few wealthy planters.

But Tillie and Harvey Ball and their nine children got by, cutting wood for fuel and supplying most of their own food. On Sunday mornings Tillie Ball sold bouquets cut from flower beds she lovingly tended in front of the family's unassuming three-bedroom house, where the four girls shared one bedroom and the five boys shared another, sleeping two and sometimes three to a bed. "When I look back, I don't see how we stayed there, how we did that, but we did it," said Herbert Ball, oldest of the nine.

He continued, "We didn't have any money or anything, but we had plenty to eat. My daddy, he had like six acres of truck patch. He raised corn and peas, butterbeans, watermelons, and all that type of stuff. We didn't have to buy any food; we raised all of it. We had like 400 or 500 head of chickens, 15 or 20 head of hogs, and about 15 cows. We had everything we needed back then; we just didn't have any money." Chores—a constant for all but the youngest children—included the splitting of wood into sufficiently small pieces to fit the fire chamber of the cookstove. Herbert Ball still fondly recalled the day in 1955 when the family moved to a different house that had propane gas. "Man, I thought I was in heaven," he says. "I didn't have to cut any stove wood."

The Balls never engaged in "public work," that is, work beyond the farm. They were among some 50 Black families that earned their keep by picking and chopping cotton on Johnny Montgomery's sprawling plantation. Harvey Ball's father lived on a patch next door. Later the Balls moved to Leon Sheffield's nearby place and were similarly employed.

Sharecropping had succeeded slavery as a form of economic bondage for African Americans in the rural South, and nowhere was the practice of working someone else's land for a small share of the proceeds more pervasive than in the cotton-dependent Delta in western Mississippi. "Not only did the system deny economic opportunity, it positively pushed the Negro backwards," argued John Ray Skates in his bicentennial history of Mississippi. As late as 1960 the median income of black families statewide was $1,444. It is unlikely the Balls managed that much. "It was all that we knew back then," said Idella Ball, one of Coolidge's sisters.

There were few ready routes to a better life for Blacks in the Deep South. Simple escape became a popular option following World War I, a trend reversed only recently. At least 315,000 African Americans left Mississippi alone between 1940 and 1960. More than a few departures from Southern states were coerced, matters of immediate survival. Cal Irvin, a former NC A&T State basketball coach, said his father fled Alabama just ahead of the Ku Klux Klan after having the audacity to challenge the business practices of the white planter for whom he sharecropped. "He thought that the man was cheating him, because he was getting nothing out of it in terms of money," Irvin said. "He spoke to this grievance. A Black man in those days wasn't supposed to speak to anything."

Public education also provided a potential and quintessentially American escape route, except that path was intentionally constricted by neglect and outright discrimination. "The real trouble is that you have given us schools too long in which we could study the earth through the floor and the stars through the roof," an African-American minister told Mississippi whites soon after the *Brown* decision was rendered. Certainly the elder Balls never had a chance at a quality education. Harvey, a native Mississippian, worked the fields from an early age, never attended school, and could not read or write. Tillie, raised in southwestern Alabama near the Mississippi line, finished the sixth grade. They were typical of their generation. As the 1960s dawned the average African American living in Mississippi had attended school for six years; only 7 percent of Black state residents had graduated high school, compared to 42 percent of whites.

Federal demands for equal educational opportunity caused immediate and profound change, as attested by the Ball family's experience. Given a chance, Harvey and Tillie Ball not only kept their children fed and clothed and sheltered, but also saw that each one finished high school. All but two of the nine attended college.

Meanwhile, in a nimble dance of survival endemic to the Deep South, the Balls also steered clear of the harshest aspects of law and custom that might swallow an African American straying from the well-worn grooves of the status quo. "If there were a racial bog in America it was Mississippi," E. Culpepper Clark said in *The Schoolhouse Door.* Claude Sitton, who covered Meredith's enrollment and other civil rights–era confrontations for the *New York Times,* said years later, "Mississippi is no longer the state that it was in that day, and neither is Alabama. But I always felt that Alabama was sorta mean, but Mississippi could be deadly."

The Balls did not spell out the rules of survival for their children; the parameters were obvious. "We come up knowing these things on our own, that certain places we just didn't go," Herbert Ball said. "There was just a line drawn there; you could see it. You had a water fountain over here that said 'white' and one over here that said 'colored.' That's the way it was." Although it may seem strange that parents would not explicitly warn their children of imminent danger, Jordana Shakoor explained in her memoir, *Civil Rights Childhood,* that such cautions were largely unnecessary: "Colored children might not be given all of these instructions literally; they also learned how to behave around whites by observing their parents. When they asked why, as my father did, they were told that this was how Negroes were supposed to behave. And it was strongly suggested that they act accordingly if they wanted to have a long life in Mississippi."

Adults of both races knew the social order would be enforced with singular brutality. "When the niggers get so that they are not afraid of being lynched," said a white man from Oxford, "it is time to put the fear in them." Between 1890 and 1910 an estimated 200 black people were lynched in the Delta, on average one every 37 days. Statewide, 534 lynchings of African Americans were recorded between 1882 and 1952. "Nothing so dramatically or forcefully underscored the cheapness of black life in the South," observed Leon Litwack in *Trouble in Mind.* Any lynching statistics were mere estimates. No authorities kept strict account of this ultimate weapon of intimidation; neither did they tally the numerous other forms of legal murder and mayhem visited upon African Americans in a state where James K.

Vardaman, a former Mississippi governor and U.S. senator, chillingly declared, "If it is necessary every Negro in the state will be lynched; it will be done to maintain white supremacy."

The county, where the Balls lived had an ample history of violence tied to defense of the social order. A Black couple was brutalized and lynched near Doddsville in the county's northern reaches in 1904, a year before Harvey Ball was born, for allegedly shooting to death a prominent white planter. Several African-American bystanders were killed almost casually by armed whites in pursuit of the suspected killers. Once returned to Doddsville, the apprehended man and woman had their fingers and ears slowly chopped off and distributed to bystanders. Then their bodies were gouged by corkscrews that removed chunks of living flesh. Finally, the pair was burned to death, the woman first, before a thousand onlookers. There was never a trial, either to prove the pair guilty or, later, to punish their unabashed executioners.

Perhaps recalling that heritage but getting the tormentors and victims confused, Theodore G. Bilbo, U.S. senator from Mississippi from 1935 to 1947, later denounced equality for the Black man by pointing out that he was "only one hundred-fifty years removed from Africa where it was his great delight to cut him up some fried nigger steak for breakfast."

Come the civil rights era, the Balls' neck of the woods was knee-deep in blood. Reverend George Lee was shot and killed in the spring of 1955 while driving his car in Belzoni, a few minutes' drive south of the Balls' home. Lee, vice president of the Regional Council of Negro Leadership and a member of the NAACP, had the temerity to register Blacks to vote despite warnings to desist. No one was prosecuted for his murder. Nor was anyone punished for the shooting that fall of another NAACP stalwart in Belzoni, where today the Catfish Museum is a tourist attraction.

A half-hour drive northeast of the Balls' place, several white men tortured and murdered a visiting Black teenager from Chicago after he made an innocently flirtatious gesture toward a married white woman. "The brutal slaying of Emmett Till in 1955 was but one instance in a centuries-old tradition of maintaining racial order by castrating, literally and figuratively, the Black male population," Clark said. The message was underlined when an all-white jury acquitted the murderers, who later sold a detailed account of their crime to *Look* magazine.

The slaying of Till caused a national sensation, as did photographs of his mutilated body printed in *Jet* magazine. For some African Americans his death was, as intended, a cautionary tale. "You didn't become a smart aleck, because we knew of situations throughout the South and throughout the country where young, smart-aleck Black boys didn't survive sometimes," said Harold White, who at the time was a youth in Columbia, South Carolina. "I guess the most alarming case was Emmett Till, who was my age."

Civil rights leader Julian Bond, then a teenager, was likewise anxious. He feared journeying to downtown Atlanta when his mother wanted him to purchase a suit. "I said, 'Why don't you go? They won't hurt you. They might hurt me.' Emmett Till was conscious in my mind. If they'd do that to him, they'd do it to me."

For others Till's murder, a case the U.S. Justice Department reopened in 2004 and closed again in 2007, was a galvanizing event. "I've talked to many people who were involved in the [civil rights] movement, and that comes up all the time," said South Carolinian Cleveland Sellers. "We were not going to allow Emmett Till to die in vain. That was just not going to happen. Whatever those systems were, those ideas were, those philosophies were, we were going to attack them on all fronts. We were going to change America."

While violence crackled like perpetual lightning on the Delta's steamy horizon, the atmosphere took on a more ominous cast after what Mississippi congressman (and future governor) John Bell Williams called "Black Monday," the day in May 1954 when the U.S. Supreme Court delivered a mortal blow to institutionalized segregation.

Resistance to the *Brown* verdict found ready ground in the Delta. Sunflower's own James Eastland, nephew and namesake of the murdered plantation owner of 1904, made notable rhetorical assaults and erected legislative roadblocks. A U.S. senator and owner of a 5,400-acre spread, Eastland was dubbed the "nation's most dangerous demagogue" by *Time* magazine.

In the summer of 1954, whites gathered at Indianola—just up the road from the Ball home and the town where the Ball children attended high school—and formed a new national organization to promote and protect existing racial norms. These White Citizens' Councils were composed primarily of middle-class businessmen and professionals who eschewed overt violence in favor of the more socially acceptable route of enforcing "orthodoxy through economic pressure, political intimidation, social ostracism, and a vigorous campaign dedicated to the idea that 'if you're not with us, you're against us,'" author Skates explained.

The effort by a White Citizens' Council to crush a 1954 petition drive to integrate schools in Yazoo City, another Delta community, is instructive. The Council published the names of those involved in the drive. They were promptly fired from their jobs, refused credit or supplies, evicted from their homes, or otherwise harassed into submission. Such tactics later backfired as African Americans launched counterboycotts, but simple pressure often was sufficient to stifle dissent. White citizens straying from the appointed path were often ostracized as well. "By 1962 Mississippians lived as nearly under an enforced orthodoxy as have any Americans," said Skates, a native son. Among whites driven from their community were the parents of the reigning Miss Mississippi of 1964. They had made the mistake of extending a dinner invitation to visiting civil rights workers.

The demand for conformity had pervasive effects. According to the 1970 census, only 14 percent of Mississippi residents were born outside the state, the same as in 1900. "Contemporary Mississippians, perhaps more than other southerners, feel for their state a tension between love and frustration, fascination and rejection," Skates wrote in 1979. "Compelled by his heritage to guard the racial status quo first in a disastrous defense of slavery, then a century later in an equally unsuccessful resistance to desegregation, and in the interim largely ignored by the dominant sections of the nation, the white Mississippian developed a sense of isolation, a parochialism bordering sometimes on paranoia, unfamiliar to most Americans."

One might well argue, and many do, that such contortions warped and retarded Mississippi's development. To this day, those in other Southern states lamenting their poor national rankings in education, health, income, and other quality-of-life indicators commonly exclaim, "Thank God for Mississippi!" Susan M. Glisson, director of the William Winter Institute for Racial Reconciliation, located at Ole Miss, said, "We can't thank God for anybody. We're generally last. A joke I've heard is '50th and rising.'"

Amid this less-than-nurturing environment, the Balls kept to the farm and led a quiet, disciplined life. Located adjacent to their flower beds and well-tended lawn was a dirt basketball court that became a magnet for visitors and thus eased any sense of isolation. Friends came from Indianola, Belzoni, Inverness, and Hallendale. The competition attracted even the Italian boys whose "rolling store" selling potato chips, ice cream, and the like—a precursor of modern food trucks—announced its arrival in the fields with blasts from the vehicle horn.

The Balls played sports whenever they could, mostly on weekends, forming the nucleus of their own basketball team. Mrs. Ball put out a keg of water, and her sons drank and took on all comers in the stifling Delta heat. "Me and my brothers, couldn't nobody beat us," Herbert Ball said. "We had some set plays. They couldn't do nothing with us, but they'd be trying. We always had fun out there."

Brother Roosevelt notably shared several qualities with Coolidge, his immediate junior: He was not named for a president, although he shared a name with one. He was a gifted ballplayer. And he was an extraordinary leaper. This last trait always intrigued media members and school sports flacks; when Coolidge attended Ole Miss, he was predictably touted as a "jumping jack," a common appellation for Black athletes.

"There weren't many activities in the rural area, with us not having a car," said soft-spoken Coolidge, who runs Ball Sign Company on the outskirts of Oxford. "When you're a young kid, you always want to go, but as you look back, you appreciate it more now—not having a lot of those things to do. You could concentrate on your schoolwork or just enjoy shooting the hoop. Shooting the hoop—that's just something I really liked, my art and playing basketball. I had guys come around and say I should be going to town. They'd come by the window and ask me. 'Coolidge!' Did I want to go with them? I said, 'No, I've got to practice.' All the practice actually paid off. I'm glad I spent that time playing."

The Ball boys cultivated young Coolidge's game with a devotion resembling the care their parents lavished on the immaculate lawn, shrubs, and flowers in their yard. The brothers encouraged Coolidge to shoot and shoot and shoot when he was so small that he could barely manage to heft the ball. Coolidge gamely persevered until he could reach the rim. Once he had the range, a brother would put up a hand to contest his shot. Soon he was playing with and against older boys. "They were pretty physical," Coolidge said of his brothers and their high school friends. "I always enjoyed playing against somebody that's better than me." Hooked on basketball, he grew into the family's best player.

Outsiders took notice of Coolidge's prowess when illness sidelined several teammates at school, allowing him to start during an eighth-grade tournament. Apprenticeship on the family's dirt court translated into consecutive 16-point performances. Ball recalled that his coach told him, "Wow, if I had known you could play like that, you would have been playing a long time ago." He identified that moment as "the turning point of my basketball."

Ball was an All–Delta Valley Conference selection each year he played on the Gentry High School varsity. By his junior season recruiters had taken notice. He was avidly sought by midlevel schools such as New Mexico State, Middle Tennessee State, historically Black Mississippi Valley State in near-by Itta Bena, and Mississippi.

Membership in the SEC did not automatically mean Ole Miss had a big-time basketball program. In fact, few places in the football-fanatical confer-ence had a lower regard for the sport. Football was central to life at the uni-versity, whereas basketball was treated "just like a recreation sport, intramu-rals or something," Ball said. Vaught-Hemingway Stadium seats 60,580 and looms over the oak- and magnolia-lined campus, clearly visible from the portico of the redbrick Lyceum at the historic center of the university. The campus speed limit was set at 18 miles per hour, supposedly to honor the jersey number worn by Archie Manning, a two-time All-American at quar-terback in 1969 and 1970. "Basketball has never been really anything much that they cared about," said Robert "Cob" Jarvis, who was the head coach during Ball's career as a Rebel. "In fact, all it is was something to play between football and baseball season."

Jarvis, a former All-SEC player at Ole Miss, became the school's first full-time assistant basketball coach when hired in June 1966. He was elevated to head coach about two years later. The circumstances of his advancement reveal everything you need to know about the hierarchy of sports at Mississippi in those days. The athletics department proudly announced for instance, the promotion of head basketball coach Eddie Crawford—to freshman football coach. "They promoted him, and I guess they promoted me to head basketball coach," Jarvis said. "I don't know whether you'd call that a promotion or not."

Under orders from superiors (presumably administrators, not football coaches), the new head coach immediately sought Black players. "They wanted us to recruit them," Jarvis said. "They wanted me to because we needed to get integrated and go on. I think they thought I was the best one to recruit because basketball's got a small group. Let [African Americans] work in that way, and then we can get some for football and stuff."

The basketball staff preferred African-American prospects from Mississippi. They struck out the first year, then focused on Ball, an all-state performer who averaged 28 points and 20 rebounds as a high school senior. He, however, cast his lot with New Mexico State. The Aggies had plenty of athletes and played an up-tempo style uncommon in the staid SEC, where zones and patterned offenses ruled. New Mexico State also was where Ball's hero, Sam Lacey, a 6-foot-10 Gentry High graduate, played his college ball. Lacey, chosen fifth in the 1970 NBA draft, went on to a 13-year NBA career. "They called me another Sam Lacey," Ball recalled of the Aggies.

Ball's commitment was not final when he left home for Las Cruces in early summer, and he confided to his mother that he might not stay. Indeed, he quickly realized he wanted to come home. "I just really wanted to make my own mark," he said, explaining his change of heart. "I don't think I would have made my mark if I had gone there." So he phoned Ole Miss, discovered that a scholarship remained, and became the sixth and final member of the recruiting class of 1970–71.

Herbert Ball said community support for his brother's choice of Ole Miss was strong, although it derived from an unlikely source. "The white people in Indianola, they pushed for him to go there." Black people were not as supportive. "I did have some say I had to be crazy to go to a white school and be the first Black, that I might not be treated right," Coolidge Ball said. "A lot of people said it. I talked to a couple of them and said, 'How do you know I won't be treated right? Have you been up to Oxford?' 'No.' 'Well, why do you say it?' 'Well, I've heard.'"

Such skepticism was not unreasonable, given the school's history and its ties to white supremacy. Even the familiar nickname "Ole Miss" derives not from an abbreviation of the state's name but from the obsequious title routinely accorded the mistress of a plantation. The Confederate flag and the song "Dixie" were embraced as athletic symbols after being employed by the segregationist Dixiecrats in 1948, the year of the university's centennial anniversary. "It was a happy marriage of politics and school spirit, a way to celebrate white southern pride in the safe confines of a stadium," Nadine Cohodas says in *The Band Played Dixie*.

(Trent Lott, the U.S. senator from Mississippi and a former Rebel cheerleader, harkened to that segregationist heritage in 2002 upon the death of Strom Thurmond, the former standard-bearer for the Dixiecrats. Mississippi was one of four states Thurmond carried in 1948, when he ran for president. Referring to that time, Lott said, "If the rest of the country had followed our lead, we wouldn't have had all these problems over all these years." A visitor to the contemporary campus will note that the Trent Lott Leadership Institute symbolically resides just around the corner from the Lyceum, the antebellum administration building before which tear gas and bullets flew when James Meredith enrolled in the fall of 1962.)

As for an African American being crazy to attend Ole Miss, that was exactly the verdict in 1958 when Clennon King tried to become the first Black student to enroll. King was examined by two physicians in the presence of the UM chancellor and then committed briefly to the state mental hospital on the grounds that any African American who would seek admission to the all-white school was not in his right mind.

Other African Americans applied to Ole Miss, including Medgar Evers, the civil rights leader murdered from ambush in his Jackson, Mississippi, driveway in June 1963. He was rejected upon applying to the law school during the mid-1950s. It was left to Meredith, a 30-year-old Air Force veteran, to finally force a place for himself at what he called "the very symbol of institutional White supremacy, the University of Mississippi." Meredith's enrollment precipitated an ugly, violent reaction from approximately 1,000 white protestors, many from beyond the campus of 5,500.

An assault on 500 lightly armed federal marshals protecting Meredith came barely two weeks after Mississippi governor Ross Barnett told television viewers, "We must either submit to the unlawful dictates of the federal government or stand up like men and tell them 'Never!'" Upon graduating from Ole Miss in August 1963, Meredith wore upside down on his lapel a button that said NEVER.

The first time Meredith came to campus to register, Barnett comically surveyed his small escort of white federal officials and said, "Which of you is Mr. Meredith?" Once informed, he denied Meredith admission.

(The use of "mister" was itself sardonic mimicry of the respect not often accorded African Americans. In 1964 the U.S. Supreme Court overturned a contempt conviction from Alabama imposed on a woman who refused to respond in court when addressed only as "Mary"; the high court ruled that taking liberties with black defendants' first names was a key to repression in the South. Fred Cox, Ball's teammate, recalls a freshman-level course he took six years later at Ole Miss in which a department head referred to everyone in the class as Mister or Miss except the sole African-American student.)

Barnett threatened to close the university rather than allow its desegregation. He vainly attempted to strike a face-saving deal with President Kennedy's administration whereby the governor would physically block Meredith's path until asked to step aside at gunpoint. "A practical politician in the Deep South would no more advocate school integration," Ole Miss president John B. Williams explained in a 1963 speech in San Francisco, "than a candidate for mayor in your city would run on a platform advocating earthquakes."

As dark approached on September 30, 1962, the crowd in front of the gracious Lyceum, which once served as a Civil War hospital, heard Barnett announce on statewide radio that the "armed forces and oppressive power" of the federal government had forced his hand. Shouts and chants of "Go to hell, JFK!" gave way to tossed objects, from bricks to Molotov cocktails. Federal vehicles were attacked. Rifle bullets and shotgun pellets flew at the marshals long into the night; scars from the gunfire still pock the neoclassical columns of the Lyceum. A bystander and a French journalist were killed, and 160 marshals were hurt during the 15-hour melee.

Kermit Davis was among the National Guard troops dispatched to Ole Miss to assist the marshals. His unit of military police was not trained in riot control, yet its members arrived around midnight with weapons loaded. Davis, a former Mississippi State basketball player who would become head coach at his alma mater in 1970, said his unit was confronted by a scene at once chaotic and "organized to a frenzy," as he put it. "They were throwing brickbats. They even had two-by-fours. They had broken park benches, concrete, trying to throw them into vehicles. We roll in there, and they had barricades on fire. There were three to five cars burning. We had to stop in the middle of all that. Besides that, the marshals had fired tear gas. We didn't even have our gas masks on."

Federal power ultimately prevailed, prompting the Mississippi senate to adopt a resolution in November 1962 expressing "entire and utter contempt for the Kennedy administration and its puppet courts." Almost exactly a year later, when President Kennedy was assassinated, students at Ole Miss openly celebrated, joined by schoolchildren across the South in places as disparate as Asheboro, North Carolina, and Dallas, Texas, where he was shot.

Shortly after the riot the Mississippi State Junior Chamber of Commerce issued a pamphlet entitled "OXFORD, A Warning for Americans." It declared the melee "one of the most tragic events" in American history due to the use of "federal forces against a sovereign state." Signs soon sprouted on campus and around Oxford that read OCCUPIED-MISSISSIPPI. The following year, the student yearbook included a photograph of an armed, helmeted marshal and the mock score "U.S. 1, Mississippi 0."

The sports theme was appropriate. Football, of all things, eased tensions during the fall of 1962 and made it more difficult to contemplate closing the university. Coach Johnny Vaught's squad, described in his memoirs in a chapter entitled "Football Saves a School," achieved the only undefeated season in Ole Miss history. Led by a pair of All-Americans, the Rebels won the SEC title and the Sugar Bowl and finished third in the national polls. Vaught was no friend of integration. Years after his most glorious season, he let slip to reporters regarding Black athletes, "By the time we find one good enough, I'll be gone. Let somebody else do that."

Meredith graduated in late summer 1963. A trickle of African-American students followed him at Ole Miss. By the time Coolidge Ball was introduced to the crowd at the school's basketball arena during the winter of 1970, there were about 200 Black undergraduates.

Ball did not then, and does not now, place himself among militants intent upon forcing open doors unfairly closed to African Americans. But he did attend Ole Miss with the intention of making a contribution that would benefit others. "Whether I did good or I did bad, I was an example," he said. "I wanted to make a good example for other Black athletes coming along when they said, 'Who was the first Black athlete here at Ole Miss? What did he do?' And they could say good things about me and what I did and my record here at Ole Miss. As far as being a pioneer, I didn't think anything about that. But I wanted to make a difference—talk to the students, meet new friends whether they were white friends or Black friends. I did all that. I think I did make a difference."

Ball also made good on his education, to the satisfaction of his family. "We talked to his coaches," said Herbert Ball of his brother's recruitment, "and I told them I didn't want him to go up there and play basketball four years and get no degree." Coolidge graduated in 1975, returning to earn his final credit hours after a year's sojourn in minor league basketball. The path he blazed soon led to predominantly Black basketball squads at Mississippi. Among the players who succeeded him was Rod Barnes, class of 1988 and the program's head coach from 1998 to 2006.

Ball's successful adjustment also encouraged the football program to recruit its first Black player. Referring to Ole Miss's head football coach and its athletics director, respectively, Cob Jarvis said, "Occasionally I would talk to Coach Vaught and Coach [Tad] Smith, just tell them everything was going fine, no problems, everything was working smooth. That's the reason I think they went out and recruited Ben Williams, from Yazoo City, because everything was working smooth with Coolidge."

Both Jarvis and Ball understood the potential for trouble, and they discussed the matter during Ball's recruitment. "I said, 'Coolidge, as long as you will behave yourself and be like a gentleman, we'll have no problems,'" Jarvis said. "'If whites get mad, I'll go to bat with you and fight the whites. If Blacks get mad about it, we'll go there.' Because the Blacks really didn't want us to get anybody. I'm sure they didn't, because a lot of the whites didn't."

Ball attended segregated schools in Indianola. He did not know what to expect upon reaching Oxford, other than he would be surrounded by white people. Uncertainty is a factor for any 18-year-old going off to college. Focused on that commonality of experience, he mounted a characteristically low-key assault on the barriers he encountered. He particularly recalled the surprised reaction of a fellow student when Ball engaged him in extended conversation without ever discussing basketball. As they parted, the student admitted that his parents had not allowed him to associate with African Americans. "He said, 'It's been an honor talking to you.' Just by him talking to me, he had a better outlook on things," Ball said.

Cox, an Indiana native, was far more unsettled by his experience at Ole Miss. There was the shock, he said, of "going from a state where basketball was number one to a place where it took a back burner to almost everything." More striking, though, was the racism that pervaded northern Mississippi. Cox visited his grandparents during the summer and said of their home: "Greenville, South Carolina, was more advanced as far as race and discrimination were concerned than Oxford, Mississippi, was in 1970."

Raised within a cocoon of sports and farm life, Cox learned of James Meredith's experience at Ole Miss only after arriving on campus. Once matriculated, Cox quickly came to appreciate the difficulties faced by the university's first Black student. "I admire Mr. Meredith for having the courage, or the stupidity, whichever is the better phrase, to do what he did," Cox said.

Attitudes were equally regressive in class, town, and surrounding countryside, where the displaced farm boy went to tinker with equipment or to relax among rural folks. Ball, his neat and similarly quiet junior-year roommate, was glad to have escaped that world. "Coolidge's outlook on farming was, he knew what it consisted of and he didn't want to have anything to do with it," Cox said.

Ball's understated manner certainly eased his acceptance off the court. Playing a starring role on a winning basketball team did not hurt, either.

The 200-pound forward was a good ball handler, a tough defender, and a productive scorer. He was quick, strong, and had a vertical leap of around 40 inches, putting him in a rarefied class with NC State's like-sized David Thompson and Alabama's Wendell Hudson.

Ball led a 20–3 freshman squad in scoring, trailed only the sleepy-eyed Cox in rebounding, and was considered one of the SEC's top freshmen. He paced the 1971–72 varsity in scoring, again nearly matched Cox on the boards, and made the All-SEC second team. Ole Miss finished 13–12, its first winning record in five years.

Ball's junior year, the team was 14–12 and he again made second team All-SEC. Only Cox was a better scorer and rebounder among the Rebels. As a senior on a frontline that former Tennessee coach Ray Mears remembered as "extremely physical," Ball led the squad in rebounding while dropping to third in scoring. He gained third-team All-SEC recognition as Mississippi went 15–10, the most victories at the school since 1960.

"He probably turned out to be as good an all-around player as we had," Jarvis said. "He ended up being, probably, a better all-around basketball player than I thought he might be. A lot of boys that score points in college and high school, they don't like to play defense. He was one of the best defensive players that we had."

Ball appeared in every game Ole Miss played for which he was eligible, averaging 14.1 points and 9.9 rebounds. He was "excellent, a true competitor," Cox said. Ball scored more than 1,000 points during his three-year turn on the varsity and still ranks among the school's all-time career and single-season rebounding leaders. He took pride in thinking the game and worked at it with singleness of purpose. "I remember Fred Cox told me, 'Coolidge, you're one of the luckiest guys. You're always around the ball.' But you've got to know where the ball is coming up. You can't just stand there and say, 'All right, here it comes.' You've got to be moving."

Ball also was a good passer and a clutch scorer. He led the team to an upset of a top-10 Alabama squad in 1973 and to the school's first win over Kentucky since 1927, prior to the founding of the SEC. The Rebels repeated their triumph over the Wildcats in 1974. (Mississippi would not defeat Kentucky again in consecutive seasons until the late 1990s.)

"I think that's one thing that helped me here at Ole Miss, that I was a good athlete, and the way I conducted myself," Ball said. "I always conduct myself the way I want to be treated. I wasn't dishing out any stuff, and I didn't take any. I think that's what really got me through." Cox, the school's first

7-footer, got more grief on the court for his size than did Ball for his race. "I never did get called out a name that I remember, or have people say bad things or throw things on the court or anything like that," Ball attested. "In fact, I always pretty much got applause."

When problems arose within the team, Ball confronted them in his unassuming but determined way. Typical was the time Jarvis, who tended to be "hot-tempered," according to Ball, began yelling at him during practice early in his sophomore year. Ball had recently advanced to the varsity after a season under the direction of humane Ken "Cat" Robbins, the freshman coach. "It looked like he was going to use me as a whipping boy," Ball said of Jarvis. "So I had to call him in the office and tell him, 'Coach, I'm one guy that really doesn't like to be yelled at.' I said, 'If I make a mistake, giving 100 percent out here, if I make a mistake I just made a mistake. And I really don't like to be yelled at.' He said, 'Oh, Coolidge, I didn't realize I was yelling.' I said, 'Well, I just want to let you know that.'"

Jarvis remembered the incident—and how much he appreciated Ball's uncommon politeness and respectful determination. "Fortunately, the first young man that we signed that was Black was Coolidge Ball, and he was an outstanding person and an outstanding basketball player, too," said Jarvis, who retired in 2007 after coaching both the boys and girls teams at Warrior Academy in Eutaw, Alabama, to state championship games in the private school division. "We were fortunate there, because imagine if we had picked up a rowdy one or something like that. You'd have had trouble. But he was a gentleman and a heck of a good basketball player."

Ball quickly became the prime intermediary between players and coach. Among his proudest achievements was his selection by teammates, most of them white, as the squad's Most Valuable Player for three straight seasons. Ball also served as team captain in 1973–74, his senior year. Given such acceptance, Ball, like Alabama's Hudson, confounded expectations by finding a home at one of the Deep South's most tradition-laden, and integration-averse, universities. "I've been interviewed several different times, and I tell people that my experience was good, that I didn't have any problems. Some just don't want to believe that," Ball said. "I told one guy, 'I know you want to know some of the bad times, but, hey, I'm sorry, there weren't any. I can't tell you any.'"

Ball's postgraduate actions support his assertions. Unlike many barrier-breaking African-American athletes, he settled in the town where he attended college. Between road trips to flea markets, arts and crafts shows, and festivals where he paints (to order) everything from banners to signs to personalized license plates, he was active in the Ole Miss Tipoff Club, which supports the basketball program.

He also remains an interested, and sometimes dismayed, onlooker as his alma mater grapples with and gradually rejected the trappings of the Confederacy.

There were hard feelings in 1982 when John Hawkins, a Black student elected as a cheerleader, refused to carry a Confederate flag onto the football field. "I read in the daily newspapers here that a negro boy is now running the University," a disgruntled Ole Miss supporter wrote to chancellor Porter Fortune. "Maybe we should just give the University to the Blacks and start anew in another location." Further clarifying his less-than-subtle message, the writer added a postscript. "Does the new king know who his daddy is?" he asked.

Six years later, a house on fraternity row was torched as a Black fraternity prepared to move in. And in 1989 members of an Ole Miss fraternity stripped two fellow whites, painted their bodies with racial slurs, and dropped them on the campus of all-Black Rust College in nearby Holly Springs.

Agitation over Confederate emblems endured. In Ball's day coaches "had to go to the extent of explaining the thing about 'Dixie' and the flag before they could even tell a kid about the university, about the athletic program," Ball said. "I think coaches got tired of it." Among that group was Ed Murphy, head basketball coach from 1986 to 1992. As quoted by school historian Sansing Murphy, "It is hard to get Black athletes to Ole Miss, but once they get here they don't want to leave."

During the winter of 1993, four Black members of the student band refused to play "Dixie" during a basketball game against Alabama, raising anew issues about symbols, tradition, and racial insensitivity. Finally, flag, song, and the Colonel Rebel mascot were set aside amidst much grumbling about lost heritage and oversensitivity. "They didn't see where it was offending anybody," Ball said of those resisting change. "It was coming to the point that something was going to have to be done sooner or later, just like segregation."

These days, about 13 percent—about the same as it has been for decades—of the Ole Miss student body of 21,000 is African American and diversity is embraced as official policy. Yet as recently as 2000, Black History

Month flyers on campus were replaced with racial slurs. Two students were expelled and their fraternity suspended for a year after a 2001 Halloween party at which one brother posed as a police officer holding a pistol to the head of a fellow member in blackface, down on his knees. In her book on the university, Cohodas makes an observation applicable to these situations as well as to the historical events she detailed: "Ole Miss was one place where appearances could be, if not deceiving, incomplete because of the chasm in perception between whites and Blacks, a chasm fueled by that dichotomy between a shared history and a divided heritage."

Lingering contradictions are never far from the surface in Mississippi. William Faulkner, the Nobel Prize–winning author who resided in Oxford, famously wrote in *Requiem for a Nun,* "The past is never dead. It's not even past." Mississippi voters reaffirmed that truth that in 2001, spurning an effort spearheaded by business leaders to remove the Confederate battle emblem from the state flag. Recent progress notwithstanding, Mississippi's avid grip on a freighted past left it as something of a backwater. The state ranks last in per capita income among the 50 states, with one of the nation's slowest growth rates.

Ball assisted those promoting a new state flag, making license plates with the slogan "A Flag for All of Us." The measure carried in Oxford, now a bastion of moderation, but failed by a two-to-one margin statewide. Ball was amazed at the zeal with which backers of the 1894 flag campaigned against the change. "I guess it's going to stay until somebody else that has the balls comes along and says we're going to get rid of it," he conceded. That moment arrived in 2020, when Mississippi voters overwhelmingly dumped their flag's Confederate symbolism in favor of a magnolia blossom signifying rebirth.

Back in Sunflower County, the population has declined since Ball left home. Wooden power poles were left leaning in drunken rows alongside the highways, as if the earth that yields cotton, rice, and catfish ponds had tired of being supportive. Still, there were signs of progress. Recently visitors to Indianola, the spawning ground of the White Citizens' Councils, were greeted by large, full-color billboards featuring the smiling Black face of "Blues Legend B. B. King," a native of nearby Itta Bena, just up the road a piece.

CHAPTER 14
EXPECTED DIFFICULTY

Al Drummond, University of Virginia, 1970–74

I had seen and known negroes since I could remember. I just looked at them as I did at rain, or furniture, or food or sleep.

William Faulkner, *Light in August*

Hank Allen came daily to practice sessions for football and basketball. He came regardless of friendships with coaches, regardless of victories and defeats. Allen, a former high-school coach and teacher in Danville, bore witness across the decades because he knew intimately the state of Virginia and its flagship institution of higher learning, the University of Virginia. "You ask yourself, what the hell's he doing that for?," Allen said of his regimen. "My hidden agenda was, after observing this university and their beginning to bring Black athletes in here, yeah, I'm going to practice. I was determined that these Black kids were not going to be ostracized and they were not going to be exploited."

No one asked Allen to watch, but UVa's Craig Littlepage, the first Black athletic director in the ACC, was glad he did. "Guys like Hank Allen are important, because they keep the institution on its toes," Littlepage said. Paul M. Gaston, a professor of history who arrived at Virginia in 1957, said institutional antagonism made vigilance necessary. "For much of UVa's history, diversity was a predicament to avoid rather than a goal to embrace," said Gaston, an active civil rights advocate articulating an unfortunate universal truth throughout the South.

Allen arrived at Charlottesville in the fall of 1969 to pursue his doctorate and to work at a federally funded center promoting public-school desegregation. A miniscule 122 African Americans were enrolled at UVa at the time.

"The University of Virginia was one of the most segregated places in the state of Virginia," said Dr. Allen, who retired as an associate professor in the

311

School of Education. "Things were so bad here at this university during that time for Black students, I knew that the ones who would finish would leave, never to return. They didn't. Most of them never came back here because of the way they were treated when they were here."

But change was in the offing a century and a half after Thomas Jefferson founded and designed the gracious campus just a few miles from his Monticello home.

The academic year prior to Allen's arrival, when there were barely enough Black students to fill a classroom (31 full-time students compared to 8,261 whites), the Virginia campus endured a wave of student protests, many concerning race relations. "In times like these, rational and compassionate men cannot afford to tolerate bigotry," declared a student coalition at the all-male school. "The days are gone in which progress can be measured by minute degrees. The days are gone when apologies are sufficient."

The school year following Allen's arrival, sexual exclusion ended as women belatedly secured freshman admittance via federal lawsuit. Previously, female applicants were shunted to Mary Washington College, a "sister" school 65 miles from Charlottesville. The arm's-length arrangement apparently suited many men on campus, among them the editors of the student newspaper, who looked "with horror" upon the prospect of a "large-scale female invasion, other than for the purposes of a party weekend." For several decades now, the majority of Virginia undergrads have been women.

"This was a prep school, for all intents and purposes," said Terry Holland, who arrived at Virginia in 1974 from North Carolina's Davidson College and began recruiting Black players in earnest as head basketball coach. And not just any prep school, but one with a "reputation for prejudice and as a country-club-like haven for the playful sons of wealthy Southerners," wrote Bryan Kay in a 1979 study of desegregation at UVa.

Virginia integrated its revenue sports in 1970–71, the same academic year it accepted women, admitting a quartet of Black football players and Al Drummond, the first African American on basketball scholarship. By then, every other university in the Atlantic Coast Conference and the majority of Southeastern Conference members had integrated their varsity programs. "It doesn't surprise me," Allen said of the timing. "This is the state that closed down their public schools" rather than integrate. Charlottesville was among the towns which took that extreme step.

Drummond hailed from outside the region, a rarity among pioneering Black players at the major Southern conferences. Most were native sons. Drummond grew up in the small town of Waverly in western New York along the border with Pennsylvania. He knew little of UVa. But the National Honor Society member sought a good education and wanted to play close enough to home for his parents, a master chef and a medical secretary, to readily see him compete. Drummond, a lightly recruited wing, also "had always heard that the ACC had the best basketball. That's what I wanted to do; I wanted to play in the ACC."

Waverly High School and the town of Waverly were predominantly white, so Drummond was accustomed to being part of a minority. Even after visiting the Virginia campus, where he played pickup ball with Black athletes from other sports, he did not give the matter of race much thought. Only later, he claimed, did he realize that he would be breaking the color barrier in Virginia basketball.

"In a way, it made me feel good because I'm thinking, 'Gosh, these guys could have Black players any time they wanted to, but now they want me.'" he said. "In that respect, I felt good. But why they weren't upfront with that kind of bothered me, because you could have come and said, 'Hey, look, you're going to be the first. It may not be the easiest thing in the world.' They did not prepare me at all, not at all."

The problems Drummond encountered had him phoning home repeatedly to seek his parents' advice. His father dissuaded him from transferring to another college at the beginning of his junior year.

Hunter "Chip" Connor, head coach Bill Gibson's primary assistant for seven years, disputed Drummond's recollection of being left in the dark about his pioneering role. "He absolutely knew that," Connor said. Then again, Connor, an All-ACC player at Virginia in 1964, was not involved in recruiting Drummond. Gibson had attended Pennsylvania State University and coached at Mansfield State College, about a half-hour's drive from Waverly. He considered the nonurban reaches of Pennsylvania and west central New York to be his recruiting turf; Gibson identified Drummond as a prospect at a summer camp the coach ran at Gettysburg College.

"He was a dominating, abrasive man when you met him on the court one-on-one," Drummond said of Gibson. "When he was just a counselor at a basketball camp, you saw sides of him you thought were characteristics of a good coach. It's almost like his plan was to calm everybody down, to get them anything they need, and I need some players for my school, so let me see what's here."

Connor returned to his alma mater in 1967–68, four years after Gibson was hired. He recalled unsuccessfully recruiting District of Columbia players Adrian Dantley and James Brown, later a television sports announcer, and making a belated inquiry about an intriguing prospect, little-known Julius Erving, already committed to the University of Massachusetts. Ultimately, however, Drummond was the sole Black to join the program during Gibson's 11-year tenure.

"Trying to convince prospective Black student-athletes that Virginia was the place for them was like trying to persuade (notorious actress) Zsa Zsa Gabor that a fortnight at a cloistered nunnery would be fun," Gary Cramer wrote in a 1983 history of the Cavalier basketball program.

School, athletic department, and community combined to pull in any welcome mat for Blacks. During the early sixties, the university chose to end a run as the host of a tennis tournament after a young Black player from Richmond, Arthur Ashe, appeared in the event, attracting local African Americans as spectators. A Charlottesville restaurant refused to serve Nigerian diplomat C. C. Uchuno unless he ate his food outside. Demonstrations aimed at ending Black exclusion from a movie theater at The Corner, a business section just off campus, were dismissed in early 1961 by the *Cavalier Daily*, the student newspaper, as the work of "a bunch of unrealistic Yankee troublemakers." Later that year, chemistry major Amos Leroy Willis inquired in another student publication how whites would feel if they "were barred from athletics, refused service at The Corner, denied a voice in choosing dormitory roommates, and stripped of identity?" A 1964 survey of UVa students found the majority would not want to live next door to a Black person.

Claudius Claiborne was a nationally recognized high-school scholar in segregated Danville. During the mid-sixties he and a classmate submitted to an admissions interview at Virginia. They left feeling insulted, demeaned, and angry.

"They put the two of us down at one end of the table, and there were three very elderly, white-haired gentlemen sitting at the other end of the table, and they proceeded to grill us for an hour," said Claiborne, the first African American basketball player at Duke in 1965. "It was like they were trying to be convinced that we actually had the intelligence to go to the University of Virginia. We both walked out of that interview and looked at each other and said, 'We'll never go to school here.' They were asking us, like, algebra questions, not the typical things you would ask in an interview at all. They were really trying to test our knowledge . . . I don't remember actually getting up and walking out, but I remember saying we're not going to respond to this."

A paltry 18 full-time Black students were at Virginia when a 1966 survey of off-campus housing found that more than 90 percent of recommended units would not take Blacks as tenants. A '66 student committee found that Virginia had not offered a scholarship to any African American athlete despite President Edgar F. Shannon's assurance that coaches were instructed not to discriminate. Gibson had not even attempted to sign a Black player, according to the report. Just who was giving orders to the athletics department came into question when AD Steve Sebo was asked about the delay. "Gosh, I'd really love to" sign Black athletes, he told a student, "but the Alumni Association hasn't given me the green light yet."

Two years later, even as the UVa intramural golf championship was held at a segregated country club, Shannon actively called upon varsity coaches to aggressively recruit African American athletes. The issue also was raised by the school's handful of Black students. Yet, Connor said Gibson and staff felt under no compulsion to seek African Americans. "I don't recall anybody ever saying you guys are the last school to get a Black, you'd better get moving," Connor said. "Because as far as I knew, we were trying as hard as we knew how to get the best players we could regardless of what color. We were involved with a number of Blacks."

Cavalier recruiting was handicapped by a basketball history that, until Drummond's freshman year, was little short of pitiful.

Virginia was the last ACC school to hire a full-time assistant for its head basketball coach. Resources and other institutional support were so scarce, Evan "Bus" Male, head coach when UVa joined the ACC in December 1953, likened competing in the new league to "bear hunting with a switch." Upon taking the North Carolina head coaching job in 1961, Dean Smith was told by predecessor and former boss Frank McGuire that he could count on six sure wins in the ACC—home-and-home matchups with minimally supported Clemson, South Carolina, and Virginia. The tip was solid. From 1954–55, when Virginia began playing a full ACC schedule, through 1970, the Cavaliers failed to achieve a winning season or finish higher than fifth in the eight-team conference. Watching UVa lose, wrote Lawrence Maddry, a *Virginian Pilot* columnist, "was the natural order of things . . . like the way lemmings hurl themselves into the sea each year."

Bill Gibson, an astute salesman and flexible strategist nicknamed "Hoot" after the cowboy star of early cinema, arrived at Virginia in 1963 and reeled off seven straight losing seasons. Six years passed before the Cavaliers even recorded double-digit victories. Meanwhile, McGuire, formerly of the University of North Carolina and the NBA's Philadelphia 76ers, turned around fellow conference doormat South Carolina.

Several Virginia players complained to media members about Gibson's coaching following the 1969 ACC tournament, in which the Cavs completed a run of ten consecutive opening-round defeats. Foment was typical of the times, even among habitually obedient athletes. Two days prior to the tournament, Maryland's high-strung football coach, Bob Ward, resigned after 115 players signed a petition demanding his ouster.

Players presented Sebo, the athletics director, with a list of grievances against Gibson, and the *Cavalier Daily* ran a four-part series titled "Gibson Must Go" in which it alleged that players were "mishandled, misled and in some cases deceived by the coach." But Sebo backed his coach, bolstered by a supportive open letter from the 1968–69 freshman basketball squad. Gibson's leading critics were soon dismissed from the team. That did not end the unrest, as a "Boot the Hoot" campaign was mounted, and the Cavaliers finished 10–15 in 1970. Gibson also lost to Maryland in the struggle for the services of top prospect Tom McMillen, a 6-foot-11 *Sports Illustrated* cover boy from Mansfield, Pennsylvania. North Carolina, not UVa, had been McMillen's second choice.

Amid unrest, Drummond arrived to little fanfare in 1970–71. "I thought that it was smart for me to play with a team that was on the way up, because you wouldn't have the extra pressure on you expecting you to win," Drummond said. His father had been raised in St. Augustine, Florida, and Drummond was unfazed by the prospect of moving to the South. He claimed he had a single serious run-in during his sophomore year, one he addressed with a crowbar deftly wielded. "I was treated pretty good, really, overall. People used to talk to me. I could go out socializing, and people would pick up the tab and stuff like that. I could go just about anyplace I wanted to. Plus, I wasn't a nut. I didn't drink. I didn't smoke. I didn't do any of that stuff. I never caused any problems."

But Drummond soon came to rue his decision to attend Virginia, one he said he would not repeat if given the chance. The problem was Gibson, according to Drummond, Hank Allen, and Barbara Drummond, the player's mother. "He thought he was a smooth operator, but I was an even smoother operator," Barbara Drummond said. "I got my licks in, let's put it this way, before the man went to hell." Shortly after Drummond's career concluded, Gibson took the head coaching job at South Florida. He lasted a season before dying of a heart attack.

Drummond said it was only on the court that he felt out of place at Virginia. "Then it became quite obvious why I was there," he said. "Keep everybody happy. Hey, Virginia's got one, too. So, hey, it's cool. Keep the heat off. I knocked the door down. That was pretty much it."

That lack of impact, like a stone skipping off water, was not lost on Connor. Recalling a recent conversation with other Virginia players from that era, he said, "We don't have any Drummond stories that would say, 'Yes, there was a time when this happened and this happened, and this was the impact of him being the first Black basketball player on scholarship at Virginia.' We don't have any of those."

Drummond's personal style contributed to a very low profile. "He was so nice and so consistent and so completely, completely noncontroversial, I just can't think of anything that he ever did that you would say, 'Hey, that was way out there on the limb,'" Connor said. "I think Al chose a very conservative, middle-of-the-road, not-to-create-any-waves approach."

Perhaps as a result, Drummond disappeared from common memory, said Dan Bonner, a teammate from Pennsylvania. "Nobody knows Al Drummond's name. I think you would be hard-pressed to ask anybody at the University of Virginia. Is there anything in the media guide about [being the first Black scholarship basketball player]? Nothing. No mention, no mention."

Drummond made a minimal impression in part because his play was pedestrian, according to Bonner, a longtime college basketball analyst on television. "Al was very nondescript in his play," he said. "Al never really made much of an impact as a player. He was a backup guard for most of his career. He started a few games, not very many as I recall. He was a very average player. We had much better players in our program."

That was not saying much. Drummond and Bonner played on teams that struggled to compete. Their 1972–73 squad, on which Drummond was a junior guard and Bonner a sophomore forward, finished 13–12, followed by 11–16 in 1974. Bonner believed the low profile of both the Cavs and Drummond allowed his Black teammate to fly under bigots' radar, too. "We were awful, so there was no reason to heckle us," Bonner said. If anything, opposing fans concentrated on teammate Lanny Stahurski, who sported a military-style buzzcut at a time most players wore their hair long.

But the more Bonner spoke of those times, the more he was struck by his own naïveté and insensitivity. The fact that Virginia was virtually lily-white was "really a revelation to me" when he arrived, he said. Bonner was "startled" to realize that UVa was last in the ACC to integrate its basketball program, later than Deep South schools such as Alabama, Auburn, and Georgia. And, come to think of it, he had "no idea" what sorts of discrimination a pioneering Black player might face. "I was in my own little world," Bonner said. "I was worried about being away from home for the first time. I was trying to play and compete on a level that was way over my head. I didn't think too much about other people's problems."

Drummond, Bonner, Stahurski, and teammate Brian Tully shared an apartment for two years. They ate together, studied together, hung out together. Drummond was "a very interesting guy," Bonner said. "We used to say that Al's favorite song was the national anthem. You remember the days before there was cable, and all these TV stations went off the air at night? Well, when they went off the air, the last thing they had was the national anthem, and Al would stay up to watch the national anthem on every channel before he went to bed."

Yet Bonner had no recollection of any conversation in which his teammate discussed what it was like to cross the color line. "It had to be a huge thing for them," Bonner said of Black pioneers, "and yet the people that were there, that were with them, that should have been the closest people to them in the world, their teammates, it just wasn't a big deal to them. So, I don't know how I feel about that. How do I feel about that? Should I feel guilty about that? I don't know."

Teammates had little notion where Drummond went or what he did away from games and the apartment. Connor, the assistant coach, found himself similarly uninformed. If Drummond had any problems, they were news to him. "Al never came to the office and complained about anything," he said, echoing coach after coach who failed to connect with early Black players.

African Americans spent their lives then, and to a lesser extent now, adjusting to white society. Often, they were excluded altogether or admitted at some personal cost. Then, suddenly, whites wanted to include Blacks, or at least Black athletes, and discovered they did not quite know how. "I guess what I would say to him today is, 'Al, if you had a problem at any point back then, we loved you just as much as every player we had,'" Connor said. "You think about it, now that none of us can figure out what he did with his time and where he went and stuff like that, you almost say, well, why wasn't I over there knocking on his door, saying, 'Al, is everything OK?'"

Frankly, those charged with Drummond's care and guidance were learning as they went, Connor said. A telling instance occurred while Virginia was recruiting Don Blackman, an African American who chose to attend Duke in 1968. "He said to me on the phone once, 'If I go to Duke, there is a black girls' school nearby called Bennett,'" Connor recalled. "'What exists in the Charlottesville area for me in that regard?' I didn't know the answer to it."

Drummond said his town-oriented social life was fine, thank you. His problems centered around his role on the court, a realm where complaints are not apt to elicit much sympathy from coaches. "As far as open-door policy, yeah, you could go in there and talk to the coaches any time you wanted to, but . . . I never went," he said. "Even if I had any questions about anything, I never went there because I knew I was either going to get lip service or just be pacified."

The 6-foot-3 guard was considered a good defender but an indifferent offensive player. Drummond's shooting form was imperfect, his control sporadic, his assertiveness inconsistent. He averaged a modest 6.7 points in three years on the varsity, about half his output on the freshman team. An inability to hit the boards or attack off the dribble was reflected in only 70 trips to the foul line in 79 varsity games. His most notable offensive trait was an ability to create scoring opportunities with his defense.

"When you think about Al Drummond, the first thing that comes to mind is speed," Connor said. "And I would say the second is probably quickness. He could get from one end of the court to the other. He was lightning fast. He also had great quickness and was a terrific athlete. What he was not, he was not as gifted shooting the ball offensively as some of the other players. We found usage for Al throughout his career whenever we needed quickness, speed, defense. He was a great player to put in the game because he could cause stuff to happen."

Besides, Virginia did not require a great deal of additional backcourt scoring or leadership when it had Barry Parkhill, the player responsible for first putting Virginia on the basketball map.

Every coach dreams of striking gold where others see only stone. Parkhill was such a find for Gibson, Connor, and company, so overlooked as a 6-foot-4 inside player at a small high school in State College, Pennsylvania, that he was not recruited by Penn State, located in the same town. Even better,

Parkhill arrived during the dark days of the "Boot the Hoot" campaign, when Gibson had a year remaining on his contract. By his junior season, Parkhill was ACC player of the year, a first for a Cavalier, and an All-American. His jersey number, 40, was retired at the conclusion of his career.

Parkhill led the 1970–71 squad in scoring as it finished 16–11, Virginia's best record since 1954. Success-starved fans flocked to see the "Amazin' Cavaliers." Attendance nearly doubled at University Hall, where only a season earlier Parkhill recalled "you could count the people in the stands on your fingers for the freshman games and a crowd of 5,000 was a big one for a varsity game." A visit by sixth-ranked South Carolina in January 1971 precipitated the first advance sellout in U-Hall's six years of existence. The Cavaliers rose to the occasion, with Parkhill's baseline jumper the decisive basket in a 50–49 victory that earned the first top-20 ranking in school history. Formerly derisive crowds now chanted "Hoot! Hoot! Hoot!" as they awaited Bill Gibson's pregame arrival on the court.

Drummond joined the varsity the next season. He was a reserve on a '72 squad that opened with a dozen victories, the best start by the Cavaliers since 1915. Along the way they broke a 28-game ACC road losing streak with the program's first win at Duke's circa 1940 Cameron Indoor Stadium. Drummond's jumper, his only points of the game, ignited a second-half rally in a victory at Wake Forest, and he had fourteen points in a thumping of archrival Virginia Tech. "The sophomore guard played the last 13 minutes of the game and put on an absolutely stunning show down the stretch," wrote Bob Lipper in the *Virginian Pilot*, "collecting eight points and a couple of steals in a period of two minutes as Virginia bolted to a 96–76 spread with 2:30 to go."

The Cavs' undisputed star remained Parkhill. The junior led the team in assists and the league in scoring. "B. P. For President" signs sprouted throughout the Charlottesville area. "Barry turns the key and then the other guys have to keep the engine from misfiring," said Gibson, rewarded by appreciative boosters with a red Mercury automobile at the conclusion of the '71 season. By mid-February 1972, UVa was 18–1 and ranked sixth in the national polls. "I've never enjoyed a season more," Gibson told Paul Attner of the *Washington Post*. "This is delightful. I hope it never comes to an end."

Not even a late slide dimmed pleasure in a 21–7 record, a third-place ACC finish, and Virginia's first 20-win season in 67 years of playing basketball. The region's media voted Gibson the 1972 ACC coach of the year.

"The Parkhill phenomenon is what it really was," said Terry Holland, Gibson's successor. "It showed that Virginia could win at a high level, and it got people in the seats. Really, that's what I looked at when I took the job." By 1976, Holland had won an ACC title and in 1981 and 1984 took Virginia to the Final Four. "Without Parkhill and those teams coached by Bill Gibson, nobody would have ever had a chance to turn this around," he said.

Thirty-five years would pass before UVa won a first national championship under coach Tony Bennett.

The magic of the Parkhill era dissipated in 1973. Virginia slid to 13–12 as four of the top six players graduated, and Parkhill failed to recapture the precision and dramatic flair that previously had marked his career. Drummond appeared in every contest, averaging nearly 27 minutes per game as Parkhill's backcourt mate. His 50 assists ranked behind only Parkhill among the Cavaliers, and he was the team's most accurate foul shooter with an 87.5 percent conversion rate. He wanted to do much more but diplomatically masked his frustrations. "Drummond candidly admits that he is under some pressure playing in the same backcourt with Barry Parkhill," Steve Gaske wrote in the *Cavalier Daily*. "'I try to get the ball to Barry first, then set up the rest of the team,' Drummond said. A complete player who is already being watched by the pros, Drummond is criticized by his coach, but for not shooting enough."

Drummond derived most of his praise on defense. "Make sure you tell Drummond that I think he did a great job," a Penn State player said after being held to six points in a UVa win at Charlottesville. Drummond scored fifteen. "All I know is, I could play some D," said Drummond. A highlight came when he recorded steals on three consecutive possessions in a win over North Carolina that broke a 30-game Virginia losing streak at Chapel Hill. As a sophomore, Drummond notched steals and baskets on four consecutive possessions in a victory over Virginia Tech.

"It used to tick me off, if I'd steal the ball and start dribbling down, all of a sudden I was supposed to hold it and set it up," Drummond said. "Come on! By the time we come down and set it up, I already had it in the hole. I just think that it was meant for me not to shoot. It was meant for me to get the ball into somebody else's hands." Somebody else meaning Parkhill, whom Drummond called "a very skilled ballplayer."

The interplay between Drummond and Parkhill, as orchestrated by Gibson, increasingly disturbed Hank Allen, casting his watchful eye on Virginia basketball in his self-appointed role of conscience and protector.

"Let me tell you something," Allen said. "I played basketball for a long time myself, from a little grade school through junior high school through high school through college. Then I coached for 17 years, so I know a little bit about it, know something about talent when I see it. Drummond came here, and Gibson was coach. Gibson was a redneck, pure redneck. He buried that kid. That boy came here, all you heard was Parkhill, Barry Parkhill. That's all they heard about, Barry Parkhill.

"Now, I'm sitting there looking at both of them in practice and play. Drummond had more skill, quicker than Parkhill. But Drummond never scored anything. Because why? Because Gibson wanted the ball in Parkhill's hands . . . Drummond, he knew and didn't know. He knew what was going on, but he couldn't deal with it outwardly. He couldn't deal with it with anybody, because nobody's going to believe what he's going to say but me. I know what's happening to him, I know exactly what's happening to him."

Drummond was not then, and is not now, apt to say he was a better player than Parkhill, although he did offer that Allen's analysis "hit the nail right on the head." Certainly, scant evidence supports a claim that Drummond was Parkhill's on-court equal. His senior season, with Parkhill gone, Drummond predicted that it would be "easier for me because I felt so much pressure last season playing beside Barry." Instead, he showed minimal statistical improvement.

"I think it sunk in my junior year that my role was just to shut down the other players but don't shoot the ball," Drummond said. "Every time I had the opportunity to shoot, I would shoot, and if I made it, I would be (relegated to) sitting on the bench. So that kind of spelled everything out for me. So, I just said to myself, 'I'm just going to finish this out, get the hell out of here, and just do my thing.' And I had spoken to some of the other (Black) players in the league and got similar stories."

Drummond did not entirely maintain a low profile, as he became the central figure in the most disputed officiating call of Virginia's 1973 season.

The Cavaliers put up an unexpectedly tough battle at U-Hall against second-ranked NC State, on the way to an undefeated year behind David Thompson, a three-time All-American, and Tom Burleson. The Wolfpack possessed the ball and a tenuous 57–55 lead in the final two minutes. That year, players were required to raise a hand when called for a personal foul. Drummond was whistled for a blocking foul as he guarded tough Wolfpack playmaker Monte Towe in the backcourt. Whether in frustration or surprise, Drummond threw up both hands instead of just one. Official George

Conley immediately assessed a technical foul on the Virginia guard. Gibson denounced the call as "plain bush," but the damage was done. Towe made three straight free throws, and the game effectively was over.

Disappointing as the call was, Drummond had to endure another insult, this time from the home fans. "We were on our way up the court, and I'm thinking, 'I can't believe they called the technical foul on me,'" he said. "And I'm looking up in the stands, and some people up there are giving me the finger. I'm thinking, 'God, as hard as I busted my ass, and we're going to lose to State like this, and these guys up here are giving me the finger.'" That was the same season Gene Corrigan, Sebo's successor as director of athletics and later the ACC commissioner, decried behavior at UVa basketball games that "gives the university the reputation of having the poorest crowds in the ACC."

Drummond never reported any racial component to interactions with Virginia fans. The same could not be said by other African Americans, according to Maryland's George Raveling and Len Elmore. They found University Hall stunningly hostile to Blacks during a 1971 visit by the Terrapins to play Drummond's freshman squad. "It was the worst language and racial taunts I've ever heard in my life when we played them at Charlottesville, and part of it I think is because (Tom) McMillen didn't go there," said Raveling, who coached the Terp freshmen. "That was one of the most racist places I'd ever seen." Considering that McMillen is white, the derision was bizarrely misplaced.

Elmore, not playing while he recovered from a knee operation, found the experience "amazing" as fans behind the Maryland bench called the Black visitors "every name from coons to Leroy." The New Yorker had heard stories about the South, but "I just never expected that to happen." When the 6-foot-9 Elmore turned and suggested that fans "just chill out," one reached into his jacket threateningly and, as if cradling a pistol, said, "I've got something here for you." Raveling insisted that his reserve players were so incensed by the Virginia spectators, they refused to go into the lopsided game. "They said, 'Leave the starters in there. Let's kill them,'" the coach recalled was their explanation.

Virginia fans were not averse to turning on their own Black players, as Drummond had discovered. Harrison Davis III was one of four players to integrate the Cavalier football program, along with halfback Kent Merritt and two others. Davis was a quarterback, then a rarity for an African American, and not a particularly successful one. "I think they were very resistant to him being a quarterback," Merritt, the team's leading rusher in 1971 and

1972, said of his housemate some 30 years after the fact. "He'd been booed, that sort of thing. I understand things were said in the stands. So, I think he was treated pretty harshly. As a matter of fact, Harrison has not come back since graduation. All of us kind of have a bitter taste in our mouths from our experiences here. Not necessarily racial experiences, but personal."

Harrison started as a sophomore in 1971. He was the team's total offense and passing leader but threw 14 interceptions compared to 3 touchdowns. After throwing several interceptions in the 1972 Homecoming game against Maryland, he was booed and benched. George Allen, son of the Washington Redskins head coach of the same name and later a U.S. senator from Virginia, replaced Harrison and likewise was intercepted as the Cavaliers lost, 24–23. Hank Allen remembered that "not a damn soul said a word" when the white player failed. "Harrison, he caught hell."

Overt racial hostility is at odds with the notion of the mannerly cavalier, emblematic of Virginian gentility at the northern terminus of the old Confederacy. But in many respects the state that produced four of the nation's first six presidents—George Washington, Thomas Jefferson, James Madison, and James Monroe—matched the Deep South in the vigor of its opposition to equal rights. That white leaders usually chose words and laws rather than violence to assert their superiority was less a sign of moderation than a reflection of traditional methods for expressing racial prejudice.

"The fact that it's Southern and Virginian gives it a distinction, because white Virginians, their whole attitude toward race is 'We're the descendants of presidents; we have to act in a kind of genteel way,'" said Julian Bond, former executive chairman of the NAACP. Bond had taught a civil rights course at UVa. "Everything is treated with a kind of politeness and a kind of gentility here, as opposed to Mississippi State or Ole Miss or Alabama or Georgia. What happened at Georgia with Charlayne Hunter and Hamilton Holmes couldn't have happened here, I don't think. It wouldn't have been allowed to happen here."

Clamping down without blowing up characterized Virginia's reaction to the Supreme Court's *Brown* decision; the ruling included among its five amalgamated cases a challenge to unequal facilities in Prince Edward County in southcentral Virginia.

Political scientist V. O. Key Jr. observed, "Of all the American states, Virginia can lay claim to the most thorough control by an oligarchy." He also noted chidingly in his classic study, *Southern Politics in State and Nation*, that "Mississippi was a hotbed of democracy" compared with Virginia. The controlling presence in the Old Dominion was U.S. Senator Harry F. Byrd, who first coined the phrase "massive resistance" to describe the organized reaction against desegregation that engulfed the white South. "No man did as much to move the front lines of opposition from the Deep South to Washington, D.C., and the Potomac River," Numan V. Bartley wrote of Byrd in his 1969 classic, *The Rise of Massive Resistance.*

The threat of integrated schools posed "the most serious crisis that has occurred since the War between the States," Byrd declared. "If Virginia surrenders, if Virginia's line is broken, the South will go down, too." Byrd worked to make massive resistance the central issue in the state's 1957 elections, and succeeded. "Let there be no misunderstanding, no weasel words, on this point: We dedicate our every capacity to preserve segregation in the schools," stated the Virginia Democratic party platform.

Virginians, particularly editor James J. Kilpatrick of the *Richmond News-Leader,* revived pre-Civil War notions of "nullification" and "interposition" to rationalize their intransigence, claiming that a state had the right to interpose its will to protect the populace from unconstitutional acts by the federal government. Harry Ashmore, in *Civil Rights and Wrongs,* wrote that Kilpatrick, later a nationally syndicated columnist of unabashedly conservative bent, "attempted to provide sociological underpinning for his legal theory."

"The Negro is fundamentally and perhaps unalterably inferior; he is also immoral, indolent, inept, incapable of learning and uninterested in full racial equality," Kilpatrick said, sounding his kinship with the worst the South had to offer. "The segregationist South has no guilt about keeping the Negro in his proper place—that is to say, in separate schools."

Virginia went to greater lengths than most to achieve that result. Many Southern states threatened drastic steps, but only Virginia and Arkansas shut down public schools in the name of perpetuating racial separation. Virginia developed a plan, financed by public tuition grants akin to today's voucher arrangements, that allowed whites to continue their education even as public schools were closed to avoid desegregation. "Any parent whose child did not attend the public schools in their hometown could receive a tuition grant merely by presenting evidence to the local government," wrote Andrew B. Lewis in *Preserving Public Education in Charlottesville.* Whites attended private schools, schools in other parts of Virginia, or even schools in other states at public expense while African American students were shut out.

Charlottesville's board of education predictably fought an NAACP desegregation suit for two years. During that time a cross was burned at the home of Sarah Patton Boyle. The civil rights activist had dared write in the *Saturday Evening Post* that "the Southwide conviction that everybody else is prejudiced is like a sodden blanket over each individual's impulses towards democracy."

When federal courts ordered immediate desegregation in the fall of 1958, Virginia governor J. Lindsay Almond Jr. closed nine schools in Norfolk, Front Royal, and Charlottesville, affecting approximately 13,000 students. Within a year federal judges forced the affected schools to reopen with mixed enrollment. That was the signal for leaders in Prince Edward County in south-central Virginia to make good on the South's favorite post-*Brown* threat—they simply abandoned their commitment to public education and closed the schools.

Prince Edward County's schools stayed closed for five years, leaving 1,800 African American students to fend for themselves. Black students at vastly overcrowded Robert Russa Moton High School in Farmville had no gymnasium or cafeteria and were forced to attend class in a school bus. State and local tax dollars, as well as funds from donors throughout the country, were applied to underwrite vouchers for white students attending private academies. That practice persisted until 1964 when the U.S. Supreme Court declared the setup unconstitutional. Today, Moton High, where students first protested their curtailed educational opportunities in 1951, is a National Historic Landmark.

The reaction to mandated school integration in Charlotteville was less extreme but hardly generous. Removal of racial barriers was grudging at best, delayed as usual by the charade of freedom of choice. "Token desegregation remained the norm in Charlottesville from 1959 to 1965," Andrew B. Lewis stated in a chapter in *The Moderates' Dilemma, Massive Resistance to School Desegregation in Virginia*. The facade of gentility slipped repeatedly: Shots were fired into the home of the NAACP's local branch president in 1959, and bomb threats plagued integrated Lane High School nearly a decade later.

Dallas R. Crowe, in a 1971 doctoral dissertation in education at UVa, noted, "The School Board did little or nothing to prepare teachers and staff for the consequences of total school desegregation until after the (May 1968) walkout of Black students at the formerly-white high school." Footballer Kent Merritt shifted to Lane as a sophomore in 1967–68 and said the integration process was punctuated by daily fights between Blacks and whites. "I don't think I remember a single day when something didn't happen," he said. "It was horrible. They put (Blacks) into an environment, it was not welcoming and had not planned for them to be a part of the school. Blacks didn't want to be there in the first place."

Remarkably, the experience did not cause Merritt to shy from similar situations. Soon he was among the first athletes to cross the color line at the University of Virginia, which fancied itself the "Princeton of the South."

UVa, the town's largest employer, had a distant relationship with the local African American community, providing menial jobs but little support or sense of connection. In partial response, many Blacks rooted against Virginia's all-white athletic teams, much as fans in Columbia, South Carolina, supported the visitors when the University of South Carolina played. When Merritt signed with Virginia in 1970, that animosity began to change.

"UVa was the last school in the ACC to integrate," Merritt said. "A big part of it was the fact they claimed they could not get a qualified Black student-athlete. I'm at Lane High School. I had good grades. I was a good athlete . . . Somebody in their own backyard seemed to fit those qualifications." Once at Virginia, the football star reported that he was the beneficiary of the same extracurricular largesse offered white teammates. In fact, his athletic status served as protective coloration. "It enabled us to have a much more pleasant experience than most of the Black kids," Merritt said, including his football classmates. "We didn't necessarily have to socialize with the Black students if we didn't want to. You'd go to restaurants. We were all known. You just had kind of the easy access. But we wouldn't have had that access had we not been athletes."

Drummond enjoyed similar freedoms but had a bit more difficulty establishing himself with his UVa peers. Shooting baskets alone at one end of an outdoor court on campus during his sophomore year, he said three whites repeatedly but coyly threw their ball at him. Finally, one tormentor brandished a stick, so Drummond went to his car, returned with a crowbar, and "kicked the crap out of them," he claimed. "I never had a problem from that point on."

The residue of those times lingered. Former teammates had not spoken with Drummond in years and had no idea he managed a restaurant, handled real estate, and owned a commercial cleaning business in the Philadelphia area. "When I think about Virginia, I'm bitter, but I think I've gotten over a lot of it," Drummond said. "I had the opportunity to come down there and play, not the way I wanted to, but when I think about how it was when I got there and how it was when I left, I think that all the players I was involved with were pretty cool."

Drummond and Merritt were just finishing college as Terry Holland arrived in Charlottesville, replacing Gibson as head basketball coach. Holland, 32, was immediately struck by what he called "the lack of a Black presence" at Virginia. Coach and university intensified efforts to attract African American students and faculty, and by 1976–77, Holland's third season, he was among a trio of ACC coaches with a Black majority on his squad, according to research by Tony Britt. (Clemson's Bill Foster and Maryland's Lefty Driesell, Holland's former coach at Davidson, were the others.)

The competitive breakthrough came in 1979, when the Cavaliers signed 7-foot-4 Ralph Sampson, a Black Virginian and the nation's premier recruit. "This is a young Black male who could have gone anywhere he wanted to, and he chose to go to the University of Virginia," Holland said. Sampson was an instant star, a three-time ACC and national player of the year. The Cavs won the 1980 NIT and finished in first place in the conference each season from 1981 through 1983, posting a cumulative 88–13 record. That established the program at the forefront of the ACC, at least temporarily.

Merritt said that Virginia athletics' enthusiastic outreach to Blacks was not necessarily reflected elsewhere. The former running back returned to UVa after a quarter-century and found that the intervening years brought minimal improvement in the relationship between Charlottesville's Blacks and the school. On campus, too, Merritt saw modest change. "I think there's more effort being given to make African Americans comfortable here, but the same things that students were complaining about then, they're still complaining about," said Merritt, an administrator in Virginia's philosophy department. "No social life. Nothing oriented toward Blacks. Those are things that people have talked about for thirty years."

The outlook appeared brighter to Bond, a nationally prominent civil rights activist before Merritt was old enough to attend high school. That he and Merritt were employed at Virginia was itself testament to change, he said. "I don't think we're living in the promised land by any means, but I do think this is a much different and better time." Bond, as others, credited presidential leadership at the university with advocating forcefully for change. Where once students led the way, said Gaston, the historian, "Now it's the administration scurrying about and the president, John Casteen, scurrying about."

Under Casteen's leadership (1985–2010), the last ACC school to cross the color line on the court was the first to do so in athletic administration, employing Littlepage as athletics director from 2001 to 2017. He, in turn, hired Dave Leitao as head basketball coach in 2005. Leitao was the school's first African American head coach in any sport.

Littlepage did not consider himself a one-man antidote to the good old boy network. Rather, like Maryland pioneer Billy Jones, he believed in setting examples, cultivating internal candidates, and rewarding merit regardless of the package it came in. Tellingly, Littlepage was succeeded as UVa's athletic director by Carla Williams, the first Black woman to serve as an AD at a Power Five school. "If the only (Black) people that our young student-athletes see are people who are doing our classified work—cutting the grass, doing the laundry, that sort of thing—and that's not balanced with the models of the professionals," Littlepage said, "then we're not doing our jobs. We had not fulfilled what I think is a fundamental responsibility."

CHAPTER 15

MOVING ON

Wilbert Cherry, University of Tennessee, 1971–73
Larry Robinson, University of Tennessee, 1971–73

We do not serve mustard, ketchup, or Negroes.

Sign at McDonald's in Knoxville 1960

Theirs was an accidental pairing—the powerful frontcourt player and the slight guard; the Virginia transplant and the east Tennessee product; the starter and the afterthought; the quiet country workman uncomfortable wearing shorts in public and the theatrical extrovert; the junior college transfer and the walk-on; the celebrated team captain and the player spurned by his coach and ignored by his school. Yet, for a season, Larry Robinson and Wilbert Cherry were equals in blazing a trail on the 10-man Tennessee varsity, plunging together through the towering "T" by the home team's locker room door prior to games, emerging on the other side with their teammates to the glare of spotlights amid the acclaim of an adoring crowd in a roaring orange sea.

The orange "T" they burst through marked the center of a color-coded universe. The team warmup outfits were striped orange and white, in keeping with the passable version of a Harlem Globetrotters routine the squad immediately launched—"our little circus act," said embarrassed seven-footer Len Kosmalski—whipping orange-and-white-checked basketballs through their legs, behind their backs, and over their shoulders.

The 70-piece pep band that accompanied them, playing the Globetrotters' signature song, "Sweet Georgia Brown," and the dancing "Rally Girls" and majorettes cavorting amid waves of sound, were all swathed in orange. Thousands of fans wearing all manner of orange garb ringed the court at the 12,700-seat Stokely Athletics Center, the "Orange Tie Club" perched conspicuously in its own seating area. And of course, head coach Ray Mears and his assistants plied the sideline in matching orange blazers, clothing that advertised "Big Orange Country" wherever they went. ("It was good for going through airports," said Harris "Bud" Ford, a longtime program publicist, "because you'd never lose anybody.")

Halftime sideshows included a unicyclist riding backwards while juggling three checkered basketballs, cloggers, and the occasional bear-wrestling exhibition. During years when dunking was banned even in warm-ups and punishable with a technical foul, Mears had nine-foot portable baskets, one foot short of regulation height, rolled out so that Tennessee players could circumvent the rule and entertain with legal dunks prior to games.

"We had a lot of fun," said Mears, an admirer of iconoclastic baseball impresario Bill Veeck. "We did it to get the crowd fired up, and it intimidated the other people. We had kids from other teams just turn around and watch us go through our warm-ups."

The circus-like schtick vastly irritated some rivals, among them Georgia coach Ken Rosemond. "He just despised Mears and didn't like all that showman stuff," said Gino Gianfrancesco, a Bulldog guard. "We never went on the court until the tip-off. We stayed in the tunnel so they could do all their hoopla and all that crap."

The color scheme, rituals, and tumult accompanied the Volunteers on the road, where fans roused by Mears's provocations pelted the team with boos, incentive, and oranges. Barrages of fruit became routine on visits to archrival Vanderbilt, thanks to Mears's deliberate pregame strolls the length of the playing floor. "He invited it. He knew. He was a showman, an instigator," Larry Robinson said. Tennessee players waiting in the locker room enjoyed the boos and catcalls that announced their coach's progress.

"That was Coach Mears' way, in my mind, of taking some of the attention off us and put it on him," said Robinson, later an AAU summer ball coach with the well-respected Tennessee Travelers. "He did everything he could to try to beat the other team, to try to get an advantage. In his mind, I think he was doing everything for his team. That's how he was, and they hated him so hard they didn't have time to hate the team."

Mears, called by some "the Barnum of Basketball," did not care what others thought. That included his embrace of Black players.

If his antics irked opponents, all the better. He was fighting for attention at a school where football dwarfed all other sports, and in a league where

Kentucky dwarfed all other basketball programs. For 15 seasons, the longest tenure in the program's history, Mears escaped those enormous shadows, winning both attention and games. In the process the University of Tennessee men's basketball program achieved a measure of competitive equality and respect infrequently duplicated before or since. Only the program directed by the late Pat Summitt, until the 2020–21 season the most successful women's basketball coach in history, could regularly compete with football for the spotlight in a city that hosts the Women's Basketball Hall of Fame.

Basketball's secondary status was long manifest at Tennessee, as at other SEC schools, by requiring the men's head coach to serve double duty as a full-time football assistant. Sometimes the dual role compromised the basketball program. John Mauer, Mears's most successful predecessor, was compelled to ask a coach from another college to direct the Volunteers at Madison Square Garden, then the mecca of the basketball world, while he accompanied the football squad to the 1945 Rose Bowl. Then again, perhaps Tennessee was onto something. The basketball squad beat national powerhouse New York University, an eventual Final Four entrant that season, without Mauer while the football Volunteers lost to Southern California, 25–0, with him.

The balance of athletic power at UT remained unchallenged under the rule of Bob "The General" Neyland, the football coach, athletics director, and World War II brigadier general for whom the 104,079-seat campus stadium is named. The university intentionally delayed hiring Mears in 1962 while the legend lay dying.

Basketball had sunk so low, the year prior to Mears's arrival the team finished 4–19, last in a 12-team SEC, and attracted approximately 400 fans to the final home game of the season. "The program was way down at the bottom," Mears said. "The reason I took this job is because I always wanted to play against Adolph Rupp. I knew so much about him. I played against him in college. Adolph had the name. Everybody wanted to play against Adolph." Mears was the rare coach who held his own against "The Baron," famous for his brown suits and perpetual success.

Ever provocative, Mears arrived for a game at UK in 1966 dressed in a brown suit, mimicry that caused an ultimately victorious Rupp to pitch a fit in private. "I was sort of an ornery guy," Mears cheerily said years later. Tennessee got even in the last game of the '66 regular season, handing Kentucky its sole loss until upset by a predominantly Black Texas Western squad in the NCAA final.

Mears, whom one writer said "wears the friendly, padded look of a successful young insurance salesman," was a hot coaching commodity when he arrived in Knoxville for the 1962–63 season. He had been featured in *Sports Illustrated* as "Mr. Wonderful of Wittenberg" after capturing a college division championship, dominating the 15-member Ohio Conference, winning 56 consecutive home games, posting a 114–22 record, and creating fan interest with a gaudy pregame ritual at Wittenberg University.

Neyland left basketball "starved for money, for players, and for coaching talent," according to the authors of *To Foster Knowledge*, a history of the university written by James R. Montgomery, Lee S. Greene, and Stanley J. Folmsbee. Mears, then 35, took the Tennessee job with the assurance of generous financial support, reflected in a doubled salary, first-class hotel accommodations for his team on the road, and a pair of assistants, just like Rupp. He also brought his pregame rituals, including snacks of green Jell-O and oatmeal cookies for his players prior to taking the court. "The kids hated it," an unconcerned Mears said of the lime gelatin.

But Tennessee had one restriction that Mears had not previously encountered. "I recruited Black players," he said of his tenure at Wittenberg. "We won the national title with them. When I came down here, the athletic director said we can't recruit any Blacks. It sort of stunned me. I didn't know that. I took the job anyhow. It didn't make any difference to me. He said it was a league rule. It may not have been in writing: I don't know. I never saw it in writing. My AD told me you can't do it. So, I said, 'You're the AD.' That was Bowden Wyatt, who hired me. I just assumed he knew what he was talking about."

There was no written policy, just an understanding that SEC schools were located in states governed by laws and customs that prohibited the mixing of races. Racial separation extended even to opponents played outside the region. Thus, SEC basketball teams periodically went through the spectacle of withdrawing from games rather than face an opponent with an African American player.

Such was Tennessee's fate when the team traveled to McKeesport, Pennsylvania, on December 23, 1946, to play Duquesne. With a crowd of 2,600 waiting expectantly for the contest to begin, John Mauer protested that he could lose his job if the Dukes used center Chuck Cooper. Duquesne would not relent. "We do not bar anyone because of race, creed, or color," declared the chairman of the home team's athletic committee. "Therefore, we cannot jeopardize our principles by agreeing to Tennessee's demand."

The game was reported as a 2–0 forfeit by Tennessee, but the result does not appear in the records of either school. Cooper went on to become the first Black player drafted by an NBA team.

One might have expected better from Tennessee, a university located in a community that, on racial matters, was "a border city in its ways of thinking," according to *Diary of a Sit-In* by Merrill Proudfoot.

Blacks operated with caution in rural sections of the east Tennessee mountains. Winston-Salem State head coach Big House Gaines called the "hill country" a dangerous place; traveling through the region to games he employed a light-skinned bus driver and made sure that only a team manager went into restaurants to order food. But Knoxville, as large as Atlanta, Nashville, or New Orleans as the Civil War ended, was different. The city and surrounds never lent themselves to a slave- and cotton-based plantation economy—unlike the state's more westerly so-called grand divisions and most of the Deep South—and so had a modest Black population and a relatively tolerant racial climate. The region so differed from the rest of Tennessee, it harbored strong pro-Union sentiment during the Civil War.

Still, Knoxville was the site of a race riot in 1919, one of 26 in the United States during what became known as the "Red Summer," with the bloodiest disturbances in Chicago, Washington, D.C., and Elaine, Arkansas.

The federal government, with its nearby Tennessee Valley Authority and Oak Ridge Laboratories, had a leavening effect as the area's largest employer. "Segregation in Knoxville wore a polite face," Proudfoot wrote, a fact he admitted "made Knoxvillians extremely timid about suggesting changes in the inherited racial patterns." When change came, resistance was muted. Mayor John Duncan was publicly supportive of lunch counter protests in 1960 and made sure police protected demonstrators, the reverse of treatment accorded civil rights advocates, then and now. "A lot of people said, 'Well, you're going to politically cut your throat,'" Duncan said. "I said, I don't care if I do." Violence was averted, and Duncan went on to be elected to the U.S. House of Representatives.

Tennessee athletics, pressured by university administrators, did eventually emulate programs in border towns in its outreach to African Americans. UT trailed only Kentucky among SEC schools in signing a Black football player, Lester McClain, in 1967. The Vols in 1972 had one of the SEC's first starting Black quarterbacks, Condredge Holloway, later a Hall of Famer in the Canadian Football League. Only Maryland of the ACC beat the Volunteers to the punch in hiring a Black man to direct a major sports program at a historically white Southern school. Alumnus Wade Houston became Tennessee's head basketball coach in 1989; Maryland hired Bob Wade in 1986.

But Tennessee was no avid trailblazer, certainly not when Neyland ruled. Resistance to change was strong, and Vanderbilt's Perry Wallace and Louisiana State's Collis Temple remembered suffering race-based verbal abuse from Stokely Center fans.

The first three Black undergraduates enrolled at Tennessee under court order in January 1961. The following fall an African American, Avon Rollins, was among about two dozen players trying out for the freshman basketball squad. To that point, no other school in the SEC or ACC had breached the color barrier in a major sport, and few SEC student bodies had been integrated. Typical of press treatment at the time, the potential racial breakthrough attracted little notice beyond a small story in Knoxville's *News-Sentinel* under the unobtrusive headline "Austin High Guard Is Frosh Candidate." Knoxville's Austin High School was all Black. The article marking the start of 1961–62 basketball practice noted in its final paragraph that "Rollins is the first Negro to go out for an athletic team at U-T."

Rollins grew up in segregated Knoxville near the university campus. "The onliest [*sic*] thing I ever saw that was white in the school system was a piece of paper," he said. Among the first Black students to enroll at Tennessee, Rollins played intramural basketball with the Air Force ROTC and was sufficiently impressive to win encouragement from several people, including UT varsity coach John Sines, to go out for the school's freshman team.

"I tried out, and I was doing quite well," Rollins recalled. Neyland was among those who watched the closed-door sessions. The coach of Tennessee's undefeated 1951 football squad did not have a sympathetic reputation within Knoxville's Black community, according to Rollins, and was an unabashed critic of integration. That stance was reinforced when, while also serving as athletics director, he canceled a track meet in the spring of 1961 because a visiting team brought Black athletes.

Neyland made it clear, loudly and emphatically, he did not want an African American on the Tennessee basketball squad, either. "Neyland was very ruthless in terms of his verbalization, using the N-word," said Rollins, who for years ran Knoxville's Belk Cultural Exchange Center, which preserves and researches African American history and culture. A leader in the

Student Nonviolent Coordinating Committee (SNCC), Rollins died in 2014 and has a Knoxville highway overpass named in his honor.

Following Neyland's outburst at practice, Rollins was cut from the squad. As Robert T. Epling put it dryly in a 1994 PhD dissertation on the integration of Tennessee football, "After the reign of the venerable General Neyland as athletic director had come to an end in 1962, the University became more receptive to the idea of integrating sports."

Had Rollins stuck, he'd have reached the varsity the same year Mears launched Tennessee's transformation into the primary threat to Kentucky's SEC hegemony. For all the glitz, Mears was an intense, highly prepared, control-oriented coach. "You couldn't get him in a hurry," said Dick Davis, a Florida assistant. Mears relied on rigorous definition of roles and minimized mistakes. He employed unconventional alignments—a 1-3-1 offense and a matchup zone defense—to dictate tempo. "I have always felt that the unorthodox method of coaching, while controversial, is the most stimulating and successful," Mears wrote in a chapter on "Tennessee's Zone and Combination Defense" in a 1965 coaching compendium edited by Hardin McLane.

Motivational speeches and devices were integral to Mears's arsenal. Wil Cherry, assuming a gravelly voice, mimicked the coach's masterful use of the upcoming Kentucky Derby to spark his team prior to one game. "It's the greatest horse race in the world," he quoted Mears. "Not the biggest, but it's the greatest. And just imagine that steed, that big horse, he goes to the winner's circle, and they place that big bouquet of roses around the stallion's neck. That is the smell of victory." Mears then produced a rose. "Smell it! Can you smell it? The smell of victory!"

Mears appropriated the logo created for the 39th Infantry Regiment in World War II by Colonel Paddy Flint: "Anything, Anywhere, Anytime, Bar Nothing." Don Quixote, Miguel de Cervantes's knight-errant, was often mentioned. So was the thinking of football coach Vince Lombardi.

"He was fiery, demanding," said Kosmalski, the center. "Every little part of the game, any little thing that you could do that would better yourself, that would help you win, he was for." Mears conjured competitive squads with few prominent recruits until his later years, when he brought in New Yorkers Ernie Grunfeld, a white player from Queens, and Bernard King, a Black player from Brooklyn, and went to a fast-paced style dubbed "The Ernie and Bernie Show." Said former assistant Marty Morris, "We certainly didn't have six high-school All-Americans coming in every year like Kentucky did."

Mears's Vols averaged a handsome 19 wins per year. Tennessee never lost more than nine games in a season after his debut effort. His winning percentage was comparable to contemporaries John Wooden of UCLA and Dean Smith of North Carolina, both Hall of Famers. By 1967, Mears's fifth season, the Volunteers were alone in first place in the SEC. Their first league championship in more than two decades secured a number eight finish in the final Associated Press poll. Two other times Tennessee tied Kentucky for the league's top spot under Mears; in 10 of his last 14 seasons the Vols finished no lower than second in the conference. His record against UK was 15–15.

Mears coached at Tennessee for nearly a decade before Cherry and Robinson became the school's first Black varsity players, although the Vols came tantalizingly close to breaking the color barrier the same year the football program added running back Lester McClain. Spencer Haywood, a powerful 6-foot-8 inside player from Detroit, committed to Tennessee and came to Knoxville for three months in 1967, creating a hopeful stir. "He was fantastic," Mears said. "Our players were ecstatic. They thought they'd win a national title." The coach thought so, too. "We'd have been a frontrunner all those four years he was here."

But following Haywood's summer in the mountains, he failed to qualify for admission and departed for a Colorado junior college. The next summer, he led the 1968 U.S. Olympic team in scoring. Haywood spent a season at what is now University of Detroit Mercy, where he paced the nation in rebounding and was selected a unanimous first team All-American. Then he leaped to the pros, outraging college leaders by defying draft restrictions on undergraduates. Signed by the ABA's Denver Rockets, Haywood enjoyed a 13-year career in professional basketball.

A 6-foot-11 transfer from Cincinnati was next chosen to integrate the Tennessee program but ran afoul of the law and, like Haywood, never appeared as a Volunteer. That left it to Larry Robinson, a transfer from Ferrum College in Virginia, to become the first recruited African American to play at UT.

"They needed to have somebody who was going to break some barriers and somebody who would set some good examples," Morris said. Morris had been Robinson's coach at the junior college prior to joining Mears's staff. He and Robinson claimed their simultaneous arrival at Knoxville was coincidental. Mears was less certain. "We'd do anything," he said, laughing. "That's the reputation I probably got."

Robinson arrived at Tennessee in the fall of 1971 with two years of eligibility remaining, having used Ferrum as a bridge from the sequestered life of a Virginia sharecropper's son.

For Robinson, life centered around family and farm in an area where little had changed in the century since ancestors witnessed Robert E. Lee and his decimated Army of Northern Virginia run to ground by Ulysses Grant's Union troops. Lee's surrender in April 1865 at Appomattox Court House, a sylvan site now preserved as a national historic park, effectively marked the end of the Civil War. "A lot of people come through there," Robinson said. "It's in every history book, and most people like to come by and see it. If you grew up there, we just see it as 'The Surrender Grounds.'"

The passage of tourists and ancient armies was far less important to locals than the progress of the tobacco crop they tended and cured. Sometimes the annual fall opening of the all-Black rural school, with seven hundred students in grades kindergarten through 12, was delayed so children could finish bringing in the tobacco—picking leaves and helping to hang them in log curing barns. The work was strenuous, the food homegrown, the entertainments simple as the family demonstrated when a brother who had moved to New York brought his city wife for a visit. "She came down to Virginia for the first time, and he had her convinced that the black cows gave the chocolate milk," Robinson said. "We had lots of fun with her."

The Robinsons' four-bedroom home was a center of constant activity. "There was always a yard full of kids at our house," said Robinson, the 11th of 15 children. "Our house was usually the gathering house, because I had brothers and sisters with kids my age. They lived around. Then you've got cousins and nephews and friends and that sort of stuff." Ballgames were common around the yard, baseball the favored sport.

Robinson did not take up basketball until the summer following the eighth grade, when the coach at Carver Price High School helped erect a hoop and a board on a pole in the family yard. By then Robinson was at least six feet tall, among the tallest students at his school. But shyness, as well as a sense of responsibility for helping the family earn its livelihood, threatened to keep Robinson from joining the basketball squad. The farm boy admittedly was daunted by the prospect of getting onto a basketball court wearing the abbreviated basketball shorts of the era. "It wasn't that big a deal once I understood what the culture was," Robinson said. A man who projects a sense of assurance and strength, he was not eager to discuss this subject. "I don't recall being in public in short pants up to that time. You just didn't do it. It was awkward. You're running around in short pants? Are you kidding me?"

Robinson did join the basketball team, and with his quickness, work ethic, and large hands evolved into a star. He also pitched and played first base, shortstop, and outfield on the baseball squad. He was good enough to try out for the Pittsburgh Pirates prior to his senior season. He ran track, and played tackle, fullback, flanker, and wingback on a football team that once lost 63–0. "Football wasn't our strong suit," Robinson said of a core group of players at their small school. They were good at basketball, though, making the segregated district playoffs Robinson's junior and senior years. An all-state performer, in consecutive playoff games his senior season Robinson scored 50 points, 46, and 44.

He was recruited by moderate-profile schools in the region such as William and Mary, Catawba, Richmond, and Virginia Tech but chose to attend Ferrum, where he had previously gone to summer basketball camp. Robinson regarded his two years at the school of about 1,200 students as "developmental time, a kind of spread-your-wings-but-not-too-far kind of thing." His wingspan proved impressive—Robinson averaged double figures in points and rebounds, made junior college All-American, was selected by the faculty for the "Catlin Award" for outstanding citizenship, and was voted "Mr. Ferrum" as the premier male student at the predominantly white school.

He also impressed coach Marty Morris with his dedication to self-betterment. "He was sort of an Abraham Lincoln sitting at the table by the candlelight," Morris said. "You could just tell that he had a burning desire for an education to improve himself."

Robinson, the big man on the Ferrum team at 6-foot-5, excelled in Morris's up-tempo, trapping system. Ferrum averaged more than 100 points per game and reached the national junior college playoffs, where its lack of frontcourt height proved fatal.

Out of junior college Robinson attracted attention from larger schools, among them Pepperdine, Marshall, Clemson, and Virginia. He went with Tennessee. "He was an easy one to recruit. He was a nice boy and a good student," Mears said.

"I was just comfortable," Robinson explained. "I came and hung out with the guys. We went around campus, it seemed to be a comfortable place.

It was far enough away from home that I could do my own thing. Then again, it wasn't too far away from home."

Robinson knew his arrival for the 1971–72 season signaled change, a topic he and Mears did not explore. Breaking barriers was not something Robinson discussed readily, then or later. Even the term "pioneer" made the calm man squirm. He accepted the label reluctantly, "in that obviously being a pioneer kind of has the connotation of being the first and leading in opening the door." But he shrugged off any suggestion that he played a special or significant role in breaking a racial barrier.

"I didn't feel any extra responsibility," he said. "I took it as a responsibility to be a solid citizen. Just kind of like what my dad had told me. That didn't matter whether I was at Tennessee or Appomattox. Just be a solid citizen, and let your actions that you demonstrate speak for you and speak for your family. I think that's the way I approached it, and hopefully it worked out OK."

Kosmalski, who said Robinson "was probably the closest guy I was with (during) my four years" at Tennessee, remembered his friend enduring a more painful process.

The big man played with numerous African Americans at home in Cleveland, Ohio, and was surprised to find a different situation at Tennessee. "Being in the South, I thought it would be more prevalent, having Black players on teams, because they are more prevalent in the South," Kosmalski said. He and Cherry, a point guard, played together on the freshman squad. Then, while Cherry rode the bench their sophomore year, Kosmalski started alongside Robinson in the frontline. Calling themselves "the chairmen of the boards," the tall pair stuck together at home and on the road, leaving arenas prior to games to walk outside and share thoughts in the cold. "He was soft-spoken," Kosmalski said. "Just a genuinely nice guy. Would do anything for you."

Race was among the topics the friends discussed, although Kosmalski "had to pry it out of [Robinson] because he wouldn't say a whole lot." Just as the Ohioan shared a certain naïveté about race with whites such as Indianan Fred Cox (Ole Miss) and Pennsylvanian Dan Bonner (Virginia), so Robinson quietly endured the sense of isolation that Vanderbilt pioneer Perry Wallace and North Carolina's Charles Scott reported. "He would feel lonely, a kind of outsider," Kosmalski recalled. "I said I hoped I didn't make him feel that way. He told me I didn't. That would have to be tough."

Kosmalski once accompanied his friend into a Mississippi shop to get a shoeshine, only to be rebuffed by the proprietor. The man told Robinson, "We like Blacks, but we don't shine their shoes." Robinson said the incident took place on a trip to Starkville to face Mississippi State. "We just left. I've told a few people since then, but I didn't tell any of the coaches or anybody. I just went on and played." Kosmalski recalled the venue as Oxford, the opponent as Ole Miss, the language as coarser, and Robinson's reaction as far less matter-of-fact. "Rob took a step forward, and I grabbed his arm. He knew better than that. I felt angry for him and embarrassed for him. He was very quiet after that. I remember it like it was yesterday. I felt hurt. I knew him enough to know he was hurt."

Robinson let his work on the basketball court provide a more eloquent rebuttal than anything words offered, as his father would have wanted. "You never hear much about him but he seems to handle whatever job he's given," Mississippi State coach Kermit Davis told Marvin West of Knoxville's *News-Sentinel*. "He is one of the most underrated players in the Southeastern Conference."

Recognition came Robinson's way his senior season. He was elected team captain and voted both Tennessee's most valuable player and third team All-SEC. Mears praised him as an exceptional leader who effectively performed "unspectacular" but essential tasks without complaint. "The coach knows his team wouldn't be where it is as SEC leader if Robinson had not been so brilliant and so consistent," F. M. Williams wrote in Nashville's *Tennessean* before UT faded to second. "He is the man, says Mears, who has taken charge every time the Vols have gotten into serious trouble."

The forward notched a double-figure scoring average and led Tennessee in rebounding both years he was on the varsity. "I've never seen anybody take the ball off the glass as softly," Cherry said. "It was like cotton. I mean, he had a touch." A tough defender, Robinson "took the challenge of the best player and tried to stop him," publicist Bud Ford said. Robinson played so hard, teammate Rodney Woods confessed, that he "started asking myself if I was trying as hard as Larry Robinson was trying. I got to wondering if I was giving as much of me as he was giving."

Tennessee finished tied with Kentucky for first place when Robinson was a junior, finished tied for second when he was a senior. He appeared in every game the Vols played in each of those seasons.

"He was a great rebounder and a good scorer," Mears said. "He was good enough to make all-league but not good enough to be All-American.

He helped us the way he played." Mears designated certain players as shoot-ers and expected others to defer; Robinson fell into the latter category. "Some guys were more of the rebounders," Robinson said, calling to mind the role that Maryland's Billy Jones played more reluctantly. "In his system, I wasn't designated as the shooter, which was neither here nor there. If there was a shot and I was open, I was free to take it. I think you just buy into those kind of philosophies . . . He never told me that you couldn't shoot."

Kosmalski, with his sweet jump hook, led the team in scoring and made All-SEC each year on the varsity. Guards Mike Edwards and John Snow also had favored offensive status. Robinson accepted a supportive role, probably more than he should have, in retrospect. "I know I gave up some offense or some stuff that I could have done, making sure I was getting the other play-ers in the position to do what they could do," Robinson said. "There wasn't a player on the team, and they'll tell you, that one-on-one, that I couldn't defeat. But in the team concept, that wasn't what we were about."

The blend player was chosen in the 16th round of the 1973 NBA draft by Philadelphia. (There are two rounds today.) Cherry thought his team-mate's failure to develop a better offensive profile doomed his chances at a fruitful basketball career. "Maybe I was just a little out of touch with real-ity," the playmaker said. "I used to encourage Larry to shoot. Larry should have been one of the leading scorers for us. He wasn't the go-to guy. Larry, he was a junk man, scrap man. Rebound what you got off the boards, what you got off the floor. Larry had one of the softest touches."

Rather than chase a longshot NBA career, Robinson accepted a tryout offer from football's Dallas Cowboys. He fashioned a two-year career as a special teams' player under coach Tom Landry, then returned to serve briefly as an assistant football coach at Tennessee. These days he is recog-nized as "the first black ever to play varsity basketball for the Vols," as Ben Byrd wrote in his book *The Basketball Vols*. Ford, longtime keeper of Ten-nessee's basketball records, likewise credited Robinson. "We relate to the scholarship player we signed," he said.

The official version of events was blind to the fact that Cherry, another African American and a lifelong resident of Tennessee, first took the court at the same moment Robinson did. A simple glance at a team photograph from the 1971–72 season, when the Vols were SEC cochampions, reveals two Black players in the back row. Next to an assistant coach and a manager on the left side stood Larry Robinson, number 55. Next to an assistant and a manager on the right stood Wilbert Cherry, number 31.

"It's like an admission ticket, and I paid the price," said an aggrieved Cherry, who wore a championship ring from that '72 season. "I dare anybody to try to bastardize the history of that and take that away from me. I paid for it. I earned it, and a portrait that reflects anything other than that is nothing but a damned lie. The truth will stand when a lie will fail. Whoever the naysayers are, to them I say, 'Bullshit!' That's another reason why Wil Cherry does have an attitude. I'm a right-thinking person. I'm a fair-minded person. I don't give anybody crap, and I take no crap off anybody. That doesn't sit well with a lot of people."

Cherry was convinced that his lack of recognition, his inability to beat out a white guard of comparable ability, and Robinson's subservient role in Mears's system all pointed to a racial subtext. And who could tell? "You hear people say that I don't see color. I saw it. I had to watch how I conducted myself at all times. But, at the same time, I would step further out. If there was a place for a Black man to be, I stayed further away from that place than Larry would ever stride because my place, in my thinking, is anybody's place."

Cherry spent his early years in Dayton, Tennessee. The town 82 miles southwest of Knoxville hosted the famous John Thomas Scopes "Monkey Trial" in 1925, a major battle in the enduring rearguard action against the theory of evolution. The Cherrys moved when Wil was five. His father's work for TVA took the eight-child family to Morristown, about a half-hour drive northeast of Knoxville. There Black children mingled freely with whites, up to a point. The movie theater was segregated, with Blacks relegated to the balcony, and so was the public swimming pool across the street from the Cherrys' house. "The bottom was painted blue and just looked so cool," Wil Cherry said. "And the water would sit there sometimes, and you just watch the people enjoy that cool water and you ask, 'Why can't we do that?' 'Well, you just can't, son.'"

That sense of hurtful exclusion arose frequently in populous, segregated areas, where proximity provided African Americans with vivid examples of the privileges reserved for whites. Perry Wallace recalled walking past three white schools on the way to his elementary school in Nashville. One was North High School, where on Friday nights the football games were clearly visible but off-limits to Blacks who lived nearby. Wallace, the SEC icebreaker, said the experience exemplified the damage segregation could do to a person's psyche.

"We sat there watching North High play football, but what we were also doing was watching white America from the other side of a fence. Not in the arena, unable literally to go in, and if you didn't watch it, that would shift your view of yourself and your position in America and where you stood as a human being. Here we were, going up to the grocery store to buy some sodas, and some Cracker Jacks, and some baloney and cheese and crackers, then sitting to watch the game. To in effect watch a world that was going on that looked big and shiny, all in lights, people were there and they were doing dates and doing bands and all of that. And here we were on the side, just some little colored people. I guess I'm saying, whether anyone wants to admit it or not, that can be defining unless you do something about that."

Cherry, younger than Wallace, took advantage of integration's first trickle through the membrane of separation while still in public school. He was the first Black basketball player at his junior high in Morristown and among a handful of Blacks at the high school he attended when the family moved to Knoxville. He thrived on being popular and visible and accomplished, on being "the bomb," as he put it. Sports participation brought special treatment, and he liked it. "The athletic experience is wonderful," Cherry said, frequently punctuating his remarks with laughter. "It opens doors. It softens attitudes. It changes attitudes. You're not like the rest of us. You're different."

The point guard and captain of the basketball team in high school, Cherry was president of the junior class, participated in the choir, acted. "I'm a damn good ballplayer," he said. He cited his quickness, "great vision," determination, ball-handling ability, selflessness, and long-range shooting ability. "I was the man, but I wasn't a selfish player. It was about winning the game." But his high-school coach thought the all-regional guard was not good enough to play in the SEC, and recruiting feelers appeared to substantiate that assessment.

Cherry, intent on defying doubters and on following his girlfriend ("Let's have some truth here," he said), enrolled at Tennessee. Nine years after Avon Rollins, with no Blacks yet on the UT roster, he went out for the freshman basketball squad. "The gym was full," he said of tryout day. He does not recall the presence of any other African Americans. "There may have been others, but your focus is on doing what you can do. I didn't care who was there. I just wanted to play a little ball."

The 5-foot-11 guard caught the eye of freshman coach A. W. Davis, a first team All-American in 1965 known in Tennessee circles as "The Man with the Golden Arm." Davis "let me play a lot," Cherry said. "Coach Davis liked me. That's why I got invited to go over to the varsity."

Kosmalski, a freshman teammate, recalled Cherry as "fun-loving, personable, very quick. Nice guy." Cherry appeared in most of the team's games as a first-year. He tried about two shots per contest and averaged 2.5 points. The highlight of his season was a 12-point effort against the talent-rich Kentucky junior varsity.

Cherry joined the varsity in 1971–72. "People used to yell for Cherry," he recalled. "They loved me. They did." Playing for Tennessee "was a wonderful experience," he said. "Even as a practice player, it's still one of the greatest experiences of my life."

The '72 season ended with Tennessee and Kentucky tied for first. The Vols had a chance to win the title outright at home in the final regular season game, but Edwards, their best free throw shooter, missed a potentially decisive one-and-one attempt with five seconds to go. UK got the league's single NCAA invitation. Several disappointed regulars voted not to accept an NIT bid, and the season was over.

Cherry got into four games that year, among them the opening rout of the visiting Anteaters of the University of California-Irvine. That was the night he ran onto the Stokely floor with Larry Robinson as the Volunteers first appeared as a racially integrated unit. By then, every ACC program and the majority of the SEC had already broken the color barrier.

"He was there when I got there," Robinson said of Cherry. "Nice guy. Had some skills. I think his size was a problem. After his sophomore year, I think he left the team."

Mears was cut from his Miami of Ohio basketball squad as a senior after the school made a coaching change. "The experience taught me that you can't always be a winner, and I think that helped me in later years when it came to dealing with adversity," Mears told author Ben Byrd. He had no compunction about cutting Cherry following the '72 season. "Wilbert Cherry was just another ballplayer for us," the coach said. "He was a walk-on, good for a walk-on. Didn't start. He hustled a lot for us. Good man to have on the ballclub."

Neither coach nor player remembered the reason Cherry was dropped from the team. Cherry had sacrificed to make time for basketball, even as he worked to support himself and pursued a degree in business administration. He recalled feeling stunned when told the bad news in Mears's office. "I was just very hurt and very shocked," he said.

Cherry's wounded feelings endured as he earned his degree, worked for TVA, and became an attorney in Knoxville. A photograph of Cherry in his

Tennessee jersey hung in his law office bearing the number 31. That matched his jersey numeral in a team photograph, but the shorts showed the number 33. Mention of the incongruity rekindled his anger. "That was crap. I didn't want my picture taken with two different numbers. Damn it! That was an indignity."

He counted as a further indignity the continued recognition of Robinson, and Robinson alone, for crossing the color line at Tennessee basketball.

"I've heard him say that," Robinson said. "I don't get involved in that. Was he on scholarship? I think what most people say, I've heard them say the first scholarship player, basketball player, at UT. I know he has some heartaches about that. I always tell him . . . let's just move on. It's not going to change anything. It's not going to make any difference. Let's just move on."

CHAPTER 16
LATER GATORS

Steve Williams, University of Florida, 1970-74
Malcolm Meeks, University of Florida, 1970-72

---

*It would be interesting to know what it is men are most afraid of. Taking a new step, uttering
a new word is what they fear most.*

Fyodor Dostoyevsky, *Crime and Punishment*

The addition of African Americans to previously all-white Southern collegiate athletic programs doubtless would have occurred eventually without
pressure from outside, if only for competitive reasons. Yet, clearly, a generation of whites accustomed to racial exclusion was in no hurry to make significant changes.

Federal power in 21st-century America is often wielded to reduce constraints on corporations and institutions, in distinct contrast with the role
played in the 1960s and early 1970s when a spate of legislation was enacted
to protect individual and collective rights. Armed back then with tools such
as the Civil Rights Act of 1964 and Title IX of the Education Amendments
of 1972, federal authority was applied to challenge a status quo that systematically denied opportunity to Blacks, women, the handicapped, and the
elderly.

Movement was not achieved in many cases until the threat of losing federal funds caught the attention of university administrators. "The U.S. Office
of Education thinks it is about time some Negro athletes, especially football
players, start showing up on grant-in-aid lists," Jim Minter wrote in the
Atlanta Journal and Constitution in 1967. To which an unnamed SEC official
responded, "They'll be telling us what to do on fourth down and two next."

Publicly SEC commissioner Arthur "Tonto" Coleman contradicted
repeated assertions of racial prohibitions by the likes of Kentucky coach

Adolph Rupp and Tennessee athletics director Bowden Wyatt by insisting there were no constraints on signing players based on race. "I have never heard any school say they wouldn't give an athletic scholarship to any person academically and athletically qualified," Coleman said. "My office makes no distinction as to race on the scholarship blank."

Of course, silent practice and public posture were two different matters.

The University of Florida, which accepted its first Black undergraduates in 1962, exemplified the difference. Two years after desegregating the student body, there were only 20 Black undergrads, the school had not even hired Black clerical staff, Black grounds workers were barred from riding in the cabs of university trucks, and the school's hospital remained segregated. Five years after the Gainesville campus was integrated, of 19,000 Florida students, only 80 were African American. No Blacks were in athletics, fraternities, sororities, student government, or other student organizations.

Joel Buchanan, an early Black undergraduate whose father was the head cook in the school cafeteria, said "you didn't feel safe" at Florida. "Certain parts of campus, you didn't go," said Buchanan. "The average Black came on campus, went to class, and left." Another Black undergrad from Jacksonville, Florida, told the *Florida Alligator*, the student newspaper, in November 1967, "High school advisors tell us not to come to UF if we want to go to an integrated school."

Florida A&M, a historically Black public university in Tallahassee, established a faculty committee charged with making exceptions for applicants who "demonstrate the ability to do successful work in the college classroom." The University of Florida, in contrast, asserted that it could find few African Americans qualified for admission and trailed all Florida public universities in its percentage of enrolled Black students. As late as spring semester 1970, Florida was admonished by federal authorities for its weak Black student recruitment efforts, its failure to hire full-time Black faculty, and for the fact that all 151 "persons with authority to initiate personnel actions" on campus were white.

Leaders frequently set the tone for the institutions they direct. Recruiting African American athletes "never came up" in discussions with superiors, said Tommy Bartlett, Florida's head basketball coach from 1966 to 1973. "I never had any conversation from the athletic director or the president that we had to have Black players."

Steve Williams and Malcolm Meeks joined the basketball program as its first Black players in the fall of 1970. Three years earlier, Stephen C.

O'Connell took office as president of the University of Florida. O'Connell, an alumnus and former boxer for the Gators, had previously served on the state supreme court. His judicial election in 1956 marked the first time a Catholic won a statewide race in Florida. O'Connell joined a supreme court majority that invoked the discredited principle of interposition, then claimed desegregation would cause "great public mischief" and defied federal court orders allowing a Black applicant to enter the University of Florida Law School. "He shared that he did what was right for the period of time," said Buchanan, who assisted O'Connell during his presidency. The law school was desegregated in 1958.

As UF president, O'Connell and his white dean of university relations, who doubled as chief officer in charge of minority affairs, flatly refused to resign from the segregated Gainesville Golf and Country Club. O'Connell also parsed language rather than face the issue when objections were raised to playing "Dixie" at halftime of football games, when "everyone stood as though it were the national anthem," according to a history of the university by Samuel Proctor and Wright Langley. Defending the song, O'Connell said he could find "no inflammatory racist statement within its traditional lyrics," ignoring the symbolic meaning.

During O'Connell's first year as president, concerns about the slow pace of desegregation at the University of Florida drew federal civil rights investigators. "Among other things, the investigators will ask why there are no Negroes attending the university under athletic grants-in-aid, and why there are no Negro students living in university dormitories," reported the *Tampa Tribune-Times*. All 300 athletic scholarships were held by whites, as were all 8,000 student assignments in campus dorms. To be fair, Florida State University, until 1947 the Florida State College for Women, was marginally better that winter of 1968, with 3 African Americans among 334 scholarship athletes and 38 Blacks living in its dorms.

The specter of civil rights troubles sparked a spate of internal memoranda within a Florida athletics department run by football coach/AD Ray Graves. Coaches were asked to report the details of their efforts "recruiting colored athletes." The word use in the memos was itself revealing of attitudes at the university. The Black power movement was ascendent by that time, and it was no secret that African Americans seeking respectful treatment bridled at being called colored. Yet that wording was employed by the department, coaches, and others. What's more, as the Tampa newspaper article indicated, a respectful rendering of the term "Negro" required that it be capitalized, a battle that Blacks fought since the turn of the 20th century. Yet memos from two men who would later recruit pioneering Black players to Florida, track coach Jimmy Carnes and basketball assistant Dick Davis, referred to "negro" athletes.

Carnes landed the school's first Black scholarship athlete, long jumper Ron Coleman, in May 1968. The following December the football program brought in a pair of Black players, and in the spring of 1970, basketball signed Williams and Meeks.

Coleman, who attended an integrated high school, vividly recalled the first time he walked into Florida's athletic dining facility. He was the only Black person present not in a service capacity, and upon his appearance the room crowded with football players hushed in a hurry. "They're all looking and they're all not saying anything," Coleman said. "OK. I'm a high-school graduate. I can read that much body language. I sit down at my own table, and I'm about to eat when, all of a sudden, from behind me, over my right shoulder, obviously coming from the end of the line there's a huge shadow. Huge shadow! I'm going, oh, boy, I never thought I'd die while I was sitting at this table eating." The shadow belonged to defensive end Jack Youngblood, a future NFL Hall of Famer. "He goes, 'Mind if I sit down?'"

Youngblood's gesture of acceptance, reminiscent of football coach Bear Bryant sharing a snack with Alabama pioneer Wendell Hudson, dissipated any hostility directed toward Coleman. "From that day on, I never had a problem with any particular athletes at the University of Florida," he said.

Ordinary Black students were not so fortunate when assigned dorm rooms with whites during that same 1968–69 academic year. "My first roommate moved out in about 60 seconds," an African American told the *Florida Alligator*. "He almost broke his neck trying to get out the door." Whites were apologetic about their aversion to sharing a room with a Black person but undeterred in their avoidance. "My mother didn't want to write to all my relatives that I had a colored roommate," a freshman explained of her departure. A sophomore admitted she was "shocked" when she saw her roommate. "I almost cried. It's the last thing you expect . . . I really wanted to stick it out. She's just as much a human being as I am."

Bigotry and lack of understanding were surprisingly prevalent in Florida, contradicting popular impressions of the South's most urbanized state after Texas. "Florida, in fact, has had a long and troubled history in the area of race relations," Raymond A. Mohl and Gary R. Mormino wrote in *The New History of Florida*, published in 1996. "In the past, the legitimacy of its role as a 'real' southern state was the subject of frequent debate, but the history of race relations in Florida leaves little doubt as to the answer."

Ron Coleman was raised in Ocala, about equidistant from Gainesville and Orlando in northcentral Florida. "When I was growing up in Ocala, a big deal was a fire truck going down the street," Coleman said fondly of the quiet, nearly crime-free community. The city and its surroundings accommodated nearly 62,000 residents in 1969, and held about 366,000 in 2019. Small as Ocala was, Coleman recalled stern warnings from his parents, who'd seen racial violence firsthand, about the dangers lurking at the periphery of his pleasant world. "They said, 'Boy, everybody thinks Florida's sunshine, tourists, la, la, la, la. But, let me tell you, son, it's bad out in those woods. And it wasn't just out in those woods. It's just all around, right here in Marion County. You just have to be careful, and you can't just do things rambunctiously.'"

Florida, particularly the Panhandle nearest Georgia and Alabama, long endured a rate of lynching that rivaled the Mississippi Delta, the Georgia piedmont, and the other most violent reaches of the Deep South.

Florida led all states with a rate of 79.8 lynchings per 100,000 Blacks between 1882 through 1930, as reported by the Southern Commission on the Study of Lynching. Next-closest was Mississippi at 52.8 lynchings per 100,000 Black people. From 1900 through 1930, Florida's rate of lynchings per 10,000 Blacks (4.5) was nearly double that of any other state and included the leveling of the town of Rosewood in 1923. "Many of the lynchers were unquestionably former Klansmen or sons of Klansmen, but no hoods were required in those days when local lawmen either led the mobs or stood aside and granted them free rein," said Michael Newton in *The Invisible Empire, The Ku Klux Klan in Florida.*

The KKK—anti-Black, anti-Jewish, and anti-Catholic—operated more openly in Florida than in other supposedly moderate Southern states. Emblematically, in 1924 a Catholic priest active in local theater in Gainesville was abducted by three Klansmen, then severely beaten and castrated before being dumped on the steps of a church in another town. Two of his attackers were later identified as Gainesville's mayor and chief of police. No one was prosecuted for the crime.

Mainstream politicians did not shy from the Klan. George Smathers, running for the U.S. Senate from Florida in 1950 against Claude Pepper, accepted KKK support and offered free legal services "to any Florida lawman charged with brutalizing Blacks," Newton wrote. "If this were not enough, Smathers made further headway with his rural audiences by deliberately playing on their ignorance, attacking Pepper as 'a shameless extrovert' who 'practiced celibacy' before marriage and whose sister was 'once a thespian in wicked New York.'" The following year was Florida's first in modern times without a recorded lynching. Instead, state NAACP leader and voting rights advocate Harry T. Moore and his wife, Henriette, were murdered, their house dynamited on Christmas evening. Klan members were strongly suspected, but no one was ever arrested.

As late as 1952, the Grand Dragon of the Klan was invited to address the Florida Sheriffs' Association.

Consistent with its racial landscape, Florida's official reaction when the U.S. Supreme Court mandated an end to segregation in 1954 largely matched that of its Southern brethren. All but two of its 10 congressmen signed the "Southern Manifesto" denouncing the *Brown* decision, and the governor declared that Florida was "just as determined as any other Southern state to maintain segregation." Defying both federal law and "its reputation as a liberal Southern state," as one history put it, Florida established a new, segregated community college system in 1957. The University of Florida and Florida State, the state's most prominent public institutions of higher learning, did not integrate their undergraduate ranks until 1962. That year, only 648 of Florida's 242,097 Black public-school students attended class with whites.

Steve Williams's experience was typical. Growing up in Pensacola near the western terminus of the Panhandle, he had no white classmates until 1969–70, his senior year at Booker T. Washington High School. There was some informal contact across racial lines, primarily via pickup basketball games. "We never played with a white kid before," Williams said. "Well, that didn't matter. We played ball, and if you could play ball, you were OK with us."

Mostly, though, Williams operated within segregation's circumscribed boundaries. Blacks were prohibited from using Pensacola Beach, so Sundays during warm weather were spent at a stretch of Gulf coast reserved for Blacks where Williams and his older brother bobbed in inner tubes and ate hot dogs and hamburgers that their grandmother and aunt grilled. Williams could shop at Newberry's and the other chain stores downtown, free to spend money on clothes and other items, but could not visit the lunch counter for a snack or use water fountains designated for whites only.

Williams nevertheless spoke well of his youth in Pensacola, where his grandmother, Myrtle Brown, raised him after his parents divorced. Among the gifts Williams most appreciated was the message from family and community that, despite the constraints of segregation, there were no limits to what he could achieve. "I always remember them instilling in us you can be anything you want to be. That's the one thing about the segregated schools, is that they pounded that into our heads, that you can be anything that you want to be. You can remember signs that say, 'Without an education, you'll always be called a boy.' Those are the ones that really stuck: You can be anything you want to be."

Williams, later an assistant principal at Howard W. Blake High School in Tampa, aspired to become a good basketball player. The seed was planted in the fifth grade when he began accompanying his aunt, head of Washington High's math department, to sell tickets at ballgames. Some friends with whom he watched those games subsequently formed the nucleus of a potent high school basketball squad that went 31–1 in Williams's senior year, capturing a state championship.

Williams, a 6-foot-1 wing, and Lawrence McCray, 6-foot-11, starred on an integrated team that won all but four games by at least 17 points. "We were special. It was a sight for sore eyes," Williams said of the squad. Many years after he finished school, he is still recognized by strangers in Pensacola because of his high-school playing exploits. "It was really something special for everyone. A lot of schools were having racial problems. We did not have a problem, and I think that basketball team had something to do with it, just pulled everybody together. Now, a few years down the road, they did have some racial problems here, but that one year, that first year, everything was smooth sailing."

Williams and McCray, named Florida's "Mr. Basketball," decided to attend college together. The pair went through the recruiting process in tandem, and narrowed their choices to three schools—Alabama, Florida, and Florida State.

Alabama was the third choice, a finalist because of coach C. M. Newton. "If there's a greater guy in the world, I don't know him," Williams said. During that period, the Crimson Tide paced Southern schools in assembling Black players. Florida State and coach Hugh Durham, similarly noted for a roster packed with African Americans, appealed to McCray. "The man offered Steve a lot of money," Williams's grandmother said of the FSU coach, "but he didn't fall for that." Durham did incur a three-year probation for recruiting violations, but followed by taking the independent school to the 1972 NCAA championship game with McCray as a starter. That '72 squad, led by Black Louisville Central High products Otto Perry and All-American Ron King, handed Adolph Rupp the last loss of his 41-year career at the University of Kentucky.

Florida appealed most to Williams, twice an all-state selection. The Gators, too, were enjoying a successful run. Norm Sloan posted three straight winning seasons prior to leaving for NC State. His successor, Tommy Bartlett, a former Ray Mears assistant at Tennessee, posted three more successful years from 1967 to 1969 with teams built around All-American center Neal Walk. The 1967 squad finished second in the SEC, best at Florida since 1941. The 1969 team was invited to the National Invitation Tournament, the first postseason appearance in school history.

Dick Davis, Bartlett's chief assistant, did not recall pursuing any Black players in their early years coaching at Florida. "We didn't even think about it when we first came here," he said. "Number one, it hadn't been done. Number two, nobody said anything about it." When the Gators did look for Black athletes, it was on their home turf, the largest state east of the Mississippi River but with minimal popular interest in basketball. Half the schools in the ACC integrated their programs with players imported from other states. SEC schools stayed home, either because it was less trouble and expense or because they placed greater emphasis on mining untapped local talent. Of ten conference members, only Georgia and Tennessee went beyond their borders.

"We felt like that, because we were a state university, we wanted the first Black player to be from this state," Davis said. "We knew that we had to get a player first that could play. Second, he had to be academically sound. And, third, we felt like we needed to get a guy that would blend in with our team and be coachable and have an opportunity to graduate."

Florida's coaches, like many SEC staffs, also believed the first African American must be an impact player. "Remember now, you're talking about the sixties," Davis said. "You know what the world was like in the sixties. We didn't want any problems with anybody saying, 'Well, you've just got a guy sitting on the bench as a token that ain't going to play.'"

An alumnus tipped Bartlett's staff to Williams and McCray as prospects able to meet Florida's academic standards. "We also found out that they had a heck of a basketball team," Davis said of Pensacola Washington, "and so we went up there and we found out, these guys are pretty good. So, we went back and back and back and back and back and back. At one time we thought we were going to get both of them, and we tried and tried and tried."

McCray was the plum of the pair in the coaches' estimation. "Of course, we would rather have had him," Bartlett said. "We wanted them both, and if we had to pick, I'd have to be crazy not to take the 6-10 guy who could really play." When McCray went elsewhere, Florida took Williams and Malcolm Meeks, a lesser-known wing from Daytona Beach on the Atlantic coast. Uncertain how the white players would react, "we felt like we needed to recruit two Blacks," Davis said. "Back in those days, I could say, 'Tony, you're going to room with Steve.' What if Tony said, 'No, I don't want to'? I didn't have a clue."

The coaches avoided that modest test of their resolve and authority by having Meeks and Williams room together. "He was a nice guy, a really nice guy," Williams said of Meeks. "He was a hard worker. Just energy galore. On the basketball floor, I've never seen anybody play harder than Malcolm Meeks. Boy, he played hard!"

Meeks averaged 13 points and 14 rebounds his senior season at Mainland High School, where his team won the Metro Conference championship. Known for his leaping ability, the 6-3 Meeks was named an honorable mention high-school All-American. "He was a good kid, but he wasn't a first-teamer in the SEC," Bartlett said of Meeks.

Williams was the better player, averaging 15 points and seven rebounds as a high-school senior. He described himself as no more than an average student, however. "I did enough to get where I was trying to go," said the player nicknamed "Grump" in high school "because I was always quiet." He placed his primary emphasis on learning the game he loved. He qualified for admission to Florida anyway. Under the circumstances, he wondered if the assertion that the school's standards were more stringent than competing institutions was an excuse to delay recruiting African Americans.

Despite those suspicions, and the coaches' clear preference for McCray, Williams said they "made me feel they wanted me." So did the handful of other Black athletes at Florida, one of the nation's largest state universities and a famed party school. Football pioneers Leonard George and Willie Jackson showed Williams the campus and town. He attended a number of football games and got a glimpse of the legendary campus swimming pools thronged with scantily clad coeds.

Overall students, faculty, and boosters were welcoming at a school where many fraternities still flew Confederate flags well into the 1970s.

Coleman, the athletic program's racial icebreaker, said it was easy to accept Williams. "He had this scholarly demeanor. I don't know what that is, but he had it. He didn't appear to be the jock or the star athlete that he apparently was in high school. He was rather unassuming, quiet, not boastful and arrogant."

Coleman added, "Steve to me was just a role model. He was just a living role model. He was a guy that, you know, that you could emulate and not have a problem if you followed him. He was that kind of guy. Some folks are just full of air. This guy was true; he was sweet."

Meeks struck Coleman as the more overtly confident of the pair, if only as a facade. "Malcolm seemed to exude it a bit more in his walk, in his talk, in his appearance. He knew what he could do on the court, but it seemed like he wasn't as comfortable off the court as Steve was. Maybe not as well-rounded or something like that. You could tell a difference. But when they got on the court, it was head-to-head. We're ballplayers, we're playing some ball. They were both good."

Black athletes tended to stick close to campus in those early years of integration, and for good reason. "It was known that there's certain places you don't go, certain things you don't do without expecting some kind of problem or trouble or interference," Coleman said of Gainesville.

Charles Chestnut III, a longtime local civil rights leader, was born in Gainesville in 1940. During his youth, Gainesville was a typical Southern town where limits for African Americans were well-defined. "You knew where to go, and you knew how far to go in this community and where not to be caught after 6 p.m. or after dark. You best be back on this side of town."

Those strictures included avoiding the University of Florida campus at night, much as was the case all day at the University of South Carolina at Columbia, and steering clear of white females altogether. Chestnut, a contemporary of Emmett Till, often went on his own to the corner grocery. He recalled vividly when that privilege was revoked. He was about twelve and exchanged smiles and pleasantries with the white girl his age who rang up his purchases. He returned several days later with his grandmother. "We ended up in the same line, and the girl smiles at me and bowed her head and said, 'Hi,' and I smiled and said 'Hi' back. My grandmother wouldn't let me go in that store any more. She was afraid that something was going to happen to me. That was her mind-set, and it was based upon experience; it was based upon the life she had lived."

During the early sixties Chestnut was among a handful of college-educated Black men who challenged the segregation of Gainesville's downtown commercial establishments, as well as the perceived passivity of their elders in the face of discrimination. Change was slow and sometimes accompanied by violence. A white mob attacked protestors trying to integrate the Florida Theater in June 1963, leaving one person shot and two beaten. Militance that demonstrators displayed shocked whites taken in by the propaganda of racism, which held since slavery that Blacks were satisfied with their inferior status.

Chestnut said unrest that pitted whites against the established order in May 1972 hastened understanding. "I think one of the most striking things in this town that helped tremendously was during the Vietnam War when the sheriff's department, the police department, and the highway patrol were down there at 13th Street and University Avenue whipping up on young white kids' heads with batons just like they used to do us in Alabama. I think that helped in some way to reshape the picture that people were seeing and thinking about."

Integration also reshaped the landscape in unintended and ironic ways. The push for open public accommodations irrevocably altered consumer support for African American commerce. "We destroyed a lot of Black businesses," said Chestnut, who long directed the family funeral home, opened in 1914. "And that was one of the things I most regretted in that struggle. I think most of the guys feel that way."

Black schools were similarly vitiated. Newly constructed Lincoln High School, a center of community activity and pride, was immediately closed, even though the result was double sessions at suddenly overcrowded Gainesville High. "That was a real shot in the head," recalled Chestnut, later a member of the school board for sixteen years. Chestnuts have been prominent in town politics since Reconstruction. Chestnut, his wife, daughter, and son held political office from the local level to the state legislature. "People do vindictive things at times," he said. "You forced me to do this, so I'm going to close your school." Typical of most Southern towns, Lincoln's athletic trophies were soon discarded.

African American athletic tradition was established at the University of Florida even as it was being obliterated off campus. Leading the way for the Gators was football coach Doug Dickey, class of '53. Like Bartlett, Dickey came from Tennessee, where he integrated that football program in the mid-sixties. The new coach actively reached out to African Americans and, in turn, eased the path for other sports to do likewise. "Basketball down there still wasn't a big deal, and that's why Norm Sloan left the first time," said

Dick Grubar, the former basketball assistant. "Even though he won, had good players, it was nothing. So, your football probably got all the academic exceptions. That started changing in the seventies."

Dickey also reached out to Gainesville's Black community, inviting local leaders to dine and mingle with players. "They wanted them to have some kind of inter-reaction, which was good," said Chestnut, one of the ambassadors. "These guys were walking into a total white environment and wanted to be sure that they had some conduit into the Black community, so if they were ever uncomfortable about something, they had somebody to come and talk to."

Yet at times Meeks and Williams felt very much on their own. Williams was a starter on the freshman squad and the Baby Gators' leading scorer. But acceptance was elusive. After one play a denizen of the bench observed, "Goddamn it, he's playing just like a nigger." Meeks, seated nearby, overheard the remark, and a minor confrontation ensued.

Later in the 1970–71 school year, a far more serious confrontation pitted many of Florida's Black undergraduates against president O'Connell. "During his presidency, some students and faculty felt he was too conservative on most social issues and that he was too much of a law-and-order man," Proctor and Langley wrote in *Gator History*, their 1986 book. O'Connell was not sympathetic to Vietnam protests or to attempts throughout his tenure to advance an agenda focused on African American issues: increased admissions, financial aid, and administrative support for undergraduates, and better pay and working conditions for university employees. A 1971 editorial in the *Gator* said, "it would be more than an understatement to say that President O'Connell has little rapport with black students."

O'Connell's response to student assertiveness was predictably stern. "I should not and will not negotiate demands with an individual or group," he declared. But his administration's record invited protest. Four years into his presidency, Blacks comprised 10 of 2,650 faculty members and 251 of 21,000 full-time students. A paucity of qualified candidates was a cause of slow progress, to be sure, as the state emerged from segregation and the educational limits it imposed, but the numbers also suggested a lack of urgency to change the school's racial dynamics.

Agendas advanced by Black students, only to be stonewalled, sparked demonstrations at other Southern liberal arts schools in 1969. A group at Duke including basketball player C. B. Claiborne occupied the administration building, leaving ahead of police sent to dislodge them. The University of North Carolina's demonstrations focused on treatment of cafeteria workers and used basketballers Charles Scott and Bill Chamberlain as front men. Clemson's Black students, including basketball's Craig Mobley, walked off campus to protest a perceived lack of safety.

Florida athletes got a taste of protest during the fall of 1970. A handful formed the short-lived League of Athletes after two tennis players lost their scholarships because their hair was deemed too long. All-American flanker Carlos Alvarez was the most prominent member of the group, which sought a broadened dress code, open housing, and later curfews.

Matters reached a head between O'Connell, then being mentioned as a U.S. Senate candidate, and Florida's Black students in April 1971. Several attempts to present the president with demands at his Tigert Hall office were rebuffed during the morning of April 15. Around noon 72 people, mostly Black UF freshmen who had come through the school's "Critical Year Program," filled the Tigert corridors and O'Connell's office and refused to leave. "There weren't athletes involved," Dick Davis, the assistant basketball coach, said.

Actually, there were. Keeping a low profile were Williams, a freshman on the basketball squad, and Coleman, a junior and an SEC champion in several track events. "Everybody felt that this is the way to get the attention of the people in charge so they'll understand we're serious about things," Williams said of the demonstration.

One building exit was left uncovered by police. "When they came with the bullhorns and said you have so much time to get out, and I was in there, I left at that time," Williams said. "A lot of my friends stayed and were arrested." Athletes were unobtrusively reminded of their vulnerability. "Well, here comes a city bus, a jail bus," Coleman said, "and here come the coaches from the athletic association. And they were pretty quiet about it, pretty discreet: 'Hey, look, all you scholarship athletes, you're going to have to get out of here. You cannot go to jail because you'll lose your scholarship.' Really? OK, we're going to kind of ease out of here. And we stood around watching our fellow classmates and schoolmates being arrested one by one."

The arrests sparked a supportive demonstration outside Tigert Hall involving approximately 2,000 students, most of them white, that was broken up by tear gas. The main consequence of the day's events was the withdrawal from school of 123 Black students, about half of the number enrolled at the university, and the resignation of three Black faculty members. Football stars George and Jackson picked up withdrawal forms but never submitted them. Williams told a reporter, "I'm definitely going to stay. By withdrawing, I think we are running away from what we are really fighting for." Privately, he considered transferring to Atlanta's Morris Brown College, but his grandmother reminded Williams that "you committed yourself to go [to Florida], and you need to stay there until you receive your diploma."

Williams again seriously questioned his Florida career the following January after he endured the most frightening racial incident of his life, one that alienated him from his coach and for years left him uncharacteristically angry. "I was a grown man before I got past this," Williams said. "I just think in the back of my mind, sometimes, I could have died that night."

The trouble occurred in Baton Rouge, where Florida traveled to play Louisiana State in late January 1972. The Gators lost, 84–73. Following the game, no food was brought into the Florida locker room. Team members were instead given meal money and told to feed themselves. A few coaches, notably Alabama's Newton and North Carolina's Dean Smith, took pains to anticipate and avoid situations that might prove embarrassing, humiliating, or threatening to early Black players, particularly on the road. That was not the case with Bartlett, despite his belief that "I bent over backwards to make sure" Williams was treated properly.

Williams was the sole African American on the Florida team once Meeks quit the squad. Meeks began disappearing overnight from the dorm room he shared with Williams midway through their freshman season. The unexplained absences soon became frequent and lengthy. "Then, after about three weeks, I ran into Malcolm on campus and Malcolm said, 'Hey, man, I got married three weeks ago,'" Williams recalled. "I was like, 'What?!'" Meeks led the freshman team in rebounding and was fifth in scoring but was a deep reserve as a sophomore. He appeared in eight games for the varsity in 1971–72, then dropped basketball. "I know his dad wanted him to continue to play," Bartlett said of Meeks. "He was a super-nice kid, but he knew and I knew he wasn't a very good player."

So, Williams was the only Black in the group when he, teammate Dan Boe, and two others went in search of food in Baton Rouge. A year earlier Collis Temple, the first African American athlete at LSU, caught static because of his race when entering several establishments near campus. Apparently, little had changed. As soon as the small Florida contingent entered a restaurant and sat at a table, all but one person in the room moved to surround Williams where he sat. The tone was decidedly hostile.

"One guy said to me, 'You've got to go,'" Williams recalled. "And I looked up at them and said, 'Why?' He said, 'Because there are too many white people in here.' So, the first thing that goes through my mind is if I stay in here, they're going to hang me. If I go outside, they can get me outside and hang me."

That's when Boe, a 6-foot-7, 227-pound senior from Wisconsin, spoke up. "I haven't had a good old bar brawl in a long time!" he announced. Recalling his teammate's declaration, Williams laughed with delight. "And that might be why I like Dan so much today."

Williams did not want to fight. Instead, he walked outside, where he was joined by a white pool player who remained aloof during the confrontation. Williams never caught the man's name but expressed eternal gratitude for the simple kindness he demonstrated that night. "We talked. He had been at that game. 'Man, don't worry about that,'" the stranger said to Williams of the restaurant confrontation. "'All those people, don't worry about that stuff. I was at the game, that was a heck of a game.' That kind of thing. That was kind of comforting in a situation like that, because I was scared then. That was one time I was scared."

None of the Florida quartet ate dinner that night. More important, the incident left a scar, if only on Williams's relationship with Bartlett.

Williams devoted considerable time and thought to the nuances of coaching basketball, the focus of his postcollege career. He adroitly climbed the professional ladder from high-school coach to major-college assistant at Florida State to head coach at the University of Maryland-Eastern Shore. But UMES is a coaching graveyard, and after four years of struggle, Williams was fired. He returned to Pensacola, where he coached at a new version of Booker T. Washington High School. From 1990–91 until 2003, when Williams retired from the sidelines, his Wildcats were a combined 376–167, a handsome .692 winning percentage.

So, Williams understood the competing demands on a coach's time and attention, the dynamics of molding a team, the highs and lows of competition, the worries about job security. And even as he recognized the premise that every player merited equal treatment, he also knew from experience that teams are composites of individuals. Further, he knew firsthand that early racial pioneers faced special challenges. "I felt he should have been more understanding," Williams said of Bartlett, "because it was the year I was the only Black person on the team, and he should have understood where we were. Now, if we'd been in Nashville or Lexington, no problem."

There were other, more pedestrian rough spots in Williams's relationship with his coaches. From his earliest days at Florida, they found him overly sensitive to being singled out for correction. "It took him awhile to get over a mistake," Dick Davis said. "If you corrected him, he understood it but he didn't understand it. And, if he was playing in a game and he made a mistake, he thought everybody was watching him, and he dropped his head. But he got over that." Bartlett suspected Williams resented such treatment but thought any hurt feelings were misplaced. "I probably gave him more breaks than I would have a white kid," the coach said. "I gave him more chances."

Bartlett noted proudly that he brought in several Black players after Williams, including future All-SEC performer Gene Shy. That trend pushed the limits of acceptance in some quarters, Bartlett said. "The feeling I had and the people around here, being in the South, I kind of felt like they wanted you to have three white guys on the court." For his part, Williams wondered of coaches from Bartlett's generation, "if, in a lot of situations, they could have continued on with just nothing but white players if they could have done that."

Any differences between coaches and players were not immediately apparent on the court. Williams started as a sophomore, averaging 12.8 points per game, third-best on a team that finished 10–15. The Gators failed to win an SEC road contest but continued to win more than they lost at "Alligator Alley," their small, hot, gloomy, loud, red-brick home, formally known as Florida Gym. "That was an altogether different place to play," said Kermit Davis, Mississippi State's head coach 1971–77. Smart teams changed shoes at halftime lest feet become waterlogged with sweat. "If they didn't bring in two or three pairs of shoes, they'd be sloshing around out there," Bartlett said.

Florida's home games were moved in 1980 to the Stephen C. O'Connell Center, which officially seated 12,000, almost double the capacity of its predecessor. (O'Connell remained so unpopular with African Americans, former aide Joel Buchanan said, "I was called a maggot for going to his funeral and sitting with his family" in 2001.)

Williams played immediately at Florida because "he was smart, smart," Davis said. Despite his size and deployment at wing, Williams used his quickness, leaping ability, and savvy to average 6.4 rebounds in 1971–72, third on the team. He compensated for a suspect jump shot with adept drives to the basket. He could pass, dribble, defend. "He was a very good defensive player, and we assigned him to the best offensive player on the other teams that we played," said Jim McCachren, a physical education teacher who coached the freshmen and assisted the varsity. "Steve was very good."

Yet, on the heels of the incident at Baton Rouge, a rupture developed that would emerge on the court in 1973, the program's fourth consecutive losing season and Bartlett's last as head coach. Listed as a starter, Williams insisted that he was buried on the bench for reasons he did not understand. He expected to build on his sophomore performance, perhaps attracting notice from the pros, but instead he saw his scoring and rebounding averages plummet. "When the clock was running out, he'd put me in and say, 'Stay away from the ball.' That's what Coach Bartlett said: 'Stay away from the ball when you get in there.'"

Williams led the 1973 team with 108 assists, including an impressive 15 in a victory over Virginia Tech, the year's eventual NIT champion. But he said most of his assists came during a nine-game span when he played point guard with starter Tim Fletcher sidelined by injury. Then it was back to mop-up duty. "If [Bartlett] had stayed, I probably would have transferred somewhere or given up basketball, because I don't know if I could have taken another year of that," Williams said. "I didn't care who was going to be our coach. I felt like just a change was needed."

Bartlett's successor was John Lotz, a former Dean Smith assistant at North Carolina. Lotz had been a confidant of basketball pioneer Charles Scott and understood the racial tenor of the times. He brought Grubar, Scott's former Tar Heel teammate, as one of his assistants. The new staff was immediately impressed with Steve Williams. Grubar called him "a great guy, a great kid," and a godsend for the new coaches. "As successful as we were when I was at Florida, a whole lot of it had to do with him accepting the role that he had in helping us to start the program going," Grubar said. "He really accepted us and put us under his wing with the players and helped us get acclimated to who they were and how good they were."

Williams was likewise impressed with Lotz, who emulated Smith's fierce loyalty to his players. "You're talking about another great guy in that class with C. M. Newton," Williams said. "For me as a person, he couldn't have come at a better time." Early in Lotz's tenure, Williams was asleep in his locked dorm room when a football assistant coach let himself in and proceeded to berate the startled basketball player. "I sent for you today, and anytime I send for you, boy, you come to my office right then!" he shouted.

The summons had conflicted with an English class, and Williams most certainly did not expect his privacy and sleep to be violated over the minor matter. He shared the incident with Lotz, who returned a day later with a promise that football coaches would no longer bother members of the basketball squad.

Other changes followed as Florida notched its only winning record during a seven-season span, finishing 15–11. Key to the success was a playing system quite similar to that employed at Chapel Hill. Thirty years later, attending a practice prior to the 2003 Final Four, Steve Williams recognized the same drills that Lotz had run being employed by Kansas, then coached by former Smith assistant Roy Williams.

Florida's new coaches made Steve Williams a cocaptain, reinstalled him in the starting lineup, and in that pre-shot-clock era put the ball in his hands when resorting to Smith's infamous "four corners" delay. "I loved it," Williams said.

"We played him everywhere," Grubar said. "From inside, because he could jump, to outside to handle the ball, pass the ball. He was a pretty good all-around player." Williams's statistics improved, and he was voted to the league's all-defensive squad.

Fulfilling a promise to himself, and a sense of obligation to the supportive folks in Pensacola, Williams graduated in four years. Meeks also graduated but cut ties with the school. Lotz lasted until the 1980 season and was replaced by Sloan, returning to Gainesville from NC State. Slowly, a winning tradition was built. Fifteen years after their initial postseason appearance, the Gators got a second NIT bid in 1984. The program earned its first NCAA berth in 1987 under Sloan. Long after Sloan was gone came a pair of Final Four appearances (1994, 2000) and a brief 2004 rating at the top of the national polls, a first for the program.

The ascent culminated with consecutive NCAA championships in 2006 and 2007 under coach Billy Donovan.

Sloan said Florida's slowness to recruit African Americans hampered his in-state recruiting efforts well into the 1980s. "Where the hell were you all back in so-and-so?" the coach was asked. The issue is apparently moot these days. "I guess that surprises a lot of people that it took so long for Florida to integrate," Steve Williams said. "It was probably just a Southern attitude with a lot of folks, just that there's a place for a Black person, and at this university is not the place."

CHAPTER 17

SNEAKERS

Larry Fry, Mississippi State University, 1971–75
Jerry Jenkins, Mississippi State University, 1971–75

I was my experiences and my experiences were me, and no blind men, no matter how powerful they became, even if they conquered the world, could take that, or change one single itch, taunt, laugh, cry, scar, ache, rage or pain of it.

Ralph Ellison, *Invisible Man*

The 1970 population of Starkville would nearly have fit within the confines of the SEC's largest basketball facility, 23,500-seat Rupp Arena at the University of Kentucky. Surrounded by farmland, far from an interstate highway or major population center, the home of Mississippi State University and its 17,000 students strikes many visitors as located in the middle of nowhere. "As far as having all the lights that you have, maybe, in Baton Rouge or some places, they're not there," said Kermit Davis, an alumnus and former head basketball coach.

The out-of-the-way setting likely influenced the pace of change at Mississippi State, last in the SEC and ACC to integrate its undergraduate student body and its basketball program. Then again, location is not destiny, realtors' claims notwithstanding. Mississippi State twice broke SEC racial logjams. Most recently, in December 2003 the school hired Sylvester Croom, the first African American to serve as a head football coach in the football-crazy league. And, at the height of the civil rights era, when violence engulfed Mississippi like a brooding cloud and segregation was defended with uncommon fervor, MSU leaders deliberately and publicly broke ranks with racial orthodoxy. Their willingness to allow the 1963 basketball squad to flee Mississippi in defiance of a court order not only secured the school's first NCAA tournament appearance but arguably finished segregation's stranglehold on SEC basketball.

People associated with sports share the conceit, lent weight by a doting society, that their activities not only matter but influence social norms. To some extent that was the case with Mississippi State in 1963. Writing of MSU president Dean Colvard's actions, Paul Attner wrote decades later in the *Sporting News*, "Athletics had been his tool to break down at least some practices based on tradition and prejudice. In his mind, it would have been difficult to mobilize similar support at that time for any other aspect of university life."

That barrier-breaking role is a familiar one for college basketball, according to former Duke University head coach Mike Krzyzewski, widely regarded as the premier coach in the contemporary game until his 2022 retirement. "It's like the advertising arm for race relations," Krzyzewski said of his sport, where fan affiliation runs strong and player identity is not hidden by a helmet. Glancing at a photograph of players holding aloft one of his program's five NCAA championship trophies, Krzyzewski added, "Basketball has allowed people to see this as people, not as objects. Unless you have that forum, it's not going to happen. I'm looking at the picture right behind you. You've got all those hands. There are white ones and there are Black ones. Come on. You see that over and over again. Then kids see that and say that that's right. If they never see it, they're afraid of that interaction. It's had an unbelievable impact."

In fact, it was a handshake prior to the NCAA contest with Chicago's Loyola Ramblers, the eventual 1963 national champions, that came to symbolize Mississippi State's reach across the nation's racial divide. "It seemed like the whole floor lit up," MSU captain Joe Dan Gold said of bursting flashbulbs that helped capture the image of his shared touch with All-American Jerry Harkness, one of four Black starters for Loyola.

Mississippi State's players eagerly took the court in East Lansing, Michigan, on March 15, 1963. "They were thrilled to death to go to play," said Jack Cristil, the school's longtime radio play-by-play announcer. "Supremely confident. They happened to catch the best basketball team in America. It was a hell of a game down to the last two minutes." MSU led early, only to fall, 61–51. The following day the SEC club won a consolation matchup with Bowling Green, led by a pair of future pros in center Nate Thurmond and guard Howard Komives.

The real drama occurred before the Maroons, now known as the Bulldogs, ever left Starkville. Colvard, a North Carolinian in his third year as president at Mississippi State, announced that the squad would accept an

NCAA bid unless "hindered by competent authority." A supportive vote by the Board of Trustees for State Institutions of Higher Learning bolstered Colvard's position. Several thousand MSU students also signed a petition endorsing the NCAA trip by their basketball team, a gesture reminiscent of Georgia Tech students protesting racial prohibitions that threatened their football team's participation in the 1956 Sugar Bowl.

State newspaper editorialists were less appreciative of Colvard's decision. The Meridian *Daily Star* declared that the move "would constitute a breach in the walls of segregation" and said "as dear as the athletic prestige of our schools may be, our southern way of life is infinitely more precious." The Jackson *Clarion-Ledger* fretted over the precedent being set. "If Miss. State University plays against a Negro outside the state, what would be greatly different in bringing the integrated teams into the state, and then, why not recruit a Negro of special basketball ability to play on the Miss. State team?"

Eight years later, exactly that happened.

Larry Fry and Jerry Jenkins signed to play for the Bulldogs in 1971 and excelled. Fry's career field goal accuracy (56.6 percent) still ranks among the school's leaders, as does Jenkins's career scoring average (19.3 points per game). Jenkins twice made All-SEC.

By 1976, the majority of players on the MSU roster were African American.

The most vitriolic response to Colvard's plans was voiced by the *Daily News* in Jackson, the state capital. "When a basketball player shaves points for the benefit of gamblers, it is an act of lowest sportsmanship and a case of soul selling. To shave points in the state's unwritten law is diluting a principle that wise men of Mississippi inaugurated years ago for valid, tested reasons and all the hysterical harping over a crack at a mythical national championship isn't worth subjecting young Mississippians to the switchblade knife society that integration eventually spawns."

Rising to parry the perceived thrust against white hegemony, state senator Billy Mitts, a former student body president at Mississippi State, quickly introduced a resolution in the legislature to bar in-state teams from postseason competition against integrated opponents.

Mitts's resolution was referred to committee, where it was destined to die. So, two days prior to the Loyola game, Mitts and a former legislator went to a sympathetic judge and secured an injunction prohibiting the MSU squad from leaving the state. That prompted Colvard, head basketball coach James

Harrison "Babe" McCarthy, athletics director Wade Walker, and others to meet off campus to devise a plan to evade the reach of naysayers.

Conspiracy to break the law had become a Mississippi tradition, almost invariably as a rearguard action against the rising tide of federally mandated integration. The most notorious result of such efforts occurred the year following MSU's basketball escape. On June 19, 1964, the landmark Civil Rights Act finally passed the U.S. Senate, ending a record 75-day filibuster. Two nights later three civil rights workers—James Chaney, a local Black man, and white New Yorkers Andrew Goodman and Michael Schwerner— were ambushed and murdered by several carloads of Klansmen, including local law enforcement, off a two-lane road near Philadelphia, the Neshoba County seat 60 miles south of Starkville.

The young men had investigated the earlier bombing of a Black church, a terror tactic commonly employed in an enduring campaign of intimidation to suppress efforts to register African American voters. Five counties in Mississippi with majority Black populations were devoid of registered African American voters as late as 1962. Despite considerable effort, fewer than 4,000 new Black voters were added to Mississippi rolls over a two-year span in the early sixties. This led to the 1964 "Freedom Summer Project," a registration drive that drew some 900 mostly white youths from the North and Midwest to Mississippi, among them Goodman and Schwerner, under the aegis of several civil rights groups. A massive search was launched, lasting 44 days, for the bodies of the missing civil rights workers, decomposing deep within an earthen farm dam seven miles south of Philadelphia. A headline in the *Clarion-Ledger* surveyed the push for equal rights and warned, "A Major Purpose of Invaders Is to Attract Federal Occupation." Federal action did help to find the bodies, and after Mississippi declined to pursue murder charges, to obtain seven convictions for violating the civil rights of the slain trio.

Not until 2005 was a lone participant in the murders indicted and convicted under state law. It took until 2013 for Mississippi to erect an historical marker on Highway 19 near the site of the murders that "proved pivotal in mobilizing moderate reaction in Mississippi," according to historian John Ray Skates.

Violence certainly was not out of the question as a response to Mississippi State's much-publicized plan to defy segregation in March 1963; president Colvard received death threats, and for a time his home was placed under guard. But school officials apparently were most concerned with avoiding direct confrontation with law enforcement in the form of a deputy sheriff armed with a copy of an injunction.

Rather than be available to be served, Colvard left Starkville two days prior to the scheduled NCAA game with Loyola to deliver a scheduled address at Auburn in adjacent Alabama. The same day McCarthy, AD Walker, and an athletic department assistant drove to Tennessee. The following morning the reserve players went to Bryan Field, a private Starkville airport. No one stopped them, so a call was made to assistant coach Jerry Simmons to bring the starters to board the plane. The charter flight landed in Nashville to pick up McCarthy and the athletics staffers, then proceeded to Michigan and the Mideast Regional.

The escape ended years of frustration for a program that blossomed virtually overnight under McCarthy's guidance. Reflective of SEC attitudes toward the relative lack of importance of basketball, the charismatic McCarthy was a young SEC game official and Standard Oil salesman with no college coaching experience when hired as Mississippi State's head coach for the 1955–56 season. Almost immediately, the Mississippi native led the perennially drab Maroons to the top of the SEC. They finished first in the conference in 1959, 1961, and 1962, but each year declined the opportunity to advance to the NCAAs lest they face an integrated opponent. MSU students voted 6–1 in favor of participation in 1959 and burned the university president in effigy after he essentially told them to butt out. New governor Ross Barnett weighed in on the subject in 1961, saying he opposed the school's NCAA participation, and that trip was abandoned.

Each year that Mississippi State declined, Kentucky went instead. When Mississippi State won again in 1963, it marked one of only two times a school besides UK won three straight SEC titles. (Alabama, likewise, finished first three times in a row under C. M. Newton from 1974 to 1976.)

MSU was not the first Mississippi basketball program to have its postseason aspirations shattered against the invisible wall of segregation. The initial victim was all-Black Jackson State College, forbidden by custom to participate in the 1957 NAIA tournament. Ironically, the winner that year was a Tennessee State squad coached by John McLendon, the first time a historically Black school captured a national championship in integrated competition.

Nor was Mississippi alone in avoiding what it could not control. Alabama's "Rocket Eight" in 1956 and Auburn's "Seven Dwarfs" in 1960 had, like Mississippi State, stayed home in March despite finishing atop the SEC during the regular season.

Mississippi native Kermit Davis did not regard the maintenance of segregation as sufficient reason to decline an NCAA bid. Then again, the senior guard on the 24–1 squad of 1959 kept that opinion to himself. "In those days you didn't question things," said Davis, McCarthy's first recruit. Davis made his own wordless statement a dozen years later as head coach at his alma mater by signing Fry and Jenkins.

Davis would always wonder what the third-ranked '59 team, led by All-Americans Bailey Howell and guard Jim Ashmore, might have achieved on a national stage. "I think the older I get, the more I regret it, not having the opportunity to see if we were the best team. To have the championship ring; I can't think of anything that you'd rather have than to have that."

(Among the tools at the Maroons' disposal was an innovation first employed by but rarely credited to Black pioneer McLendon, and later made famous as North Carolina's "four corners" offense. Called "the Domino Five" by McCarthy, the alignment put players at the four corners of the frontcourt, leaving 6-foot-7 Howell isolated for long stretches with the ball at the top of the key and, in those days, no constraining shot clock. From there, the 1997 inductee into the Naismith Memorial Basketball Hall of Fame was almost unstoppable as he drove, shot, or passed.)

Avoidance of integrated competition by SEC teams was not limited to postseason play. When Tennessee coach John Mauer learned Duquesne intended to use an African American player, he forfeited the game rather than face the Dukes in Pennsylvania in December 1946. The avoidance tactics reached embarrassing, hurtful heights on New Year's Eve a decade later. Appearing in simultaneous two-game tournaments in Kentucky and Indiana, respectively, both Ole Miss and Mississippi State withdrew rather than face teams with Black players. "It was a shameful display of discourtesy and fear, not on the part of the boys but of their elders," observed the Louisville *Courier-Journal*.

Mississippi's decision was made on-site by Rebels coach B. L. "Bonnie" Graham. He evinced surprise that Iona's Gaels had an African American player. Graham was backed by athletics director Tad Smith, who said of facing a Black athlete, "We can't afford to do that." Stanley Hill, the Gael at the center of the storm, told Ian O'Connor of the *Journal News* of Westchester, New York, "I was shocked, enraged, humiliated. It was a terrible, sinking feeling. I remember everybody just looking at me—the fans, players, everyone. The crowd started booing Mississippi. When we got back to the hotel, some Mississippi players came to my room to apologize." During the

2001 NCAA tournament, when the schools finally faced each other on a basketball court, Hill watched the game as the guest of Ole Miss chancellor Robert Khayat.

Mississippi State's McCarthy did not want to quit the Evansville event. Mississippi was relegated to a consolation game; the Maroons qualified for the championship contest in the Indiana tournament after defeating Denver, which had two Black forwards. But when MSU athletics director C. R. Noble read game accounts, he ordered the team home before it could play an integrated Evansville College squad. "It took us awhile to get over that," recalled Davis, a sophomore in 1956–57. "Most of us were from rural areas. Here we were, either Ashmore or Howell were [*sic*] going to be the most valuable player of the tournament. We were all going to receive watches, and we'd have got a trophy, which was a big, big deal for us back then."

Over time, segregation's constricting dictates eased, helped along by Mississippi State's well-publicized defiance in 1963. Barely a decade later, when James W. Loewen and Charles Sallis edited a history, *Mississippi, Conflict and Change*, they noted, "Most voters in the state now realize that desegregation is here to stay."

McCarthy was forced out at MSU in 1965—coincidentally, the same calendar year the school was integrated—after suffering consecutive losing seasons. Even finishing on a sour note, the three-time SEC coach of the year won two-thirds of his games over a decade at Starkville. McCarthy paused briefly at the University of Georgia, coached for a year at George Washington University, then became a coach in the fledgling American Basketball Association. Nicknamed "Old Magnolia Mouth," McCarthy delighted the pros with his country colloquialisms, from "We've got to get after them like a biting sow" to "We're going to cloud up and rain all over them."

Davis, meanwhile, directed Tupelo High School in Elvis Presley's hometown to a pair of state championships and a four-year record of 132–23. (For years visitors could follow the musical notes affixed to light poles along East Main Street and Elvis Presley Drive in Tupelo to reach the Elvis Presley Birthplace and Museum, which boasted "long-hidden treasures from Elvis's early life" as well as a memorial chapel and a park.) When MSU assistant coach Jerry Simmons was killed in an auto accident during a recruiting trip, Davis took his place on the staff of Joe Dan Gold, the '63 captain hired to succeed McCarthy.

Almost immediately the young coaches began scrutinizing Black athletes as possible prospects.

Davis had competed as a youth against African Americans despite attending school in a state so devoted to segregation, even warehoused textbooks were separated by law based on the race of their eventual recipients. A pitcher with a good curveball, Davis was the sole white on a team of older Blacks just across the state line in Memphis until his father put a stop to it. In 1954, Davis's junior year at Walnut High School, his team won the state basketball championship. When the local Black high school also won a state title, the squads defied custom and met informally on an outdoor court one Sunday afternoon to see who was best.

Racially separate high-school basketball tournaments remained the norm in Mississippi when Davis became an MSU assistant in 1966. He began attending both the Black and white versions and quickly discovered a wealth of talent untapped by integration-averse SEC schools. He was not alone in that assessment. George Raveling, then a Villanova assistant, happily haunted the African American tournaments of the Deep South. "It was just incredible the talent that you would see," he said. "Going throughout the South, I'd see so many guys there was no way we could get them all."

Word of Mississippi State's 1963 defiance of segregation did not smooth the school's recruiting path among African American prospects, as Dean Smith's more modest resistance did at North Carolina. Not until the media-saturated nineties, when the Bulldogs made consecutive NCAA appearances, culminating with a Final Four berth in 1996, did popular attention return to those earlier events. "I didn't know any history about Mississippi State," said Jerry Jenkins, who grew up in the southern part of the state. "I knew about the Black schools, Jackson State and Grambling and stuff, but Mississippi State, no. I didn't hear anything. Bailey Howell, I knew about, but the team itself, no."

Davis and Gold, his boss, concentrated their efforts within Mississippi but had little success luring African American athletes to Starkville. "We were getting our toes in the water. I knew in my own mind, and Joe Dan did," Davis said, "if we were going to compete in the SEC, all coaches will tell you, you better get your home folks and then go out and recruit outside the state."

Practicality confirmed that strategy. Difficulty attracting interest from Blacks within Mississippi was nothing compared with the skepticism rampant beyond its borders, as Davis discovered at a well-regarded high-school all-star game in Pittsburgh. "We have such a bad name," Davis said of the state, which took until 2020 to remove a Confederate emblem from its flag.

"I remember when I went to the Dapper Dan, I was talking to a Black player up there. I mentioned Mississippi, and he put his hands up and he said, 'Wait a minute, coach! Wait a minute! I don't want to go down there!' He had heard so many stories about Mississippi."

Cristil, the radio voice of MSU football and basketball for 58 years, said there also were barriers to success at Mississippi State that existed apart from race and reputation. "You've got to understand, first and foremost, the economic situation in the state," the Tupelo resident said. "This is not a rich state. You cannot compete with the Tennessees, the Georgias, the Floridas, Kentuckys on a dollar-wise basis. You've got to spend every dollar you've got very, very wisely and then invest it wisely in your personnel and in your people.

"You've got to understand the political situation in the state of Mississippi," continued Cristil, citing ubiquitous tension among Southern educational institutions. "Our state is controlled by the legislature, most of whom are attorneys. Most of them have an Ole Miss background, and they're your principal rival. And you've got to understand this: You won't get any help out of the legislature. Whatever you generate, you're going to generate yourself through your own abilities to be successful in whatever the endeavor is.

"And you still have that unfortunate group of people that think they're holier than thou, that they're better than anybody else, and they want to live in the antebellum days which no longer exist, haven't existed for a half a century or longer. But they still want to live that way. These things you've got to understand, and if you don't understand those things, then you're not going to be successful in the state of Mississippi."

Nor was Starkville an easy sell, although life in town was perhaps a bit kinder for African Americans than elsewhere in rural Mississippi. "Starkville was better than most small country towns because of the influence of what was then called Mississippi A and M College, now Mississippi State University," Sayde H. Wier wrote in her book, *A Black Businessman in White Mississippi, 1886–1974*, with John F. Marszalek. "There was a good atmosphere here, and I liked the class of people—even the working people were influenced by the college."

But folks were less hospitable during the civil rights era, when Black athletes were coming onto the scene. Norm Sloan was the coach at Florida in January 1965, and the memory of Chaney, Goodwin, and Schwerner was still fresh when the chartered bus carrying his all-white team was stopped by a state trooper as it approached Starkville. "This guy motioned us down. We opened the door, and he stood there. He had two guns on, like a Wild West guy, and he said, his opening remark was"—here Sloan affects an exaggerated Southern drawl—'Are y'all an integrated athletic team passing through Mississippi?' Well, I was dumbfounded."

Segregation remained a fact of life in Starkville long after it began unraveling in most Southern communities. Wier's husband was a barber in town for 46 years but was proficient only at cutting the hair of whites. Serving men of his own race might have hurt or ruined his business.

Integrated SEC teams found Starkville—population 11,369 in the 1970 census—particularly inhospitable compared to other venues. Jimmy Walker, who played with Henry Harris at Auburn in 1970 and 1971, recalled that finding a place to eat in Starkville was a particular challenge. "We'd go in a white restaurant, they'd say we're too busy or whatever, wouldn't serve us because of Henry. So, let's go to a predominantly Black restaurant. We'd go there, and they wouldn't serve us because I was with him. And we'd keep bouncing around. In Mississippi, we'd have to go three or four places before we ever found a place that would serve both of us. So, I got a little different perspective on what some of the Blacks go through. But it wasn't a big deal to either one of us. It was more of a joke than anything." Similar conditions persisted in Starkville through the decade.

Mississippi State basketball did boast several notable advantages.

The first was a replacement arena for the so-called New Gym, opened in 1950 with seating for about 5,000 spectators. The raucous, intimidating arena was among the last of the older generation of SEC facilities to be replaced. "They were more of a country group," Alabama's Wendell Hudson recalled of Mississippi State fans. "They were yipping and yapping about everything."

Adding to the ambience were agriculture-related noisemakers, later banned. "People would pack in there, I mean literally," Cristil said. "When they said people hang from the rafters, that was true. Any spur or stanchion that was available, by God, they were hanging on it. And they brought cowbells and plowshares, and they hit them with ball-peen hammers. It was madness. You couldn't even hear yourself think. Quite an atmosphere."

Fans were particularly rude to Kentucky and coach Adolph Rupp. "If they treat me and my boys like that now, what do you think they would [do] if I brought a Negro there?" Rupp asked. Once, MSU fans placed a skunk under Rupp's seat on the sidelines.

A major goal under Davis was achieved with the 1975 opening of "The Hump," the Humphrey Coliseum, which seated 10,500. "I was proud to get the new coliseum, but I'd like to recruit the players there and then play in the old 'Pit' because we did have an advantage," Davis said. "Really, you just about had to read lips when you called timeout to understand what the coach was trying to tell you."

MSU's other advantage was Davis himself, at least as far as Fry and Jenkins were concerned. Or, rather, as far as their mothers were concerned.

"He took a chance to sign Black players," Jenkins said of Davis, the 1971 Associated Press coach of the year in the SEC. "I have a lot of respect for him. I think my mother had more respect for him than I do. They liked each other. That's all they kept talking about. They were always praising each other." Larry Fry, too, was pushed toward Mississippi State because of the impression that Davis made. "My mother said something that I'll never forget—'There's something about him that I like that I don't see in these other coaches.'"

Fry and his eight siblings were raised by his mother, Virginia Yarbro, and her parents at the rural edge of Lexington, a small town in western Tennessee. Days began at 5 a.m. with stoves to be stoked and lighted and hogs to be fed. There were more chores to be performed after the long walk home from the distant, segregated school; not until 1967 did Fry attend previously all-white Lexington High School.

Yarbro, a worker at a munitions plant, was a stern disciplinarian. She often meted out punishment with a switch, a willow branch cut for the occasion. "My mother was basically a person that didn't spend that much time talking to you about what you did wrong. She believed in taking care of business," said Fry, a career educator later noted in Mississippi as a get-tough high-school principal. Virginia Yarbro also believed in the power of prayer, and every Wednesday evening devoted several hours with her children to Bible readings and discussion of everyday problems. The life lessons included how to cope with taunting by white students who called her son "nigger" and how to understand why local restaurants would not allow his family and friends inside. "My mother tried to guide us through it," said Fry. "My mother was a very, very strong religious person. She believed that things were there for a reason but prayer would change those things."

Hard work was another transformative element in the Fry arsenal. Once he settled on basketball as his sport of choice, Fry made the best use of what became a burly, broad-shouldered, 6-foot-5 frame. Davis long kidded Fry that "you're the first Black I ever knew that had the white man disease and couldn't jump." Or, as the coach told one reporter in more complimentary fashion, "He couldn't jump out of the gym, but he jumped every time."

Fry mastered a low-post game, tailoring his skills to position himself for rebounds and to score close to the basket. Easing the task, he was tutored by Jerry Graves, a former Bulldog big man who lived in Tennessee's Lexington. Graves played at Mississippi State during its segregated heyday under McCarthy, and helped steer his young protégé toward Starkville. Fry "is one of the greatest guys I've ever known," Graves told Thomas Warner of the Pascagoula *Mississippi Press.* "I would have liked to play with Larry. We were similar-type players." Graves twice made All-SEC and paced his team in scoring, rebounding, and foul shooting in 1960 and 1961.

Fry, the only African American on his squad in ninth grade and part of tenth, also benefited from his relationship with Sammy Fisher, the Lexington High coach. Fry's parents were divorced, and although he knew his father, the youngster saw him infrequently. "Sammy Fisher more or less treated me just like I was his son. This was a guy that looked beyond color. He just wanted you to be the best basketball player you could. He was the one that really drove me." Fry's senior year at Lexington High, he averaged 26 points and 15 rebounds and made all-state in Tennessee.

During his recruitment, Fry heard nothing from Mississippi State coaches about the absence of Black basketball players in the Bulldog program. "I could come in and play next to Jerry Jenkins. That's the only statement (Davis) ever made." A close observer of the civil rights movement, Fry knew the score, anyway. And, if he did not, Norm Stewart, the head coach at Missouri, made sure to raise the issue during recruiting. "I was willing to take on the challenge, that's the way I would sum it," Fry said of his choice of MSU. "My mother asked me, 'Do you think that you would make a difference?' If I could do something like that, maybe it would open the doors for someone else."

That Fry would not be the sole African American at Mississippi State was underscored when he made his all-expense-paid visit to campus. Jenkins was present that weekend, and the pair spent time with the school's first Black football players, enrolled for the 1969–70 academic year.

One obstacle to Fry's basketball career remained after he cast his lot with Mississippi State—the Vietnam War was in full swing, and his draft board twice called him for active military duty. Each time Kermit Davis found a way to intervene, avoiding a considerable moral dilemma for Fry, who opposed the war as "totally uncalled for," not to mention seeing all the young men who looked like him "brought back in the body bags."

Fry went on to enjoy a solid career on Mississippi State teams that were a combined 36-42. He twice led in field goal accuracy, led in rebounding once, and was second twice. He was among the top three scorers each year on the varsity. "Fry, he was tough," Jenkins said of his teammate. "He was limited in a lot of things. He just battled. He was strong, he was strong as an ox. Good team player. For his abilities, I thought he was one of the best."

Where Fry was the mule, stolidly carrying the load, Jenkins was the show horse setting the pace. "He could shoot outside, he could take it to the hole," Davis said. "He was really, really, really a great prospect as far as having all the tools."

Jenkins led the Bullpup squad in scoring and rebounding in 1971–72, the last year in which freshmen were ineligible for the varsity. The 6-foot-7, 180-pound wing, nicknamed "Slim" in college, scored in double figures in all but three games during his varsity career and made all-tournament in every in-season event in which he appeared at Mississippi State. "We did a lot of isolation stuff for him. He was very good one-on-one," said teammate Steve Steinwedel. "Coach gave him some freedom to put in on the floor and drive it." Quick and an exceptional jumper, Jenkins averaged seven rebounds per game despite being stationed on the perimeter.

Scoring was what Jenkins did best, finishing several seasons among the SEC leaders. His 575 points in 1974–75, long prior to the advent of the three-point shot, still ranks among the top 10 in school history. Only Bailey Howell totaled more points during a three-year career. Jenkins was an All-SEC selection as a junior and senior, leading MSU in scoring both seasons.

Jenkins also was a good defender, a skill that earned him playing time as a ninth grader at Gulfport High School. Nicknamed "Spider" in those days, as a sophomore the long-armed Jenkins played on both the junior varsity and varsity. He sprouted by his junior prep year into a 6-foot-3 forward and a starter on a team that won the state championship. Suddenly, Jerry Jenkins's personal horizons broadened considerably, a transformation he credited to Bert Jenkins, the Gulfport High coach. "He loved to spend time with people that were dedicated and want to play," Jerry Jenkins said. "We spent more time together in that gym, just me and him, than anyone, because I was hungry."

Bert Jenkins was a towering figure in Mississippi high-school basketball, inducted in 1999 into the Mississippi Sports Hall of Fame after a career in which his teams won seven state titles and posted a cumulative 866–180 record. (Jenkins's best-known player was Chris Jackson, later Mahmoud Abdul-Rauf. Jackson, a two-time consensus All-American and SEC player of the year at LSU, led the Admirals to a 1988 Mississippi state championship.) "He just discovered me from scratch, from a beggar, I would say," Jerry Jenkins said of his coach, who was white and no relation. "I didn't have any idea I was going to go to college. It didn't even cross my mind about a scholarship. I just loved the game. And, then, all of a sudden, my senior year everyone wanted me. Which was down to Coach Jenkins. It had to be him, because I had no idea about it."

Among the recruiters who came calling, MSU's Davis and Houston's Guy Lewis made strong but opposite impressions on Annette Jenkins, mother of the All-American. "The coach from Houston, he was here, he was here, he was here," she said. "He promised me so much. Davis didn't promise me anything." That made Davis the trustworthy one, in her estimation. "If someone gives you something, you don't trust them because there must be a reason why they're giving it," Jerry Jenkins explained.

Annette Jenkins passed along not only values but an aptitude for basketball; her four sons each earned a college scholarship in the sport. Annette and her two sisters had grown up playing the game, usually on outdoor courts, around Mount Olive in southern Mississippi. There, relations between Blacks and whites were cordial, far better, she said, than in the northern reaches of the state.

Jerry was her oldest child, born when she was 16. "I was like a ride in the haystack," he said with a laugh. His mother soon moved to Gulfport and got married. Her eldest child followed after spending his early years with grandparents.

Early settlement by the Spanish and French immediately distinguished the Gulf Coast from other parts of Mississippi. "Partly because of the diversity of its population, the coast has always been more tolerant in its politics and folkways than other areas of the state," according to the Loewen-Sallis history of the state. Convention hotels along the coast accepted integrated groups in the 1950s, unlike the rest of Mississippi. Games of chance were overtly tolerated. Statewide prohibition was in effect until 1966, yet coastal counties openly sold liquor, with the state levying a 10 percent tax on the illegal commodity. Today the Gulf Coast hosts a cluster of legal gambling casinos, and the roads are lined with a parade of billboards advertising lounge acts.

The coast's divergence from Mississippi's racial norms had its limits during Jerry Jenkins's youth, however. "You didn't go to the beach unless you took the white folks' daughters to the beach," Annette Jenkins said. "If their child wanted to go on the beach, you took their child on the beach. Other than that, you weren't caught on the beach."

Unless, of course, you wanted to protest segregation. That was the case in April 1960 when Dr. Gilbert Mason, a physician, was arrested for disorderly conduct for swimming in the Mississippi Sound at Biloxi. The following week approximately four dozen African Americans of all ages conducted a "wade-in" on the same beach. Young white men quickly attacked with sticks, clubs, rocks, and chains while police looked on or arrested Dr. Mason, this time for "fighting and disrupting traffic." Later, a large-scale riot erupted in which ten people were shot, none fatally.

Segregation's grip eased along the Gulf by the mid-sixties, and Jerry Jenkins was able to attend previously all-white Gulfport High. Often the only Black member of the basketball team, he did not consider himself a pioneer then, or later. "That wasn't one of the reasons I signed with Mississippi State; do I want to be the first Black and play?" Jenkins said. "That didn't come into it. People ask me, 'Do you know you were the first Black?' I say, 'Yeah, what am I supposed to do about that?' I didn't even think about it. It didn't cross my mind."

He quickly hooked up with Fry, who had given the matter of breaking the school's color barrier considerable thought. "Jerry and I were like brothers," Fry said of his roommate. Their freshman year at college, Jenkins introduced Fry to his future wife, a fellow graduate of Gulfport High whom he knew well. Another of Jenkins's high-school classmates was Melvin Barkum, the first Black quarterback for MSU. In 1972, he and Tennessee's Condredge Holloway became the first to play the position in the SEC.

As close as Jenkins and Fry were, they were opposites in more than playing style and views on crossing the color line.

"Jerry was much more serious and introverted and quiet, less outgoing," teammate Steinwedel said. "Larry was very outgoing, made friends very quickly." Jenkins was a solid student in high school, attracting interest from Harvard, among others universities, yet it was Fry who earned the credits to graduate on time from MSU with a degree in physical education. Steinwedel also found Fry, an Indianapolis native, less concerned than Jenkins with matters of race. "Jerry was more sensitive, not more militant, but more in touch with his Blackness, if that's the right way to put it." That sensitivity became an issue early in their careers, when the basketball freshmen were supposed to endure a hazing ritual, or "tallying."

The practice was unfamiliar to Jenkins. Loath to subordinate himself physically to seniors who might dislike Blacks, he balked at being hit. After getting tallied once, he reconsidered his college choice. "I did it, and then I said I would never do it again. That's when I said, I don't think Mississippi State is for me, and I was ready to go home," Jenkins said.

Kermit Davis remembered receiving an urgent, late-night telephone call from an upset Larry Fry. "He said, 'You've got to get up here quick.' He might have said Jerry's going to go home." Davis promised to put a stop to the practice of tallying, and did. Jenkins decided to stay, and just as Mississippi State quietly, if belatedly, desegregated its student body, so it transformed its basketball program.

Davis was forced out in March 1977, two years after Fry and Jenkins concluded their careers. The next season, 1977–78, Mississippi State finished second in the SEC. But, despite an expanded NCAA tournament field that allowed multiple entrants from the same league, the Bulldogs did not get a bid.

The snub completed an ironic circle. Once, legislators fighting to protect a dying system strove mightily to block MSU from participating in integrated postseason play. Fifteen years later, the racial center of gravity had shifted to the extent that a member of the Mississippi House of Representatives protested the Bulldogs' dastardly exclusion from NCAA competition, and called for an investigation of the selection process.

APPENDIX

First Black Players, By Year Arrived And League

Year	ACC	SEC
1964	Maryland	
1965	Duke	
1966	North Carolina, Wake Forest	Vanderbilt
1967	N.C. State	
1968		Auburn
1969	Clemson, South Carolina	Alabama, Georgia, Kentucky
1970	Virginia	Florida, Louisiana State, Mississippi
1971		Mississippi State, Tennessee

Players by School, Freshman Season

League	School	Player	Freshman Season
ACC	Clemson	Craig Mobley	1969–70
	Duke	C. B. Claiborne	1965–66
	Maryland	Billy Jones, Pete Johnson	1964–65
	North Carolina	Charles Scott	1966–67
	N.C. State	Al Heartley	1967–68
	South Carolina	Casey Manning	1969–70
	Virginia	Al Drummond	1970–71
	Wake Forest	Norwood Todmann	1966–67
SEC	Alabama	Wendell Hudson	1969–70
	Auburn	Henry Harris	1968–69
	Georgia	Ronnie Hogue	1969–70
	Florida	Malcolm Meeks, Steve Williams	1970–71
	Kentucky	Tom Payne Jr.	1969–70
	Louisiana State	Collis Temple Jr.	1970–71
	Mississippi	Coolidge Ball	1970–71
	Mississippi State	Larry Fry, Jerry Jenkins	1971–72
	Tennessee	Wilbert Cherry*	1970–71
	Vanderbilt	Perry Wallace	1966–67

*Teammate Larry Robinson was a junior college transfer.
Note: Freshmen were not eligible for varsity competition until 1972–73.

Players by First Year of Varsity Participation

Year	Player	School	Home State
1965–66	Billy Jones	Maryland	Maryland
1966–67	C. B. Claiborne	Duke	Virginia
	Pete Johnson	Maryland	Maryland
1967–68	Charles Scott	North Carolina	New York
	Norwood Todmann	Wake Forest	New York
	Perry Wallace	Vanderbilt	Tennessee
1968–69	Al Heartley	N.C. State	North Carolina
1969–70	Henry Harris	Auburn	Alabama
1970–71	Ronnie Hogue	Georgia	Washington, D.C.
	Wendell Hudson	Alabama	Alabama
	Casey Manning	South Carolina	South Carolina
	Craig Mobley	Clemson	South Carolina
	Tom Payne Jr.	Kentucky	Kentucky
1971–72	Coolidge Ball	Mississippi	Mississippi
	Wilbert Cherry	Tennessee	Tennessee
	Al Drummond	Virginia	New York
	Malcolm Meeks	Florida	Florida
	Larry Robinson	Tennessee	Virginia
	Collis Temple Jr.	Louisiana State	Louisiana
	Steve Williams	Florida	Florida
1972–73	Larry Fry	Mississippi State	Tennessee
	Jerry Jenkins	Mississippi State	Mississippi

All-Conference Players

League	Player	School	Seasons League Honors Earned
ACC	Charles Scott*	North Carolina	1968: First team
			1969: First team
			1970: First team
			1970: Academic
	Al Heartley	N.C. State	1970: Academic
SEC	Perry Wallace	Vanderbilt	1970: Second team
	Tom Payne Jr.	Kentucky	1971: First team
	Wendell Hudson**	Alabama	1972: First team
			1973: First team
	Ronnie Hogue	Georgia	1972: Second team
	Coolidge Ball	Mississippi	1972: Second team
			1973: Second team
			1974: Third team
	Henry Harris	Auburn	1972: Third team
	Larry Robinson	Tennessee	1972: Academic
			1973: Third team
	Collis Temple Jr.	Louisiana State	1973: Academic
			1974: Third team
	Jerry Jenkins	Mississippi State	1974: Third team
			1975: Second team

*Also named to All-America second team in 1968, first team in 1969 and 1970, and Academic All-America team in 1970.

**Also named to All-America team in 1973.

BIBLIOGRAPHY

BOOKS

Applebome, Peter. *Dixie Rising: How the South Is Shaping American Values, Politics, and Culture.* San Diego: Harcourt Brace, 1997.

Ashby, Warren. *Frank Porter Graham: A Southern Liberal.* Winston-Salem, NC: John F. Blair, 1980.

Ashmore, Harry S. *Civil Rights and Wrongs.* New York: Pantheon Books, 1994.

Baker, Kent. *Red, White and Amen: Maryland Basketball.* Huntsville, AL: Strode Publishing, 1979.

Barnhart, Tony. *Southern Fried Football: The History, Passion, and Glory of the Great Southern Game.* Chicago: Triumph Books, 2000.

Barrett, Russell H. *Integration at Ole Miss.* New York: Quadrangle Books, 1965.

Bartley, Numan V. *The Rise of Massive Resistance: Race and Politics in the South During the 1950s.* Baton Rouge: Louisiana State University Press, 1969.

Barton, Don, and Bob Fulton. *Frank McGuire: The Life and Times of a Basketball Legend.* Columbia, SC: Summerhouse Press, 1995.

Beckum, Leonard C. *Legacy, 1963–1993: Thirty Years of African-American Students at Duke University.* Durham: Duke University, 1995.

Berry, Wendell. *The Hidden Wound.* Boston: Houghton Mifflin, 1970.

Bettersworth, John K. *People's University: The Centennial History of Mississippi State.* Jackson: University Press of Mississippi, 1980.

Bolton, Clyde. *The Basketball Tide: A Story of Alabama Basketball.* Huntsville, AL: Strode, 1977.

Bradley, Bill. *Values of the Game.* New York: Workman, 1998.

Briggs, Mark D. "A Tale of Two Pioneers: The Integration of College Athletics in the South During the 1960s in the Age of the Civil Rights Movement." Master's thesis, School of Journalism and Mass Communication, University of North Carolina, 2000.

Brown, Mary Jane. *Eradicating This Evil: Women in the American Anti-Lynching Movement, 1892–1940.* New York: Garland, 2000.

Browne, C. A. *The Story of Our National Ballads.* New York: Thomas Y. Crowell, 1919.

Brugger, Robert J. *Maryland: A Middle Temperament, 1634–1980.* Baltimore: Johns Hopkins University Press, 1988.

Bryan, Wright. *Clemson: An Informal History of the University, 1889–1979.* Columbia, SC: R. L. Bryan, 1979.

Bryant, Paul W., and John Underwood. *Bear: The Hard Life and Good Times of Alabama's Coach Bryant.* Boston: Little, Brown, 1974.

Burt, Al. *The Tropic of Cracker.* Gainesville: University Press of Florida, 1999.

Byrd, Ben. *The Basketball Vols: University of Tennessee Basketball.* Huntsville, AL: Strode, 1974.

Cady, Edwin H. *The Big Game: College Sports and American Life.* Knoxville: University of Tennessee Press, 1978.

Cahill, Mary, and Gary Grant. *Victorian Danville.* Danville, VA: Womack Press, 1977.

Calcott, George H. *Maryland and America, 1940 to 1980.* Baltimore: Johns Hopkins University Press, 1985.

Carleton, Mark T. *River Capital: An Illustrated History of Baton Rouge.* Woodland Hills, CA: Windsor Publications, 1981.

Carter, Dan T. *The Politics of Rage: George Wallace, the Origins of the New Conservatism, and the Transformation of American Politics.* New York: Simon & Schuster, 1995.

Chace, William M., and Peter Collier, eds. *Justice Denied: The Black Man in White America*. New York: Harcourt, Brace & World, 1970.

Chafe, William H. *Civilities and Civil Rights: Greensboro, North Carolina, and the Black Struggle for Freedom*. Oxford: Oxford University Press, 1980.

Clark, E. Culpepper. *The Schoolhouse Door: Segregation's Last Stand at the University of Alabama*. Oxford: Oxford University Press, 1993.

Cleaver, Eldridge. *Soul on Ice*. New York: Dell, 1968.

Cohodas, Nadine. *The Band Played Dixie: Race and the Liberal Conscience at Ole Miss*. New York: Free Press, 1997.

Coleman, Kenneth, ed. *A History of Georgia*. 2nd ed. Athens: University of Georgia Press, 1991.

Collier-Thomas, Bettye, and V. P. Franklin. *My Soul Is A Witness: A Chronology of the Civil Rights Era, 1954–1965*. New York: Henry Holt, 1999.

Cone, Carl B. *The University of Kentucky: A Pictorial History*. Lexington: University Press of Kentucky, 1989.

Conroy, Pat. *My Losing Season*. New York: Doubleday, 2002.

Cramer, Gary. *Cavaliers! A Pictorial History of UVa Basketball*. Charlottesville, VA: Spring House Publishing, 1983.

Creekmore, Betsey Beeler. *Knox County Tennessee: A History in Pictures*. Norfolk, VA: Donning Company, 1988.

Crowe, Dallas R. "Desegregation of Charlottesville, Va., Public Schools, 1954–1969: A Case Study." Doctoral dissertation, School of Education, University of Virginia, 1971.

Cutrer, Thomas W. *Parnassus on the Mississippi: The Southern Review and the Baton Rouge Literary Community, 1935–1942*. Baton Rouge: Louisiana State University Press, 1984.

Dabney, Virginius. *Mr. Jefferson's University: A History*. Charlottesville: University Press of Virginia, 1981.

D'Emilio, John. *Lost Prophet: The Life and Times of Bayard Rustin*. New York: Free Press, 2003.

Dickerson, James L. *Dixie's Dirty Secret: The True Story of How the Government, the Media, and the Mob Conspired to Combat Integration and the Vietnam Antiwar Movement.* Armonk, NY: M. E. Sharpe, 1998.

Doyle, Don H. *Nashville Since the 1920s.* Knoxville: University of Tennessee Press, 1985.

DuBois, W. E. B. *The Souls of Black Folk.* New York: Alfred A. Knopf, 1976.

Dufour, Charles L. *Ten Flags in the Wind: The Story of Louisiana.* New York: Harper and Row, 1967.

Dunnigan, Alice Allison. *The Fascinating Story of Black Kentuckians: Their Heritage and Traditions.* Washington, D.C.: Associated Publishers, 1982.

Dyer, Thomas G. *The University of Georgia: A Bicentennial History, 1785–1985.* Athens: University of Georgia Press, 1985

Edgar, Walter. *South Carolina: A History.* Columbia: University of South Carolina Press, 1998.

Ehle, John. *The Free Men.* New York: Harper & Row, 1965.

Epling, Robert T. "Seasons of Change: Football Desegregation at the University of Tennessee and the Transformation of the Southeastern Conference, 1963 to 1967." Doctoral dissertation, University of Tennessee, 1994.

Fairclough, Adam. *Race and Democracy: The Civil Rights Struggle in Louisiana, 1915–1972.* Athens: University of Georgia Press, 1995.

Fitzpatrick, Frank. *And the Walls Came Tumbling Down: Kentucky, Texas Western, and the Game That Changed American Sports.* New York: Simon and Schuster, 1999.

Fleming, Cynthia Griggs. "White Lunch Counters and Black Consciousness: The Story of the Knoxville Sit-Ins." In *Trial and Triumph: Essays in Tennessee's African American History,* ed. Carroll Van West. Knoxville: University of Tennessee Press, 2002.

Folmsbee, Stanley J., Robert E. Corlew, and Enoch L. Mitchell. *Tennessee: A Short History.* Knoxville: University of Tennessee Press, 1969.

Fountain, Clara G. *Danville: A Pictorial History.* Virginia Beach, VA: Donning, 1979.

Frady, Marshall. *Wallace.* New York: World Publishing, 1968.

Franklin, John Hope. *Race and History.* Baton Rouge: Louisiana State University Press, 1989.

Gannon, Michael, ed. *The New History of Florida.* Gainesville: University Press of Florida, 1996.

Garrow, David. *Birmingham, Alabama, 1956–63: The Black Struggle for Civil Rights.* New York: Carlson, 1989.

George, Nelson. *Elevating the Game: Black Men and Basketball.* New York: HarperCollins, 1992.

Glass, Mary Morgan, ed. *A Goodly Heritage: Memories of Greene County.* Eutaw, AL: Greene County Historical Society, 1977.

Grundy, Pamela. *Learning to Win: Sports, Education, and Social Change in Twentieth-Century North Carolina.* Chapel Hill: University of North Carolina Press, 2001.

Gunther, John. *Inside U.S.A.* Rev. ed. New York: Harper & Brothers, 1951.

Hagan, Jane Gray. *The Story of Danville.* New York: Stratford House, 1950.

Hampton, Henry, and Steve Fayer. *Voices of Freedom: An Oral History of the Civil Rights Movement from the 1950s to the 1980s.* New York: Bantam Books, 1990.

Harper, Frederick D. "Black Student Revolt on the White Campus." *Journal of College Student Personnel,* Vol. 10, Issue 5, September 1969, 291-95.

Harrison, Lowell H., and James C. Klotter. *A New History of Kentucky.* Lexington: University Press of Kentucky, 1997.

Herakovich, Doug. *Pack Pride: An Illustrated History of N.C. State Basketball.* Cary, NC: Yesterday's Future, 1994.

Hitchcock, Susan Tyler. *The University of Virginia: A Pictorial History.* Charlottesville: University Press of Virginia, 1999.

Hubbard, Jan, ed. *The Official NBA Encyclopedia.* 3rd ed. New York: Doubleday, 2000.

Hughes, Langston. *The Panther and the Lash: Poems of Our Times.* New York: Knopf, 1967. Reissue, New York: Vintage Books, 1992.

Hunter, Bruce. *Don't Count Me Out: The Irrepressible Dale Brown and His LSU Fighting Tigers.* Chicago: Bonus Books, 1989.

Hunter, Bruce, and Joe Planas. *Fighting Tigers Basketball: Great LSU Teams, Players and Traditions.* Chicago: Bonus Books, 1991.

Jacobs, Barry. *Golden Glory: The First 50 Years of the ACC.* Greensboro, NC: Mann Media, 2002.

Johnson, Elmer D., and Kathleen Lewis Sloan, comps. *South Carolina: A Documentary Profile of the Palmetto State.* Columbia: University of South Carolina Press, 1971.

Johnson, Erle. *Mississippi's Defiant Years, 1953–1973: An Interpretive Documentary with Personal Experiences.* Forest, MS: Lake Harbor, 1990.

Jones, Dorothy Phelps. *The End of an Era.* Durham, NC: St. Joseph's Historic Foundation, 2001.

Jones, Lewis P. *South Carolina: A Synoptic History for Laymen.* Columbia, SC: Sandlapper, 1971.

Kay, Bryan. "The History of Desegregation at the University of Virginia: 1950–1969." Senior thesis, Department of History, University of Virginia, 1979.

Kean, Melissa Fitzsimons. "'At a Most Uncomfortable Speed': The Desegregation of the South's Private Universities, 1945–64." Doctoral dissertation, Department of Philosophy, Rice University, 2000.

Kennedy, Stetson. *Jim Crow Guide: The Way It Was.* Boca Raton: Florida Atlantic University, 1959.

Klebenow, Anne. *200 Years through 200 Stories: A Tennessee Bicentennial Collection.* Knoxville: University of Tennessee Press, 1996.

Lamon, Lester C. *Blacks in Tennessee, 1791–1970.* Knoxville: University of Tennessee Press, 1981.

Lassiter, Matthew D., and Andrew B. Lewis, eds. *The Moderates' Dilemma: Massive Resistance to School Desegregation in Virginia.* Charlottesville: University Press of Virginia, 1998.

Lewis, Andrew B. "Emergency Mothers: Basement Schools and the Preservation of Public Education in Charlottesville." In *The Moderates' Dilemma: Massive Resistance to School Desegregation in Virginia*, eds. Matthew D. Lassiter and Andrew B. Lewis. Charlottesville: University Press of Virginia, 1998.

Litwack, Leon F. *Trouble in Mind: Black Southerners in the Age of Jim Crow.* New York: Alfred A. Knopf, 1998.

Locke, Tates, and Bob Ibach. *Caught in the Net.* West Point, NY: Leisure Press, 1982.

Loewen, James W. *Lies My Teacher Told Me: Everything Your American History Textbook Got Wrong.* New York: Simon & Schuster, 1995.

Loewen, James W., and Charles Sallis, eds. *Mississippi: Conflict and Change.* New York: Pantheon Books, 1974.

Marcus, Laurence R., and Benjamin D. Stickney. *Race and Education: The Unending Controversy.* Springfield, IL: Charles C. Thomas, 1981.

McCarthy, Kevin M., and Murray D. Laurie. *Guide to the University of Florida and Gainesville.* Sarasota: Pineapple Press, 1997.

McFall, Pearl Smith. *So Lives the Dream: History and Story of the Old Pendleton District, South Carolina, and the Establishment of Clemson College.* New York: Comet Press Books, 1953.

McKale, Donald M., and Jerome Reel Jr., eds. *Tradition: A History of the Presidency of Clemson University.* 2nd ed. Macon, GA: Mercer University Press, 1998.

McLane, Hardin, ed. *Championship Basketball by 12 Great Coaches.* Englewood Cliffs, NJ: Prentice-Hall, 1965.

McWorter, Diane. *Carry Me Home. Birmingham, Alabama: The Climactic Battle of the Civil Rights Revolution.* New York: Simon & Schuster, 2001.

Meredith, James. *James Meredith vs. Ole Miss.* Jackson: Meredith Publishing, 1995.

Mills, Nicholaus. *Like a Holy Crusade: Mississippi 1964—The Turning of the Civil Rights Movement in America.* Chicago: Ivan R. Dee, 1992.

Mohl, Raymond A., and Gary R. Mormino. "The Big Change in the Sunshine State: A Social History of Modern Florida." In *The New History of Florida*, ed. Michael Gannon. Gainesville: University Press of Florida, 1996.

Montgomery, James Riley, Stanley J. Folmsbee, and Lee Seifert Greene. *To Foster Knowledge: A History of the University of Tennessee, 1794–1970*. Knoxville: University of Tennessee Press, 1984.

Moore, John Hammond. *Albemarle: Jefferson's County, 1727–1976*. Charlottesville: University Press of Virginia, 1976.

———. *Columbia and Richland County: A South Carolina Community, 1740–1990*. Columbia: University of South Carolina Press, 1993.

Morris, Ron. *ACC Basketball: An Illustrated History*. Chapel Hill, NC: Four Corners Press, 1988.

Murray, Pauli. *Proud Shoes: The Story of an American Family*. New York: Harper and Row, 1956.

Muse, William V. *Auburn University: An Alabama Treasure and an International Resource*. Princeton: The Newcomen Society, 1998.

Myrdal, Gunnar. *An American Dilemma: The Negro Problem and Modern Democracy*. With Richard Sterner and Arnold Rose. New York: Harper and Brothers, 1944.

Neel, Roy M. *Dynamite! 75 Years of Vanderbilt Basketball*. Winter Park, FL: Burr Oak, 1975.

Nelli, Bert, and Steve Nelli. *The Winning Tradition: A History of Kentucky Wildcat Basketball*. Lexington: University Press of Kentucky, 1998.

Newton, C. M. *Newton's Laws: The C. M. Newton Story*. With Billy Reed. Lexington: Host Communications, 2000.

Newton, Michael. *The Invisible Empire: The Ku Klux Klan in Florida*. Gainesville: University Press of Florida, 2001.

O'Connor, Adrian. *River City: Stories of Danville*. Danville, VA: Danville Register & Bee, 1993.

Oliphant, Mary C. Simms. *The History of South Carolina*. River Forest, IL: Laidlaw Brothers, 1964.

Opdyke, John B., ed. *Alachua County: A Sesquicentennial Tribute.* Gainesville, FL: Alachua County Historical Commission, 1974.

Peeler, Tim. *Legends of N.C. State Basketball.* Champaign, IL: Sports Publishing, 2004.

Perkins, David. *Raleigh: A Living History of North Carolina's Capital.* Winston-Salem, NC: John F. Blair, 1994.

Pratt, Robert A. *We Shall Not Be Moved: The Desegregation of the University of Georgia.* Athens: University of Georgia Press, 2002.

Proctor, Samuel, and Wright Langley. *Gator History: A Pictorial History of the University of Florida.* Gainesville, FL: South Star, 1986.

Proudfoot, Merrill. *Diary of a Sit-In.* Urbana: University of Illinois Press, 1962.

Radoff, Morris L., ed. *The Old Line State: A History of Maryland.* Annapolis: Hall of Records Commission, State of Maryland, 1971.

Raines, Howell. *My Soul Is Rested: Movement Days in the Deep South Remembered.* New York: G. P. Putnam's Sons, 1977.

Raper, Arthur F. *The Tragedy of Lynching.* New York: Negro Universities Press, 1969.

Reed, Billy. *Transition Game: The Story of S. T. Roach.* Lexington: Host Communications, 2001.

Ruffin, Thomas F. *Under Stately Oaks: A Pictorial History of LSU.* Baton Rouge: Louisiana State University Press, 2002.

Rupp, Adolph. *Rupp's Championship Basketball for Player, Coach and Fan.* Englewood Cliffs, NJ: Prentice-Hall, 1948.

Russell, Bill. *Go Up for Glory.* With William McSweeny. New York: Coward-McCann, 1966.

Sansing, David G. *The University of Mississippi: A Sesquicentennial History.* Jackson: University Press of Mississippi, 1999.

Seymour, Robert. *"Whites Only": A Pastor's Retrospective on Signs of the New South.* Valley Forge, PA: Judson Press, 1991.

Shakoor, Jordana Y. *Civil Rights Childhood*. Jackson: University Press of Mississippi, 1999.

Shaw, Bynum. *The History of Wake Forest College, 1943–67*. Winston-Salem, NC: Wake Forest University, 1988.

Shipp, Bill. *Murder at Broad River Bridge: The Slaying of Lemuel Penn by Members of the Ku Klux Klan*. Atlanta: Peachtree Publishing, 1981.

Siegel, Frederick F. *The Roots of Southern Distinctiveness: Tobacco and Society in Danville, Virginia, 1780–1865*. Chapel Hill: University of North Carolina Press, 1987.

Skates, John Ray. *Mississippi: A Bicentennial History*. New York: W. W. Norton, 1979.

Sloan, Norman. *Confessions of a Coach*. With Larry Guest. Nashville: Rutledge Hill Press, 1991.

Smith, Dean. *A Coach's Life*. With John Kilgo and Sally Jenkins. New York: Random House, 1999.

Snider, William D. *Light on the Hill: A History of the University of North Carolina at Chapel Hill*. Chapel Hill: University of North Carolina Press, 1992.

Stokes, Durward T. *The History of Dillon County, South Carolina*. Columbia: University of South Carolina Press, 1978.

Storey, Jeffrey J. "Building Basketball Success in Big Orange Country: The Ray Mears Era in Tennessee Basketball." Master's thesis, University of Tennessee-Knoxville, 1996.

Thomas, Frances Taliaferro. *A Portrait of Historic Athens and Clarke County*. Athens: University of Georgia Press, 1992.

Tolnay, Stewart, and E. M. Beck. *A Festival of Violence: An Analysis of Southern Lynchings, 1882–1930*. Urbana: University of Illinois Press, 1995.

Tygiel, Jules. *Baseball's Great Experiment: Jackie Robinson and His Legacy*. New York: Vintage Books, 1983.

Wall, Bennett H., ed. *Louisiana: A History*. Wheeling, IL: Harlan Davidson, 1984.

Warren, Robert Penn. *Who Speaks for the Negro?* New York: Random House, 1965.

Weisbrot, Robert. *Freedom Bound: A History of America's Civil Rights Movement.*
New York: W. W. Norton, 1990.

West, Carroll Van, ed. *Trial and Triumph: Essays in Tennessee's African American
History.* Knoxville: University of Tennessee Press, 2002.

White, Theodore. *The Making of the President 1964.* New York: Atheneum
Publishers, 1965.

Wier, Sadye H., and John F. Marszalek. *A Black Businessman in White
Mississippi, 1886–1974.* Jackson: University Press of Mississippi, 1977.

Wolfe, Suzanne Rau. *The University of Alabama: A Pictorial History.*
Tuscaloosa: University of Alabama Press, 1983.

Woodward, C. Vann. *The Strange Career of Jim Crow.* Oxford: Oxford
University Press, 1966.

Wright, George C. *A History of Blacks in Kentucky, Vol. 2. In Pursuit of Equality,
1890–1980.* Frankfort: Kentucky Historical Society, 1992.

Wright, Louis B. *South Carolina: A Bicentennial History.* New York: W. W.
Norton, 1976.

Wright, Richard. *Black Boy.* New York: Harper & Row, 1945.

NEWSPAPERS

Advocate (Baton Rouge, La.)

Anderson News Leader (S.C.)

Anderson Independent (S.C.)

Atlanta Constitution

Atlanta Journal

Atlanta Journal and Constitution

Augusta Chronicle

Baltimore Sun

Banner-Herald (Athens, Ga.)

Birmingham News

Birmingham Post-Herald

Carolina Blue

Cavalier Daily (UVa student newspaper)

Chapel Hill Weekly

Charlotte News

Charlotte Observer

Chronicle (Duke U. student newspaper)

Clarion-Ledger (Jackson, Miss.)

Columbia Record

Commercial Appeal (Memphis, Tenn.)

Courier-Journal (Louisville, Ky.)

Daily News (Jackson, Miss.)

Daily News (Los Angeles, Calif.)

Daily Progress (Charlottesville, Va.)

Daily Reveille (LSU student newspaper)

Daily Star (Meridian, Miss.)

Daily Tar Heel (UNC student newspaper)

Danville Register

Danville Register & Bee

Diamondback (U. Maryland student newspaper)

Durham Morning Herald

Durham Sun

Evening Bulletin (Philadelphia, Pa.)

Evening Star and Daily News (Washington, D.C.)

Fayetteville Observer

Florida Alligator (U. Florida student newspaper)

Florida Times-Union

Gainesville Sun

Greensboro Daily News

Greensboro News and Record

Greensboro Record

Greenville News

Gwinnett Daily News (Ga.)

Herald (Rock Hill, S.C.)

Huntsville Times

Hustler (Vanderbilt U. student newspaper)

Journal News (Westchester, N.Y.)

Kansas City Star

Kentucky Kernel (U. Kentucky student newspaper)

Knoxville Journal

Lexington Herald-Leader

Marietta Daily Journal

Milwaukee Journal

Milwaukee Sentinel

Mississippi Press

Montgomery Advertiser

Nashville Banner

New Orleans States-Item

New York Daily News

New York Post

New York Times

News and Courier (Charleston, S.C.)

News and Observer (Raleigh, N.C.)

News of Orange County (N.C.)

News-Sentinel (Knoxville, Tenn.)

North Carolina Anvil

Plainsman (Auburn U. student newspaper)

Raleigh Times

Red and Black (UGA student newspaper)

Roanoke Times

Salt Lake Tribune

Selma Times-Journal

Shreveport Times

State (Columbia, S.C.)

Tampa Tribune-Times

The Technician (N.C. State U. student newspaper)

Tennessean

Tiger (Clemson U. student newspaper)

Times-Picayune (New Orleans, La.)

Tuscaloosa News

USA Today

Virginian-Pilot

Washington Post

Winston-Salem Journal

Winston-Salem Sentinel

INTERVIEWS

The author conducted interviews with the following persons during the course of writing this book: Farra Alford, Hank Allen, Bev Ashbury, Lee Baker, Coolidge Ball, Herbert Ball, Idella Ball, Rita Barnes, Tommy Bartlett, Tim Bassett, Greg Bernbrock, Julian Bond, Dan Bonner, Dale Brown, Myrtle Brown, Vic Bubas, Joel Buchanan, Lawrence Campbell, Larry Chapman, Wilbert Cherry, Charles Chestnut III, C. B. Claiborne, Claudia Claiborne, Bob Cole, Ron Coleman, Oscar Combs, Chip Connor, Phyllis Hancock Cooper, Fred Cox, Bobby Cremins, Jack Cristil, Rudy Davalos, Charlie Davis, Dick Davis, Kermit Davis, Jimmy Davy, Godfrey Dillard, Al Drummond, Barbara Drummond, Mike Dunleavy, Paul Ellis, Len Elmore, George Felton, Bud Ford, Phil Ford, Maxie Foster, Ralph Foster, Marvin Francis, William Friday, Larry Fry, Clarence Gaines, Tom Gardner, Howard Garfinkel, Paul Gaston, Artie Georges, Gino Gianfrancesco, Pete Gillen, Susan Glisson, Dick Grubar, Chester Grundy, Ferrell Guillory, John Guthrie, Joe B. Hall, Sandra Hall, Thomas Hearn, Al Heartley, Harvey Heartley, Paul Hewitt, Darryl Hill, Ronnie Hogue, Terry Holland, Irwin Holmes, Gene Hooks, Mildred Hudson, Wendell Hudson, Whack Hyder, Cal Irvin, Samuel Isaac, Ernie Jackson, Cob Jarvis, Annette Jenkins, Jerry Jenkins, Mary Johnson, Pete Johnson, Billy Jones, Tom Konchalski, Josie Knowlin, Len Kosmalski, Mike Krzyzewski, Harry Lesesne, Mike Lewis, Fred Lind, Craig Littlepage, Tates Locke, Casey Manning, Leon Marlaire, Jim McCachren, Jim McCloe, Jack McCloskey, Gilbert McGregor, Bill McLellan, Ray Mears, John Mengelt, Kent Merritt, Bud Millikan, Craig Mobley, Ernie Morris, Marty Morris, Mark Murphy, C. M. Newton, Bill Overton, Billy Packer, Darrell Payne, Elaine Payne, Tom Payne Jr., Dan Pollitt, Dennis Powell, Tom Price, George Raveling, Robert Raymond, Charles Reynolds, Guy Rhodes, Cornelius Ridley, Charlie Riley, Larry Robinson, Avon Rollins, David Sanders, Charles Scott, Cleveland Sellers, Roy Skinner, James Slade, Norm Sloan, Irwin Smallwood, Dean Smith, Larry Smith, Tubby Smith, Steve Steinwedel, Pat Stephens, Bill Tate, Vince Taylor, Collis Temple Jr., Collis Temple III, Dick Toth, Brenda Temple Tull, Hub Waldrop, Jimmy Walker, Solly Walker, Perry Wallace, Donnie Walsh, Bob Warren, Bucky Waters, Harold White, Gary Williams, Steve Williams, Brian Winters, Al Young Jr., and Bernice Young.

INDEX

A

Abdul-Rauf, Mahmoud (Chris Jackson), 288, 380
Abele, Julian Francis, 68
ACC. *See* Atlantic Coast Conference
African Americans: athlete difficulties, xiii, xxi–xxii; athlete performance, 130; athlete treatment, 229; athletics directors, xv, 20, 311, 328–29; Black Lives Matter for, xxiii; Black Power movement for, 114, 117, 160, 166, 351; civil rights era and, 84; as coaches, statistics, xv; in Durham, North Carolina, 69; institutions, xiii–xiv; out-of-state scholarships for, 275–76; pride, 147; quotas, 158–60; recruitment of, xviii, 107, 109–10, 153–54, 155; sports and, 149, 214; style of play, 203–4; veterans, 227; women, discrimination of, 161. *See also specific topics*
Alabama: Birmingham bombings in, 132; Bloody Sunday violence and, 138–39; Greene County, 78–80; integration, 79–80, 87–89, 124–25, 128, 129, 133, 144, 145–46, 244, 247, 259–60; Ku Klux Klan, 125, 132, 139, 294; racism and, 88, 138–39; Reconstruction and, 79; segregation, 86–87; Selma, 137–39, 145; Tuscaloosa, 140. *See also* Auburn University; University of Alabama
Alcindor, Lew (Kareem Abdul Jabbar), 46, 117, 153, 155, 187, 262
Alexander, Lamar, 40
Alford, Farra, xx, 130, 134, 136–37, 140, 142, 143, 177
Ali, Muhammad, 19
Allen, Forrest "Phog," 179
Allen, George, 324
Allen, Hank, 56, 61, 203, 316; on integration, 52, 68, 311–12; on racial hostilities, 324; University of Virginia and, 311–12, 321–22
Allen, Lucius, 117
Almond, J. Lindsay, 326
Alvarez, Carlos, 361
Andrews, Jim, 188

Angel, David, 252
Anheuser, Rick, 215
Applebome, Peter, 139
Armwood, George, 4
Arnholt, Tom, 46
Artest, Ron, 211
Asbury, Bev, 29, 30, 40–41, 42
Ashe, Arthur, 314
Ashmore, Harry, 132, 175, 325
Ashmore, Jim, 372, 373
Athens, Georgia: culture of, 218; integration, 232; Ku Klux Klan, 218; segregation, 233
athletics directors: African American, xv, 20, 311, 328–29; racial prejudice denial by, 349–50; women, 3, 329. *See also specific individuals*
Atlantic Coast Conference (ACC): African American leadership statistics, xv, 311; African American players, 152–53; basketball, xv–xviii, xxi–xxiii; Billy Jones on, 2, 20–21; color barrier in leadership, xv, xxiii; formation of, xvi; history and, xiv–xv, xvii, xxi–xxii; integration and, xiv–xv, xvii, 356; members of, xvi–xvii; minorities and, 20–21; 1970 Tournament, 214–15; University of South Carolina withdrawal from, 264
Attner, Paul, 320, 368
Auburn University: atmosphere of, 84–85; basketball program, 82–83; Bill Lynn and, 92–93; coaching staff, 92–93; current culture of, 86; diversity at, 87; integration, 85–89, 124; recruiting, 81–82, 83; Rudy Davalos and, 76; "Seven Dwarfs" squad at, 92, 371

B

Bailey, Thurl, 207
Baker, Kent, 11
Ball, Coolidge, xxii; athletic abilities, 306; character of, 293, 305; childhood, 293–94, 298–99; early career, 299; family, 293–94; high school career, 300; honors, 307; pioneering role, 304, 305; player statistics, 292, 306; postgraduate life, 308–9; reception of,

291–92; recruitment of, 292, 300–301; Robert Jarvis coaching and, 305, 306–7; siblings, 299; support for, 301
Ball, Harvey, 293, 295, 296
Ball, Herbert, 293, 294, 295, 299, 301, 304
Ball, Idella, 294, 295
Ball, Roosevelt, 299
Ball, Tillie, 293, 294, 295, 299
Banks, Eugene "Gene," 73
Barkum, Melvin, 154, 381
Barnes, Rod, 304
Barnett, Dick "Skull," 35
Barnett, Ross, 302–3, 371
Barnhart, Tony, 246
Barrows, Frank, 118
Barry, Marion, 40
Bartlett, Tommy, 158, 350, 359, 362; on program funding, 238; recruiting, 356–57, 364; Steve Williams relationship with, 363–64, 365
Bartley, Numan, 198, 200–201, 228–29, 325
Bass, Brandon, 274
Bassett, Tim, 189, 221, 224, 225, 235, 236, 237, 239, 273
Baylor, Elgin, 10, 100, 105
Beauregard, Pierre, 277
Beck, E. M., 162, 175, 226
Bee, Clair, 17, 234
Bellamy, Walt, 191
Belmont, Joe, 246
Bennett, Brian, 171, 189
Bennett, Tony, 321
Bernbrock, Greg, 281, 282
Berry, Wendell, 174–75, 195
Bible. *See* religion
Bilbo, Theodore G., 296
Bing, Dave, 8, 10
Birmingham, Alabama, 132, 259–60
Birth of a Nation, 243
Bishop, David, 8
Black Boy (Wright), 51, 217
Black Lives Matter, xxiii
Blackmon, Don, 319
Black Power movement, 114, 117, 160, 166, 351
Bloody Sunday, 138–39
Boe, Dan, 362–63
Bolton, Clyde, 123, 127, 135
Bond, Julian, 297, 324, 328
Bonner, Dan, xix, 317–18, 341

Boone, Daniel, 48
Bootle, W. A., 230
Bostic, John, 141
Bowie, Sam, 186
Boyd, Alexander, 79
Boyle, Sarah Patton, 325, 326
Bradley, Bill, xxiii
Bradshaw, Charlie, 183
Bragg, Braxton, 277
Branscomb, B. Harvie, 38, 40
Breathitt, Ned, 183
Brennan, Pete, 255
Brewer, Jim, 144
Briggs, Mark, 117
Briggs v. Elliott, 257
Britt, Tony, 328
Brown, Dale: coaching jobs, 280; coaching records, 288–89; hiring of, 287–88; on Temple family, 276
Browne, C. A., 247
Brown, Henry Billings, 138
Brown, Hubie, 62
Brown, James, 314
Brown, Larry, 108, 254
Brown, Myrtle, 354
Brown v. Board of Education, 6, 14, 33, 34; athletic programs impacts with, xiv–xv; Duke University compliance with, 61; Florida response to, 354; Georgia, 228–29, 230; Maryland, 4–5; Mississippi, 294–95, 297; North Carolina State University, 200–201; South Carolina and, 244, 259; University of Virginia, 324; Vanderbilt School of Religion response to, 39; Wake Forest and, 151, 152, 162. *See also* integration; segregation
Bryant, Paul "Bear," 124, 127–28, 135–36, 144, 180, 182, 246, 352
Bubas, Vic, 64, 184, 195, 204, 215; Claudius Claiborne relationship with, 71–72; coaching style, 63, 65; integration and, 59, 61; last year for, 66, 101; recruiting methods, 62; team marketing, 63
Buchanan, Joel, 350, 351, 364
Budd, Dave, 210
Bulkley, Joel, 113
Burleson, Tom, 22
Burt, Al, 161
Butler, Bill, 220

Byrd, Ben, 343, 346
Byrd, Harry, 324–25
Byrnes, Jimmy, 258, 260, 261

C
Calhoun, John, 261
Cameron, Eddie, 60
Campbell, Lawrence, 52, 53, 55, 57
Carleton, Mark, 278
Carlos, John, 117
Carmichael, Stokely, 29, 71
Carmody, Tom, 62, 63, 64
Carnesecca, Lou, 254
Carnes, Jimmy, 352
Carnevale, Corky, 264
Carter, Dan, 139
Carter, Jimmy, 224
Case, Everett, 63, 195, 196, 208, 209, 215, 216, 280
Casteen, John, 328–29
Central City, Kentucky: culture of, 169; demographics, 169; economy, 170; lynchings, 169–70
Central Intercollegiate Athletic Association, 202–3
Cervantes, Miguel de, 337
Chafe, William, 198, 200, 201
Chamberlain, Bill, 101, 119, 361
Chamberlain, Wilt, 34, 189, 262, 263
Chaney, Don, 281
Chaney, James, 370, 375
Chapel Hill, North Carolina, 110–12
Chapman, Larry, 77, 82, 90, 91
Chappell, Len, 151
Chenault, Ken, 41
Cherry, Wilbert "Wil," 331, 338, 341, 342; background, 344; feelings about leaving team, 346–47; Larry Robinson and, 343, 347; pioneering role, 343–44; player statistics, 346; on Ray Mears, 337; segregation experience for, 344–45; team tryout, 345
Chestnut, Charles, III, 358–59, 360
Christian, Bob, 191
Christianity, 23, 25–26, 61, 85, 133, 151, 377
Churchill, Winston, 230
Claiborne, Claudia, 62, 73
Claiborne, Claudius "C. B.," 2, 68, 114, 184; academics, 67; background, 51, 55–56; college career, 65–66; criticism of, 64; current interests, 73; Duke

University experience, 51, 55, 61–62, 73–74, 360; Durham, North Carolina and, 69; exclusion of, 64–65; freshman year, 63–64; graduation, 72–73; on Hank Allen, 203; high school career, 56–57; Horace McKinney and, 58–59; protests, 71–72; racism and, 57–58, 210, 257, 314–15; recruitment of, 61–62; segregation and, 53, 64–65; Vic Bubas relationship with, 71–72
Claiborne, Jerry, 128
Claiborne, "Pop," 56
Clark, E. Culpepper, 125, 295
Clark, George, 79
Clark, Jim, 138
Cleaver, Eldridge, 64
Clemson University: athletic program changes, 266–67; atmosphere of, 241–43, 249; basketball program, 245–46; Confederate flag and, 245, 246–49; Craig Mobley on, 241–42, 249; "Dixie," 245, 247, 248–49; facilities, 246, 266; football program, 246–47; Frank Howard and, 246; Harvey Gantt and, 260, 275; integration, 244, 260; protests, 242; segregation, 259; student population, 261; University of South Carolina and, 268; Wake Forest University and, 260
Cleveland, Charles, 129, 140
coaches: African American statistics for, xv; Auburn University, 92–93; integration compliance and, xx; Louisiana State University, 284, 287–88; University of Georgia, 220–21; University of Tennessee, 332. *See also specific individuals*
Cohen, Robert, 219
Cohodas, Nadine, 301, 309
Cole, Bob, 245, 253, 263, 264
Coleman, Arthur "Tonto," 349, 350
Coleman, Ron, 119, 140, 141, 352, 353, 357–58, 361
Cole, Nat King, 132
Cole, William P., Jr., 10
Colvard, Dean, 368, 369, 370, 371
Combs, Oscar, 172
Confederate flag: Alabama showing of, 249; Clemson University and, 245, 246–49; at Duke University, 37–38, 67–68; as racist symbol, xx, 247–48, 282; South Carolina displays of, 244–

45, 247–48; at University of Florida, 357; University of Mississippi use of, 301, 308; at Vanderbilt University, 42
Conley, George, 323
Conley, Larry, 181
Conner, Theophilus Eugene "Bull," 132
Connor, Hunter "Chip," xi–xii, 13, 199, 209, 313–15, 317–19
Conroy, Pat, 246
Cooper, Brent, 113
Cooper, Chuck, 334–35
Cooper, Phyllis Hancock, 145
Cooper, Tonya, 113
Cooper, Willie, 113
Cooper, Willis "Breeze," 205, 206, 207
Corey, Irwin, 76
Corrigan, Eugene "Gene," 115, 323
Covington, Wes, 106
Cox, Fred, 292, 293, 302, 305, 306–7, 341
Cramer, Gary, 314
Cremins, Bobby, 215, 254, 255, 262, 264
Cristil, Jack, 368, 375, 376
Crockett, Davy, 48
Crockett, Manuel, 197
Croom, Sylvester, 126, 367
Crowd, Horace, 234
Crowe, Dallas R., 326
Cunningham, Billy, 255
Cunningham, Sam "Bam," 128
Curran, Jack, 235
Currie, Bill, 215
Cutrer, Thomas, 278, 279

D
Dampier, Louie, 181
Dandridge, Bob, 203
Dantley, Adrian, 314
Danville, Virginia: atmosphere of, 53–54; Confederacy and, 51–52; integration, 52, 57–58; protests, 54–55; segregation, 52–53
Daugherty, Brad, 115
Davalos, Rudy, 76, 80, 81, 82, 83, 84, 94
Davidson College, 107–8
Davidson, Donald, 39
Davis, A. W., 345
Davis, Charlie, 116, 158, 205, 212; on Charlie Scott, 103; on Jack McCloskey, 165–66; on North Carolina racism, 106, 113; Norwood Todmann and, 148–49, 156, 157,

160–61, 165, 167; Player of the Year award and, 120–21, 214; on student protests, 119; on Wake Forest racial safety, 164
Davis, Dick, 141, 180, 337, 352, 356, 357, 361, 363
Davis, Harrison, III, 323
Davis, Jefferson, 51, 104, 124
Davis, Kermit, 342, 364, 367, 379; basketball background, 373–74; on Humphrey Coliseum, 376–77; on Mississippi racism, 374–75; player advocacy of, 378, 382; recruitment approach, 374, 377, 380; on segregation, 372, 373; University of Mississippi riots and, 303
Davis, Walter, 115
Davy, Jimmy, 43, 188; on color line, xii, 31–32; on Pearl High School, 35; on Perry Wallace, 28, 37, 38, 45, 47
Day Law, 175
Dedmon, Lee, 264
Dee, Johnny, 142
D'Emilio, John, 110
Dennard, Kenny, 73
Derrick, Mel, 101, 120
Dickey, Doug, 359
Dickey, Frank G., 183
Dietzel, Paul, 256
Dillard, Godfrey: activism and, 29; background, 29; racism and, 42, 44, 48; temperament, 29–30; Vanderbilt University and, 38, 40, 42
Dillon County, South Carolina, 252–53
Dinsmore, Jim, 89
Dix, Bennie, 61
"Dixie" (song): at Clemson University, 245, 247, 248–49; Craig Mobley on, 251; at Duke University, 67; as racist symbol, xx, 185, 245, 247–48; at University of Florida, 351; at University of Mississippi, 301, 308; Wake Forest protest of, 166–67
Dixie Classic, 208–9
Dodd, Bobby, 229
Donovan, Billy, 366
Dooley, Vince, 233
Dostoyevsky, Fyodor, 349
Douglas, Leon, 129, 140
Douglass, Frederick, xii, 4
Doyle, Don, 31
Draughton, Ralph Brown, 89

Driesell, Charles "Lefty," 104, 107, 108, 109, 197, 253, 264, 328
Drummond, Al, xix; academics, 313; athletic abilities, 317, 319, 320, 321, 322; Barry Parkhill and, 321–22; childhood, 313; on college experience, 313; on fans, 323; memories of, 13, 317, 318; postgraduate career, 327; reception of, 316, 323, 327; recruitment of, 313, 314, 315; on role, 322
Drummond, Barbara, 316–17
Du Bois, W. E. B. (William Edward Burghardt), xii, 31, 69, 97, 269
Duke, James B., 59
Duke University: academics, 66–67; attractions of, 63; Claudius Claiborne and, 51, 55, 61–62, 73–74, 360; dominance and titles, xvi–xvii; Durham history and culture, 68–69; integration, 59, 61, 64–65; player alienation, 67–68; protests, 70–71, 72; racist symbols at, 37–38, 67–68; recruiting, 73; Willis Smith and, 59, 60
Duncan, John, 335
Dunleavy, Mike, 255
Dunning, Joe, 214
Dunn, T. R., 129
Durham, Hugh, 355
Durham, North Carolina: African American community, 69; history and culture in, 68–69; integration and, 69–70; protests, 70, 71, 72. See also Duke University
Dwyre, Bill, 76
Dyer, Thomas, 231

E

Eastland, James, 297
Easy Rider, 237
Eaves, Joel, 92, 224, 238
Edens, A. Hollis, 61, 64
Edgar, Walter, 244
Edwards, Mike, 343, 346
Edwards, Robert C., 242, 248, 249, 260
Ehle, John, 110, 111
Eisenhower, Dwight, 230
Ekker, Ron, 191
Elkins, Charles, 97
Ellis, Cliff, 92
Ellison, Ralph, 367

Ellis, Paul, 88, 129, 131, 134, 136, 137, 140, 142, 143
Elmore, Len, 323
Emmett, Daniel David, 247
English, Alex, 262–63
Ennis, Reginald, 203, 204, 205
Epling, Robert T., 337
Erving, Julius, 314
Esposito, Sam, 196, 205, 207
Evans, Damon, 220
Evans, Mike, 106
Everly Brothers (Don and Phil), 169
Evers, Medgar, 125, 302

F

Fairclough, Adam, 175, 270, 275
Fats Domino, 272
Faubus, Orval, 230
Faulkner, William, 309, 311
Fellows, Frank, 11
Fisher, Sammy, 378
Fitzpatrick, Frank, 158, 182
Fleming, Vern, 222
Fletcher, Tim, 365
Flint, Paddy, 337
Florida: Brown v. Board of Education response in, 354; integration, 354, 359; Ku Klux Klan, 353; lynchings, 353, 354; race relations, 353–54, 359. See also University of Florida
Fogler, Eddie, 115
Folsom, James "Kissin' Jim," 88
Fonda, Peter, 237
Ford, Danny, 136
Ford, Harris "Bud," 332, 337, 342, 343
Ford, Phil, 115, 197
Forrest, Nathan Bedford, 139
Fortune, Porter, 308
Foster Auditorium, 123–24, 145–46
Foster, Bill, 328
Foster, Maxie, 222, 231, 232–33, 236–37
Foster, Ralph, 83, 85, 87
Frady, Marshall, xxii, 145, 247
Francis, Marvin "Skeeter," 260
Franklin, Harold, 89
Franklin, John Hope, xii, 247
Frazier, Walt, 65
Friday, William, 208, 209
Fry, Larry, 367; athletic abilities, 369, 377–78, 379; childhood and mother, 377; Jerry Jenkins friendship with, 381–82; recruitment, 378; signing of,

369, 372, 377; Vietnam War
opposition, 378–79
Fuller, Howard, 70

G

Gabor, Zsa Zsa, 314
Gaines, Clarence "Big House," 192, 203;
Billy Packer and, 152, 153; on
Kentucky racism, 27; on racism, 27,
161, 198, 335; recruitment approach,
157–58, 161; on Tennessee racism,
335; Wake Forest and Winston-Salem
State rivalry and, 162–63
Gandhi, Mohandas, 40
Gantt, Harvey, 244, 260, 261, 275
Garber, Mary, 211
Garfinkel, Howard, 209
Garrett, Glenn "Goober," 137, 144
Garr, Homer, 44
Gaske, Steve, 321
Gaston, Paul M., 311, 328
Gee, Gordon, 49
George, Bill, 150
George, Leonard, 357, 361
George, Nelson, 149, 158
Georges, Artie, 167
George Washington High School, 57
Georgia: *Brown v. Board of Education* and,
228–29, 230; education system, 227–
31; integration, 229–31, 232; Ku Klux
Klan in, 218, 231–32; lynching, 227;
racism, 226–27; segregation, 230–31,
233. *See also* University of Georgia
Georgia Tech: John Hyder and, 223–24;
postgame fight, 224–26; protests, 229;
Sugar Bowl (1956), 229; University of
Georgia rivalry, 223–26
Gianfrancesco, Gino, 223, 224, 225, 235–
36, 332
Gibson, Bill "Hoot," 166, 313–17, 319,
320, 321, 322, 323, 328
The Gift of Good Land (Berry), 174–75, 195
Gillen, Pete, 164
Gilliam, James William "Junior," 32
Gilliam, Joe, 34
Gilmore, Artis, 130
Glisson, Susan M., 298
Gold, Joe Dan, 368, 373, 374
Goodman, Andrew, 370, 375
Graham, B. L. "Bonnie," 372
Graham, Frank Porter, 59–60, 110, 111
Graham, Marian, 60

Grant, Joseph, 241, 248
Grant, Robert, 154
Grant, Ulysses, 339
Graves, Jerry, 378
Graves, Ray, 351
Greene County, Alabama, 78–80
Green, "Jumping Johnny," 209
Gregory, Dick, 70
Grier, Bobby, 229
Griffin, Marvin, 228–29
Griffith, D. W., 243
Grubar, Dick, 99, 101, 102, 109, 115,
246, 360, 365
Grundy, Chester, xiv, 171, 172, 184, 185–
86, 188, 190, 193
Grundy, Pamela, 118
Grunfeld, Ernie, 337
Guerin, Richie, 191
Guillory, Ferrell, 279
Gunther, John, 243
Guthridge, Bill, 102
Guthrie, John, xxii, 219; coaching style,
238; concern for players, 239; on
Georgia Tech fight, 224; recruiting,
220–22, 235; on Ronnie Hogue, 234

H

Hagan, Cliff, 185
Hall, Joe B., 182, 183, 187, 189–90
Hall, Sandra, 271, 272, 273, 274, 285,
287
Hamer, Fannie Lou, 70
Hannah, John, 136
Harkness, Jerry, 158, 214, 368
Harris, Dickie, 256
Harris, Henry, Jr., xxi, 28, 89, 130, 143;
background, 78–81; Bill Lynn on, 77,
83, 90, 91, 94; coaching position, 94;
college career, 91–92, 93–94; college
experience, 76; high school career, 78,
81; injuries, 78, 91, 94; NBA and, 94;
Perry Wallace Jr. on, 84–85;
personality, 77–78, 90; player statistics,
91, 94; playing style, 91–92;
recruitment of, 81–82, 83; suicide, 75–
77, 85, 94–95; treatment of, 84, 85,
90–91, 376; War Eagle scholarship for,
87
Harris, Henry, Sr., 80
Harris, Willie Pearl, 80, 81
Hartsfield, William B., 230
Haskins, Clem, 186

Haskins, Don, 16, 181
Hatton, Vernon, 181
Hawkins, John, 308
Hawkins, Virgil, 161, 162
Hayes, Elvin, 117, 281
Haywood, Spencer, 117, 190, 338
Heard, Alexander, 29
Hearn, Thomas, 150, 151
Hearst, Patti, 76
Heartley, Al: academics, 216; ACC
    Tournament (1970), 214–15; athletic
    abilities, 196, 205, 212, 213–14;
    college career, 205–6, 215–16; defense
    skills, 211–12; family life, 202; high
    school, 201–2, 204; honors, 196; New
    York University and, 212; on Norman
    Sloan, 216; Norman Sloan on, 196,
    205–6, 213–14; offense and, 213;
    professional career, 216; role of, 195–
    96; team tryout, 196–97, 205;
    treatment of, 211
Heartley, Harvey, 202, 205–7, 210; on
    integration, xiv–xv; on North
    Carolina racism, 198–200; on "smoke
    and smother" style of play, 17, 204
Heartley, Matthew, 204
Heisman, John, 246
Helms, Jesse, 60, 110, 198
Henry, Butch, 154
Herbert, Dick, 210
Hewitt, Paul, 112
Heyman, Art, 59
Heys, Sam, 42
The Hidden Wound (Berry), 174
Higbe, Kirby, 53
Hill, Cleo, 152–53, 163
Hill, Darryl, 5, 154, 249
Hill, Palestine, 249
Hill, Stanley, 372, 373
Hinkle, Tony, 212
Hitler, Adolph, 279
Hodges, Luther, 200–201
Hogue, Gaylord, 234
Hogue, James Albert, 233
Hogue, Lucille, 233, 234
Hogue, Ronnie, xxi, 7; academics, 239;
    athletic abilities, 223, 225, 238–39;
    childhood, 233; college career, 222;
    college experiences, xxiii, 219; family,
    233–34; Georgia Tech fight, 224–26;
    high school career, 221; honors, 222,
    223; Lemuel Penn and, 217–18, 234;

Malcolm X and, 225; personality,
    235–36, 237; player statistics, 239;
    recruitment of, 221–22; on role of
    pioneer, 239; on safety of campus,
    237; student organizations, 236–37;
    women and dating for, 235–36
Holland, Terry, 107–8, 312, 321, 328
Holloway, Condredge, 154, 335, 381
Holmes, Hamilton, 220, 226, 230–31,
    232, 324
Holmes, Irwin, 196–97, 206
Hood, James, 124, 125
Hooks, Gene, 155
Hopper, Dennis, 237
Horner, Jack, 210
Houston, Wade, 177, 336
Howard, Frank, xx, 256, 266, 267;
    coaching career, 246; protests and,
    242, 248
Howell, Bailey, 372, 373, 374, 379
Hudson, Lou, xxi, 113, 153
Hudson, Mildred, xxi, 126, 128, 131–34,
    143–44, 145
Hudson, Vanessa, 133
Hudson, Wendell, xviii, xx, 306, 352;
    acceptance of, 134–36; athletic
    abilities, 130–31, 136, 142–43;
    childhood, 133–34; college career,
    129; college experience, xxii, 134–35,
    143–44, 307; friendships, 139–40;
    high school career, 126; honors, 142,
    144; on Mississippi State University
    fans, 376; NBA career, 145;
    personality, 129–30; player statistics,
    136, 239; recruitment of, 128, 131;
    University of Alabama and, xxi, 124,
    126, 307; on University of Mississippi
    racism, 137
Humphrey Coliseum, 376–77
Hunter, Bruce, 280, 281
Hunter, Charlayne (Hunter-Gault), 220,
    226, 230–32, 324
Hunter, Leslie, 35
Hurston, Zora Neale, 75
Hutchinson, Bud R., 89
Hyder, John "Whack," 223–24, 225, 226,
    228
Hyder, Tommy, 224

I

Iba, Henry "Hank," 10, 17
Ingram, Cecil "Hootie," 267

Institute for Diversity and Ethics in Sport (TIDES), xv

integration: ACC and, xiv–xv, xvii, 356; Adolph Rupp and, xx, 171; Alabama, 79–80, 87–89, 124–25, 128, 129, 133, 144, 145–46, 244, 247, 259–60; armed forces, 174; athlete performance and, 130; athletics and, xiii, xiv–xv, xx–xxii, 326–27, 349–50, 368; Auburn University, 85–89, 124; Brenda Temple Tull on pressures with, 84; Clemson University, 244, 260; coaches compliance with, xx; Dean Smith and, 25, 111–12, 374; Duke University, 59, 61, 64–65; education and, xiii–xv; Florida, 354, 359; Frank McGuire and, 261–62, 263; Georgia, 229–31; Hank Allen on, 52, 68, 311–12; Herman Millikan and, 13; Louisiana State University, 275, 277; Louisville, Kentucky, 176–77; Maryland, 6; Mississippi, 294–95, 297–98, 370; Mississippi State University, 367–69, 382; Nashville, Tennessee, 34; Norman Sloan experience of, 207, 211, 375–76; North Carolina, 69–70, 111–12, 200–201; North Carolina State, 195–96, 197; SEC and, xiv–xv, xxi–xxii, 356; South Carolina, 244, 257–58; University of Alabama, 124–25; University of Florida, 350–51, 354, 358, 359–60, 366; University of Georgia, 219, 226, 232; University of Kentucky, 182–83, 186–87; University of Maryland, 4–5; University of Mississippi, 291–92, 302–3; University of North Carolina, 25, 111–12, 374; University of South Carolina, 244, 256–57, 260–61; University of Tennessee, 335–37; University of Virginia, 312–13, 314, 326–27; Vanderbilt University, 28–29, 39–41; Virginia, 52, 57–58, 324–26; Wake Forest University, 150–51, 153–55, 159, 160, 161. *See also Brown v. Board of Education*

Invisible Man (Ellison), 367
Irvin, Cal, 55, 203–4, 294
Irvine, Weldon, Jr., 164
Isaac, Samuel, 77, 80, 92
Issel, Dan, 121

J

Jabbar, Kareem Abdul (Lew Alcindor), 46, 117, 153, 155, 187, 262
Jackson, Chris (Mahmoud Abdul-Rauf), 288, 380
Jackson, Ernie, xviii, 67–68, 71, 119, 214, 256
Jackson, James H., 16
Jackson, Jesse, 41
Jackson, Maynard, 70
Jackson, Wilbur, 128
Jackson, Willie, 357, 361
Jamison, Antawn, 115, 121
Jarvis, Robert "Cob," 45; Coolidge Ball and coaching of, 305, 306–7; recruiting, 300–301, 304
Jefferson, Thomas, 312, 324
Jenkins, Annette, 380, 381
Jenkins, Bert, 379
Jenkins, Jerry "Slim" (also "Spider"), 367, 377, 378; athletic abilities, 369, 379; childhood, 374, 380–81; Larry Fry friendship with, 381–82; sensitivity, 381–82; signing of, 369, 372
Jim Crow, xiv, 31, 138, 175
John 4:20, 23
Johnson, Bob, 41
Johnson, Frank, 88
Johnson, Joseph A., 39
Johnson, Julius "Pete," Jr., 4, 16; academics, 14; college career, 8–9; family, 6–7; pioneering role of, 2, 3, 5–6; player statistics, 11–12, 19; racism and, xix, 2, 12–13, 15; strengths, 12; style of play, 18–19
Johnson, Julius, Sr., 6
Johnson, Lyman, 188
Johnson, Lyndon, xx, 56, 89, 108
Johnson, Mary, 139
Johnson, Susie, 6
Johnston, Joseph, 68
Jones, Billy, 4, 65, 329; academics, 14; on ACC, 2, 20–21; on authority, 19–20; background, 7–8; college career, 2, 9; as color barrier pioneer, xv, xxi, 2–3, 5; injuries, 16; isolation, 15; player statistics, 11; racism and, xix, 12–13; social life, 15–16; strengths, 12; style of play, 18, 343; Sugar Bowl (1965), 1
Jones, Charlie, 110, 111
Jones, Dorothy Phelps, 70

Jones, Ernest, 7
Jones, LeRoi, 70
Jones, Lewis, 243
Jones, Ruth, 7
Jones, Sam, 62, 106, 203
Jordan, Joe, 223
Jordan, Michael, 41, 81, 100, 115, 116, 118, 153, 223
Joyce, Kevin, 255, 264

K
Kaiser, Roger, 231
Kay, Bryan, 312
Kean, Melissa Fitzsimons, 39, 59
Kearns, Tommy, 254
Keech, Larry, 106
Kehoe, Jim, 11
Kemp, Joe, 181
Kennedy, John, 53, 124, 125, 236, 302, 303
Kennedy, Robert, 117, 124
Kennedy, Stetson, 138
Kentucky: ban on interracial marriage, 175; Day Law, 175; Louisville, integration in, 176–77; lynchings, 169–70; racism, 27; segregation, 174–75; slavery, 175; Wendell Berry on, 174–75. *See also* University of Kentucky
Kessler, Alec, 222
Key, V. O., Jr., 324
Khayat, Robert, 373
Kilpatrick, James J., 325
Kindred, Dave, 181
King, Bernard, 337
King, Clennon, 302
King, Martin Luther, Jr., xxiii, 133, 162, 202, 225, 230; assassination, xxi, 70, 117, 206–7; on Birmingham race relations, 132; Danville, Virginia and, 53, 54, 55; holiday, 198, 243; on non-compliance, xx, 123; Raleigh, North Carolina and, 206–7
King, Riley "B. B.," 310
King, Ron, 356
Knight, Douglas, 70
Knowlin, Josie, 66, 67, 68, 71, 72
Knoxville, Tennessee, 331, 335
Komives, Howard, 368
Kosmalski, Len, 143, 331, 337, 341–42, 343, 346
Kretzer, Bill, 215

Krzyzewski, Mike, xvii, xx, 73, 165, 178, 368
Ku Klux Klan: Alabama, 125, 132, 139, 294; Florida, 353; Georgia, 218, 231–32; Mississippi, 370; North Carolina, 69, 198; in South Carolina, 243, 247–48; University of Georgia and, 231–32; white allies murdered by, 79

L
Lacey, Sam, 301
Lancaster, Harry, 182
Landry, Tom, 343
Langley, Wright, 351, 360
Langston High School, 55, 56
Langston, John Mercer, 56, 57
Larese, York, 255
La Traviata, 33–34
Lattin, Dave "Big Daddy," 46
Laurinburg Institute, 105, 106–7, 108
Lawson, Harbin "Red," 231
Lawson, James, 40
Lee, Clyde, 44, 49
Lee, George, 296
Lee, Harper, 1, 7
Lee, Howard, 118
Lee, Robert E., 104, 145, 339
Leftwich, Ed, 213, 215
Leitao, Dave, 329
Leonard, Willie, 357
Lesesne, Harry, 259, 260
Lewis, Andrew B., 325, 326
Lewis, Anthony, 44
Lewis, Bob, 99, 235
Lewis, Guy, 380
Lewis, John, 40, 54
Lewis, John Tillery, 247
Lewis, Mike, 62
Lienard, Bob, 222, 235
Lincoln, Abraham, 175, 183, 339
Lind, Fred, 63, 66, 73, 118
Linn, Bill, 142
Linn, George, 124
Lipper, Bob, 320
Littlepage, Craig, 20, 311, 328–29
Litwack, Leon F., xii, 86, 88, 176, 227–28, 295
Lloyd, Harry, 267
Locke, Taylor "Tates," 266, 267
Loewen, James W., 373, 380
Long, Earl, 278
Long, Huey, 278–79

Long, Paul, 163
Lott, Trent, 301
Lotz, John, 108, 114, 365–66
Louisiana: education system, 275; Huey Long, 278–79; lynchings, 270; *Plessy v. Ferguson,* 275; segregation, 270–72, 275; voting restrictions, 270
Louisiana State University: basketball program, 280; coaching staff, 284, 287–88; facilities, 281, 286; fans, 285–86; football program, 279–80, 282; history of, 277–78; Huey Long and, 278–79; integration, 275, 277; Pete Maravich and, 280–81, 282; racism and, 277, 282–83; recruiting, 269, 276, 281–82, 283; team records, 281, 288–89; Temple family legacy, 269, 276, 284; Tiger Stadium, 279; University of Kentucky and, 287
Louisville, Kentucky, 176–77
Love, Bob, 281
Lowe, Sidney, 207
Lucas, John, 102, 197
Lucie, David, 225
Lucy, Autherine, 124, 229–30, 232
lynching: assaults on women, 175–76; Florida, 353, 354; Georgia, 227; Kentucky, 169–70; Louisiana, 270; Maryland, 4; Mississippi, 295–96
Lynn, Bill, 81, 87; on Auburn, 85; on Henry Harris Jr., 77, 83, 90, 91, 94; style of play, 92–93

M
MacArthur, Douglas, 279
Maddox, Carl, 281
Maddry, Lawrence, 315
Madison, James, 324
Mahorn, Rick, 203
Malcolm X, 77, 90, 225
Male, Evan "Bus," 315
Malone, Vivian, 124, 125
Maloy, Mike, 65, 104
Manley, John R., 111
Manning, Casey, 262; athletic abilities, 254; character of, 263, 265; childhood, 252; college career, 253–54, 264–65; family, 252; high school career, 252, 253; on North Carolina State racism, 207–8; pioneering role, 263, 265; player statistics, 265; professional career, 268; recruitment of, 253–54

Maravich, Petar "Press," 280–81, 282, 284, 286, 287
Maravich, Pete "Pistol Pete," 92, 98, 280–81, 284, 286, 291
Marin, Jack, 62, 63
Marlaire, Leon, 130
marriage, 102–3, 175, 252
Marszalek, John F., 375
Martin, Charles, 229
Maryland: *Brown v. Board of Education* and, 4–5; integration, 5, 6; lynching, 4; slavery and, 4. *See also* University of Maryland
"Maryland, My Maryland," 4
Mason, Gilbert, 381
Mauer, John, 333, 334, 372
McAdoo, Bob, 115
McCachren, Jim, 365
McCarthy, James Harrison "Babe," 224, 369–70, 371, 372, 373, 378
McCarthy, Mickey, 225
McClain, Lester, 335, 338
McClain, Ted "Hound Dog," 36
McClane, Hardin, 337
McClellan, Bill, 267
McCloskey, Jack, 156, 158, 159, 160, 164–66
McCray, Lawrence, 355, 356–57
McDaniels, Jim, 44, 186
McDuffie, Frank, 106, 107, 108, 109
McDuffie, Sammie, 108
McGregor, Gilbert "Gil," 103, 158, 161; background, 262; on Norwood Todmann, 147, 148, 149, 156, 160, 165–66; on racism, xviii, 160; on Tom Payne Jr., 191; at Winston-Salem State, 163
McGrew, Alvin, 131
McGuire, Al, 254
McGuire, Dick, 120
McGuire, Frank, 124, 220, 265, 315; integration and, 261–62, 263; personality, 255, 256; recruiting, 253–54, 255; at St. John's University, 184–85, 235, 255; style of play, 254; team records, 254–55; University of North Carolina and, xvii, 99, 103, 111, 112, 195, 247; University of South Carolina and, 214–15, 263–64, 266, 268; Wilt Chamberlain and, 262, 263
McGuire, Frank, Jr., 268
McKeithen, John, 269

McKinney, Horace "Bones," 58–59, 151, 153, 155, 195, 260
McKissack and McKissack, 34
McLendon, John, xiii, 35, 60, 116, 184, 203, 216, 371
McLennon Junior College, 146
McMillen, Tom, 316, 323
McMillian, Jim, 98
McNeir, Waldo F., 275
McWhorter, Boyd, 273
McWhorter, Diane, 260
Mears, Ray, 180, 306, 356; coaching approach, 332–34, 337, 338–39, 346; on Larry Robinson, 342–43; recruiting, 334; team records, 334, 338
Meeks, Malcolm, 349, 366; athletic abilities, 357, 362; confidence of, 358; racism experienced by, 360; recruitment, 350, 352, 357
Mengelt, John, 77, 82, 87, 90–92, 93, 94, 142, 291
Meredith, James, 23, 89, 292, 295, 301, 302, 304, 305
Merlene, Davis, 187
Merritt, Kent, 323–24, 326–27, 328
Middleton, Troy H., 275
Miles College, 131
Miller, Larry, 99, 116
Millikan, Herman "Bud," 15, 63; on Billy Jones, 2, 12; death, xix; integration and, 13; recruiting, 8; style of play, 17–18; team records, 10–11; treatment of players and, xix, 9, 19–20
Minnifield, Dirk, 189
Minter, Jim, 349
Mississippi: *Brown v. Board of Education* and, 294–95, 297; demographics, 294; education system, 294–95; heritage of, 298; integration, 291–92, 297–98, 370; Ku Klux Klan, 370; lynchings, 295–96; progress in, 382; racial violence, 295–97, 370; racism, 23–24, 44, 374–75; segregation, 295–96; sharecropping, 294; Starkville, 44, 287, 367, 375–76. *See also* University of Mississippi
Mississippi State University: facilities, 44, 367, 376; fan behavior, 376; hazing at, 381–82; Humphrey Coliseum opening, 376–77; integration, 367–69, 382; recruiting, 376–77; segregation, 367, 369, 373, 382
Mitts, Billy, 369
Mobley, Craig, 361; academics, 250; Casey Manning and, 252; childhood, 250; on Clemson University, 241–42, 249; college career, 267; on "Dixie," 251; family, 249; high school career, 250–51; honors, 251; player statistics, 267; popularity of, 266–67; protests and, 242; recruitment of, 251–52
Moe, Doug, 254, 255
Mohl, Raymond A., 352
Monroe, Earl "The Pearl," 163, 203
Monroe, James, 324
Montgomery, Johnny, 294
Moore, Archie, 192
Moore, Harry T., 354
Moore, Henriette, 354
Mormino, Gary R., 352
Morocco, Zippy, 222
Morris, Ernie, 147
Morris, Jim, 101
Morris, Marty, 337, 338, 339
Morrison, Helen, 61
Mount, Rick, 108
Mousa, Rick, 264
Mullins, Jeff, 59
Murphy, Calvin, 98
Murphy, Ed, 308
Murphy, Mark, 78, 85, 93
Murray, Donald, 4
Murray, Pauli, 69, 241, 243
Musselman, Art, 266
Myrdal, Gunnar, 261

N
Namath, Joe, 216
Nash, Diane, 40
Nashville, Tennessee: culture of, 30–31; integration, 34; interracial competition, 32; Pearl High School in, 25, 27, 32, 34–37, 126; politics of, 31; protests, 39–40; segregation, 30–32, 33; tolerance, 32. *See also* Vanderbilt University
Nelli, Bert, 179
Nelli, Steve, 179
Neumann, Johnny, 291
Newton, Bill "Fig," 286
Newton, Charles Martin "C. M.," xvii, 136, 137, 181, 182, 239, 362, 365; impact of, 124, 128, 355; recruiting,

127, 128, 130, 131, 159, 183; sensitivity of, 141–42; tolerance and, 140–41; as University of Alabama coach, 82–83, 124, 126–27, 128, 144–45, 239, 371

Newton, Deb, 140

Newton, Michael, 353

New York University, 212

Neyland, Bob "The General," 333, 334, 336–37

Nixon, Richard, 76, 120

Noble, C. R., 373

Nordan, Lewis, 291

North Carolina: Central Intercollegiate Athletic Association, 202–3; Chapel Hill, 110–12; education system, 200–201, 202; integration, 69–70, 111–12, 200–201; Ku Klux Klan, 69, 198; media coverage, 210–11; Pearsall Plan, 201; protests, 70, 71, 72; racism, 69, 106, 113, 198–200. *See also* Duke University; Raleigh, North Carolina; University of North Carolina; Wake Forest University

North Carolina State University: ACC Tournament (1970), 214–15; attractions of, 204–5; *Brown v. Board of Education* and, 200–201; Dixie Classic, 208–9; fans, 209–10; integration, 195–96, 197; New York University and, 212; protests, 206–7; racism at, 207–8; student body, 198

Northington, Nat, 154, 183

O

Oakley, Charles, 203

O'Connell, Stephen C., 350–51, 360, 361, 364

O'Connor, Ian, 372

Odom, Ernest, 129, 140

Odums, Raymond, 129

Olympics, 117–18

O'Neal, Shaquille, 288

Oswald, John, 182

"O Tannenbaum," 4

Outlar, Jesse, 219

Overton, Bill, 87, 155, 157, 256

Owens, Jesse, 232

Owens, Ted, 283

Owens, Tom, 255

P

Packer, Billy, xv, 126, 158, 165, 213; on Charles Scott, 98, 100, 103, 116;

Clarence Gaines and, 152, 153; on Norwood Todmann, 149, 156, 164; on racism, 159, 209; at Wake Forest University, 151, 152–53, 155, 163, 205

Page, Greg, 154

Parker High School, 126, 130, 133

Parkhill, Barry, 319–22

Parks, Rosa, xxii, 188

Patterson, Eugene, 210–11

Payne, Darrell, 172, 173, 178, 192

Payne, Elaine, 172, 173, 174, 187

Payne, Margie, 187

Payne, Thomas, Sr., 173

Payne, Tom, Jr., 130, 222, 276, 286; academic career, 187, 188; Adolph Rupp and, 171, 172, 173, 179, 187–88, 191; athletic abilities, 189; character of, 173; childhood, 173, 174; college career, 172, 179, 188–89; criminal activity, 78, 170, 172–73, 191, 192; early career, 178; family, 173–74, 178–79; high school career, 177–78, 187; on imprisonment, 170; Joe Hall and, 189–90; legacy of, 192–93; physical attributes, 173; on pioneer role, 178–79; potential of, 192; professional career, 190–92; on racism, 171; recruitment of, 178, 187; University of Kentucky and, 170–71

Pearl High School, Nashville, 25, 27, 32, 34–37, 126

Pearsall Plan, 201

Peeler, Tim, 208

Penn, Lemuel, 217–18, 234

Pepe, Phil, 212

Pepper, Claude, 353

Perry, Otto, 355

Pettijohn, Samuel, 89

Pettit, Bob, 280

Phillips, Bruce, 115, 212

Piccolo, Brian, 154

Planas, Joe, 281

Plessy v. Ferguson, 138

Polk, Bob, 37

Pollitt, Dan, 108, 111, 119

Populism, 227

Porter, Will, 169–70

Powell, Colin, 41

Powell, Dennis, 265

Pratt, Robert, 218

Presley, Elvis, 373

Price, Tom, 255, 256

Proctor, Samuel, 351, 360
protests/student protests: Birmingham, Alabama, 132; Charles Scott and, 119–20; Claudius Claiborne and, 71–72; Clemson University, 242; Craig Mobley and, 242; Danville, Virginia, 54–55; Duke University, 70–71, 72; Durham, North Carolina, 70, 71, 72; Frank Howard and, 242, 248; Georgia Tech, 229; Nashville, Tennessee, 39–40; North Carolina State University, 206–7; South Carolina, 245; Steve Williams and, 118–19, 361, 362; University of Florida, 360–62; University of Georgia, 231; University of North Carolina, 118–19; Wake Forest University, 166–67
Proudfoot, Merrill, 335
Proud Shoes (Murray), 69, 241, 243
Providence College, 105, 106, 164
Pynchon, Thomas, 76

Q
Quinn, Boyce, 202
Quixote, Don, 337

R
racism, 147; Alabama and, 88, 138–39; Billy Jones and, xix, 12–13; Billy Packer on, 159, 209; Bloody Sunday, 138–39; Charlie Scott and, xxiii, 90; Clarence Gaines on, 27, 161, 198, 335; Claudius Claiborne and, 57–58, 210, 257, 314–15; Confederate flag as symbol of, xx, 247–48, 282; "Dixie" as symbol of, xx, 185, 245, 247–48; at Duke University, 37–38, 67–68; Georgia, 226–27; Gilbert "Gil" McGregor on, xviii, 160; Godfrey Dillard and, 42, 44, 48; Julius Johnson Jr. and, xix, 2, 12–13, 15; Larry Robinson experience of, 341–42; Louisiana State University and, 277, 282–83; Malcolm Meeks experience of, 360; Mississippi, 23–24, 44, 374–75; Norman Sloan experience of, 207, 211, 375–76; North Carolina, 69, 106, 113, 198–200; Perry Wallace and, xxi, 23–24, 29, 41–45, 47–48, 226, 336, 344; Ralph Ellison on pain of, 367; Roy Skinner on, 27; social settings and, 86–87; in South Carolina, 243; Steve Williams experience of, 362–63;

Tom Payne Jr. on, 171; at University of Florida, 351, 357, 360–61; University of Maryland and, xix, 12–14; at University of Mississippi, 137, 301, 308–10; Vanderbilt University and, 23–24, 41–43
railroad tracks, 86
Raines, Howell, 211
Raleigh, North Carolina: atmosphere of, 198; education system, 201–2; Martin Luther King, Jr. and, 206–7; media coverage, 210; segregation, 198–200
Raper, Arthur, 175
Raveling, George, 3, 83, 86, 162, 186–87, 209, 323, 374
Raymond, Robert, 75, 77, 78, 79, 81, 84, 93, 94
Reeder, Tony, 223
Reed, Willis, 281
Reese, Harold "Pee Wee," 26
religion, 23, 25–26, 61, 85, 133, 151, 377
Reynolds, Charles, 86
Reynolds Coliseum, 208, 209
Reynolds, Edward, 151
Rhodes, Guy, 77, 83
Rice, Condoleezza, 41
Richardson, Nolan, 204
Richmond, Chris, 5
Rickey, Branch, 195, 209
Ridley, Cornelius, 27, 34, 36, 43
Riker, Tom, 255
Riley, Charlie, 158, 163
Riley, Pat, 181
Ritchie, Albert, 4
Robbins, Ken "Cat," 307
Roberts, Bobby, 251, 266
Robertson, Oscar, 8, 16, 156, 208–10, 211
Robinson, Jackie, xiv, xxii, 5, 15, 26, 27, 61, 104, 118, 178–79
Robinson, Larry, 331, 332, 344; athletic abilities, 342–43; childhood, 339–40; honors, 340; pioneering role of, 338–39, 341; player statistics, 340; racism experience for, 341–42; recruitment, 340–41; Wilbert Cherry and, 346, 347
Roche, John, 103, 104, 120, 121, 214, 215, 255, 263
Rocket Eight, 123, 124, 130, 142, 371
Rollins, Avon, 336–37, 345
Rollins, Wayne "Tree," 266
Roosevelt, Franklin, 258, 279
Rosemond, Ken, 219, 288, 332; coaching

style, 237–38; recruiting, 220–21, 234–35; team records, 238

Rosenbluth, Len, 255

Rouse, Vic, 35

Rucker, Holcomb, 149

Ruffin, Ben, 70

Rupp, Adolph, 16, 82, 115, 142, 178, 190, 219, 234, 238, 266; background, 179; career end, xvi, 356; coaching style, 17, 46, 127, 180–81; fans treatment of, 376; integration and, xx, 171; personality, 180; racial attitudes, 171, 177, 181–84, 186–87, 349–50; Ray Mears on, 333; team records, 27, 179–80; Tom Payne and, 171, 172, 173, 179, 187–88, 191

Russell, Bill, xxiii, 84, 158, 160, 182, 184, 281–82

Russwurm, John, 58

Rustin, Bayard, 110

S

St. John's University, xxiii, 184–85, 195, 199, 235, 255

Salk, Jonas, 230

Sallis, Charles, 373, 380

Sampson, Ralph, 328

Sanders, Al "Apple," 286

Sanders, David, 250

Sanderson, Winfrey "Wimp," 83

Sansing, David, 292, 308

Sayers, Gale, 154

Schafer, Alan, 253

Schweitzer, Albert, 230

Schwerner, Michael, 370, 375

Scopes, John Thomas, 344

Scott, Charles "Charlie," xvii, 131, 257, 361, 365; breakout game, 100–101; childhood, 105; color barrier and, 2–3; culture shock, 105–6; Dean Smith and, 108–9, 114–15, 116–17, 119–20; Durham, North Carolina and, 69; friendships, 103; honors, 97, 103, 116, 120; impact of, 97–98, 104, 113; isolation for, 101–2, 341; Laurinburg Institute, 106–7; on marriage, 102–3; NBA, 121; on Norwood Todmann, 156; Olympic team, 117–18; on opportunity, 105; on pioneer role, xix, 113–14; player statistics, 100–101, 103; protests and, 119–20; racism and, xxiii, 90; recruitment of, 107–9; on scholarships, 97; skills as player,

115–16, 157; on University of North Carolina, 99, 195; visibility of, 98

Scott, Shannon, 121

Scott, Shawn, 121

Scott, Simone, 121

Scott, Trudy, 121

Sebo, Steve, 315, 316, 323

SEC. See Southeastern Conference

segregation: Alabama, 86–87; Arkansas, 230; Claudius Claiborne and, 53, 64–65; Clemson University, 259; geography and, xiii; Georgia, 227–28; Kentucky, 174–75; Kermit Davis on, 372, 373; Louisiana, 270–72, 275; Mississippi, 295–96; Mississippi State University, 367, 369, 373, 382; Nashville, Tennessee, 30–32, 33; North Carolina, 106, 110–11, 198–201; political correctness and, xix–xx; psychological damage of, 14, 344; South Carolina, 243–44, 252, 257–58; tradition of, xi–xiii; University of Alabama, 124–25; University of South Carolina, 257–58; Virginia, 324–26; Wake Forest University, 162–63; Wilbert Cherry experience of, 344–45

Sellers, Cleveland, xii, 245, 247–48, 297

Selma, Alabama, 137–39, 145

"Seven Dwarfs" (Auburn squad), 92, 371

Severance, Alexander, 162

sexual assault, 170–71, 172, 175–76

Seymour, Bob, 25, 110, 111, 112

Shabel, Fred, 62

Shakoor, Jordana Y., 271, 295

Shannon, Edgar F., 315

Shaw, Bynum, 151

Sheffield, Leon, 294

Sheinin, Dave, 44

Shelton, Robert, 125

Sherman, William Tecumseh, 68, 277, 278

Shetler, Carl, 92

Shipp, Bill, 218

Shue, Gene, 10

Shuttleworth, Fred, 132

Shy, Gene, 364

Simmons, Jerry, 371, 373

Simone, Nina, 164

Sines, John, 336

Sirica, John, 76

Sitterson, J. Carlyle, 118, 119

Sitton, Claude, 295

Skates, John Ray, 294, 297, 298, 370
Skinner, Roy, 27, 30, 36–38, 46, 47
Slade, James, 57, 58
Slaughter, John B., 3
slavery, 4, 175
Sloan, Joan, 215
Sloan, Norman, 198, 264; ACC
  Tournament (1970), 214–15; on Al
  Heartley, 196, 205–6, 213–14; Dixie
  Classic, 208–9; integration and racism
  experience for, 207, 211, 375–76;
  1970–1971 season, 214–16; recruiting,
  195, 366; style of play, 212–13; at
  University of Florida, 356, 359, 366
Smallwood, Irwin, 153
Smathers, George, 353
Smith, Alfred, 110
Smith, Dean, 65, 129, 235, 315; Charlie
  Scott and, 108–9, 114–15, 116–17,
  119–20; coaching record, 99–100,
  179, 338; on conference honors, 104;
  Craig Mobley relationship with, 251;
  on Frank McGuire, 254–55; as guard,
  185, 197; integration and, 25, 111–12,
  374; player support of, 115, 116, 119–
  20, 362, 365; recruiting, 108–10, 112–
  13, 220; sensitivity of, 114–15; style of
  play under, 99, 366
Smith, Orlando "Tubby," 3, 141, 186,
  187, 192, 239–40
Smith, Tab, 304, 372
Smith, Tommie, 117
Smith, Willis, 59–60
Smokey Robinson and the Miracles, 109
Snow, John, 343
"Snow White and the Seven Dwarfs"
  (Auburn squad), 92, 371
The Souls of Black Folk (Du Bois), xii, 97,
  269
The Sound of Music, 107
South Carolina: atmosphere in, 243;
  Briggs v. Elliott, 257; Brown v. Board of
  Education and, 244, 259; character of
  citizens, 260, 261; Confederate flag
  and, 244–45, 247–48; demographics,
  243; Dillon County, 252–53;
  education system, 243–44, 257–59;
  integration, 244, 257–58; Ku Klux
  Klan, 243, 247–48; protests, 245;
  racism in, 243; segregation, 243–44,
  252, 257–58. See also Clemson
  University; University of South
  Carolina

South Carolina College, 257–58
Southeastern Conference (SEC): African
  American leadership statistics in, xv;
  basketball, xv–xvii, xvi, xvii, xxi–xxiii;
  color barrier, xv, xxiii, 23–24;
  formation of, xv; history and, xvii,
  xxi–xxii; integration and, xiv–xv, xxi–
  xxii, 356; members of, xv; recruiting,
  28
Southern Manifesto, 354
Spence, Phil, 197
Spencer, Lyle, 101
Spivey, Jim, 181, 187
Stackhouse, Jerry, 115
Stahurski, Lanny, 317, 318
Stallworth, Isaac "Bud," 81, 82, 130, 283
Starkville, Mississippi, 44, 287, 367, 375–
  76
Steele, Larry, 115
Steinwedel, Steve, 379, 381
Stephens, Pat, 235, 238, 280
Stillman College, 140, 146
Stokes, Durwood, 252
Sugar Bowl, 1, 229, 256, 304, 369
Sullivan, Ed, 216
Summers, Freddie, 154, 257
Summitt, Pat, 333
Sutherland, Frank, 42

T
Talmadge, Eugene, 138, 228
Tate, Bill, 154
Taylor, Richard, 277
Temple, Collis Benton "C. B.," 269–74,
  275, 276, 283, 287, 288, 289
Temple, Collis, III, xxii, 276, 284
Temple, Collis, Jr., xxi, 225; academics,
  283; athletic abilities, 282–84, 289;
  character of, 273; on Charlie Scott,
  97–98; childhood, 271; college career,
  286–87; community service, 274; Dale
  Brown and, 288; family life, 271, 272;
  fighting, 273; high school career, 284;
  on Louisiana State University
  coaching staff, 284; personal habits,
  287; pioneering role, 274; professional
  drafts, 284; recruitment of, 269, 276,
  282, 283; siblings, 273, 275–76;
  teammate confrontations, 285;
  treatment of, 284–85, 336, 362; work
  ethic, 273–74
Temple family legacy, 269, 276, 284
Temple, Garrett, 276, 284

Temple, Ida B., 276
Temple, Shirley, 269, 271, 283, 289
The Temptations, 109
Tennessee. *See* Nashville, Tennessee;
    University of Tennessee; Vanderbilt
    University
Their Eyes Were Watching God (Hurston), 75
Thompson, David, 97, 100, 143, 153,
    197–98, 207, 211, 213, 306, 322
Thompson, John, 10
Thurmond, Nate, 368
Thurmond, Strom, 200, 243, 301
TIDES (Institute for Diversity and Ethics
    in Sport), xv
Till, Emmett, 296–97, 358
Tillman, Ben "Pitchfork," 176, 243, 261
Tiny Tim, 216
Todmann, Norwood, xxiii, 78, 113;
    arrest, 148; athletic abilities, 156, 157–
    58; character of, 147–49, 160–61,
    167; Charlie Davis and, 148–49, 156,
    157, 160–61, 165, 167; drugs and,
    147, 148, 167; Jack McCloskey and,
    164–66; player statistics, 156–57;
    public service work, 148–49;
    recruitment of, 155–56
To Kill a Mockingbird (Lee), 1, 7
Tolnay, Stewart, 162, 175, 226
Toth, Dick, 189, 222, 223, 225, 226, 235
Towe, Monte, 213, 322, 323
Towns, Forrest "Spec," 232–33
Transylvania College, 127
Tribble, Harold, 150, 159
Truman, Harry, xiv, 40, 174, 258
Tull, Brenda Temple, 280; activism in
    college, 273; childhood, 270–72, 276;
    on integration pressures, 84; on
    Louisiana State University racism,
    277, 282–83
Tully, Brian, 318
Tureaud, Alexander Pierre, Jr., 275, 277
Tuscaloosa, Alabama, 140
Tuskegee High School, 89

U
Uchuno, C. C., 314
Umstead, William, 200
University of Alabama: Bear Bryant and,
    127; Charles Newton and, 82–83,
    124, 126–27, 128, 144–45, 239, 371;
    fan behavior, 141; Foster Auditorium,
    123–24, 145–46; George Wallace and,
    124–25; integration, 124–25;
recruiting, 127–28; Rocket Eight, 124;
    scholarship athletes, 135; segregation,
    124–25; team records, 142, 144–45;
    travel arrangements, 141; Wendell
    Hudson and, xxi, 124, 126, 307
University of Florida: campus
    atmosphere, 350; championships, 366;
    integration, 350–51, 354, 358, 359–
    60, 366; Norman Sloan at, 356, 359,
    366; racism at, 351, 357, 360–61;
    reception of athletes, 351–52, 357,
    359–60; recruiting, 351–52, 356–57,
    359–60, 366; student and faculty
    protests, 360–62
University of Georgia: attractions of, 219;
    basketball program, 234, 238; campus
    organizations, 236–37; coaching staff,
    220–21; diversity and, 220;
    dormitories, 222; drawbacks of, 219;
    Georgia Tech rivalry, 223–26; Hunter
    and Holmes, 220, 226, 230–32;
    integration, 219, 226, 232; Ku Klux
    Klan and, 231–32; Maxie Foster and,
    232–33; minority enrollment, 219–20;
    protests, 231; recruiting, 235; riots,
    231–32, 260; Stegeman Coliseum,
    234; team records, 223, 238–39;
    Tubby Smith and, 239–40
University of Kentucky: basketball and,
    xvii, 171; boosters, 180; campus life,
    185–86; environment of, 172;
    integration, 182–83, 186–87;
    Louisiana State University and, 287;
    NCAA violations, 180; recruiting, 180,
    186–87; reputation of, 186; St. John's
    and, 184–85; Texas Western and,
    185–86; Tom Payne and, 190; Tom
    Payne Jr. and, 170–71. *See also* Rupp,
    Adolph
University of Maryland: African-
    American athletes and, 5–6; Billy
    Jones and, xix, 1–2; Herman Millikan
    and, xix, 10–11; integration, 4–5;
    minorities and, 3; racism and, xix, 12–
    14; social life, 15–16; style of play, 17–
    19; Sugar Bowl (1965), 1; tournament
    play, 16–17
University of Mississippi: basketball
    program, 300; Confederate flag and,
    301, 308; "Dixie" played at, 301, 308;
    football program, 303–4; integration,
    291–92, 302–3; racism at, 137, 301,
    308–10; recruiting, 292, 300–301;

riots, 260, 303
University of North Carolina: Charles Scott and, 99, 195; culture of, 110; dominance and titles, xvi–xvii; fans and, 102; Frank McGuire and, xvii, 99, 103, 111, 112, 195, 247; integration, 25, 111–12, 374; protests, 118–19; recruiting, 108, 109; tournament play, 99, 116–17. *See also* Smith, Dean
University of South Carolina: ACC withdrawal, 264; Casey Manning and, 253–54, 264–65; Clemson University and, 268; facilities, 255–56; Frank McGuire and, 214–15, 263–64, 266, 268; integration, 244, 256–57, 260–61; North Carolina State and, 263–64; recruiting, 262–63; segregation, 257–58; student population, 261; team receptions, 264; team records, 263–64
University of Tennessee: basketball program status at, 332–33; basketball program style, 331–32; Bob Neyland and, 333, 334, 336–37; coaching staff, 332; integration, 335–37; racial hostilities at, 336–37; recruiting, 334
University of Virginia: Al Drummond and, 313, 327; *Brown v. Board of Education* and, 324; championships, xvii; Craig Littlepage as athletics director at, 20, 311, 328–29; diversity and, 311–12, 328–29; fans, 323–24; Hank Allen and, 311–12, 321–22; integration, 312–13, 314, 326–27; progress of, 328–29; racial hostility and, 312, 314–15, 323–24; recruiting, 314, 315–16, 319; team records, 315–16, 320–21; women admittance to, 312
Unseld, Wes, 177, 184, 186

V
Vaccaro, Sonny, 190
Vacendak, Steve, 62, 63
Valvano, Jim, 207
Vanderbilt, Cornelius "Commodore," 38
Vanderbilt University: culture of, 25, 27–28; history of, 38–39; integration and, 28–29, 39–41; Perry Wallace and, 48–49; racism and, 23–24, 41–43; recruiting, 27, 37–38

Vandiver, Ernest, 230
Vardaman, James K., 295–96
Vaughn, Tom, 88
Vaught, Johnny, 204, 304
Veeck, Bill, 332
Verdi, Guiseppe, 33
Verga, Bob, 62
veterans, 227
Vietnam War, 242–43, 248, 378–79
Virginia: Danville history and culture in, 51–55, 57–58; integration in, 52, 57–58, 324–26; segregation, 324–26. *See also* University of Virginia
Voting Rights Act, 139

W
Wade, Bob, 3, 336
Wake Forest University: athlete compensation, 164; athletic program funding, 158–59; Billy Packer and, 151, 152–53, 155, 163, 205; *Brown v. Board of Education* and, 151, 152, 162; campus, 150; Clemson University and, 260; culture of, 149–50, 163–64; football program, 154–55; integration, 150–51, 153–55, 159, 160, 161; Jack McCloskey and, 165; press coverage of, 151, 152; protests, 166–67; segregation and, 162–63; starting lineup, 158; team records, 151–52, 157, 166; Winston-Salem State rivalry with, 162–63
Waldrop, Herb "Hub," 84, 85, 89, 93, 95
Walker, D. C. "Peahead," 150
Walker, Jimmy, 90, 91, 94, 376
Walker, Jimmy (Providence), 105, 106
Walker, Solly, xxiii, 184, 185, 199, 208, 261–62
Walker, Wade, 370, 371
Walker, Wyatt T., 53–54
Wallace, George, 104, 260; Alabama integration fought by, 87–89, 124–25, 128, 129, 133, 144, 145–46, 244, 247; apology from, 145; on Auburn integration, 87–88, 124; Bloody Sunday violence and, 138–39; political support in 1964, 5
Wallace, Grady, 255
Wallace, Mattie, 32, 33
Wallace, Perry Eugene, Sr., 32, 33
Wallace, Perry, Jr., 116, 190, 345; academics, xv, 28; background, 23–

24, 29, 31–33; church and, 25–26; color barrier broken by, xv, 2, 40, 65, 76, 98, 129, 183; dunking, 43–44, 46; family, 32–34; on Henry Harris Jr., 84–85; high school career, 25, 34–37; honors, 48–49; as inspiration, 49; isolation, 24, 42, 341; player statistics, 24–25, 43–46; professional career, 48; racism and, xxi, 23–24, 29, 41–45, 47–48, 226, 336, 344; recruiting and, 37–38, 107; on segregation damage, 344; temperament, 27–28, 30; on University of Mississippi, 291–92

Walsh, Donnie, 113, 254, 264
Ward, Bill, 166
Ward, Bob, 316
Ward, Clara Singers, 272
Ward, Horace, 230
Warner, Thomas, 378
Warren, Bob, 26, 37
Warren, Mike, 117
Warren, Robert Penn, 278
Washington, Booker T., 69
Washington, George, 324
Washington, Walter, 48
Waters, Harold "Bucky," 61, 63, 64, 65
Waters, Raymond "Bucky," 61, 62, 63, 64, 166, 255, 266
Watson, Tom, 227
Weisbrot, Robert, 201
West, Marvin, 342
White, Harold, xxi, 257, 258, 262, 263, 265, 297
Whitehead, Eddie, 177
White, Joseph "Jo Jo," 283
White, Theodore, 5
Wicker, Tom, 88
Wiedeman, Dave, 151
Wier, Sayde, 375, 376
Wilkins, Dominique, 222
Williams, Ben, 305
Williams, Carla, 329
Williams, F. M., 342
Williams, Gary, 3, 9–10, 15, 17, 63, 163
Williams, John Bell, 297, 302
Williams, Roy, xvii, 366
Williams, Steve, 349, 350; athletic abilities, 357, 360, 364–65, 366; childhood, 354–55; coaching career, 363; college experience, 354; demeanor of, 357–58; racist threat experienced by, 362–63; recruitment of, 352, 355–57; sensitivity, 364; student protests and, 118–19, 361, 362; Tommy Bartlett relationship with, 363–64, 365
Williams, T. Harry, 278
Williford, Vann, 215
Willis, Amos Leroy, 314
Wilmore, Henry, 262
Wilson, Roy S., 275
Wilson, Steve, 288
Winfield, Dave, 144
Winston-Salem State, 7, 17, 27, 152–53, 161–63, 198, 335
Winters, Brian, 254, 255
Wise, Albert Harper "Skip," 266
Wolf Whistle (Nordan), 291
women, 49, 85; African American, discrimination, 161; athletics inclusion of, 64–65, 118; athletics leadership and, xv, 3, 329; basketball, 145, 333; dating/socializing with white, 60, 175, 236, 243, 287, 358; lynching assaults on, 175–76; Ronnie Hogue and, 235–36; sexual assaults on, 170–71, 172, 175–76; University of Virginia admittance of, 312
Wooden, John, 263, 338
Woodruff, Robert, 260
Woodward, C. Vann, 105, 227
Wood, Wendy Scholtens, 49
Wooten, James T., 104
Worthy, James, 115
Wright, George, 176
Wright, Joby, 81, 235
Wright, Louis B., 257
Wright, Richard, 51, 217
Wyatt, Bowden, 334, 349

Y

Yarbro, Virginia, 377
Young, Al, Jr., 78, 80, 81, 93
Young, Bernice, 79
Youngblood, Jack, 352
Yow, Debbie, 3

Z

Zilko, Steve, 236

ABOUT THE AUTHOR

Barry Jacobs is a freelance journalist who has covered sports, history, the environment, and politics for more than 30 years. His articles have appeared in dozens of regional and national publications, including the *New York Times,* to which he was a regular sports contributor from 1981 through 2001.

Jacobs's published works include the annual *Fan's Guide to ACC Basketball* (1984 through 1998 editions) and the books *Golden Glory: The First 50 Years of the ACC, Coach K's Little Blue Book, The World According to Dean,* and *Three Paths to Glory.* Jacobs also is an online columnist for wral.com, tarheeldaily.com, and dukebasketballreport.com. He lives near Hillsborough, North Carolina, with his wife, Robin, serves as an Orange County commissioner, and is the caretaker of Moorefields, a 1785 estate on the National Register of Historic Places.